Psychoanalytic Anthropology After Freud

PSYCHOANALYTIC ANTHROPOLOGY AFTER FREUD:

Essays Marking the
Fiftieth Anniversary of Freud's Death

David H. Spain
Editor

New York **Psyche Press** *1992*

Published by
PSYCHE PRESS
P. O. Box 780
New York, NY 10024
(212) 721-4466

Designed and Computer Typeset by
THE ACADEMIC FACTOR, New York City
(212) 684-0983

Library of Congress Cataloging in Publication Data

Spain, David H.
Psychoanalytic anthropology after Freud: essays marking the fiftieth anniversary of Freud's death. David H. Spain, ed.
Includes bibliographical references and indices.
ISBN 0-9622885-4-3 (cloth)
1. Ethnopsychology. 2. Psychoanalysis and culture. I. Freud, Sigmund, 1856-1939. II. Spain, David H.
[DNLM: 1. Anthropology, cultural—essays. 2. Psychoanalytic theory—essays. WM 460 P9774485]
302—dc20
DNLM/DLC

For Library of Congress 91-35094
CIP

1. Psychoanalysis and culture. 2. History of psychoanalytic anthropology. 3. Field- and Clinic-based studies.
4. Theoretical and critical studies.

For Norman Miller Spain and
Ruth Ann Polley Spain

with love and deep appreciation

CONTENTS

ACKNOWLEDGMENTS

My most immediate and greatest debt is to my wife, Jannie, who has put up with me and otherwise supported this and my other endeavors, professional and avocational, to an extent that, I am convinced, few could match and fewer still would even want to try. I am also grateful for the patience shown me, during my times away from family life while this book was being prepared, by all three of my children but especially by Rachel, who is yet quite young (Andrew and Ryan, I suspect, were quite happy to have me out of their hair). Like her brothers before her, she has already given me more than I can ever return.

Although too numerous to mention one by one, I also owe a great deal to the generosity of friends and neighbors. I particularly want to thank Ralph and Colleen Rosinbum and Jack and Danie Carr for the use of their cabins for several very productive periods of writing relating to this book and several other projects.

In recent years, I have received much support and encouragement from a number of friends in the Seattle psychoanalytic community. In addition to my fellow candidates at the Seattle Psychoanaltyic Institute who so warmly helped me to become a part of their world and to the members of the faculty who taught classes that were so helpful to me, I particularly wish to thank Mike Allison, Bob Bergman, Bob Campbell, Ted Dorpat, Roger Eddy, Ron Furedy, Rob Janes, Charlie Mangham, Gerry Olch, Damaris Rice, David Rowlett, Sr., Werner Schimmelbusch, and Larry Schwartz. I am also grateful for the many stimulating evenings I have had in activities organized by various psychoanalytic study groups and organizations in the Seattle area. I have found this environment most rewarding and look forward to more of the same, especially from the Seattle Psychoanalytic Society, the Northwest Alliance for Psychoanalytic Study, and the Anthropology and Analysis Study Group.

Other teachers will know the extent of my debt to my students and colleagues. I particularly would like to thank those many students who have kept me alert with their unending supply of questions, expressions of annoyance and doubt, and scholarly sources that I "must read." Many of those sources were helpful but none so much as the students themselves, especially Debra Boyer, JoAnn Campbell, Heidi Kelley, Bruce Saari, Jeanette Schimmelbusch and Shusuke Yagi. Most of my colleagues, I am glad to say are my colleagues and I owe much to all of them. My greatest debts are to those who have truly listened to me, who actually read what I wrote and who, thereby, were able to help me with well-timed and much-deserved criticisms. In this regard, I wish to thank, from my university, Carol Eastman, Simon Ottenberg, Lorna Rhodes, Pierre van den Berghe, Jim Watson and Bud Winans. From around the country and abroad, I wish to give special thanks to Christopher Badcock, Jim Bohannan, Val Daniel, Marvin Harris, Francis L.K. Hsu, John Ingham, L. L. Langness, Bob LeVine, Bobby Paul, Daniel Rancour-Laferriere and Mel Spiro.

Finally, I wish to thank Jean Langford and Elaine Durall for their help with the preparation of the manuscript, Robert Endleman of Psyche Press, and all the contributors to this volume. It is because of their faith and patience that this book exists at all.

Introduction

Psychoanalytic Anthropology After Freud: A Personal and Appreciative Introduction

David H. Spain

The principal objective of this essay is to introduce you, the reader, to the papers in this volume. In doing so, however, I also wish to say some things about psychoanalytic anthropology in general—especially for those readers who may have had little previous exposure to the field. I do so hoping that this introduction will give such readers greater appreciation of the aims and scope of psychoanalytic anthropology, including that portion represented by the papers in this volume. I hope also that some of the enthusiasm of those working in this field will come through to, and rub off on, those who will take the time to study this book.[1]

This is, in fact, a wonderful time to be involved in psychoanalytic anthropology. The field has never been more dynamic and robust than it is today. The number of well-trained, serious psychoanalytically oriented anthropologists is *much* larger than it has ever been; indeed, although I know of no precise accounting, the number surely exceeds, by far, the total from all previous periods put together. This has resulted in a level of productivity and enthusiasm that is unprecedented and, frankly, quite exciting.

---

[1]I thank John Ingham for his many extremely helpful substantive and stylistic comments on the first draft of this introduction. For help on certain aspects of the writing, I also thank Ryan G. Spain. For help with the references, I am indebted to Jean Langford.

There is, however, more than a growth in numbers. Those working in this field are being stimulated by diverse intellectual developments within psychoanalysis itself, where virtually every facet of theory and method has, in recent years, been re-evaluated and, in many cases, reformulated. As a consequence, psychoanalytic anthropologists can do their work using a great many theoretical viewpoints. Although this has already led to many interesting, unexpected innovations, bearing on the general scientific goals of both psychoanalysis and anthropology, my sense is that it will be many years before the crest of this trend is reached.

Psychoanalytic anthropology: some definitional matters

As the words imply, psychoanalytic anthropology is that subdiscipline of anthropology devoted to the use of psychoanalytic concepts, method and theory in the study of culture. Many of the papers in Part I of this volume illustrate this. Psychoanalytic anthropology also has another, somewhat less well-known but equally important goal—namely, using the ethnographic and theoretical works of anthropology to foster the development and clarification of psychoanalytic theory. The authors of many of the papers in this volume have had this as one of their major goals (see Part II, especially).

The terms "psychoanalytic" and "psychoanalysis," which are central in the previous paragraph, are familiar words to most people. I have found, however, that many people are unaware of a well-established albeit largely tacit convention governing certain aspects of their use. It is worth presenting this convention explicitly not only because it too often is an unstated part of a scholarly oral tradition, but also because those unfamiliar with it may, as a consequence, be confused by some of the discussions in this volume. Note, then, that when the words "psychoanalysis" and "psychoanalytic" are used without modifiers, not only in this book but in the scholarly literature generally, the *usual* referent (cf. "unmarked" in linguistics) is to the psychological theories and methods developed by Sigmund Freud *and* to concepts derived from and closely related to them.

Although simple enough to state, this convention reflects, in part, the rather complex situation arising from the relationship between Freud and some of his early followers—notably Jung and Adler. They developed views which, in important ways, were derived from Freud's work (as were some of his from theirs), but which are generally thought to be distinctive enough to merit terminological marking (cf. "marked" in linguistics). Thus, the psychological theories developed by Jung and Adler are usually referred to as "Jungian analysis" or "Adlerian analysis," and the (unmarked) term "psychoanalysis," as usually used, *excludes* their views.

Although this convention is so well established it is rarely noted explicitly, it is far from a perfect system. It works well enough for the two examples given but there are other cases that are much less clearcut. For example, some would insist that theoretical developments initiated by Melanie Klein, Karen Horney, Heinz Kohut and Jacques Lacan are so far-removed from and/or fundamentally at odds with Freud's views that they should be terminologically distinguished the way Jung's and Adler's views are. Others, however, strongly dispute this.

This convention, as well as some of the debates engendered by it, has seemed odd to some but it does occur in other sciences. In biology, for example, when the term "evolution" is used today, one may safely assume the reference is to Darwin's theory and certain, but not all, of its derivatives. Only if there is a modifying term (e.g., "Lamarckian evolution"), or if the context suggests otherwise, will this assumption be invalid.

The marking of a theoretical variant in this way can be a very sensitive issue because more than communicative precision may be involved. Terminological marking is often associated with an opinion about the relative worth of the marked and unmarked terms. As in the example from biology, most if not all non-Darwinian (marked) evolutionary theories are thought, by biologists, to be fundamentally incorrect. Similarly, in psychoanalysis (in the unmarked sense of the term), the marked varieties of the discipline are thought to have less value than the unmarked ones. Because of this, it can matter a great deal whether or not one insists that the views of, say, Lacan or Kohut should be terminologically marked.

Although many varieties of psychoanalysis are identified by name in this book, most are not "marked" in the sense just described. In some cases, however, there is an evaluative dimension. Thus, the theories developed by Jung and Adler (among others) are marked and excluded.

Although this fact reflects, in part, the scholarly record of psychoanalytic anthropology which, by-and-large, has not drawn upon these theories (for reasons that ought to be but have not yet been explored in detail), this also reflects a judgment regarding the relative worth of these particular variants of psychoanalysis—a view that is widely shared among psychoanalysts and psychoanalytic anthropologists. On the other hand, when the variants of psychoanalysis developed by (among others) Lacan, Kohut, and M. Klein are distinguished terminologically, it is almost always simply for the sake of clarity. Indeed, this book as a whole, it may be emphasized in this context, is an expression of the view that a convincing case has not yet been made that such variants are as distinct from the unmarked theory as are the marked variants by Jung or Adler.

In sum, the term "psychoanalysis" (and variations such as "psychoanalytic") refers to the psychological concepts, methods and theories developed and amended by Sigmund Freud and to the accumulated knowledge based upon observations made in light of those ideas. Included also are those modifications of Freud's ideas that have been and continue to be made by those of his colleagues and intellectual descendants who acknowledge Freud's central role in founding the branch of psychology in which they continue to work. Finally, in terms of goals, the term refers to the discipline that has, as its primary goal, the development of a science of the structure and function of the human psyche, an endeavor undertaken for both theoretical and applied—i.e., for non-clinical and psycho-clinical (therapeutic)—purposes.

An historical sketch of the field

The first scholarly works in psychoanalytic anthropology—i.e., the first attempts to use psychoanalytic theory in the study of culture and the first attempts to use ethnographic data and anthropological theory to foster the development of psychoanalytic theory—were not undertaken by an anthropologist. They were carried out by a psychoanalyst who used his knowledge of myth and other forms of expressive culture (e.g., sexual beliefs and behavior, jokes, folktales, beliefs about the dead) to inform nascent theoretical developments in psychoanalysis; he also used that newly developed theory in his studies of culture. The person who first did this was Sigmund Freud (see, in this regard, his *The Psycho-*

pathology of Everyday Life, 1901; *Three Essays on the Theory of Sexuality*, 1905; *Jokes and Their Relation to the Unconscious*, 1905; and, of course, *Totem and Taboo*, 1913).[2]

From very early on, anthropologists paid attention to the more important psychoanalytic ideas, often by attempting to use ethnographic data to show the distributive limits of developmental milestones which Freud and others had claimed were human universals. The most famous instance of this, by far, was Malinowski's suggestion (Malinowski 1927) that the psychodevelopmentally central relationship among the matrilineal Trobriand Islanders was not the oedipal triangle of mother, father and child but a "nuclear complex" involving the child, mother, and mother's brother.

In the first few decades of this century, numerous anthropologists read seriously in the psychoanalytic literature and at least one anthropologist of great intellectual stature (A. L. Kroeber) became, for a time, a lay analyst. In general, however, the relationship between anthropology and psychoanalysis was strained. Indeed, for many years, there was not more than a handful of anthropologists at any one time who published regularly in psychoanalytic anthropology. In no small measure, this was due to the success of Malinowski's work—a fact that itself was a product of another, even more important one: nearly all anthropologists had rejected the general evolutionary and universalistic theories that had been used by Freud in developing his views.

Even so, important work in psychoanalytic anthropology was being done during this period and, fortunately, by exceptionally gifted scholars. Two of the earliest were Géza Róheim and Abram Kardiner. Although both men had been trained, academically and clinically, in Europe, they were quite different, intellectually and otherwise. Kardiner (1891-1981), a practicing psychoanalyst who had been analyzed by Freud himself, never did ethnographic fieldwork. Rather, he used psychodynamic principles to interpret data gathered by cultural anthropologists (e.g., Ralph Linton and Cora Du Bois). He did this in a series of seminars at Columbia University in the 1930s (for an informative review and assessment of his work, see Manson 1988). His views, especially regarding Freud's theories, were decidedly revisionist. Indeed, because he and

---

[2]See Bibliography.

others, such as Erich Fromm and Karen Horney, proposed and adopted rather extensive modifications of classical theory during this period, they are usually designated as "neo-Freudians."

Kardiner's major work, *The Individual and His Society*, was published the year Freud died (1939). In it, and in later works such as *The Psychological Frontiers of Society* (1945), he presented his particular version of what may be termed the "culturalist" and/or "adaptationist" stance regarding the relationship between culture and personality. Although some versions of this viewpoint are still popular in psychological and psychoanalytic anthropology (the work of the Whitings and many of their students comes to mind; for an overview, see Whiting 1978), Kardiner's version, as Manson notes (1988:xiii), has been "largely misinterpreted and unappreciated." It is somewhat surprising that this should be so since in his "neo-Freudianism," Kardiner had rejected many of the more controversial claims of psychoanalysis—a move that clearly was an outgrowth, at least in part, of his close association with mainstream, relativistic anthropologists, such as Linton, who had rejected universalistic theories of human behavior.

All of this is in striking contrast to the position taken by Géza Róheim (1891-1953) a thorough-going universalistic psychoanalytic reductionist. For him, the worldwide ethnographic record was an expression, in public and relatively enduring form, of myriad private solutions to panhuman neurotic conflict engendered by human nature and the vicissitudes of human development (e.g., see Róheim 1943). Although his PhD was in geography, Róheim read thoroughly in and was deeply committed to anthropology. He also was a fully trained psychoanalyst who, for many years, saw patients in his private practice in New York. He is generally recognized as the first person with such dual training to undertake long-term ethnographic field research (in 1929, in Australia; see Róheim 1934 and 1945).

For many years, Róheim was virtually the only deeply committed psychoanalytic voice in anthropology—and what a voice it was: he published over 150 papers and more than a dozen books in his lifetime (and more have been published posthumously). It must be said, however, that his many and provocative words fell largely upon deaf ears—in part, one suspects, because his psychoanalytic orientation was, as La Barre once put it (1980a:170), "vigorously intransigent."

Two years before Róheim's death, the anthropologist George Devereux (1908-1985) published *Reality and Dream: The Psychotherapy of a Plains Indian* (Devereux 1951) and thereby began to carry, with a vigor quite equal to Róheim's, the psychoanalytic flame. This work, which he would later describe (1978b:367) as "probably . . . the only published verbatim account of any psychotherapy," was the first of approximately a dozen books and more than 200 academic papers in psychoanalytic anthropology and related topics that he would publish—an outpouring that, in quantity, significance, and range, few (except La Barre, on whom see below) can hope to match.

Although Devereux, like Róheim, was a Hungarian by birth, his skills in mathematics and his Francophilian leanings led him to Paris where, in the late 1920s, he studied mathematical physics with Mme. Curie. In the early 1930s, he Gallicized his name (it had been Dobo) and left Paris to participate in Leslie White's field laboratory in New Mexico, where he arrived wearing leather chaps, cowboy boots, and a ten-gallon hat (for this and other information on Devereux's life, I rely upon Devereux 1978b, and La Barre 1985). He did fieldwork with the Mohave in 1932-33 and, in 1935, took his PhD in anthropology at Berkeley.

Devereux's route to psychoanalysis is surely unique for, as he put it (1978b:366) "I remained an anti-Freudian until, in 1938, my Mohave informant taught me psychoanalysis." He undertook formal psychoanalytic training at the Topeka Institute where he graduated in 1952. He practiced privately from 1959 through 1963 and then returned to Paris where, in addition to his work in psychoanalytic anthropology, he taught himself Greek philology and began publishing highly regarded works in that field as well.

In the opinion of many (myself included), his greatest work is *From Anxiety to Method in the Behavioral Sciences* (1967)—a complex epistemological critique of the social sciences. It is couched primarily in terms of the psychoanalytic concept of counter-transference and illustrated with material he had gathered from his research in both the clinic and the field over a period of three decades. Although the importance of his work had long been recognized by psychological anthropologists, he did not garner truly world-wide critical acclaim until the last decade of his life.

Unlike Róheim, Devereux did not have to carry the flame of psychoanalytic anthropology alone. He was joined in this effort by Weston

La Barre (b. 1911) who can be described, with intended irony, as the first mainstream psychoanalytic anthropologist who, at the same time, was a true maverick—a character trait he himself acknowledges (with obvious relish) and traces, with tongue only partly in cheek, to an ancestor who was burned at the stake in France in 1766 (La Barre 1978c:282) and to whom he dedicates what surely is his most important work, *The Ghost Dance: The Origins of Religion* (La Barre 1970).

La Barre was trained in anthropology at Yale, principally by Leslie Spier and Edward Sapir. It was Sapir who encouraged La Barre to undergo a didactic analysis and to read seriously in the works of Freud and the other great early psychoanalysts such as Abraham, Jones and Ferenczi. La Barre, like Devereux, had formal training in psychoanalysis at the Menninger Clinic in Topeka and was in analysis several times (La Barre 1978:281). At about the time Devereux began publishing on the Mohave (an article on institutionalized homosexuality—Devereux 1937), La Barre published his first professional paper—on Native American beers (La Barre 1938a). His first book, *The Peyote Cult*, which has been reprinted a dozen times (La Barre 1978c:283), was also published in 1938 but it was not explicitly psychological. The first of his more than 100 scholarly publications that was overtly psychological (not to mention uncounted others on his "five-foot shelf of unpublished manuscripts" (La Barre 1978c:296) was "The Psychopathology of Drinking Songs" (La Barre 1939).

For psychoanalytic anthropologists, however, one of La Barre's most important early works was *The Aymara of the Lake Titicaca Plateau, Bolivia* (1948)—the first of a series of publications on this group by La Barre that have been the focus of much debate. Another landmark work was *The Human Animal* (1954)—a hugely successful, integrative study of the relationship between human biology and culture that, as with so much of the work of both Devereux and La Barre, was about 20 years ahead of its time. The general themes of this covertly psychoanalytic classic achieve their fullest flower in 1970, in La Barre's magnum opus—*The Ghost Dance: The Origins of Religion*, a work that dares to discuss the phylogenetic and ontogenetic roots of religion and magic, a topic first broached by Freud and that La Barre continues to explore in this book and also in *Muelos: A Stone Age Superstition about Sexuality* (1984) and *Shadow of Childhood* (1991).

Psychological anthropology in general had been "declared dead" (Spindler 1978:3) by many anthropologists in the 1960s. Insofar as, up to then, very few scholars were really active in the psychoanalytic branch of that subdiscipline, one might have confidently predicted that the demise of psychoanalytic anthropology would be swift and sure. It turns out, however, that such a prediction would have been completely incorrect. By 1973, psychological anthropology was vigorous enough to start its own journal (*Ethos*) and, a few years later (1978), to support a journal specifically devoted to psychoanalytic anthropology (*The Journal of Psychoanalytic Anthropology*, which merged with *The Journal of Psychohistory* in 1988). Correspondingly, the number of people working in psychoanalytic anthropology and the number of anthropologists who have graduated from psychoanalytic institutes or who have made extensive and important use of psychoanalytic ideas has vastly increased in the past few years—so much so that a single volume such as this one can represent only a fraction of the people and ideas that invigorate the field today.

These anthropologists have been quite productive and, in recent years, have published extensively. A good portion of that mountain of literature was reviewed recently by Robert A. Paul in the *Annual Review of Anthropology* (1989). That essay is essential reading for anyone seeking an overview of recent developments in psychoanalytic anthropology. In addition to Paul's review, there are several other very useful sources that should be consulted to find the more-or-less anthropological contributions to the literature in "PASO" (Endleman's acronym for "**P**sycho**A**nalytic **SO**cial Science," Endleman 1991).

Some of the more recent general sources would include, for example, Stein and Apprey's *From Metaphor to Meaning: Papers in Psychoanalytic Anthropology* (1987); Rabow et al.'s *Advances in Psychoanalytic Sociology* (1987); Chodorow's *Feminism and Psychoanalytic Theory* (1989); Endleman's *Love and Sex in Twelve Cultures* (1989), *Deviance and Psychopathology* (1990), and *Eros and Evolution* (1991); Hunt's *Psychoanalytic Aspects of Fieldwork* (1989); Dundes's *Analytic Essays in Folklore* (1975); a collection of some of LaBarre's papers in *Culture in Context: Selected Writings* (LaBarre 1980); a collection of some of Spiro's papers in *Culture and Human Nature* (Kilborne and Langness, eds. 1987); Roland's *In Search of Self in India and Japan: Toward a Cross-Cultural Psychology* (1988); Devereux's *Problems in Ethnopsych-*

iatry (1980); Stein's *The Psychoanthropology of American Culture* (1986); and DeVos and Boyer's *Symbolic Analysis Cross-Culturally: The Rorschach Test* (1989). A vital series published annually is *The Psychoanalytic Study of Society*, now edited by the Boyers; a notable, almost always controversial journal is *The Journal of Psychohistory*, founded and edited by Lloyd deMause.

Psychoanalytic anthropology: some basic themes

Anyone who reads all the papers in this volume or even a 10% sample of the material cited above will surely come to appreciate that anthropologists who commit psychoanalytic anthropology do a multitude of rather disparate things. There are, however, some patterns in the variety that, once identified, may enhance one's ability to appreciate the works in this complex field. There are, it can be suggested with reasonable evidential support, four basic approaches to the psychoanalytically informed study of culture (cf., the somewhat different classification of psychoanalytic models in, as well as those reviewed by, Pine 1990). Defined in classical terms and Freudian texts, these are (1) the "drive" or bioevolutionary-instinctual approach fostered by *The Three Essays on Sexuality* (1905) and *Totem and Taboo* (1913), (2) the "ego" or adaptationist approach grounded in *Beyond the Pleasure Principle* (1920) and *The Ego and the Id* (1923), (3) the hermeneutic or interpretative approach originating in *The Interpretation of Dreams* (1900), *The Psychopathology of Everyday Life* (1901) and *Jokes and Their Relation to the Unconscious* (1905), and (4) the object-relations/self-psychological approach inspired in part by Freud's essay "On Narcissism" (1914b). These are not, it must be emphasized, stand-alone viewpoints. Indeed, this was particularly true for Freud himself who, to take but one example, drew very heavily on drive theory in his dream book in attempting to develop a general framework for interpreting dreams and other expressive materials. These general approaches also have many variants, of course, and there are, as well, other key developments not derived from these works. From the very beginning, psychoanalysis was far more than Freud's brainchild.

As important as such Freudian sources may be for some key works in psychoanalytic anthropology, what is most noteworthy about the field in recent years is the prominence of psychoanalytic works not written by Freud. Very often, these sources are as central now to ongoing research as were Freudian sources of the sort just mentioned. It is in this development that we encounter one of the central reasons for the organization of the panel that led, in time, to this book. We are now seeing, in psychoanalytic anthropology, truly fruitful developments by scholars whose work is rooted in theoretical formulations that, although ultimately Freudian, are distinctive enough to warrant being referred to in ways which usefully separate them from the discipline's omnipresent founder. As such, this is a development in psychoanalytic anthropology that is not so much new, given the precedent of the work of neo-Freudians like Kardiner, but of unprecedented frequency and salience.

If this is correct, then the future of psychoanalytic anthropology, though it may continue to be rooted in, and even dominated by, the work of Freud mentioned above, will more and more be informed by the views of such conceptual innovators as Bion (1963, among others), Kernberg (1975), M. Klein (1948), G. Klein (1976), Kohut (1971, 1977), Lacan (1966), Langs (1976), Mahler, Pine and Bergman (1975), Peterfreund (1983), Sandler (1987, among others) and Winnicott (1965, among others)—to mention only some of the more prominent. Some of these viewpoints are already on the way to becoming reasonably well-established in psychoanalytic anthropology and, happily, are represented in this volume. Others, although incredibly rich, are almost entirely untapped resources that future students of the field will, we may hope, soon be turning to for inspiration.

The roots of this book

In the broadest sense, this book emerges from basic developments in the history of psychoanalytic anthropology sketched above. This introduction is also, at least partly, a personal one and so, with that in mind, I want to mention some of the more personal experiences that led to this book. For example, this book is a product of my genuine surprise that the training I received while a candidate at the Seattle Institute for Psychoanalysis was not simply a close reading of the definitive, 23 volume (plus a 24th index volume) *Standard Edition of the Complete Psychological Works of Sigmund Freud*. Indeed, if anything, it may be that we read too little of Freud during the years I spent there (1980-1986). Be that as it may, one fact is incontrovertible: it was there that I came to appreciate how true it is that *psychoanalysis today is far more than the collected works of Sigmund Freud.*

Second, this book is a product of my discovery that I am not the only one surprised by this fact. Repeatedly, students and others show me, sometimes directly but more often indirectly, that they accept one version or another of a crude stereotype: that being a psychoanalyst or a psychoanalytic anthropologist means no more nor less than being slavishly devoted to each and every one of Freud's utterances. It might perhaps be of interest to tarry and consider the origins of such a view, but I will instead simply point to the contents of this volume and assert that these papers are only the tip of what is in fact a remarkably heterodox mountain of psychoanalytic thought available today, not just within psychoanalysis proper but in the main disciplines of the humanities and in several of the basic social sciences besides anthropology.

Finally, the idea of organizing the panel was reinforced when it occurred to me, one day, that 1989 would be the fiftieth anniversary of Freud's death (and not uncoincidentally for the origin of that thought, the year of my own fiftieth birthday). Given my views about the richness and diversity of psychoanalytic thinking, both within and outside of anthropology, I felt that a presentation of some of the recent, lively psychoanalytic ideas developed during the period after his death would be a fitting celebration of Freud's legacy.

To have papers representing all the rather diverse and distinctive varieties of psychoanalytic work being done in anthropology these days, it would have been necessary to invite a surprisingly large group. Although such a group is wonderful to contemplate, it would have been far too large for the venue—the 1989 Annual Meeting of the American Anthropological Association where all save one of the papers in this volume were first presented together.[3]

Ultimately, I selected a panel of sixteen—twelve who gave papers and four discussants. As I started putting the panel together, I was surprised to find that having a large number of people to choose among

[3]For various reasons, the papers presented by E. Valentine Daniel and Gilbert Herdt could not be included in this volume.

actually made it more difficult to decide whom to ask. Decisions were made largely in terms of five goals. First, I wanted people who would present views rooted in newer and less straightforwardly Freudian theoretical terms. In this volume, progress toward this goal is made in many of the papers but especially in those by Badcock, Campbell, Kilborne, LeVine, Spiro, Trawick and myself. Second, I wanted a nearly equal balance of papers grounded deeply in clinical or ethnographic field work on the one hand and, on the other, those that were more exegetic and/or theoretical. The division of the papers into Parts I and II in this volume reflects this.

Third, I wanted to have on the panel as many as possible who were doing clinical work and/or who had undertaken formal training in a psychoanalytic institute. This was a goal not only because clinical work is central to psychoanalysis but also because it is important for it to be more generally known that quite a few anthropologists have had rather extensive and formal (if not "full") psychoanalytic training. Six of the thirteen anthropologists who participated have had such training—five who gave papers (LeVine, Kilborne, Johnson, Spiro and myself) plus one of the discussants (Robert A. Paul). In addition, and quite intentionally, three of the participants were full-time clinicians (Ramanujam, who read a paper and the psychoanalysts Stanley Greenspan and Vamik Volkan, who were discussants).

Fourth, I wanted near numerical parity between well-known psychoanalytic anthropologists and newer people and/or those who either were not anthropologists or who were not usually or had not until recently been identified as being psychoanalytic anthropologists. For me, this was important because I felt the composition of the panel itself should show not only that psychoanalysis is receptive to many viewpoints but also that very good work is being done in psychoanalytic anthropology by many quite talented "new faces."

Fifth, and perhaps most important of all, I wanted some of those on the panel to do more than merely use psychoanalytic theory to speak to scholarly issues in anthropology. Rather, I wanted panelists who could and would use their expertise to speak to psychoanalysts. This was in response to well-known hegemonic tendencies among psychoanalysts which seriously undermine not only their ability to be heard by, but also to listen to, others. Although psychoanalysis is, as one of my students put it, "an interpretive strategy that precludes closure [and which, therefore,] anthropologists can not afford to ignore,"[4] I sense that psychoanalysis is all too willing, at times, to ignore what is being said about and to it from perspectives afforded by other disciplines. I therefore wanted the papers in this volume to provide psychoanalysts with one or two difficult-to-ignore suggestions. Virtually all the papers make some contributions toward this goal but those by Badcock, Campbell, Ingham, Kirschner, Spiro and myself seem especially salient in this regard.

In sum, I saw the panel, much as I see this introduction, as an *appreciation* of Freud and also, but more importantly, as something other than an elegiac memorialization of the "father who doesn't die" (to borrow Gombaroff's eerie phrase, in Wallerstein 1988:9). I wanted to honor Freud by showing how fruitful the many ideas have been that he planted throughout his long and distinguished career. I hope and trust that this spirit, which was so clearly in evidence on the day these papers were first presented together orally, will come through in this medium.

And with that, let me now offer some appreciative comments about those papers.

LeVine and Kohut

The first chapter is Robert LeVine's genuinely wise essay in which he both looks back with insight at several themes in the history of psychoanalytic anthropology and forward with optimism to the future of our endeavor. In doing so, he offers important suggestions about how to approach the subject when doing fieldwork. In this, he not only provides valuable advice but also makes a point that I did not fully appreciate until I became a psychoanalytic candidate—namely, the importance of clinical work for psychoanalysis. Somehow, and like many others, I tended to think of psychoanalysis (in spite of its obvious clinical reputation—a not always flattering one to be sure) as an almost theological endeavor, with its most lauded practitioners being those who labored long and hard to produce what I imagined were arcane, impossibly dense, jargon-filled, exegetical re-re-re-readings of Freud's sacred words. In fact—and in a

---

[4]Quoted from a 1991 unpublished term paper on psychoanalytic anthropology written by Malcolm Shelley.

manner not at all unlike that routinely seen among anthropologists—the psychoanalysts I came to know held clinical aptitude, not theoretical rectitude, in highest regard, and for essentially the same reasons anthropologists have such high regard for their colleagues known to be skilled fieldworkers: it is by far the most difficult part of the professional role, it is central to the discipline's progress and, alas, excellence as a fieldworker or clinician appears to be all too rare.

LeVine's topical concerns pertain to an important, much discussed subject on the cutting-edge of psychological anthropology these days: the nature, development and cultural vicissitudes of the "self." Given the prominence of this topic, it is surprising that the work of Heinz Kohut (1913-1981) is not better-known than it is in anthropology, for he has provided one of the more comprehensive theories available regarding both the development and psychopathologies of self (see Kohut 1971, 1977, 1984, and 1985; in addition to LeVine's recent publications that are informed by aspects of Kohut's thought, see Ewing 1990).

Kohut's ideas, while initially located clearly within the general Freudian paradigm, grew steadily further from this so-called orthodox center. As in the case of others who greatly modified Freud's theories (see, for example, the discussion of Lacan, below), this trend ultimately led many to question whether Kohutian views were "really" psychoanalytic. To this day, the matter remains unsettled. Although I have no tabulatable data with which to bolster my view, I think most analysts believe the whole question is silly—about half because it is obvious that Kohut's views fall within Freudian psychoanalysis, broadly defined, and the other half because it is just as obvious that they fall well outside the admittedly fuzzy Freudian boundary.

As with Lacan, there can be little doubt that Kohut's way of talking and writing about human development, clinical method, oedipality and culture is quite distinctive. Gone (or at least apparently missing) are such Freudian mainstays as repression of instincts, of oedipal urges as normal features of a "stage" of human development and the locus classicus of the neuroses, of cool clinical neutrality as a way of fostering the transference neurosis, and the conception of civilization as the price we pay to avoid letting our instincts create a savage Hobbesian world.

In their place we hear about the role of parents and analysts as mirrors (cf. Lacan on the "mirror stage") and of the central importance, clinically, of the idealizing or mirror transference, of "selfobjects" and of self-selfobject relationships, of the developmental line of narcissism, of the way Freud's "Guilty Man" in fear of injury has been supplanted by "Tragic Man" in search of succor, of empathy as the matrix of psychological survival, and of life and civilization as, potentially, at least, a joyous experience.

In Freud's formulation, childhood vicissitudes and the press of phylogenetically grounded impulses are the source of neurotic psychopathology. For Kohut, childhood events are still important but, in contrast to Freud's views on the stages of psychosexual development, the central task of human development lies on the developmental line of narcissism and the formation of a cohesive self. For Kohut, therefore, what Freud described as the normal features of the oedipal years, including lustful, murderous unconscious wishes, while common, are thought of instead as pathological byproducts of failed self-selfobject relationships.

Some anthropologists will, I should think, find value in the debate about whether such views should properly be seen as supplements to or supplantings of Freud's framework. I hope, however, that most will adopt a stance closer to the one taken on this issue by Kohut himself, viz.:

> A worshipful attitude toward established explanatory systems--toward the polished accuracy of their definitions and the flawless consistency of their theories--becomes confining in the history of science--as do, indeed, man's analogous commitments in all of human history. Ideals are guides, not gods. If they become gods, they stifle man's playful creativeness; they impede the activities of the sector of the human spirit that points most meaningfully into the future [Kohut 1977:312, quoted in Muslin 1985:228-229].

This attitude, especially when understood as applying as much to Kohutians and the ardent proponents of various other psychoanalytic "isms" as it does to its ostensible primary target—i.e., classic (orthodox) Freudians, is clearly preferable to other possible attitudes to "heterodoxy."

It also is a very good rendition of both the outlook behind the organization of the 1989 panel whose papers are collected in this volume and of Robert LeVine's approach to the task of bringing a theory to bear on the formulation of his research—in this instance, carried out with Sara LeVine among the Gusii. The opening pages of LeVine's essay will have some of the comfort of a familiar easy chair to those who have read his powerful and important *Culture, Behavior and Personality* (1982). Those unfamiliar with it may be expected, upon finishing this essay, to want to rectify this situation, for they surely will recognize the value of further exposure to the kind of thinking about the nature of psychoanalytic anthropology with which LeVine begins his essay. And, if not then, then surely after seeing the sagacious and even-handed manner he adopts in presenting what are, in fact, rather striking and sensitive ethnographic data.

Trawick and Lacan

For reasons I shall provide shortly, I recently found myself wondering what American anthropologists would think about their French colleagues if, in a relatively sudden move, they were to insist that there were many profound, virtually paradigm shattering ideas in the work of Margaret Mead. This obviously quite hypothetical and admittedly rather odd question occurred to me as I pondered the phenomenal surge of interest, in America (but by no means only here), in the ideas of Jacques Marie Émile Lacan (1901-1981).

For me, and apparently for many others, Lacan's ideas are still largely at the horizon. With even minimum exposure to them, almost anyone can sense that his was a grand vision and so one can understand the appeal. And yet, as one struggles toward this horizon, especially through the work of Lacan *himself*, the goal of understanding never seems to get any nearer. Even so, it seems, at times, that there are legions who, for many reasons, persist in their efforts to reach that horizon. Many do so, I believe, because some of those in the vanguard for whom we have the highest respect, such as Margaret Trawick, continue to urge us onward. And so we try to move ahead, worried all the while that, for us, Lacan's ideas will forever remain an unsatisfied Desire in the realm of the Real or, what probably is worse, that for us his ideas will never leave the realm of the merely "New."

Because of this (to return to my initial, rather strange hypothetical question), it can be quite surprising, if not downright shocking, to learn that Mead and Lacan were born just 8 months apart (Lacan in Paris on 13 April; Mead in Philadelphia on 16 December 1901). Even though Mead's role in the discipline of anthropology was huge and her ideas continue to this day to have an impact within and outside the discipline, one can hardly imagine, as one enters the 1990s, calling her ideas "new." And yet, what Jacques Lacan had to say is now and, for most of us, will likely remain for some time, quite New.

For mainstream psychoanalysts of the 1950s and 1960s, however, Lacan ultimately was far more than merely new. His views were thought to be so at odds with those of his French colleagues that, in 1952-53, he resigned from the Paris Psychoanalytic Society and formed the French Psychoanalytic Society which, by 1962, was expelled from the International Psycho-Analytic Association (for unorthodox practice and teaching methods). Throughout these battles many of the most important leaders of the psychoanalytic mainstream were some of his closest (non-French) associates, including Heinz Hartmann, the IPA president, and Rudolph Loewenstein, his former analyst. Although they were, by then, a part of the immigrant psychoanalytic community in America (on which subject generally, see Kirschner's essay in this volume) and adherents of "ego psychology," most Lacanian experts assert that this had nothing to do with Lacan's scathing denunciations of this variant of Freudian thought.

Lacan's rise, by the 1970s, to the exalted status of French intellectual celebrity, to being, as Plottel puts it, "a household word in households where nobody had [read] a single one of his paragraphs" (1985:335) was, in a sense, rather gradual in that his greatest impact, in France, was achieved over a period of about 30 years prior to the 1970s. Lévi-Strauss was his friend and his "seminars" clearly were *the* place to see and be seen, as evidenced by the attendance of such luminaries (or is it the luminosity of such attendants?) as Barthes, Derrida, Jakobson and Kristeva. In any case, Lacan's forced departure from the International—and there can be little doubt that Lacan genuinely wanted to remain a part of the mainstream and, indeed, was always convinced that his ideas were not only faithful to Freud but also more faithful than were those of his bête noire, the "American" ego psychologists—did little to diminish his influence and, as is often the case, it may have done much to enhance it.

Experts warn that "clear and complete" summaries of Lacan's theories would be a "contradiction in terms" (e.g., Ragland-Sullivan

1987:xi). They also note that, given the linguistic foundation of his theory, it is "impossible" to explain Lacan fully in Anglophonic terms because doing so provides only the "*illusion* of understanding" (ibid.:x). Even so, at the moment, I "hear" Lacan (all too dimly, I suppose) as offering a reasoned blend of topographic and structural Freud with entirely new (and, often, improved) metaphors. Lacanians, I realize, are likely to find this claim fatuous, if not worse but, so far, this stance has contributed to my relative comfort with what others take to be the unbearable challenge and unwarranted influence of his unbareable thought.

Lacanian exegetical sources abound. I have yet to find one, however, that says as much so insightfully about Lacan in so few words as does Margaret Trawick's essay in this volume. Nevertheless, the key to her essay, as I read it, is not her presentation of some of Lacan's most basic ideas but, rather, her precautionary comment about her aims. Note, then, that she is not attempting to use Lacan's ideas to penetrate the logic of Dravidian kinship systems; neither is she hoping that her ethnographic data from Tamil Nadu will permit one to "test" Lacan's formulations. To attempt either would be to violate the counterhegemonic stance that is central in both world views. Given this, readers with an aversion to Lacan may, if they prefer, turn first to the Tamil ethnographic data on pages 55-61 and then to the discussion of Lacan on pages 49-55, for, given her counterhegemonic intent, it can and does not matter where one starts. Those who, at the end of her paper, desire to know more about Lacan, should consult (among others) Crapanzano (1978), Lemaire (1977) and Ragland-Sullivan (1987); those who want more and even richer data about life and love in a Tamil family will find it if they read Trawick's *Notes on Love in a Tamil Family* (1990).

Campbell and Mahler

Mahler's framework, although not without its critics (e.g., Stern 1985), is the product of extended naturalistic observations of normal child development—work of the sort that Freud, unfortunately, seldom did. Mahler began her career in Vienna as a pediatrician directing a well-baby clinic. In the 1930s, she did what so many other analysts did in the face of Nazi persecution: emigrated to the United States (on the significance of which, see, again, Kirschner's paper in this volume). In 1959, she and her associates (notably Fred Pine and Anni Bergman) began the studies that would result in what many would argue is one of the most important psychoanalytic books ever written: *The Psychological Birth of the Human Infant* (Mahler, Pine and Bergman 1975).

JoAnn Campbell's research, although thoroughly informed by Mahler's formulations, was carried out, it is important to note, as much to question and refine them as anything else. Her paper in this volume is striking for a number of other reasons, however. First, the ethnographic data are comparatively fine-grained and of a sort all too rarely seen in the anthropological literature. In a manner reminiscent of the much-admired work of Jean Briggs (1970), Campbell focuses on myriad small, intrafamilial details of life bearing on the psychological development of two Nigerian children. In contrast to the usual anthropological habit of emphasizing the grand, the exotic, and the public, Campbell zooms in on the minute, the ordinary, and the relatively private moments in their lives. Second, she does not wait until after she has presented all the observational data before providing her interpretive thoughts. Rather, she puts forward her hunches about the significance of the material close on the heels of the presentation of each part of it, thereby allowing the reader to see clearly the data in which her thoughts are grounded and, in this way, making it easier to evaluate her claims.

Third, she was attuned to the transferential strands of the children's relationships to her—a move that is as important for and neglected in anthropology as the recognition and use of the observer's counter-transference reactions (Devereux 1967), something Campbell also did, although this is not shown explicitly in this paper. Fourth, *when asked by the parents*, she shared with them her thoughts about how they might make changes in their approach to childcare—opinions that were carefully limited in scope, sensitive to the cultural backgrounds and personal circumstances of the individuals involved and, perhaps most significantly, were clearly grounded in her in-home observations of the children—methodological advances that could, one suspects, be adopted more widely (e.g., by child therapists).

Fifth, her work is provocative for the way she *selectively* makes interpretation-like statements to the children she observed (e.g., her comment to Sharif acknowledging his wish not to share), an empathic move designed to be helpful to the child in his attempt to cope with particular circumstances but that turned out to be helpful to Campbell in her attempt to understand those same events. Finally, and more particularly from the perspective of the way this paper fits into this volume as a whole, Campbell's use of Mahler's framework can be thought about more deeply in light of Kirschner's essay on Protestant values and the history of psychoanalysis and, by the same token, one can, from the perspective of Campbell's essay, appreciate more fully than otherwise would be possible the complexity of the issues in Kirschner's paper. Moreover, because Campbell uses her study of the psychological impact of multiple mothering to discuss key biographical and intellectual events in the lives of both Anna Freud and her father, her essay resonates especially well with Ingham's paper in this volume.

Kilborne and shame

Benjamin Kilborne's essay for this volume is important for at least three reasons. First, it is an example of what we may expect will be a growing trend in psychoanalytic anthropology: theoretical papers by, and of relevance for, anthropologists that are grounded, at least in part, in psychoanalytic clinical work by the anthropologist-author. As it stands, papers of this sort are not so much unprecedented, given the work of Devereux (one of Kilborne's mentors), as far too uncommon. Since there are today several anthropologists who are engaged in the clinical practice of psychoanalysis, we may hope to see more anthropological essays informed by this venue for gathering data about the human condition.

Kilborne's paper also is important because of the way it brings together so many of the issues raised and developed in other papers in this volume. His discussion of shame and early infant research, for example, brings to mind some of the ethnographic data in Campbell's essay. His theoretical review of narcissism and mirroring complements LeVine's discussion of Kohut and Trawick's of Lacan. And his hypothesis that personal factors may have led Freud to neglect shame and his comment that clinical work seems, increasingly, to pertain to shame foreshadows the essays by Ingham and Kirschner.

Finally, Kilborne's paper is important because its central topic is one for which there is a need, within anthropology, for much refinement. Although it is true, as noted in the opening line of the essay, that Freud devoted relatively little of his published work to the study of shame, the same cannot be said for anthropologists. Ever since Benedict's

Chrysanthemum and the Sword (1946), anthropologists have struggled with a variety of issues that surround this concept. Of these, certainly the best known, if not the most important, is whether shame is more predominant than guilt in typical individuals and institutions in certain societies and, therefore, that such groups may be said to have a "shame culture."

For several reasons, the anthropological approach to this topic has always seemed a bit odd to me. In the first place, far too few of the anthropological discussions are informed by the extensive and quite sophisticated theoretical literature on shame—much of which, it may be noted, is reviewed by Kilborne in his essay. One may hope, therefore, that future anthropological inquiries into shame will be based on this more detailed theoretical foundation.

Second, the anthropological data on "the shame question" are infrequently systematic. Rather, much of the discussion in anthropology is grounded in essentially anecdotal data—e.g., claims that, in a given culture, there is no word for guilt or that there are many well-known and much discussed notions about what is shameful but that guilt is seldom if ever discussed. There are few, if any, anthropological studies that use precise and otherwise well developed measures of shame and guilt to analyze data drawn from a carefully chosen sample. Neither can it be said that there are any truly thorough intra-cultural analyses of the relative salience of guilt and shame (with Levy's work in Tahiti [Levy 1973], being a possible exception).

Third, and most puzzling, at least to me, is how irked some become when it is suggested (e.g., in classes or at professional meetings) that shame appears, in some cultures, to be more salient than guilt. Some who react this way may, of course, be objecting to the paucity of data being used to justify such a claim. My sense, however, is that this issue runs a distant second to another one—namely, that an invidious distinction seems all but inevitable when guilt and shame are discussed. When asked, most of those I have discussed the matter with cannot say why they think this is so; they are, nonetheless, convinced psychoanalytically oriented anthropologists think guilt is, somehow, "better" than shame.

In part, this hypothesis may well be rooted in their sense, however tacit, that Freud not only did not discuss shame as much as he discussed guilt but also that he saw civilization itself as originating in human-kind's attempt to obliterate an original, guilt-inducing sin (on which, see also

Ingham's paper in this volume). Or, it could be an example of the process described in Kilborne's paper where one can be ashamed that one is ashamed (and so on, ad infinitum). In any case, it is an issue that merits further research.

Ramanujam and India

One of my colleagues, on learning that I had become a candidate at the psychoanalytic institute in Seattle, said with rather noticeable emphasis: "Good. They need an anthropologist over there." From contextual information I have not supplied, it was obvious to me that he meant that psychoanalysts could benefit from more exposure to anthropological thought—and, then as now, I have no doubt about it: he was right.

At the time, however, my motives were essentially the opposite of those envisioned by my colleague. I became a candidate primarily because I felt—and still feel—that anthropology and the other social sciences could benefit greatly from more exposure to both the methods and theories of psychoanalysis. It may be, of course, that I had this view simply because I was already an anthropologist; it was psychoanalysis that was new to me and that I wanted to add to my viewpoint. In any case, this attitude was, I soon sensed, neither more nor less appropriate than the one expressed by my colleague. It was, I realized, not a case of deciding which discipline needed the other more; rather, I discovered what is perhaps obvious—that there is a *mutual* need. The two disciplines are like the two halves of an arch; they will need to lean on each other to support anything.

Although attractive, this compromise position is, I have come to appreciate, more easily conceived than achieved. There are, I believe, two reasons for this. First, psychoanalysis can be and often is both incredibly provincial and hegemonic—a deadly combination if ever there was one. Second, and possibly even worse, anthropology can be and often is both incredibly cosmopolitan and anti-nomothetic. Thus, in extreme cases, psychoanalysis becomes "the" Freudian view which can explain everything and anthropology becomes an endless parade of particularisms amassed in the service of thwarting all attempts to generalize.

We all have had some exposure to these tendencies but there are few, I suspect, who have had more experience with these stultifying disciplinary potentials than people with non-Euro-American cultural roots who try, in their work, to speak to both camps. I first began to sense this through the teaching and publications of one of my mentors, Francis L. K. Hsu, who has been tireless—and not surprisingly, given the magnitude of the problem, all too unsuccessful—in his efforts to point out blind spots to Euro-American anthropologists and, less often, to psychoanalysts (see Hsu 1979). It is through him that I began to grasp the seriousness of the problem and, at the same time, to have a greater appreciation for the efforts of those who, like B. K. Ramanujam, continuously risk being marginalized by both anthropology and psychoanalysis. The efforts of such individuals to speak to us are, therefore, of considerable importance.

Through B. K. Ramanujam's essay, in a manner that reminds one of the powerful effect of the reports of clinical work by Kakar (e.g., 1978) and Roland (1988), we are permitted access to and have a far richer sense of the inner worlds of the persons who "make up" (i.e., both create and comprise) other cultures. Thus, in the case of Mr. B, presented in the latter half of his paper, we see—vividly and by no means painlessly—what anthropologists know but often have difficulty presenting so convincingly: that other cultures are, subjectively, other realities. In reading about Mr. B, I recalled my surprise on reading an account of an Indian patient presented by his relatives to Sudhir Kakar. He is, they said:

> very stubborn in pursuing what he wants without taking our wishes into account. He thinks he knows what is best for him and does not listen to us. He thinks his own life and career are more important than the concerns of the rest of the family [Kakar 1990:428].

Mr. B and Dr. Kakar's patient, even with the glimpse we have of him, are also of interest for the way they resonate with the material on the Indian families in Margaret Trawick's essay and the Nigerian families in Campbell's paper. Even the dramatically different cultures and theoretical frames being used do not mask these fundamental "family resemblances" (to borrow—and play with a bit—Obeyesekere's recent and felicitous use of this familiar phrase; 1990: passim).

Dr. Ramanujam's essay also is important for the way it offers a basis for broadening Euro-American psychoanalysis conceptually, an effort that also is made in several other papers in this volume, including especially those by Badcock, Campbell, Spiro and myself. To be worthy of the term, a dialogue must be a two-way process. This sort of communication is, however and in my opinion, all too rare in the talking that anthropologists and psychoanalysts do.

Ingham and Catholicism

An important point is raised by those who object to the use of psychoanalysis in a totalizing, hegemonic manner especially vis à vis other intellectual specialties in the social sciences and humanities. Legitimately, one finds resentment when psychoanalysts act as though they have a theory which gives them exclusively the power to cast their all-knowing gaze upon, if not "into," others to reveal hidden (and, therefore, "truer") motives for the other's actions (see Paul 1987, for different but related comments about what is commonly known as applied psychoanalysis; see also Meltzer 1987).

It was satisfying, therefore, to have several persons on the panel who were using their scholarship to return the favor—that is, who were using some of the tenets of anthropology or other areas of expertise to gaze at psychoanalysis. Of the several in this volume who do this, two of the more sustained efforts are by Ingham and, in the paper following it, by Kirschner.

There are appealing ironies to John Ingham's paper. For one, there is irony in the fact that, although the paper is hermeneutic (itself an intellectual development generally traced to biblical scholarship), Ingham's aim is to show, contra many anti-generalizing interpretivists, that there really is something to Freud's theory of human nature and the Oedipus complex (Ingham, personal communication). For another, there is irony in his observation that one of the first works in psychoanalytic anthropology was *Totem and Taboo*. This was, of course, Freud's study of, among other things, the neurotic origin of religious belief. Accordingly, in his personal and professional life, Freud made every effort to exhibit what, one surmises, he felt any psychosexually mature, well-analyzed, scientific psychoanalyst should show—namely, that, at a personal level, Freud had neither a need for nor had his mature, scholarly opinions in any significant way been influenced by religion (cf., Rizzuto 1979). The irony, then, stems not from Ingham's convincing demonstration that Freud's denunciations of religion might have other meanings—and this for reasons not all that different than those Freud himself would have brought to bear on those of his patients who might have repeatedly and vehemently denied the validity of one of his interpretations. Rather, it comes from his ability to show that the religious themes that may well have been formative for Freud, as he struggled to give birth to his particular version of oedipal theory, were Roman Catholic.

Building on but going far beyond the work of Vitz (1988), Ingham (who has published previously on Catholicism) offers a more complex reading of Catholicism beginning with his suggestion (contra Vitz) that Eden and Golgotha are opposed as well as similar scenes. The heart of his presentation, however, has to do with the biblical, Roman Catholic and personal (for Freud) meanings of such central motifs as trees, words, knowledge (especially in Scripture and Freud's dreams) and their impact on Freud's views. Also central to Ingham's discussion (and it is a point mentioned as well, but less centrally, by Campbell in this volume) is his assessment of the impact on Freud's views of his (probably traumatic) relationship with his Roman Catholic nanny. It is likely, he suggests, that Freud's well-known and much criticized over-emphasis of the father-son dyad in his theories is, in part, a product of the particular character of this period of Freud's life. Ultimately, concludes Ingham, Freud's views in general were "facilitated and constrained by an intricate and idiosyncratic blending of culture, experience, and defense" and, as any psychoanalytic anthropologist should well be able to appreciate, that this has had "important consequences for the history of psychoanalytic thought."

Kirschner and Protestantism

It is more boring than annoying to be told that Freud's theories are of limited applicability because they are so culture-bound. Boring because this argument has to be the single greatest cliché in the arsenal of critics of psychoanalysis. Indeed, it is worse than that, it is a muddled cliché since those who use it fail to distinguish two quite distinct issues—the cultural roots of an idea and the idea's empirical value.

Although the central premise of Suzanne Kirschner's essay is that psychoanalytic theory is "shot through with myriad cultural discourses," her contribution to this volume is neither muddled nor clichéd. On the contrary, it is a brisk and riveting demonstration of the influence on the history of psychoanalysis of values which derive from two of the most important strands of Protestantism which were foundational for the Anglo-American world. Interestingly, by showing how contemporary secular variants of Puritan and Nonconformist Protestantism have fostered psychoanalytic views in England and America that are, by comparison, atrophied in Roman Catholic France, Kirschner also reinforces, quite independently, Ingham's claims, in the paper discussed above, regarding the role of Catholicism in the development of Freud's oedipal theory.

Discussed in Kirschner's paper is the work of the later ego psychologists (e.g., Mahler and Kernberg), British object relations (e.g., Winnicott and Sandler), and self psychology (Kohut, on which also see LeVine's paper in this volume). All of these theorists show far less interest in oedipal conflicts and instinctual issues and, instead, provide a broadly similar chart of human development with the normal outcome being individuals with a well-, if not hyper-, developed sense of their distinctiveness and autonomy.

Kirschner notes that these "revisionists" generally have attempted to remain part of the psychoanalytic mainstream and have tended to do so in part by arguing that their new views were forced upon them by the necessities of their clinical work. A key component of this defense is the claim that today's patients, in contrast to those of Freud's day, tend not to exhibit oedipal-level psychopathology. But, Kirschner reminds us, that argument is weakened by growing evidence that even Freud's patients were not "mere" oedipal neurotics either. They too had problems linked to much earlier periods in their development.

This point is vital to Kirschner's presentation because, once the inadequacies of this virtually standard argument are recognized, the way is cleared for her assessment of the impact of cultural values on the shaping of what she refers to as the psychoanalytic lens. The result of her inquiry is impressive. She shows that the shaping of the Anglo-American psychoanalytic lens clearly is the product of research and clinical work carried out in a setting dominated by three distinctive, culture-specific values—self-reliance, self-direction and verbal expression

—not of work ground out against a neutral background.

Spain and oedipality

Gananath Obeyesekere was one of the two discussants for the afternoon session during which I presented my paper. Late in 1988, when the panel was in the final planning stage, he kindly held out some hope for me when I asked if he might do a paper. Ultimately, however, he all too modestly decided that he did not, at that time, have anything new that he wanted to say about psychoanalysis since he had spoken at length on that subject in the Morgan Lectures (see *The Work of Culture: Symbolic Transformation in Psychoanalysis and Anthropology*, Obeyesekere 1990). I had already begun writing my paper by this time—a task that, in this instance, was comparatively easy for me to do since I had given oral versions of it as lectures for several years in my undergraduate course in psychological anthropology (indeed, much of the content was developed in response to my students who, in the main, are quite happily anti-psychoanalytic).

In his comments on my paper at the session, Obeyesekere (at least as I recall it) said two things, one rather positive and the other fairly negative. He enjoyed the part where I speculated about what the history of psychoanalysis would have been like if Freud had been born in Japan. It was, he said, a good question and, furthermore, it reminded him of a similar argument he had made in what was then his forthcoming book (see 1990:84-88). As for the rest of the paper, however, he was less sanguine. In particular, he expressed considerable surprise that an anthropologist, so near the last decade of this century, should still be asserting that the Oedipus complex was universal.

During the Spring 1991 term, I used *The Work of Culture* as the main text in a seminar on psychoanalytic anthropology. Most of the handful of students in it had read my oedipality paper in a course the previous quarter. Like them, however, I did not read *The Work of Culture* until the Spring term. It was of more than passing interest to me, therefore, when several of the students opened our discussion of "Lecture Two" ("Oedipus: The Paradigm and its Hindu Rebirth," pp.71-139) by commenting on what they thought was the rather striking convergence of our views on the question of the universality of oedipality.

I could not help but agree with them. After all, several times in my paper I had said things like "oedipality is not a constant but a variable" and "*The* Oedipus complex is not a universal." And, for his part, Obeyesekere had said things like "Neither myth nor complex is universal in the sense of exhibiting an invariant pattern or structure; but they might exhibit 'family resemblances'" (p.88) and "The Oedipus complex is much more complex than the simple triangular relationship where the son hates the father and loves the mother!" (a statement that prompted me to write "Sure!" at that point—i.e., on p.86, in the margin of my copy of his book). And, even though I had also said things like "oedipality is found in all cultures," I was completely convinced (and still am) that if there are any differences in our views on this issue, they are minor (for an essay on oedipality that offers an important contrasting view, see Stanley Kurtz's forthcoming book *All the Mothers Are One*).

The moral of this story is this. One can *easily* be misunderstood on an issue such as this, so let it be noted once again: although oedipality is a human developmental universal, it is *not* a constant.

Johnson and materialism

Cultural relativism may have European roots but, in anthropology, the idea flowered most gloriously in America through the careful nurturing of Franz Boas. It is interesting, therefore, that the first really significant relativistic push against Freud's ostensibly anti-relativistic psychology was made not in the United States but in England—by, of course, Bronislaw Malinowski. Ever since, there has been, especially in America, a "persistent erosion" (to use Johnson's phrase) of Freud's materialism. An evaluation of this development is the central theme of Allen Johnson's essay.

For most anthropologists, the term materialism is often used as the shorthand for cultural materialism. As Johnson notes, however, there are at least three distinct types of materialism—a claim he establishes quite forcefully in his paper which, fortuitously, fits quite neatly between my relatively abstract ponderings about oedipality and Badcock's comparatively detailed formulation of a Darwinian psychoanalysis.

These days, if there is an admired form of psychoanalysis in academia, it would seem to be that variety which is the least biological. In contrast to the expectations of Johnson's colleagues, who apparently are caught up in the hermeneutic turn of modern anthropology and who obviously gave him the same puzzled looks my colleagues gave me when I said I had begun training in psychoanalysis, Johnson takes biostructural materialism quite seriously. In particular, he discusses it in light of his research showing that traditional oedipal stories are found in hundreds of cultures from all parts of the world. In tones reminiscent of Chomsky on language, Johnson suggests that oedipal tales are the "external reflection of some innate property of the human mind."

A key moment in Johnson's essay occurs when he acknowledges that his views are consistent with Paul's (1976) essay on the primal crime. That paper is, I continue to believe, one of the boldest, most important, and most misunderstood of the modern works in psychoanalytic anthropology, in part because (much to the consternation of many psychoanalysts and psychoanalytic anthropologists), Paul insists "something like" the primal crime actually took place. In this context, Johnson reviews basic findings on the oedipality question that are available in the literature on those primates, such as the chimpanzees, that are comparatively near humans phylogenetically. On doing so, he forthrightly reiterates his earlier view, stating: "the seemingly universal oedipal-type tale is evidence of a biostructural human [mental] substrate" or algorithm that "must be activated or completed by interpersonal experiences of the growing child."

Johnson then contrasts biostructural materialism with the ecological-functionalist form, a variety in which culture is seen as a set of defensive products and/or as made up of projective systems. It is, as Johnson documents, a view which dominated psychological anthropology for nearly 40 years, beginning in the 1930s. Although waning somewhat, it is a view that neither he nor I (nor many others) would lightly dismiss.

Historical materialism is the third type discussed by Johnson—in this instance by means of some informative vignettes from his field study of tenant-landlord relationships on a plantation in Brazil. What sets Johnson's discussion apart is the lengthy time period during which he made his observations and his use, in more recent visits, of both Marxist class analysis and psychoanalytic theory to assess not only his reactions to the residents of the plantation but their reaction to him. This strategy, it seems to me, beautifully illustrates two of Johnson's more thought-provoking concluding observations: (1) "the materialism of Freud is most valuable when placed in a context of competing orientations" and (2) that it was, after all, Freud's "willingness to accept that seemingly contrary processes may coexist" that made his ideas endlessly "dynamic and provocative."

Badcock and Darwin

"Trying to understand why men have such powerful feelings about their own penises is not quite the same thing as trying to explain the zig-zag commissures of clams." How true! But it is not utterly different, either. And that is the central point, I believe, not only of Daniel Rancour-Laferriere's exuberant *Signs of the Flesh: An Essay on the Evolution of Hominid Sexuality*, in which the sentence quoted above may be found (1985:7), but also of the profound and often provocative essay prepared especially for this volume by Christopher Badcock. That his essay eventually became a part of this volume is quite gratifying to me and is due, in no small measure, to his swift pen and most generous spirit.

Badcock's general aim is no less than to complete a synthesis of Freudian findings and modern evolutionary theory and then to develop it into a new paradigm for behavioral science. Building on the work of Trivers (e.g., 1985) and others in sociobiology, Badcock has, in his several more recent and important books (e.g., see especially Badcock 1986, 1990, 1991 and 1992) recast and largely rewritten much of the Freudian canon.

Virtually everything psychoanalytic, from such intensely controversial topics as penis envy and the primal scene to such clinical mainstays as repression and transference, is grist for his neo-evolutionary mill. And, impressively enough, Badcock here presents the heart of his views on this vast array of topics in just a few pages. In time, of course, we will know if his works will establish a new paradigm for behavioral science. Until then, however, they will give all psychoanalytic anthropologists much to think about. Indeed, so numerous and important are his insights, it may well require years to absorb them fully. But what stimulating years they are sure to be.

Spiro and symbols

In reviewing the history of psychoanalytic anthropology, I discussed the work of four individuals who made extremely important contributions to the field: Géza Róheim, the pioneer, the one who showed the way, both in the clinic and field; Abram Kardiner, the great revisionist whose impact on psychological anthropologists is far greater than many people seem to realize; George Devereux, a dazzling, creative genius whose mastery of science, language and literature yielded a scholarly oeuvre that (alas) is unlikely soon, if ever, to be matched in our field; and Weston La Barre, who, no matter what else he may astonish us with in his next publication, will always be the unsurpassable master of scholarly detail as well as an absolutely unblinking beacon—not only for psychoanalytic anthropologists but also for, as he put it so deliciously (and maliciously) in dedicating a collection of some of his papers, "the willfully blind who remain my friends" (La Barre 1980b). As the years go by, other names will be added to this list in future historical sketches of the field. First among them, I am sure, will be Melford E. Spiro. His psychoanalytically informed publications mark him, I think indisputably, as the leading psychoanalytic anthropologist today.

Like Róheim, Kardiner, Devereux and La Barre, Spiro has been both prolific and at his best when he has been most polemical. Indeed, among his contemporaries, he is virtually without peer as a fashioner of tightly-reasoned position-papers on critically important topics and arguments in anthropology generally and psychoanalytic anthropology specifically. More important, however, is his personal impact on the field: he has done far more to foster an interest in psychoanalysis among his students and anthropological colleagues than any other anthropologist. Some of Spiro's best known and most admired scholarly attributes are displayed in his contribution to this volume. It is an essay that surely is one of his more tightly-worked arguments on any subject to date and, as is typical, it is a particularly important one since both anthropologists and psychoanalysts spend the best parts of their working days engrossed in the mysteries of meaning as conveyed by signs.

The paper is grounded in *The Interpretation of Dreams*, a bio-hermeneutic work of gigantic import, in which Freud lays down the foundation for nearly a century of scholarship on human mentation. Central to this was his distinction between primary and secondary process—with dreams, of course, being "primary" in at least two senses of the term. As Spiro demonstrates, however, Freud's account of the *formal* (as opposed to the functional) differences in primary and secondary mental represental processes is "critically flawed." Spiro shows, contrary to Freud, that some very important features of the method whereby unconscious thought is represented are not unique to that mode but are characteristic of the representation of conscious thoughts also.

As I read him, there are two keys to Spiro's argument—first, the contrast that he draws between conventional and private symbols (cf. Obeyesekere 1981) and second, the use that he makes of C. S. Peirce's (1932) model of signs. It is the second of these that is the bellwether, I believe, for much that will animate our discipline in the years ahead is likely to be informed by Peirce's views. As E. Valentine Daniel noted in the Peircian essay he read at the meeting where the papers in this book were first presented (a paper that, unfortunately, could not be included here), the Peircian and Freudian triads can be made to resonate quite beautifully indeed.

Regrettably, since Spiro's paper is quite brief and addressed primarily to psychoanalysts (a move which, although attributed to a parapraxis, could hardly be more appropriate for this volume since one of my most basic aims was to foster a two-way conversation between anthropology and psychoanalysis), we must wait for the other shoe to drop since the full anthropological ramifications of his point are not spelled out. One may anticipate, however, that having cleared the air by showing the absence of a *formal* distinction between sign-substitution in primary and secondary process mentation, there will be ample room for Spiro to show us more vividly some of the implications of the *functional* (motivational) differences. May that boot drop hard and fast.

Conclusion

In the fifty years since Freud's death, psychoanalysis has been the subject of more evaluative thought and scrutiny than any other twentieth century social theory. To some, and for years, this has been taken as a sign of the theory's weakness, as an indication that psychoanalysis is moribund. I and many others, however, see this as a sign of the discipline's strength and continuing salience. Even those who appreciate this the most, however, can be and must continue to be critical. *Appreciation requires it.*

In Vienna, in Sigmund Freud Park, there is a granite memorial to the founder of psychoanalysis. The words on it, however, are not Freud's. Instead, it is Seneca who speaks to us, saying: "The voice of reason is soft." Over the years, many who have expressed their views regarding psychoanalysis have done so in a manner that can be described only as harsh. If this book, which both expresses and *is* an appreciation of Freud's legacy, is at times critical, it may be hoped that it can be said fairly that our voices were soft. It certainly was our intent.[5]

[5]Materials cited in this Introduction are listed in the Bibliography at the end of the book.

Part One

Field- and Clinic-Based Studies

Chapter One

The Self in an African Culture

Robert A. LeVine

In *Totem and Taboo* (1913), Freud wrote in two distinct voices, that of the tentative clinical observer attempting interpretations of exotic customs and that of the confident theorist offering a comprehensive account of human nature. These have inspired two tendencies of thinking and research in psychoanalytic anthropology, one more empiricist and primarily concerned with cultural variation, the other more speculative and concerned with biopsychological universals. Freud himself explicitly preferred the second of these, and those like Jones and Róheim who remained part of his circle defined an orthodox position in accord with Freud's conception of human nature, while those who sought rapprochement with the emerging cultural anthropology of the 1920s and 1930s defined a variety of revisionist positions critical of Freud.

In the revival of interest in psychoanalytic anthropology since the late 1960s, the boundaries between these two traditions of thought and research have weakened and become blurred, though they are still recognizable as tendencies. Contributors to the field have created a number of individual positions that are not classifiable simply in terms of this polarity. The substantial differences in viewpoint that persist are discussed and debated, representing progress of a sort. Furthermore, I believe there may be some common starting points, if not true unifying assumptions, for contemporary psychoanalytic anthropology as a whole regardless of its antecedents in the divisions of earlier generations.

1. *The Standard Edition of the Complete Psychological Works of Sigmund Freud*. Published between 1953 and 1966, the 23 volumes of the Standard Edition by James Strachey provided not only an improved English translation but, through the editor's notes and the inclusion of previously inaccessible works, the possibility of a clearer understanding of Freud's thought than was available to anthropologists and other

scholars of previous generations. Given the persistent confusion, *even within psychological anthropology*, about the relationship of Freud's ideas to earlier work in our field, this constitutes an advance of which psychoanalytic anthropologists have only begun to take advantage.

The importance of the Standard Edition stems in part from the lack of a genuine research tradition within organized psychoanalysis, despite its enormous output of books and journals. There is no generally agreed upon means of building knowledge from psychoanalytic observations, either as discoveries or verifications. There are many competing views among psychoanalysts of how clinical findings during the fifty years since Freud's death bear on the generalizations and theoretical models of Freud and his successors. The hope expressed in Freud's 1923 statement that "psychoanalysis is ... a collection of psychological information ... which is gradually being accumulated into a new scientific discipline" has not been borne out, as his successors tend either to treat his works as unmodifiable truth or to devise novel systems of their own. Cumulative knowledge is rarely to be found. In this confused situation, the anthropologist seeking to work with psychoanalytic concepts or methods has no choice but to begin with Freud's own writings, and the Standard Edition provides indispensable help. I believe there is general agreement that anthropological discourse about psychoanalysis not well grounded in Freud's work cannot be taken seriously.

2. *The Darwinian framework.* No valid anthropology or human psychology can be inconsistent with evolutionary biology as formulated by Charles Darwin. Freud believed this, though some of his own evolutionary hypotheses are flawed from a contemporary biological perspective, and it remains fundamental to work in the field he began.

3. *Universals.* Although the universalism-relativism debate is as vigorous as ever, psychoanalytic anthropology calls for the assumption that there *are* socially relevant psychological universals and that Freud's work is the best source of concepts with which to build theoretical models of them. It is hard to imagine a psychoanalytic anthropology, for example, without assuming transference and intrapsychic defense as universal among humans. This is not to deny that questions of the *extent* to which social behavior is attributable to species-specific universals or culture-specific traditions are among the most controversial in our field.

4. *Fieldwork.* Whatever role they assign to theoretical interpretation, contemporary psychoanalytic anthropologists put field research at the

center of their scholarly activity. Recent volumes of psychoanalytically informed ethnography conducted in cultures around the world attest to this assertion.

5. *The assumption that both cultural context and personal experience are important objects of investigation.* Most psychoanalytic anthropologists assume that symbols encountered in fieldwork must be located in what I shall call "cultural space" and "personal time," i.e., in the conceptual network of a particular culture and the sequentially experienced lifespan of an individual, and that doing so represents an essential series of tasks for the investigator.

In each of these five common starting points, there is much room for serious, even fundamental, disagreement. They nevertheless give reason to hope for an exchange of perspectives and information that will advance the field.

My own approach to psychoanalytic anthropology owes a great deal to the influence of Heinz Kohut, who is known for his psychoanalytic self psychology (Kohut 1971, 1977) but who was previously the foremost teacher of basic Freudian principles at the Chicago Institute for Psychoanalysis. Kohut's advice to those who sought a psychoanalytic social science was, "Clarify the surface before going to the depths." A surface psychology, i.e., a phenomenology of conscious experience, was the essential pathway to the depth psychology that constitutes psychoanalytic understanding. Kohut saw this simply as an explication of the Freudian clinical method, working through the conscious associations of the patient to the unconscious meanings of a symptom, a dream, or a feeling. He emphasized the importance of empathy in this process, and the importance of a common language and culture for the analyst's achievement of empathy with a patient (Kohut 1959). The greater the cultural and linguistic distance between analyst and person being analyzed, the more the analyst needs to learn of the other person's conscious point of view in order to achieve empathy. Thus anthropologists studying a culture other than their own need an extended period of contextual investigation before being able to make valid depth interpretations.

Kohut's view brings out two similarities between ethnography and psychoanalysis. First, both are methods of "empathic understanding," in which the reconstruction of the other's point of view is an essential part of the investigation; and second, both rely on contextual analysis, i.e. the establishment of subjective meanings by placing specific ideas or behaviors in a larger symbolic order. In addition, Kohut's emphasis on the self as an organizer of experience is consistent with ethnographic studies of the self in diverse cultures and constitutes a promising connection between psychoanalysis and anthropology.

A psychoanalytic anthropology should, in my opinion, be addressed to the following general questions:

1. Are there variations in emotional responsiveness, psychodynamics and other aspects of psychological organization between human populations?

2. What is the psychodynamic basis of stability and change in cultural symbols and social institutions?

3. How does childhood experience contribute to the adult psychological organization that may vary across populations and support social and cultural stability and change?

4. What universals of human development and culture are consistent with the evidence from diverse populations?

This sequence of questions, with universals at the end to be generated from cross-cultural evidence, reflects the empiricism of my approach and my skeptical attitude toward claims of phylogenetically based, species-wide universals—an attitude not shared with all psychoanalytic anthropologists.

I have long believed that what psychoanalytic anthropology needs most is a descriptive method usable in diverse cultural settings that would permit the accumulation of knowledge and the empirical testing of theoretical models. Without such a method, it is difficult to move beyond the exploratory phase of a research project that began more than 75 years ago. Although culture-specific explorations have recently become deeper and more extensive, no consensus has yet emerged regarding how we can generate valid descriptions that might be compared across cultures. We cannot expect psychoanalysts to help, given their neglect of the same problem in their own field, and we have learned from experience that solutions based on personality tests are inadequate. Anthropologists must devise their own solutions, and in fact have done so in the diverse contexts of their field research. They have shown that ethnography can be an instrument of psychoanalytic understanding, particularly when combined with other methods that extend its insights to the individual level.

A few years ago I presented in outline a person-centered approach to the ethnographic study of self that might produce cultural data of psychoanalytic significance (LeVine 1982:293-304). I assumed that the social conventions for presenting the self in social interaction and representing the self in cultural narratives reveal the wishes, fears and defenses common to the members of a community who maintain these conventions in their interpersonal communication. More specifically, I assumed that the conventions of routine interaction constitute a social code of censorship for the sexual, aggressive and self-assertive tendencies of individuals, and that cultural narratives constitute conventionalized fantasies that express wishes and fears, conflicts and defenses—including those that are censored in everyday life—by attributing emotions to personified but often disguised figures.

The ethnographer's tasks of describing and interpreting these conventions resemble the analyst's "listening to the patient," i.e., recording the patient's preoccupations as they occur in free associations, and accumulating evidence about the emotional experience of the patient on which depth interpretations can be based. The goal is not simply to record all conscious preoccupations in their sequential order, but to identify initially what leads to anxiety and to relief and protection from anxiety. Freud's model, originating in psychiatric treatment and later extended to normal development and culture, approaches mental phenomena through the disturbances of stable states—including what he called the "psychopathology of everyday life"—and explicitly assumes the salience of anxiety in organizing experience and generating cognitive rules of censorship, avoidance and disguise. Anthropologists may object to this approach as leading to the characterization of a particular culture as distinctively pathological, with the implicit presumption that the ethnographer's culture is normal, and I do not deny that psychoanalytic concepts have been used in this way. But Freud's application of this model to the dreams and slips of the tongue of normal people in his own society (including himself) shows that it need not entail such a presumption. I take a psychoanalytic approach to assume that every culture is partly designed to protect normal people from anxiety and to restore their sense of well-being when anxiety threatens, and that probing this aspect of culture can lead to a deeper understanding of the positive goals a particular people share.

An ideal strategy of psychoanalytic field research in a particular culture would, in my view, have four parts. In the first, person-centered ethnography identifies the meanings of interactive and narrative conventions current in a community, i.e., their probable psychic functions in maintaining a culturally constituted sense of self. In the second, studies of particular adults shed light on the actual psychic functions of conventional norms and representations, e.g., the degree to which rituals provide defensive resolutions for specific persons and in what situations. The third part consists of studies of children and their environments from birth onwards, to obtain independent evidence on childhood experience and the ontogenesis of the self-representation of the defenses. Finally, there is the cross-checking of interpretive conclusions by a native investigator, i.e., a trained social scientist or psychiatrist whose first language and culture were acquired in the indigenous context. By varying the analytic perspective from cultural material to individual case studies, child observations and the bicultural analyst, this research strategy provides evidence to falsify and revise psychoanalytic interpretations until an interpretation is reached that is most consistent with the multiple bodies of data.

Since the middle 1970s, when we last spent a long period of time there, Sarah LeVine and I have been working on a project of this sort among the Gusii of Kenya. The project was organized around a two-year study of infants and their parents, involving observation of children's interactions with their social environments during the first 30 months of life (LeVine et al. in press), but it also included intensive ethnographic study of routine interaction, rituals, and other cultural narratives and case studies of young mothers, families in crisis, and heavy drinkers. Some of these materials have been published (S. LeVine 1979; R. LeVine 1982), but most have not. The most difficult part has been involving bicultural Gusii able and willing to provide an insider's critique of our interpretations, but we believe this is still possible.

I shall focus on the ethnographic part of the project here, particularly the controversial idea that ethnographic description can be used for psychoanalytic interpretation. In order to do this in a brief presentation, I shall start with some conclusions from the ethnographic exercise, and then indicate some of the grounds for arriving at the conclusions.

A psychoanalytic approach asks the questions: What do these people want? What forms do their wishes and fears take? How do they maintain a sense of psychological well-being in the face of perceived threats? The Gusii—and here I speak in an "ethnographic present" of precolonial traditions dating from before 1907 that were largely intact in the 1950s but which have changed at an accelerating pace with each decade since then—are organized entirely by patrilineal kinship, with localized lineages, patrilocal residence and extensive polygyny. The domestic group serves as the prototype and idiom for social organization in general and the dwellings serve not only as spaces for routine activities but also as the stages for all ritual dramas. Burial, for example, takes place just outside the house, in specified locations for men and women, and the deceased elders are regarded as powerful kin who communicate only through omens and afflictions, demanding to be fed through animal sacrifice and threatening dire consequences if they are not. Thus there is symbolic continuity between the interactional contexts of daily life and the representational world of ritual performance. Yet no observer could fail to notice the prominence of fear and other negative emotions in Gusii rituals as a whole as explained by Gusii informants, and the minor role of positive emotions in most of them.

What is feared? First of all, incest. The Gusii practice an elaborate form of intergenerational avoidance, in which social and physical distance is mandated not only between parents and their real children but between all kin who address each other with parent and child terms. Each person's interactional world is effectively stratified into generational layers of classificatory parents and children—who must be avoided—and peers, grandparents and grandchildren, who need not be. The focus of avoidance (as Freud guessed in his discussion of mother-in-law avoidance in *Totem and Taboo*) is sexual contact, interpreted so broadly as to include touching, appearing pregnant or co-hearing an obscenity with a parent of the opposite sex. There are specific rules to avoid sexual contact between mother and adult son as well as father and adult daughter, but the most intensely prohibited contact is between father and son's wife, where the likelihood of sexual encounter is greatest, given the domestic power of the patriarch. Thus the idiom of incest is used to limit that power as well as to restrain the behavior of young adults toward their elders.

The norms that mandate joking sexual abuse between members of alternate generations—in which a boy and his maternal grandmother, for example, exchange bawdy insults—give public emphasis by way of contrast to the restraint that must prevail between generations. Accidental breaches of this restraint occasion severe embarrassment, which is regarded as a moral emotion. To fear incest in culturally specified situations and to follow rules that avoid sexual contact, is to be a good person by Gusii standards. Neighboring peoples like the Luo, Kipsigis and Kikuyu who have different rules (lacking avoidance) are regarded as morally inferior. These rules of propriety are far more salient and elaborated for the Gusii than face-to-face norms of conviviality (regulating aggression) and norms of humility (regulating self-assertion). The Gusii have created a culture in which the avoidance of incest, a human universal, has become symbolically extended and codified into a central feature of their culturally constituted sense of self and through it into a system of social control.

If incest is most feared in social interaction between the generations, it is jealousy that is most feared among peers. In Gusii ritual and folk medicine it is taken as a basic assumption that one's body is extremely vulnerable to the malevolent intentions of a jealous neighbor and that all neighbors are potentially jealous. Serious illness and other afflictions are often attributed to the malevolence of others in the community, sometimes portrayed as witches and sometimes as users of sorcery medicine. Social contact with a malevolent person translates into life-threatening illness involving a swelling of the visceral organs unless protective medicines are applied, usually rubbed into cuts made on the body. This kind of protection is also a necessary part of most Gusii rites of passage. Babies are seen as particularly vulnerable because their skin is soft and can easily be penetrated, but the most powerful men in the community require particular protection (through sorcery medicines) because their status and property arouse jealousy. A vast amount of ethnographic material supports the statement that Gusii see themselves as somatically vulnerable to ill will.

One reaction to this representation of self is to inhibit the disclosure of any information about the self that would arouse jealousy in others. Thus Gusii avoid announcing any good fortune that occurs to them, often even to other members of the domestic group. Others have to guess what the news is and ask a question to which they will get a grudging reply (see S. LeVine 1979). They consider reporting good news as "boasting," which would certainly elicit harmful jealousy in others.

There are two interpretations of this phenomenon that go beyond the statement by informants that they are realistically afraid of jealous kin and neighbors. First, the focus of their inhibition is the unsolicited announcement of good fortune, not disclosure of the information. Thus a woman would not, could not, burst out with the news that she is pregnant—this would be gross flaunting that might somehow offend someone—but she could concede that she was if questioned or permit others to find out indirectly. Thus it is the act of making the announcement, even to someone with no reasonable grounds to be jealous, that is particularly feared and avoided. This suggests a censorship of self-assertion based on the unconscious expectation that the display of a grandiose self, to use Kohut's term, will bring a negative response. We consider this a transference phenomenon that must have its roots in childhood experience, just as the opposite kind of expectation, viz. *amae*, the presumption of the benevolence of others, as described by Doi (1981) for Japanese adults, reflects a culturally constituted pattern of interaction in early childhood.

Second, there is the assumption of limitless greed. Why is everyone expected to be jealous of any improvement in anyone else's life? There is no problem understanding why those who are especially deprived, like barren women or impoverished men, might envy those more fortunate than themselves, but such persons do not account for the pervasiveness of presumed jealousy in the community. The vernacular term for murderous jealousy, *enda mwamu*, literally "black stomach," is also used to refer to a greedy child who takes all the food from the bowl for himself instead of sharing it with his siblings. The prototype of someone motivated by enda mwamu is the witch (*omorogi*), about whom there is an endless stream of gossip and rumor in a Gusii community. Many people claim to have come upon a group of witches at night exhuming corpses from graves in order to eat them and to gain potent magic from their body parts; they report that the witches were quarrelling over the distribution of the human meat, demanding better parts and complaining that the others were keeping the best parts for themselves. If we assume that this narrative represents rejected aspects of the self, then the assumption of universal jealousy is based on the persistent greed and resentment of sharing experienced in oneself but attributed to one's neighbors and kin. This suggests a greed that is repressed in the course of childhood social development and is disavowed as part of the mature self but remains unconsciously active in shaping social expectations and fantasies during the adult years.

A third answer to the question of what Gusii adults fear is: other people's eyes. Being seen or even being visible is a metaphor for danger to the self in many Gusii rituals, and being in ritual seclusion is the contrasting metaphor for safety. Seclusion in one's own house for an extended period is necessary at moments of physical vulnerability such as just after circumcision or clitoridectomy in male and female initiation or when a mother gives birth to twins or a breech-delivered or premature child. Seclusion is also prescribed by diviners as a cure for certain afflictions. The vulnerable or afflicted person is always maintained with warmth and food in this simulation of the womb for several weeks, but the most salient part of seclusion to the Gusii is the rule that no one, but particularly members of the local community, may see the person until it is over. Then there is a dramatic ceremony of emergence (*ekiarokio*), requiring animal sacrifice, libations of millet-beer and the administrations of protective medicine *before* the person emerges to be seen by kin and neighbors. The ethnographic data leave no doubt that at such moments the eyes of ordinary neighbors are considered dangerous to one's survival until seclusion and ritual protection have strengthened one physically. The eyes of neighbors and the social visibility they represent are potent, multivocal symbols of interpersonal fear in Gusii culture.

The developmental history of this fear involves the averting of gaze in mother-infant interaction, so that the child's earliest experiences with mutual gaze are not charged with the positive emotional valence they have in our own cultural experience. As the infant becomes a toddler, maternal visual attention is attracted more by misbehavior than by good conduct and becomes a symbol of reproach. Later still, as the child learns how to behave according to adult standards in face-to-face situations, visual interaction is largely excluded by the code of avoidance and respect. Given this history, it is not surprising that being seen could become a symbol of fear. Mutual gaze may lead to emotional arousal in all humans, but the specific emotion aroused is influenced by one's developmental experience in a particular cultural environment (LeVine 1990).

Having described in summary form some of the fears manifested in Gusii cultural materials, I want to end by indicating that Gusii culture also provides formulas for defending oneself against these fears. One formula is avoidance, not only in defending against the experience of incest but also as a general strategy for preventing dangerous interactions. Ritual seclusion is only the most dramatic form of avoidance in this more general sense; the reduction of social contact is the normative response to witches and others who are feared. A second formula is ritual itself, i.e., following a highly detailed set of prescriptive rules authorized by a diviner or other ritual expert in order to eliminate the dangers of ancestors, witches and sorcerers. The third is strengthening one's body through the administration of protective medicine rubbed into cuts, as mentioned above, which is part of many rituals and healing performances. By adhering to these formulas, a Gusii can gain relief from fear, or at least from the acute anxiety that arises when an adult believes himself and his family to be in danger.

The question of how effective these culturally constituted defensive formulas are in managing the fears and anxieties of Gusii individuals can only be answered through case studies of individuals. At a more general level, the effectiveness of these formulas has eroded over the decades as interpersonal competition over land, school achievement and jobs has increased fear and as the local authorities, who once regulated competition, have lost their power. The results are evident in alcoholism, family violence and other violent crime, and witchcraft suspicions, all of which increased noticeably between 1956 and 1976, but also in the rise of new social identities based largely on Protestant Christianity which offer the possibility of transcending local ties in the interests of a separate self.

Much more evidence could and should be presented concerning the features I have described, particularly in relation to the Gusii representation of self. This paper should be seen as consisting of headlines from a detailed account still in progress, suggesting how ethnography focused on social censorship can lead toward a psychoanalytic understanding of the cultural context of individual experience.

References

Doi, L. Takeo. 1981. *The Anatomy of Dependence* (John Bester, trans.). New York, Vintage.

Freud, Sigmund. 1913. *Totem and Taboo*. Standard Edition, Vol. 13. London: Hogarth Press. 1955:1-164.

Kohut, Heinz. 1959. Introspection, empathy and psychoanalysis. *Journal of the American Psychoanalytic Association* 7:459-483.

_________. 1971. *The Analysis of the Self.* New York: International Universities Press.

_________. 1977. *The Restoration of the Self.* New York: International Universities Press.

LeVine, Robert. 1982. *Culture, Behavior and Personality*, 2nd ed. New York: Aldine.

_________. 1990. "Infant Environments in Psychoanalysis: A Cross-cultural View." In G. Herdt et al., eds., *Cultural Psychology* (pp.454-474). New York: Cambridge University Press.

LeVine, Robert, S. Dixon, Sarah LeVine, A. Richman, P.H. Leiderman, and T.B. Brazelton, T.B. (in press). *Omwana: Infants and Parents in a Kenya Community*. New York: Cambridge University Press.

LeVine, Sarah. 1979. *Mothers and Wives: Gusii Women of East Africa.* Chicago: University of Chicago Press.

Chapter Two

Desire in Kinship: A Lacanian View of the South Indian Familial Self

Margaret Trawick

This paper aims to mate two large and unwieldy and to all appearances incompatible beasts, one of these beasts being Dravidian kinship (the system of cross-cousin marriage practiced by people in South India) and the other being Lacanian psychoanalytic theory (the teachings of the influential French linguistic philosopher and psychoanalyst, Jacques Lacan). Probably the first question that will come to many readers' minds is why would any sane person even dream of such a union. So I will spend much of the space allotted to me here just venturing a few answers to that question, "Why?" I will proceed by trying to describe each of these two beasts in such a way that their sites of potential communion become apparent, and I hope that in the process it will become evident what we spectators as well as the participating beasts might get out of such an endeavor.

It is important to emphasize that this exercise of juxtaposition, whatever metaphor I use to describe it, is not an attempt to apply Lacanian theory to the analysis of Dravidian kinship, nor is it an attempt to use Dravidian kinship as data against which to test Lacanian theory. It is more like a comparison of two thought systems, with the added understanding that this act of comparison is not going to leave either of the two systems unchanged. So to proceed.

First to start answering why. Why Lacan? As things stand presently, the work of Jacques Lacan is regarded with perplexity and suspicion by most English-speakers who come upon it. This perplexity and suspicion have to do with Lacan's use of words. His work seems to be written in a language close to our own, a language we may even think we "know," but when we try to study this work we have enormous difficulty trying to make sense out of it, we cannot pin down what he means, for instance, by the word "Real," and we are angered when we discover that the instability of Lacan's verbal art is intentional. We categorize Lacan as an obnoxious obfuscationist and we turn to other writers who are easier to understand.

But now, let us take another look. *Is* Lacan just trying to drive his audience crazy, or is something more therapeutic going on? Especially, I would exhort people in our particular discipline to study Lacan's work carefully before passing judgment upon it. Consider that we cultural anthropologists are scholars who take pride in our ability to question the presupposed, to embrace the seemingly wild and strange rather than trying to conquer it or dismiss it, to see that one man's absurdity is another's common sense, who take the trouble to learn the difficult tongues of obscure and marginal peoples, who take it on faith that these tongues are worth the considerable effort we must make in order to learn them. If we believe that the categories of our understanding are products of our culture and are not absolute, if we believe that we must reconsider the matter of what "truth" is by looking carefully at the various truths developed in unfamiliar worlds, then we should recognize what Lacan, during his life, was trying to do. One of his aims may have been to bamboozle us, surely. He was a trickster—but we are familiar with tricksters: they are important people. They discomfort and infuriate us but they also make us laugh and create new worlds and get us out of the straitjackets of the old. In similar fashion, Lacan aimed through his unorthodox use of our language to subvert the familiar categories in which we think, through which we communicate. Just because his work is puzzling, that is no reason not to read it. At the minimum, studying Lacan is good practice for fieldwork.

There are, as well, a number of other reasons why anthropologists, especially psychoanalytically inclined ones, should pay attention to Lacan's work.

a) One of his main aims during his life was to incorporate the insights of twentieth century ethnography into his development of Freudian theory, and in fact he did just this. His work is informed by and responds to such developments as exchange theory, structural linguistics, myth and kinship analysis, semiotics, modern studies of child development and animal behavior—all of these of course being formative influences in our own field as well (Lacan 1968).

b) He treats the matter of gender differences as both culturally determined (i.e., not basically biological) *and* culturally foundational (Mitchell and Rose 1982; Gallop 1985). He has had an enormous influence upon the development of modern feminist thought, which is of great concern to cultural anthropologists, or should be.

c) He emphasizes as central to human existence the supposedly "non-functional" aspects of life: play, theater, ornamentation, in Lacanian terminology "supplementation" and "jouissance" (Kristeva 1984). His work has many connections with performance theory in general and with the later work of Victor Turner in particular.

d) He developed the idea that Freudian theory is essentially a theory of *language*, thus creating a wide new bridge between the psychological and linguistic subfields of anthropology (Kristeva 1980).

e) His work is anti-totalizing and anti-univocal, stressing, again as central to human life, the ambiguous, the polysemous, the diverse. Though his communicative (or anti-communicative—cf. Kristeva 1984) style has come to be seen by detractors today as a kind of hegemonic discourse, like many such discourses it originated as an intentionally counter-hegemonic act. Lacan helped spearhead the rebellion within psychoanalysis against the sexist and ethnocentric valorization of "ego-integration" and "ego strength" as necessary to "health" (cf., Chodorow 1978; Roland 1988), and he privileged the split self and the decentered subject as originators of cultural process. Thus he has much to say to those of us interested in such phenomena as spirit-possession, linguistic code-switching, multiculturality, and the psychology of women, outcastes, and marginalized or colonized peoples.

f) Finally, Lacan is, with Foucault and Derrida, one of the founding fathers of the post-structuralist movement, whose impact upon our discipline, however we may evaluate it, can certainly not be ignored.

Many summaries and exegeses of Lacan's written work have been produced in the last decade, including at list one review of his *Écrits* by an anthropologist for anthropologists (Crapanzano 1978). Therefore, I will not attempt an overall digest of his writings here. What I will do is describe some aspects of his theory which I believe resonate strongly with the system of thought we call Dravidian kinship. This is, I must add, my own interpretation of Lacan, formulated as I mate him in my mind with the other object of my contemplation. I am trying not to distort, but it certainly must be true that already the changes are happening.

The Lacanian self or ego moves and develops on a continuum, beginning with the pre-self when the infant has no sense of its body as a whole or as a bounded entity distinct from the objects of its perception (Ragland-Sullivan 1987). It has no sense of itself as a whole for the simple reason that it has no control of itself as a whole; it cannot move from one place to another of its own accord or even sit up or roll over. This radical "prematuration" at birth, this relatively long period of dependency, of course distinguishes human beings from most other mammals, and it is crucial to the human sense of self. At this stage, whatever happens within my purview happens to me. I and my world (the two are one) consist not of bounded selves but only of a set of floating parts—"letters" of the body Lacan calls them—mouths, hands, breasts, genitals, urinary stream, fecal output, voice, and gaze—all of these things experienced as disconnected *pieces* which are however *significant* because each of them is *different* from its surroundings, marked off in some way (you can see Saussure coming in at this point).

One day the infant learns to roll over, and around that time it develops a sense of itself as a whole entity, and also of its mother as a whole entity. Then it enters what Lacan calls the "mirror stage." It is during this stage that the "moi" or "Imaginary self" congeals—an *image* of the self mirrored in the image of the Other, who at this stage is the mother (Lacan 1977). There is a kind of golden moment in the mirror stage, when the world seems whole and complete, when I *am* my mother, her gaze is my gaze, her heartbeat is my heartbeat, as I nurse at her breast I put my hand to her mouth and we are complete—we reflect and echo each other. But even in this golden moment there is born a sense of my own insufficiency: to *look* at, she, my mother, the Other, is perfect and whole. I should be like her but I know from experience that I am dependent, fragmented and insufficient. Thus in the very process of becoming itself, in the bodily continuum with the mother as it grows into the mirror stage, the self feels a longing, a lack.

This sense of longing and lack becomes fixed with the development of language. (Now, here comes something very important:) Lacan sees the acquisition of language as coterminous with the oedipal experience and indeed constitutive of it. Lacan's identification of language itself as the axe dividing the human soul, his assertion that *the acquisition of language is indivisible from the core tragedy of human existence* (Lacan 1968), is both what sets him apart from most other psychoanalytic thinkers and what makes him especially interesting to us anthropologists. In Lacan's theory, the (metaphorical) Father who comes between the mother and child, who breaks the psychophysical bond between them, who shatters the mirror stage, is the master of language, is (for all intents and purposes) language itself. Language in Lacan's terminology is, then, "the Law of the Father." It is, in other words, the culturally constructed order of things, the received wisdom, *seemingly* all-encompassing and eternal. As the child begins to comprehend the *systematic quality* of language (it is not just a bunch of parts, it is a totality), he recognizes that it is the marker and tool of *power* (the Phallus), he sees that it is *bigger* than him, that it encompasses him and yet is beyond him, and he desires to master it. The Law of the Father, representing itself as a totality higher than the one the child has known, calls the child to reach for it; thus it *seduces* the child away from his mother's body. Language now becomes the Other out of which the self considers itself to be made, against which it measures itself; thus the abstraction of language usurps the physicality of the mother, taking her place. The mother's body becomes something cast off, abjected—and yet one is never quite free of it. The Law of the Father, the linguistic code, now becomes the totality, the self-enclosed whole for which one reaches, *but which one is never able truly to grasp or own.* Why? Because meaning, the "substance" (Tamil *poruḷ*) of language that one would want to put into one's mouth and ingest as one ingest's mother's milk (Kristeva 1982), is not really a substance at all. It has no being in itself. It is always shifting, always multiple, and always no more than a difference, a gap, a void (Sanskrit *śunya*). It is empty.

With the development of language, the self becomes something new. Out of the "*moi*," the "imaginary" self or pre-linguistic self-image that congealed in the mirror stage, there now arises the "*je*," the "speaking subject." With the rise of the speaking subject, *self-definition* comes to prevail over *self-image*, logic to prevail over feeling, ideology to prevail over experience. At the same time, the moi, far from dead, gains access, through its connection with the je, to language, and henceforth enjoys subverting language to its own purposes. All those aspects of language that we would call poetic or expressive, as well as all the Freudian slips of the tongue, are really just the moi speaking (Kristeva 1982, 1984).

Briefly, then, in the Lacanian schema, Other and Self develop in tandem (Ragland-Sullivan 1987). In the pre-mirror stage there is no self or other, it is all one world of disconnected objects. In the mirror stage, the Other is the body of the mother. In the post-mirror stage, the Other is language, the Law of the Father. The Body of the Mother and the Law of the Father are, it would seem, not very friendly towards each other—the Law calling us to cast away the body while the body continues to cry out from its place of abjection (Kristeva 1982), challenging and sometimes throwing rocks through the windows of the Law. But both the Body and the Law are the Other, against which, and in terms of which, the Self is molded and defined.

As we grow up, we internalize the Other, and store it up somewhere different from the place where we are. Or perhaps it would be better to say that the Other enters our house before we even get there ourselves, and lives there uninvited and usually unperceived, like a ghost. We experience it as an alien presence that causes us to behave in inexplicable ways and speaks to us through the uncontrollable language of dreams. In Lacan's view (1968), the unconscious is its voice.

The unconscious, in other words, is not a set of innate biological drives pushed beneath the surface by exterior pressures. It is itself exterior in origin, like (to switch metaphors) a subterranean river or lake fed constantly from the outside. That the system of language is necessarily *both* unconscious *and* transindividual is an insight Lacan brings to psychoanalysis from anthropology and linguistics. His view of the "always alreadiness" of language within the person may shed new light on certain culture-and-personality problems that have long vexed us.

In its relationship with this Other whose being precedes its own, the Self is multiply fragmented. With respect to the Body of the Mother, the Self is insufficient, a bunch of parts held together by an external whole. With respect to the law of the Father, the Self is also not whole in itself; as a part of language, it is defined only negatively and relationally, as per the Saussurean view of language, in which "there are only differences." Moreover, in the oedipal moment the Self is torn from the Body of the Mother by the magnet of the Law of the Father, whose alternative wholeness the Self can never experience at all because, if the truth be known, this wholeness is just an illusion. The language we speak is not really the Law of the Universe, even though we are compelled to believe that it is, and even as a work of art it is not really all that perfect and symmetrical. As Sapir says somewhere, "All grammars leak." The Law of the Father is a fraud.

Now to Dravidian kinship.[1] In Tamil Nadu, the center of "Dravidian" culture, marriage is an institution in which—to put it coldly—much affect is invested. Marriage between matched partners is not merely a means of maintaining social order, it is also and more importantly the only way for an individual to achieve personal fulfillment—or so people believe. The drama of cross-cousin marriage (for it is indeed a drama) forms the emotional heart and core of a great body of Tamil myth, folklore, cinema, and ritual, as well as of much everyday discourse. Cross-cousin marriage, in turn, is considered to be built upon the brother-sister bond. Ideally, and often as well in practice, a brother and sister marry their children to each other. A powerful love binds brother and sister. This love, widely celebrated and highly romanticized, like the theme of marriage with which it is often paired, is an abiding preoccupation of Tamil art and ritual, ancient and modern. A passage from Nila Padmanabhan's novel, *Talaimuraikaḷ* (translated by Indira Peterson 1986), describes the essence of this bond. Pay attention to every word here. In this passage, a brother and sister meet by a well, just as the brother has determined to help free the widowed sister from a life of imprisonment and misery. After a long separation, they stand facing each other:

> . . . perhaps these two hearts met and communed with each other in that immortal moment when *face met face* and *eyes embraced eyes*.
>
> In those silent moments, *no words* passed between them. They felt a kind of joy sweep over them, as if, *simply through the exchange of glances*, each heart had shared with the other all its sorrows, troubles, and hopes for release. *It seems as though the most ingenious edifices of language and phrase*, the most intricate dexterities of conversation, *handed down through the generations*, through eons—it seemed as though *in the eternal*

---

[1]For a variant of this argument with more ethnography and less theory, see Trawick (1990).

> *flow of that soundless moment, all these were* blunted, rendered useless, *smashed to bits*, when they confronted the steady torrent of that wordless moment. . . .
>
> How wonderful!
>
> Tiravi [the brother] was overcome with wonder at the powerful experience of deep feeling, an experience that he could *not quite take in.*
>
> *"Is it possible that, just because the seeds of our life, our bodily substance, our very blood, and our birth itself, came out of a single source, we are blessed with the transcendent vision of uniting with the other in feeling, of intuiting the very thoughts of the other?"*
>
> [Indira Peterson, trans. Emphases mine.]

Thus, as brother and sister stand facing each other, they find that their common physical origin, their shared bodily substances drawn from the mother's womb, is all they need, as long as they gaze into each other's face, to feel whole and complete. As they dwell in this bodily unity, the power of language is broken. All the "edifices of language . . . handed down through the generations" are "rendered useless," seen to be empty, and lose their power.

Recall that in Lacanian psychoanalytic theory, the Other against which and within which the self is formed is first, the substantial body of the mother and later, the powerful but insubstantial law of the father, viz., language and with it all the rules and conventions handed down through the generations. When Language comes to be perceived as a totality, as the Law according to which the universe is ordered, it supplants the body of the mother, which previously was the world. When the Law of the Father (language) separates the self from the mother, *defining* them as *different* from one another, then desire is born in the self. The self feels torn (castrated) and not whole, and longs to unite (or reunite) with the other and so become complete. It seeks this unity through attempts at realization and appropriation of the wholeness of language, through a search for meaning. But this longing for unity will never be fulfilled, because meaning is not a substance that can be grasped; it is just a matter of differences—like the self itself, an emptiness, a void.

In Tamil Nadu, kinship is experienced first as a sharing of bodily substances. People who are kin are people who have a common bodily origin, and live together as one body. True siblings are ones who are "born together (*uḍan piṟantu*)" "of the same womb (*cahōtararkaḷ*)." Their bond to each other, called the "blood bond (*ratta pācam*)" is formed through their mother's body.

Later (in the life of the individual), kinship is experienced as a *linguistic* phenomenon. Relations are ordered according to the ideal symmetry of kinship *terminology*. One behaves toward a kinsperson in accordance with the kin term by which one calls that person. Dravidian kinship terminology, in turn, is postulated upon the "rule" of cross-cousin marriage. The term *māman* means both mother's brother and father-in-law; the term *attai* means both father's sister and mother-in-law, and so forth down the line. The daughter of the *māman* is, for a man, the *muṟai peṇ*, the "rightful woman" whom that man should marry. If he marries someone else, then his wife's father *becomes* a man's *māman*, her mother becomes his *attai*, and so forth with all the rest of her kin (she likewise addresses his kin in the same manner). The Dravidian terminological kinship order thus is realized through the institution of marriage, and the individual, male or female, becomes a fully social being, and fulfills his or her moral responsibility (*muṟai*) only when he or she marries. A certain kind of social, moral, legal, *symbolic* (in the Lacanian and Saussurian sense) wholeness is thus brought about for the Tamil individual by marriage.

And yet, marriage is at the same time a threat, indeed a rending, of the bodily wholeness that preceded it, a rending of the blood bond. Marriage is described by many Tamils (especially Tamil women) as a tearing of the self away from the mother's body. Marriage, as literate Tamil men describe it, is an "artificial union (*ceyaṟkai puṇarcci*)" that stands opposed to the "natural union" of siblingship. The natural union of siblingship, as Tamil people describe it, derives from an original oneness, and is characterized by spontaneity and love. The artificial union of marriage, on the other hand, is performed for the sake of interest and social order, and is characterized by duty and necessity. Through the institution of cross-cousin marriage, fathers of brides and grooms both perpetuate the Tamil logos (i.e., the ideal social order as encoded in language) and solidify their own political power. The personal longings of individuals are subsumed to the alleged needs of the kindred or caste, as these needs are defined by male elders.

And yet, it is through this same institution of cross-cousin marriage that siblings seek to re-establish the bodily unity that they lost when they themselves were married. In marrying their children to each other, brother and sister seek to rejoin their sundered blood bond. This motivation for cross-cousin marriage is quite conscious and explicit in Tamil Nadu. Consider, for instance, Peterson's (1986) translation of this song form the movie *Pāca Malar* ("Flower of Affection" or "Bond Flower") in which a brother and sister are tragically separated from each other in childhood. They grow up, the brother fathers a boy baby and the sister gives birth to a girl baby. Though separated, the brother and sister sing a single lullaby in harmony, in which they plan to marry the babies to each other, and so be reunited. The two sing to their respective babies:

Brother:
You were born to win many battles
with your elephants and armies
you were born to marry your aunt's daughter
and live in joyful love!

Sister:
He'll give you a gold watch and necklace,
he'll ask for your hand—
your uncle will give much wealth,
he'll offer you the whole world,
in exchange for the sister's daughter's hand
in marriage for his son.
Shall I tell you of how my brother brought me
up like a darling daughter,
sheltered me under his wing?
Shall I tell you of the unimaginable
misfortune which separated us?

Together:
We were born together
joined like the eye and the pupil,
like the pupil and the image within!
Though the earth and sea and sky should come
to an end, we shall not forget our love,
nothing can break our bond.

[Peterson, trans. Emphases mine]

In seeking to regain through marriage, the Tamil Law of the Father, the wholeness they recall in their early union with the body of the mother, brother and sister unconsciously, or half-consciously, perpetuate the psychic breach within themselves into the next generation.

According to Lacan, somatic Need (to eat, to sleep, etcetera) grows into psychic Desire when I recognize that there is another like myself, whose feelings may be the same as mine, when the world which once was one becomes two, and I understand that my mother is *not* myself but *like* myself, that I am a self and so is she. She is the Other and I desire her and my desiring her consists in my desiring her to desire me—an infinite regression. This state of mind Lacan calls the "mirror stage." It is a time when one sees oneself literally mirrored in the gaze of the other ("like the pupil and the image within"). The mirror stage begins with the recognition that there are two bodies (mother's and own), like but not like, fused in love. The mirror stage ends when language comes between, defining the self in terms of words, which take the place of sensory images. At the end of the mirror stage, identity begins—gender identity (the label "male" or "female" affixed to the self) and also the question "Who am I?"

"I raised my sister from the time she was three until the time she was twenty-two," a Tamil man told me, "about nineteen years. I carried her on my shoulders, I combed her hair and braided it and put flowers in it. If a parent raises a child so lovingly, and then sees someone beating the child, how painful it will be for the parent. So I saw her husband strike her, and when I saw that I went to strike her husband, but she stopped me, saying, 'Who are you to come between a husband and his wife?'

"'That's right,' I thought. 'Who am I? Who am I'? The words ring a thousand times inside my ears."

In Tamil culture (as abundantly attested in myth, cinema, and everyday conversation) the primordial couple are uterine brother and sister. The central kinship bond is the sibling bond. The love joining brother and sister is stronger than any other kind of love, but it is a tragic love because brother and sister are inevitably separated from each other by the fact of marriage. Often the person who comes in between (brother's wife or sister's husband) is hated for this reason. Brothers and sisters (not all, but many) think of themselves as joined by a deep spiritual bond that *comes before words* (remember the quote from *Talaimuṟaikaḷ*). When they *look into each other's face* (as they do in

Talaimuraikal, as into a mirror) full understanding flows between them. The bodily union that comes before words seems all that is needed. Conversely, when one sibling turns her back upon the other, the other may suddenly feel his identity crumbling.

For the brother-sister bond is born just at the moment of realization that the mirroring face is *not* precisely one's own; that the other is, though the same, also *different* from oneself. It is born in the moment of recognition that I am a "boy" and you are a "girl." My identity leans against yours, depends upon yours. If I am born Tamil, my sibling of the opposite sex stands for both my mother and my father; she is *both* the one in whose *image* I dwell, *and* the one by whose *words* I am named. She represents the moment of transition from the Imaginary (bodily) world to the Symbolic (language-oriented) one. She is at the center of the moment of loss and so the feeling she stands for is longing. But this same moment of loss (the oedipal moment) is also the moment of identity formation, when the self becomes defined. So the opposite-sex sibling, standing at the moment of loss, also stands at the center of the question, "Who am I?"

Lacan rejects the idea that Truth can be established with any certainty by the conscious mind. He considers that plurality and ambiguity are to be studied in their own right, not as "noise" obscuring truth but as windows providing glimpses into the true foundations of the self (Ragland-Sullivan 1987:11). He similarly rejects the idea of an "integrated ego." For him every human self is divided, fragmented, in the very process of its formation. An emptiness, Desire, is at the center of our hearts. We create everything we create in response to this Desire. Though it is pain, we need it, in order merely to be. Happiness and fulfillment, wholeness and closure, are simply not in the cards for us.

In Tamil Nadu, ambiguity is a defining characteristic of the sacred. A deity is one who dwells within a person's heart, and is more interior to the person than the person's own soul. A deity is the truth of selfhood. But every deity is sharply ambiguous. Each human spirit is likewise fluid and multiple, permeated and possessed by others, all the time (cf. Roland 1988). Spirit-possession is a love relationship, or more precisely, a relationship of Desire (Tamil *ācai*); the possessing other is often an elder kinsman or kinswoman. Time and life for the Tamils are entropic processes: one becomes less individuated, one merges more with others, the older one gets. Final fulfillment (union with God) can be achieved only through a total dissolution of the ego. In every realm of life from poetry to house construction to business transactions to religious devotion, the necessity of incompletion is a repeated theme in Tamil life. Completion means closure means stasis means death. Perennially unfulfilled desire, eternal incompletion, is what motivates the continuation of life. I would suggest that the Dravidian kinship system is posited, like many other aspects of South Indian culture, upon this principle of incompletion. For Tamils, marriage is castration—a breaking of bodily wholeness for the sake of cultural order. Brother and sister, their bodily unity divided by marriage, seek to reclaim this unity through marriage in the next generation. But in their effort to make themselves whole again, they castrate their children. Longing, in seeking fulfillment, begets only more longing. Thus through perennial incompletion, the social order continues.

A pessimistic view, perhaps, but then, Freud was pessimistic, too. Therapy lies in acceptance of the things that we can't change—acceptance of our unhealable fragmentation, acceptance of our unslakable longing to find wholeness through another. Better than acceptance is making something good out of the bad. People in Tamil Nadu excel at such arts. Their kinship order is a beautiful object woven out of pain.

References

Chodorow, Nancy. 1978. *The Reproduction of Mothering: Psychoanalysis and the Sociology of Gender*. Berkeley: University of California Press.

Crapanzano, Vincent. 1978. "Lacan's Écrits." *Canto* 2:183-191.

Gallop, Jane. 1985. *Reading Lacan*. Ithaca, NY: Cornell University Press.

Kristeva, Julia. 1980. *Desire in Language: A Semiotic Approach to Literature and Art*. New York: Columbia University Press.

_____. 1982. *Powers of Horror: An Essay on Abduction*. New York: Columbia University Press.

_____. 1984. *Revolution in Poetic Language*. New York: Columbia University Press.

Lacan, Jacques. 1968. *Speech and Language in Psychoanalysis*. Anthony Wilden, trans., comm. and ed. Baltimore: Johns Hopkins University Press.

_____. 1977. *Écrits: A Selection*. Alan Sheridan, trans. New York: W. W. Norton.

Mitchell, Juliet, and Jacqueline Rose. 1982. *Feminine Sexuality: Jacques Lacan and the École Freudienne*. New York: W. W. Norton.

Peterson, Indira. 1986. *The Tie That Binds: Brothers and Sisters in North and South India*. Paper presented at the Conference on Religion in South India, Hyannis, MA.

Ragland-Sullivan, Ellie. 1987. *Jacques Lacan and the Philosophy of Psychoanalysis*. Chicago: University of Illinois Press.

Roland, Alan. 1988. *In Search of Self in India and Japan: Toward a Cross-Cultural Psychology*. Princeton, NJ: Princeton University Press.

Trawick, Margaret. 1990. *Notes on Love in a Tamil Family*. Berkeley: University of California Press.

Chapter Three

Multiple Mothering and Separation-Individuation: Evidence from Some Nigerian Children[1]

JoAnn F. Campbell

Introduction

With its high degree of family nuclearization and comparatively few working mothers, extended family caregivers were rare in America for most of the twentieth century. Now however, as women return to the workforce before their children are three, there is increasing need for and use of daycare. Given our children's experiences with multiple caregivers during their first three years, more attention to the psychodynamics of these experiences and their effects upon psychic development is essential. We need to ask ourselves: do these experiences alter the course of the Separation-Individuation Process (Mahler, Pine and Bergman 1975)? Do they compromise superego development so self-control is externalized and the regulation of self-esteem relies upon the environment?

---

[1] I want to thank Robert Bergman, Jeanette Dyal, Gerald Olch, Robert Paul, Werner Schimmelbusch, Calvin Settlage, David Spain, Vamik Volkan, and Adolph Whiting for commenting helpfully on various drafts of this paper. Special thanks are due to Andrea Furedy and to Avrama Gingold for their helpful editorial suggestions.

The psychological literature tends to ignore the pre-oedipal development of children with multiple caregivers. In western culture, where the biological mother is most apt to be the main—or only—caregiver, researchers tend to look at pre-oedipal issues only in relation to a single primary caregiver (Spitz 1957, 1965; Winnicott 1958, 1965, 1971; Mahler, Pine and Bergman 1975; Emde, Gaensbauer and Harmon 1976; Stern 1985).

Nonetheless, the limited research on the products of multiple mothering has produced evidence that its effects are present well into adulthood. Cambor (1969) found superego impairment and lack of maturity in adult patients who experienced multiple primary caregivers early in life. They tended to externalize superego functioning to their environment, their self-affirmation and self-control coming from someone in their environment rather than from an internal source.[2] Volkan (1979) analyzed the multiple mothering experiences of Turkish children. The frustration experiences encountered during the Separation-Individuation Process were ". . . unlike those of the child constantly in a one-to-one encounter with the same mother," resulting in "typical psychological characteristics" that included the externalization of certain superego functions (1979:57).

The universality of the Oedipus complex has long been debated (Malinowski 1927, 1929; Parsons 1967; Okonogi 1978a, 1978b). For example, Spiro (1982) argues for the applicability of the Oedipus complex for Trobriand Islanders, countering Malinowski's claim that it is not applicable because of psychoanalytic theory's bias toward Viennese culture, while the Japanese psychoanalyst Kosawa substitutes the Ajase complex, with its focus on the mother-son rather than father-son relationship, because he believes it more suitable in understanding the Japanese psyche (Okonogi 1978a, 1978b).

Given these debates and the importance of the Mahler et al. formulation of the Separation-Individuation Process for understanding various aspects of Western children's pre-oedipal development, I decided to test the theory in a non-Western population (Campbell 1985) and examine some of the ways multiple mothering impacts this process. Habiba and

---

[2]Cambor notes his population experienced either abrupt and prolonged separations from one of these figures or a lack of empathy from one or both caregiver(s). Thus his study is not a commentary on multiple caregiving experience without such disruptive variables.

Sharif are Nigerian children who experienced multiple caregivers when their mothers returned to work soon after their birth but, at about 18 months of age, each was abruptly separated from the non-parental caregiver when both families moved to the United States.

From examination of the impact this separation experience had upon their Separation-Individuation Process, I have concluded that object loss may remain a salient element in ongoing developmental conflict. Such loss may interfere with psychic structuralization in ways that result in a greater need for self-control and self-esteem regulation to come from external sources. This corroborates the findings of both Cambor and Volkan. Furthermore, the time of the disruption, rather than the multiple mothering *per se*, is significant in the difficulties with establishing self and object constancy.[3]

To illustrate my formulations, I will briefly describe the Separation-Individuation Process and discuss my observations of Habiba and Sharif. Finally, I will relate my findings to children in this culture.

The separation-individuation process

The Separation-Individuation Process is a set of compromise formations (Campbell 1985) organized around dependency and autonomy as those themes relate to the primary caregiver, usually the mother, during the first three years of life. From Brenner's (1982) description, compromise formations arise from an intrapsychic conflict that allows the greatest amount of wish fulfillment to occur within a tolerable amount of displeasure.[4] Conflict arises when an individual uses a wish defensively

---

[3]In Campbell (1989), an elaboration of the Mahler et al. theory was included and the notion of the self-object illusion as the first mental representation of the self was introduced. This internal representation is essential to the child's capacity to cope with self and object differentiation, continues to undergo refinement throughout life, and is essential to the development of empathy, adult sexual relations, parenting, and group involvement.

[4]Many psychoanalysts, perhaps including Brenner, do not subscribe to the idea of compromise formations before the oedipal phase because they believe there is insufficient ego structure for their formation. Others, including Settlage,

(continued...)

to oppose another (e.g., wishes for autonomy and separate functioning oppose wishes for dependency upon and connection to another person). The Separation-Individuation Process unfolds between approximately 4 and 36 months. Object and self constancy continue to be elaborated to some extent throughout life. This process is preceded by establishing a special relationship to a primary caregiver. Hereafter, I will call this caregiver "mother." To differentiate between mother and infant, I will refer to the infant as "he."

During the first three or four weeks after birth, the infant's responses indicate little differentiation between inside and outside. Physiological processes maintain state regulation. Mahler et al. (1975) call this period the "Normal Autistic Phase."[5]

From three or four weeks through the next four or five months, the infant gradually responds to external stimuli and particularly the mothering agent. Mahler et al. postulate that perceptions of the mothering agent (as a representative of the environment) fuse or merge with the infant's experiences. These experiences originate from inside and produce a fusion of perceptual and experiential (somatic) senses of self. They refer to this period as the "Normal Symbiotic Phase."[6] The infant gradually discriminates mother from the environment and links her to his sense of well-being.

From Mahler et al.'s viewpoint the Separation-Individuation Process is a gradual differentiation of this experiential fused sense of self into

---

[4](...continued)
believe preoedipal compromise formations are possible (Settlage, personal communication 1989).

[5]My own view is that the word *normal* should be expunged from the label for this phase. "Optimal" and "good enough" development are linked to cultural ideals and the realities of that culture. A practice considered appropriate to the proper development of the individual in one culture may be considered harmful to individual development in another.

[6]The same argument (see fn.4, above) applies to the use of the word "normal" in the Normal Symbiotic Phase. Elsewhere I have posited a symbiotic developmental line, extending symbiosis to include uterine experience with its physiological nature, then the development of this kind of symbiosis into a social symbiosis, and finally a psychological symbiosis.

psychic object representations as perceptually, experientially, emotionally, and cognitively separate from the self. This process is divided into four subphases: (1) Differentiation, (2) Practicing, (3) Rapprochement, and (4) On the Way to Object Constancy. Each subphase has characteristic tasks that distinguish it from the previous subphase.

Differentiation (age 5 or 6 to 10 or 12 months). This subphase marks the beginning of the Separation-Individuation Process. The infant explores his and his mother's bodies and achieves some differentiation. Reactions to strangers indicate greater awareness of the distinctions between his mother and others. This creates inner tension and enhances his discriminatory ability before he is able to differentiate between himself and his mother. As this phase ends, the presence of separation anxiety clearly indicates the infant's awareness of concrete separateness from his mother. He will deliberately attempt to reunify with his mother. For example, fussiness brings her back, lifting his arms to be picked up restores tactile affirmation of connection, and following behaviors carry him to his separating mother. These behaviors provide the child with experiences vital to cause-effect learning.

Practicing (age 10 or 12 to 16 or 18 months). The beginning of the Practicing subphase is marked by enhanced locomotor skills (e.g., crawling, walking, and manipulating the non-mother environment). These new interests bring about a relative diminution of separation anxiety as the toddler's distance perceptual modalities become increasingly useful in keeping in touch with mother while exploring the non-mother world. By the end of this subphase he is calmer when his mother leaves the room. Mahler et al. believe this state indicates the child is trying to "image" mother (remember her via thought). At such times (states of "low-keycdness") he appears sad, diminishes activity, and directs attention inward. If disturbed while in this state he may cry as if his mother's image is lost and no longer available to ward off anxiety.

Rapprochement (age 16 to 24 or 26 months). The Rapprochement subphase begins with a resurgence of separation anxiety as anger and temper tantrums increase. Behaviors indicate a continued attempt to deny the separateness. The child actively searches for his mother when she leaves the room rather than passively trying to image her (as at the end of the Practicing subphase). This phase reaches a crisis with increasing temper tantrums as his ambivalence intensifies. His behavior indicates wishes for dependence and independence from mother have come into opposition. He deals with ambivalence by splitting his discrepant good and bad images of mother as well as his attitudes toward her. By defensively projecting these split off parts to the environment, his internal battle is mitigated. This often results in increased wariness of strangers, who become the recipients of the projections.

On the Way to Object Constancy (age 24 to 30 or 36 months). During the final subphase, opposed wishes achieve some resolution. Behaviors indicate attempts to solve dilemmas. He begins to interpret his mother's good and bad representations. These interpretations result in "good enough" differentiated representations of other and the self that have some stability even in the face of intense emotions. As tantrums diminish, he separates from his mother for longer periods. He begins to reduce the use of defensive solutions such as splitting and projection to deal with his anger, replacing them with disavowal, isolation, displacement, reversal, and undoing. In our culture many children are now considered ready to enter preschool.

Mahler et al. find that different outcomes of the Separation-Individuation Process, as well as differences in the timing of each phase, can be traced to differences in the mother's relationship with and handling of the child. Their study does not address in any detail the effect of culture, significance of father[7] and/or extended family, or other caregivers upon the process.

My observations

The families in my study are all from the same area of Nigeria, with the same tribal affiliation. The fathers were civil servants[8] on extended sabbatical leaves granted to complete graduate work in various fields that would enhance their occupations. My initial objectives in observing these families were to: (1) assess how the Separation-Individuation Process

---

[7]They do suggest the father is important during the Rapprochement subphase in helping the child separate from mother. Their observations do not include details of the father-child relationship.

[8]As civil servants, they represent a much more Westernized segment than the general population. Despite the predominance of Western ideals in the men, many of the wives maintain very traditional beliefs and practices, especially in relation to early child care.

unfolds in children with non-Western parents, (2) determine what effects separation from their native country has on this process, and (3) explore how parental adaptations to new surroundings impinge upon their children's progression through this psychological process.

I concentrated on the children's relationships to their mother, siblings, father, and, to some extent, other people with whom they had fairly regular contact. All these people contribute to the Separation-Individuation Process experience. Some fathers, by providing direct childcare, assumed the role often fulfilled by a grandmother, other female kin, or hired Nigerian caregivers. In turn, these fathers became more instrumental in their children's Separation-Individuation Process than might have been the case had they remained in Nigeria. They were, in fact, more like fathers in our culture.

The younger married women (ages 14 to 22) often visit the older more experienced and securely adapted women. These visits help them cope with their own separation anxiety and loneliness for their mothers. In turn they become somewhat more emotionally available to their infants and young children when dealing with their child's developmentally appropriate feelings. Two mothers who had experienced traumatic separations in early childhood were seriously depressed. Their depression had a dramatic impact upon their children's psychological development (Campbell 1984), who appeared to have diminished interest in other people, resembling Ainsworth's (1967) insecurely attached and unattached infants.

The following observations are of Habiba and Sharif. It is important to note how the difficulties they experience are manifested, in part, in their transference relationship to me. Both children expressed transference reactions early, with an intensity I found puzzling. In time, I came to realize they were transferring feelings and wishes for a significant non-parental caregiver left in Nigeria. My appearance on the scene and their intense interest in me was a way for them to try to complete a developmental process that had been interrupted when they were at the end of the Practicing or beginning of the Rapprochement subphase. This abrupt separation contributed to their ongoing separation-individuation conflict and interfered with the timely establishment of object constancy and early phallic phase development.

I observed them an average of 5 days a week, 1½ hours each day for 6 weeks. One year later I returned and observed Sharif daily for one week. (Habiba and her family had returned to Nigeria permanently.)

Habiba

Habiba, age 3, is the youngest of four children. She has two sisters, ages 9 and 12 (both attending school in Nigeria), and one brother, Mohammed, age 7. Her father had come to the United States alone but soon became so lonely that he had his wife and children join him here.

At first, Habiba is shy around me, although she soon begins asking her parents questions about me. On my first visit, I give Habiba and Mohammed drawing paper and crayons. She draws three circles, two of which have what look like facial features, and identifies them as herself and mother. The third circle, with no features, she identifies as her nanny. She addresses the nanny by the term used for mother and addresses her mother by name. Her mother, who is watching, says, "Habiba misses her nanny very much."

For the first week of visits, Habiba's mother has to grab her hand to stop her from following me outside when I leave. Habiba cries, stopping only when I promise to return the next day. When from the window Habiba sees me going away from her apartment, she again cries. Her mother explains to Habiba that I am going to visit Fatima but will visit her later. Still, Habiba cries until her mother brings her to where I am visiting. Once she sees me she sits very close to me, remaining silent throughout my visit. During this first week, each time I leave Habiba's distress escalates, culminating in a full-blown tantrum. Eventually, she begins to realize I will return and my leaving then becomes a game: she smiles at her mother, tries to follow me, her mother grabs her hand, and I promise to return on a specific day. Occasionally, however, when her mother is less patient or preoccupied, my leaving then creates distress.

Over the course of my observations, Habiba's mother becomes more preoccupied with her absent daughters. As a result there are more battles between Habiba and her mother. Her mother becomes more ambivalent when Habiba either wants to be closer to her or demonstrates independence by rejecting her decisions. For example, I am visiting at lunchtime when her mother offers me a plate of food and gives me a spoon. Habiba asks for a spoon and her mother says, "No, eat with your hands like a Nigerian." Habiba goes to the cupboard and gets her own spoon. This irritates her mother, but she does not take it away. Generally, Habiba is persistent and gets what she wants despite her mother's resistance. I see this persistence in her relationship with her brother. For the most part Mohammed is patient with his sister's demands and intrusions, relating to her in a tutorial manner similar to his teacher father. Sometimes, though, he complains, "Habiba always wants everything I have."

Habiba frequently seeks praise, being exhibitionistic to gain her family's attention. They usually respond warmly. When she does not get what she wants, she becomes angry. She then demands that her mother say, "Habiba is a good girl" or "Habiba is a good girl and Mohammed is a bad boy." Sometimes she commands her mother to punish her brother. Her mother complies by lightly slapping Mohammed on the leg. A "knowing" look between the two indicates this is a game to satisfy "little" sister.

Habiba loves to perform for her father. She often shows him her toys and tries to get him to "fix" something that seems broken. "Wooing" behavior, typical of the Rapprochement subphase, is often directed at both her mother and father. There is a consistently seductive quality to her relationship with her father, indicating early phallic phase interests. Occasionally, her mother gets exasperated and says, "I don't know what to do with her, she wants my attention all the time," or "It's like Habiba wants inside my skin." Habiba's requests for self-affirmation show an intensity beyond what is expected in a child this age.

In Nigeria, Habiba's mother worked full-time in a managerial role, taking three months off after the birth of each child. She always used the same nanny and plans to rehire her once they return home.

Shortly before the family left Nigeria, the oldest daughter was promoted a year early and received a scholarship to a prestigious boarding school. The mother now worries about her daughter coping alone because she is so young. The 9-year-old daughter is rarely mentioned. She is living with her maternal grandmother so the elder sister will not be lonely on school holidays. Because the father chose not to be part of the decision to accept the scholarship, her mother feels responsible for any loneliness or difficulty her daughter experiences.

When Habiba's mother was 3 her elder sister married and moved 400 miles away. She was sent to live with her sister until the first child was born "so [the elder sister] would not get lonely." The marriage produced no children and was dissolved within four years. The sisters returned to the parental home and she (Habiba's mother) stayed until entering secondary school in another city, where she lived with her uncle until she married (at age 16). After secondary school she got a job as a civil servant and attained a relatively high position for a woman in her culture.

The mother's experience of abrupt separation at age 3, her current separation from her daughters, and Habiba, now at age 3, all enhance her own separation anxiety. In trying to cope, sometimes she emotionally withdraws from her daughter, which Habiba experiences as loss of love. In turn, Habiba becomes more persistent with her exhibitionistic displays to get her mother's attention. These antics usually cause her mother to laugh. Habiba's constant demands for attention negate the fear of losing love, brought on by her mother's periodic emotional withdrawal, and fear of losing her mother as she had lost her nanny.

Habiba's mother became a full-time mother for the first time when she came to the United States. She said Habiba was very fussy at first, and could be soothed only by being carried on her mother's back in the traditional way. The mother complied with these demands, although she felt Habiba was too big. The increased fussiness was Habiba's response to being separated from her nanny (object loss) and her mother's inconsistent emotional availability (loss of love). For Habiba, being held is a compromise that resolves two issues: remembering nanny and integrating those memories into her experiences with mother. She can remember her nanny via a perceptual action mode, while allowing her to feel physically connected to her mother so as not to lose her, too. This integration is essential to development of an internal mental representation or symbol of the infant-caregiver relationship which the child can then use to mediate separation anxiety. Her mother responds to her fussiness, initially by holding and then by acceding to her demands, for example, when she brings her to see me at Fatima's apartment. Fussiness and success in being held at 18 months seem forerunners of the persistence I see at age 3. This also indicates Habiba's successful capacity for quickly getting some of her mother's emotional availability when it is not spontaneously forthcoming. This pattern of demanding self-affirmation from the environment may be a component in narcissistic character formulations seen in the clinical setting. Partial success in reaching an otherwise psychologically unavailable caregiver tends to encourage the child to continue exhibitionistic behavior in order to assure parental love. If the environment continues to be only partially responsive, instead of responsive enough, this character pattern may become fixed. This may be even more likely if the environment continues to be less responsive than the internal needs of the child. Due to the loss of nanny, Habiba's need for psychological resources are enhanced. This enhancement requires an adjustment in the mother-child relationship. Since mother is also disturbed by the separation experience, she had difficulty making this adjustment.

Habiba's mood swings are wide, with intense periods of anger. By telling her she is a "good" girl, her mother appeases her. Projection is a major defense against her own sense of being "bad," with Mohammed her target. Occasionally she chooses her mother and, once, myself. For example, she demands that her mother give her a can of Coke rather than a little in a glass. Her mother gives it to her and she spills it. She angrily says, "You should not have given me a can." Once, while playing with some toys I brought, she accidentally pulls a leg off a doll. She surreptitiously takes the doll to her father, who is babysitting, and quietly asks him to repair it. I tell her the doll has a loose leg and it had come off before. When her father cannot repair it, Habiba angrily throws the doll aside. She looks at me and says, "You should not have such a doll in your case." Her father reprimands her. She continues to ignore the doll and is surly throughout that day's observation. The next day her mood is different and she shows her mother the broken doll. Her mother sets up a tea party and includes the doll. While Habiba enjoys her mother's performance, she never again chooses the doll as a plaything. By avoiding the doll, she can avoid feeling she is a "bad" girl and protect our relationship by not getting angry with me.

Clearly, Habiba is transferring her interest in her nanny to me. She needs to avoid angry feelings toward me, fearing I might go away like her nanny. The intensity of her transference is enhanced because of the inconsistent psychological availability of her mother. My presence gives her an opportunity to be more hostile toward her mother, thus increasing her need for maternal attention to restore the good object. A defense pattern used earlier to deal with separation conflict in the mother-child-nanny relationship is reactivated. Each day, as I prepare to leave, she reenacts a scene that helps her restore the good love object relationship with her mother and let the bad love object go away. If her mother were psychologically available adequately, Habiba might be able to partially resolve her separation anxiety and fear of object loss by using me instead of nanny. Since mother is not consistently and spontaneously available, Habiba instead uses old defenses to the exclusion of developing new ways to cope.

The danger in abrupt separation from loved ones during the first few years of life stem from the meaning the child gives to such events. If the parent does not help the child bring these meanings in line with reality, he may attach meanings that do not coincide with reality. Thus, Habiba organizes the meanings of her current conflict over losing her mother's love with memories of and defenses against object loss. As a result, she cannot resolve her ambivalent feelings toward love objects and continues to use splitting and projection as a way to deny unwanted feelings. Habiba's mother is also suffering object loss, and is unable to connect her daughter's behavior and fantasies to real experience.

Early in my observations, Habiba's mother tells me about the only other American woman who has visited her home. This woman, the girlfriend of a Nigerian, said how, before meeting this family, she had thought Africans were less advanced than Americans. This outraged Habiba's mother, who no longer wanted to welcome her into her home, but because of the woman's relationship to their Nigerian friend, could not openly express this resentment. She expresses it to me by telling me that this woman asked to be given one of her Nigerian dresses when she returns to Nigeria. Habiba's mother does not want to give her one. She decides she will give her a dress she likes least.

As she is telling me this story, I feel she is unconsciously warning me to see her as an equal or stay away. Her sensitivity and way of dealing with her anger seem unconsciously connected to being sent away at age 3. She may have felt she was not "good enough" to stay with her parents. This persistent idea continues to organize her relationships and make her sensitive to comments causing her to feel worthless. Her anger makes her feel "bad," and, in turn, she projects this feeling onto others. This is like the Rapprochement subphase child who is unable to manage ambivalence. Thus, splitting and projection remain as major defenses against anger for Habiba's mother.

Both Habiba and her mother share the same style of management of anger. Although identification promotes Habiba's similarity to her mother, the abrupt and prolonged separations from a primary caregiver each experienced early in life contribute to the specific compromise formations each tends to use.

Sharif

Like Habiba, Sharif, age 32 months, was separated from his primary caregiver at age 18 months. When I first saw him, he had been in the United States for a little over one year. Sharif has a sister Aisa, age 5, and a brother Tijani, age 18 months. Before moving to the United States, his mother had worked half-time after the birth of her three children, returning to work three months after each birth.

Sharif began having tantrums shortly after moving to the United States. Just about the time that his brother started walking (about four months before I began my observations), Sharif's tantrums became more frequent. The tantrums tended to occur only when Tijani took toys with which Sharif was playing. Because he is the elder, Sharif is expected to give these toys to his brother, whom their parents still treat and speak of as a "baby."

Sharif has a natural curiosity about how things work, and because he often takes objects apart, Sharif's mother thinks he will probably become an engineer. His father, on the other hand, sees this behavior as destructive. Several times in front of Sharif, he says to me or other adults in their social network, "Sharif is so destructive and naughty, I don't know what to do about it." Sharif's response is to hang his head in shame.

During my first visit, Sharif is shy, but very quickly brings me toys and objects and performs for me. Because of his interest, his mother begins using my visits to encourage self-control in her son. For example, she says, "JoAnn will not want to see you if you continue acting this way." He will then agree to stop. She believes Sharif needs a special friend to help him with his fear of leaving her. In many ways, she encourages his interest in me. This encouragement of Sharif's attempts to identify with me is in contrast with Habiba's mother, who does not want Habiba to drink her Coke from a can or eat with a spoon as I do.

Sharif is not able to be away from his mother. Usually, she gives him the choice of staying with his father or going with her. He always prefers going with her while Tijani prefers staying with his father. Occasionally, he and his sister visit another Nigerian family in their complex. His visit generally lasts about 10 minutes before he asks to go home "to see" his mother. Sometimes, he decides to stay with me while I babysit his brother. This indicates a wish to grow up and be able to leave his mother.

Soon after arriving in this country, Sharif's parents began looking at daycare facilities. They wanted their children to have the educational advantages offered in the United States. Sharif's sister, Aisa, began attending a private daycare and kindergarten soon after moving here. The mother felt the facilities available for the younger children were inadequate, and her children would be better off at home. Although she had wanted to attend school herself, she has postponed her own education until her children are older.

Sharif wants to attend his sister's school, but would have to be three years old and toilet trained, and his urine control is still inconsistent. This distresses his parents, who say he cannot go to school until he no longer needs diapers. His parents believe he should be completely trained by now. The pressure on Sharif is amplified as other people in their social network make comments to him about his failures. His sister had ceased to soil or wet herself and her bed by age 1. His mother feels boys take longer to train, but began to worry after age 2½. Sharif's wish to be big like his sister and go to school is in conflict with his wish to remain with his mother. The resulting compromise is to urinate in his pants until he is ready to leave his mother for school.

Unfortunately, his mother feels inadequate to deal with this conflict. She says if she were in Nigeria her mother, whom she believes is more capable at childrearing, would know what to do. She credits her mother with Aisa's good nature.

Sharif's mother is clearly concerned about her son's development. She worries that his continued dependency will lead to teasing by other children, who may call him a "mama's boy." She blames the fourteen months age difference of her two sons for the difficulty Sharif is experiencing with growing up as well as for the conflict between her sons.

Her helplessness and yearning for her mother's assistance arise when both boys throw tantrums simultaneously. These tantrums generally occur when Tijani intrudes into Sharif's activities and takes his playthings. His mother usually tells him Tijani is little, does not know any better, and will soon lose interest. She tries to provide verbal information for Sharif to associate to practical experiences and help him with delaying gratification, and this strategy often does work.

When Sharif does share, which is often because Tijani is very intrusive, she praises him, causing him to look proud. When Sharif does not share, his mother shames him by saying he is acting like Tijani, and becomes angry and demanding. If he still does not comply, she shouts and calls Sharif, by now in tears, a "crybaby." At this point, she puts the item on the shelf, out of Tijani's reach but in sight. Presumably, this is for Sharif's benefit and to assuage her own guilt over losing her temper. Once Sharif sees that his brother does not get the toy, he seems satisfied. Tijani, however, who still sees the toy, whines until his mother gives it to him. She does not set limits on Tijani by saying "no."[9] Sharif becomes enraged when he sees his mother give his brother the toy. He cries, throws himself on the floor, and writhes around. Again, his mother puts the toy on the shelf. This time, Sharif stops his tantrum and Tijani starts his own. It is only when the mother leaves the room and Tijani follows her that tempers cool.

I am puzzled why this mother, generally quite competent, has such difficulty regulating sibling rivalry between the brothers. She sees Sharif as more troublesome than Tijani, but usually is successful in manipulating him by threatening loss of privilege (a form of loss of love). This pattern is consistent with the practice of other parents.

Being raised by multiple maternal caregivers in an extended household may have contributed to the difficulty Sharif's mother has with her sons' sibling rivalry. She herself had several mothers who lived within the same household. Besides her own biological mother, she had a maternal grandmother and two unmarried grandaunts. The caregiving relationships did not end with childhood. To help with her household and children after the birth of each child, a grandaunt would move into her home for two to three months, and the child sleeping in the parental bedroom would be moved into the grandaunt's room. This action mediated the separation from mother, fostered the transference of nurturing to the grandaunt, and mitigated the intensity of initial envy of the mother/baby relationship. Because she feels she cannot cope without help, Sharif's mother is so afraid to have another child while in the United States that she uses artificial birth control, although it is against her religious beliefs.

Multiple caregivers help diffuse sibling envy and rivalry by providing each child with someone special. This results in less intense experiences of object loss and loss of love. At the same time, this secondary figure orients the older child toward autonomous functioning, thus facilitating the developmental process that leads to independent functioning. Sharif's mother, therefore, has never experienced the intensity of envy and sibling rivalry she sees in her sons and thus cannot empathize with Sharif's need to keep some things for himself. This in turn interferes

---

[9]In general, these adults do not say "no" to a child under age 2 because they feel a child does not understand why he cannot have something. If they decide they do not want the child to have an item, they put it out of sight.

with discovering the cause of Sharif's refusal and helping him cope with his brother's intrusions. Her method is always the same: Sharif must give up his toys to Tijani until Tijani's interest wanes. Frequently, the child's underlying motivation in these intrusions is to restore connection to a primary love object. When there are multiple caregivers these intrusions often diminish because the younger child's needs are met by an available loving person and the older child's playthings are returned with less delay, thus diminishing the intensity of anger and frustration.

Sharif does not throw tantrums or bite or hit Tijani when their father is home. If Tijani wants Sharif's toys, Sharif's father asks him to give them to him, and Sharif usually complies. Both parents expect Sharif to give in to his brother and shame him when he fails to comply.

When the father is home, Tijani has his exclusive attention and is less apt to intrude into Sharif's activities. In our culture, competition for mother is often mediated by the father's availability to the older child, leaving the mother more exclusively available to the younger child. In this family, the roles are reversed. The father became more active in caretaking when Tijani was weaned from the breast at the age of 10 months. Now Tijani goes to his father for "libidinal refueling," or comfort, when he is ill or hurt. Only when the father is unavailable does he go to his mother. I often see Tijani snuggling into his father's shoulder. His father does not encourage autonomous activity and verbalization as a part of their relationship but appears to enjoy the snuggling. This division of dyadic pairing interferes with progress in both children's Separation-Individuation Process.

Traditionally, fathers in this tribal group do not assume a nurturing role. Rather grandmothers or other female kin fill this role. In this respect, Sharif's father is unusual. According to his wife, even in Nigeria he was involved in his children's care by feeding and changing their diapers. She says with pride, "This is unusual for fathers in my culture."

Like his wife, the father sees Tijani as a baby and Sharif as a "big boy," creating an artificial categorization without adequate consideration of the reality of their chronological age. Father expects more mature behavior from Sharif than appropriate to his age and treats Tijani like a symbiotic partner. This split relationship to his sons seems unconsciously linked to his own early experience with his parents when his father went to school abroad for a year, leaving wife and child in Nigeria. Then soon after his father returned to Nigeria the parents divorced and Sharif's father remained with his father. The current separation from home unconsciously reactivates emotions relating to these childhood experiences. His relationship to his two boys becomes a way to deal with and mediate his own anxiety. He can relate to Tijani and satisfy a wish for dependency gratification (and thus his connection to his mother) and he can relate to Sharif in a manner that satisfies independent wishes (and his identification with his father). When Sharif takes things apart, father attributes this behavior to some sort of innate "destructiveness" in Sharif. This attribution begins to make sense when we consider father's experience of family destruction following his father's education abroad. He cannot allow Sharif to take things apart and feels helpless to deal with this problem just as he must have felt helpless when his family came apart at age three or four. Father tells me how, since he has grown up, his father consults him about how to deal with his teenage brothers "since he believes I am more in tune with modern ideas." He says his father is much more lenient with them than he ever was with him, thus indicating he experienced his father as restrictive and critical as a boy.

Given father's special relationship to Tijani, his expectations that Sharif concede to his brother, and his sharp criticisms when these expectations are not complied with, it seems that Sharif tends to believe his father loves Tijani more. This idea may contribute to Sharif's inability to use his father to help him tolerate separation experiences from mother.

The transference of Tijani to father at weaning, as well as the persistence of a symbiotic relationship, complicates Tijani's separation-individuation progress. Consequently, Tijani has not moved into the Rapprochement subphase. This is, in part, because his father fosters a symbiotic relationship[10] but also because Tijani experiences daily and multiple separations from his father who travels to and from the university. Because Tijani is always upset, his father sneaks out or his mother averts his attention. If Tijani does not see his father leave, he does not

[10]Mahler et al. (1975) found that when mothers were conflicted about their child's differentiation and fostered the symbiotic relationship beyond its usual phase appropriateness, other elements of the Separation-Individuation Process lagged behind the child's ability to actually separate from her. Father's pattern of relationship was not in the service of furthering autonomy and independence, but rather it appeared to be a way to keep Tijani close and connected to him to satisfy his own emotional needs at the time.

become fussy. For Tijani, this experience is made all the more mysterious since he is given no explanation where or if his father has gone. As a consequence of this loss, each time the door opens, he darts out. This is even more of a problem in this household because visitors to it are frequent.

He also insists on searching through packages and briefcases visitors bring with them. To prevent Tijani from emptying their parcels, visitors hide them in the living room closet. This is effective since he demonstrates lack of evocative memory. Like his parents, visitors also use deception when they leave. Again, whenever the door opens Tijani dashes out. In essence the open door becomes a contextual reminder of his absent father and his darting out an attempt to find him in the hallway where he has so often found him before. When I return to follow up my observations a year later, Tijani is still upset when his father leaves. They still use deception, only now he cries for a while afterward. They can no longer distract him because he can evoke his memory of his father without contextual clues and disappointment has an enduring and painful quality.

These experiences give some insight into the driven nature of Tijani's intrusiveness. Sharif is not only a rival for their mother's attention, but is also a substitute for the missing father. Sharif and his playthings became a way for Tijani to reenact his relationship with father. By taking possession of Sharif's toys, he takes possession of father. Thus these toys, along with his relationship to Sharif, and especially the action of possession, become transitional experiences. These transitional experiences serve to mediate object loss and separation anxiety.

Tijani's intense darting, intrusiveness, and searching behaviors provide insight into Sharif's persistence in taking things apart. Both boys are attempting to cope with object loss. In view of the parents' practice to deceive Tijani, it seems likely this pattern was also used with Sharif. When his mother left for work, the searching activity became a way to cope with object loss. Therefore, when Sharif came to the United States, exploring inanimate objects became a way to locate his missing grandmother. This activity took on transitional qualities (Winnicott 1953). When Tijani interrupts Sharif's activities, he also interrupts his search for the long lost love object. Since this searching activity reconnects him to his past, it also mitigates fears of object loss and onset of separation anxiety. When Tijani takes his brother's toy, Sharif's transitional activity is interrupted and besides triggering rivalry, it also activates fear of object loss. The need to continue his search, while positively valued by his mother, is negatively valued by his father. This complicates his use of father as a secondary love object to effect separation from mother. To gratify his father he must give up his transitional activity and this intensifies his fear of losing his mother.

Three weeks following the end of my first observations, the family returned to Nigeria for Christmas vacation. Sharif and Aisa each claim a maternal aunt with whom they sleep and interact, whom they describe as being each one's "own aunt." This new division of dyads helps ease sibling rivalry as now each child has his or her own special person. This allows Tijani to return to his mother since he no longer must share her with Sharif. Father's need for dependency gratification through his nurturing relationship to Tijani abates with the return to Nigeria and he turns caregiving back to his wife.

Soon after returning to the United States, Sharif begins attending daycare at his sister's school. His mother says he likes it and adjusts easily. I suspect the trip to Nigeria and his reunification with his grandmother helped him consolidate his internal representations. He no longer needs to search for her. This consolidation not only eases fears of object loss but makes it possible for him to give up his need to "see" his mother, stop urinating in his pants, and thus enables him to enter daycare.

The next year saw a great improvement in Sharif and Tijani's relationship. This is partly due to Sharif's skill in successfully manipulating Tijani in ways his parents approve (just as Aisa manipulated him a year earlier). Sharif also has greater anticipatory skills now. He knows if he concedes temporarily, Tijani will be satisfied and leave him and his playthings alone. In contrast to the previous year, Sharif's activity no longer has such a driven quality, although he still is very curious about how things work and is persistent at figuring this out. Mother believes he has remarkable talent in this area.

With Sharif in school, Tijani and his mother's relationship seems back on track and, although delayed, he appears to be working through the Rapprochement subphase in relation to his mother. His father now relates to him in a more age-appropriate way, although, as with Sharif, he views some of his behavior as destructive and intrusive. He criticizes Tijani, as he had Sharif, to elicit more desirable behavior, but is made less upset and helpless by Tijani's unacceptable behavior.

When I was finishing my first set of observations the year before,

Sharif's father expressed concern about Sharif's behavior. I suggested ways to improve the father-son relationship. Now, one year later, he is more attentive to his son and generally tolerates occasional regression. When Sharif appears disappointed or sad, he offers more nurturing. This frees Sharif to go to his father during difficult times. For example, one day after school, Sharif was sad and disappointed. His sister, celebrating her birthday, was given gifts. He went to his father for comfort and his father held him on his lap (a kind of intimacy not permitted the year before). He now allows his son to express some regressive needs. The previous year he would have criticized Sharif's need for closeness and shamed him for being a baby like Tijani. Father is now functioning as a secondary love object and this fosters his son's identification with him. He praises Sharif's successes in dealing with his brother's intrusions.

Mother tells me that several days earlier Sharif began going into his sister's classroom. (While she is telling the story, Sharif looks down as if ashamed.) Mother says that father told Sharif that if he didn't stop going into his sister's classroom, he would not take him to school anymore, and Sharif told his father he would not do it again. She goes on to say that today he went into his sister's classroom again, only this time when his teacher collected him, he began to cry. I ask him why he goes to his sister's classroom. He smiles and says, "Because I want to be big." I ask, "What will you do if you're big?" He says, "I'll take care of my baby." "How?" I ask. He responds, "I'll tell him not to worry, mother will be back soon." His mother clarifies, "When he talks about his baby, he's talking about Tijani." Minutes later, he refuses to share with Tijani. His mother reminds him, "Remember, you said you'd take care of your baby." He looks down in shame. I say, "Sometimes it's hard to share with your brother." He looks up, nods, smiles, and plays with new enthusiasm. Soon he is sharing with Tijani. Acknowledging his wish not to share seems to diminish his conflict and reduce his shame over failing to take care of "his baby."[11]

---

[11]Furman (1978) says that feelings expressed in words as opposed to action can diminish conflicts with the environment and superego precursors. There is less need for defensive activity. Sharif's negative feelings toward Tijani were never acknowledged as legitimate. These feelings were increasingly subjected to defensive activity in order to avoid the shame he experienced when he did not want to take care of or give in to his brother.

During the next few days, Sharif's play indicates themes of identification with his father, concerns about control of oral aggression, body parts being bitten by toys, and fear of being bitten by monsters. At the time, I surmise he has entered the phallic phase and castration anxiety is playing a role in his mental life and behaviors. I feel his need to go to his sister's classroom is related to this fear. His sister, like his mother, is his defense against reactivating separation anxiety and losing self control in the face of castration worries. Clearly, in light of my previous year's observations, Sharif needs his mother or sister's presence, to be able to see them, to contain his intensely hostile aggression. A year earlier, his predominant expression of anger was biting, hitting, and temper tantrums.

A few weeks after my last visit, I telephone the family as they prepare to return to Nigeria permanently. Sharif had been circumcised at the clinic a few days earlier. His mother says he does not seem bothered by it because he was more interested in playing with the clinic's dart game than in going home.[12]

This information clarifies the behaviors I saw weeks earlier. The themes in his play reveal he knew about the impending operation. His behavior reveals that he conceptualizes this operation as having his penis bitten off. I imagine his parents tell him this surgery will make him like his father. Furthermore, his play indicates his wish for me to protect him. For example, he had asked me to make a hanger out of modeling clay for his jet. Afterwards, he asked if he could keep it, but his father says "No." I also observe his fear of losing self-control, as well as his fear of reactivating earlier solutions to his hostility by biting and hitting his rival. Another time, he enclosed a father and boy doll to protect both dolls from an enraged "Pacman" toy that is all mouth and flailing arms (presumably a projection of his hostile aggressive wishes).

Facing his impending surgery, separation anxiety emerges again in relation to castration anxiety. I believe this prompted him to go to his sister's classroom. His father's castrating threat of not letting him return to school only added to his distress. Like identification with his father, going to school makes him feel big. Being angry with his father tempor-

---

[12]From a psychoanalytic point of view, this eagerness to play the dart game can be seen as an unconscious symbolic attempt to see if his penis still works. To his mother, his interest in playing meant that the surgery was not disturbing to him.

arily interfered with identifying with him as a protective, loving object. This leads to a regressive wish for his mother's protection and help in containing his fear of losing self control, just as, a year earlier, being able to "see" her kept him from biting Tijani. In spite of being angry with his father, his play indicated a persistent wish to identify with him. Although he said the enclosed space is a protection against Pacman, we may also see it as a protection against engulfment in a maternal symbiotic relationship which, while offering him protection, takes away his sense of "bigness." Furthermore, regressive wishes for mother, as well as wishes for her strength, interfere with identification with father and hence stability of gender identify (Chasseguet-Smirgel 1985).

I see several indications that Sharif may experience more than the ordinary stress during the phallic phase: (1) an increase in fears of object loss as new conflicts arise (because of experiencing a prolonged separation from his grandmother at a crucial point in development of mental representations); (2) concerns about loss of parental love as he is criticized and shamed, especially in relation to feelings of rivalry; (3) the timing of his circumcision and the oral fantasies that become activated to cope with this event; and (4) symbolic castration threats from father which stimulate hostile aggressive wishes and promote regressions that interfere with his identification with his father. These multiple fears may compromise oedipal resolution and/or result in a harsh superego and difficulties maintaining self-esteem, especially if he experiences future traumatic events that reactivate these multiple fears.

On the other hand, a return to Nigeria may diminish the father's own regressive needs for connection, thus alleviating his tendency to be so critical of Sharif's regressive behaviors. The fact that the father's relationship to his own father is now one of mutual respect is an encouraging sign in this regard. Returning to Nigeria then may result in an improvement in their relationship so that pre-oedipal regression and conflict during the phallic phase conform more to a level that will permit further psychological elaboration and development.

Discussion

Both Habiba and her mother show a more than expected need for external sources of self-esteem regulation. Splitting and projecting help them to defensively deny their own anger and sense of personal badness. Habiba's mother often speaks about being unable to alter her circumstances: "Whatever happens is God's will." In contrast, Habiba has (some) confidence in her ability to alter events. Her persistent efforts to get what she wants render her less vulnerable to the whims of her environment than her mother, who passively accepts what happens. I suspect that this difference is in part due to the fact that Habiba did not experience separation from her mother, although she did experience inconsistent psychological availability. She can generally stimulate her mother to respond favorably to her exhibitionistic displays. Her mother, however, experienced a more prolonged physical and psychological separation at age 3. I doubt her adolescent sister could have provided her with adequate psychological support while coping with her own separation anxiety and sexual relationship to a man she did not know.

Her inability to draw her nanny with facial features makes me suspect Habiba had not established imaging before separating from her. Remembering the nanny results from direct reminders from her environment. Thus, my appearance on the scene, and special interest in her, provided a powerful remembering experience. It is important that she mold our relationship to some likeness to her relationship to nanny. Sensori-motor schemas serve as a way to link me to the mother-child relationship, just as earlier nanny had been linked to it. There is a tactile nature to her relationship to me. By grabbing my hand as I leave and being grabbed by her mother, she replicates the experience of separation and reunion with mother and nanny as mother left for work each day and again as nanny returned to her own home at the end of the day. Being held on her mother's back also serves as a sensori-motor memorial link to her nanny.

Toward the end of my observations, mother complains of her back hurting because Habiba insisted on being carried like a small child. The mother's back pain is so intense that she consults a doctor, which legitimately permits mother to stop what she views as an infantile behavior on Habiba's part. Without this permission, the mother cannot change the way she and Habiba relate.

The same nanny had been employed by this family since the birth of their first child twelve years earlier. It seems likely that she had become a maternal substitute for both Habiba and her mother. When the mother says, "Habiba misses her nanny very much," she echoes her own loneliness for and dependency upon this woman.

The mother's fulltime employment outside the home added another dimension to Habiba's relationship to the nanny, who cared for Habiba during most of her day, thus serving in a primary caregiver capacity. The intensity of Habiba's loneliness for nanny can be seen in the intensity and rapidity of her transference reaction to me.

Sharif's mother is emotionally available to him and values Sharif's searching activities, so she can help her son with his longings for his grandmother without resorting to holding. When Sharif takes things apart, he is able to explore his environment and derive more opportunities for independent functioning. Also, caregiving patterns are apt to be similar between his mother and grandmother, so the integration of nurturing experiences is easier than it was for Habiba where the child-rearing patterns of the two mothers are less apt to be the same.

In contrast to Habiba, when Sharif is angry he does not give up autonomous practicing. He manipulates perplexing objects until they work or he asks for help. This indicates a relatively mature potential for tolerating frustration. Sharif's demands for self-affirmation from external sources are typical for a child in the early phallic phase. Repetitive showing off to get attention is not necessary because both parents praise him spontaneously. In many ways, his parents are empathic and can set aside their own interests and preoccupations in favor of their children. I do feel they stress mature behaviors in relation to his brother more than necessary and foster infantile dependency in Tijani somewhat longer than necessary. It is as if the junior-senior relationship blurs Sharif's and Tijani's real ages and, likewise, their potential.

Habiba's parents also appear to operate from the same sort of principle. Often they discourage her from trying "big girl" activities that she is really capable of doing, while expecting her brother to be very mature. (I do not see the playfulness and mischievousness in him that I see in other boys his age.)

In this Nigerian culture, adult relationships are hierarchically organized at most interpersonal levels. An important motivation for this kind of social structuring is derived from the way sibling rivalry is diffused within an extended family household, and this in turn has important implications for psychological development. This early diffusion of envy, when successful, may result in diminution of the intensity of castration fear and oedipal rivalry as the intensity of pre-oedipal conflicts, reactivated during the Oedipus complex, is diminished. This diminution of pre-oedipal conflict makes it less difficult to maintain hierarchical relations in adulthood since castration fears and competitive urges are less intense within the social unit. This is in contrast to American culture, where nuclear households predominate and sibling and oedipal rivalry are intense.

With diffused sibling rivalry and diminished conflict, there is less need for regressive behaviors to restore the mother-child relationship. The child's omnipotence is maintained to a greater degree by extended family involvement with him and autonomous functioning can be resumed more quickly. The sense of maturity in relation to a younger sibling is not compromised to the same degree as for the nuclear family member where usually only one parent is available for all the children much of the time. This kind of early diffusion experience may be at the expense of complex development of internal defense strategies to cope with rivalry. American children, in the face of limited external human resources, must develop internal defenses to cope with rivalry in order to maintain their relationship with their human environment. When the external resource becomes unavailable, as happened with these Nigerians when they moved to the United States, difficulties in coping arise. Thus, Sharif's mother cannot use internal resources to help her children resolve their intense rivalry conflict. Instead she tries to replicate the missing external resources in her behaviors, which only intensifies the conflict. She tries to engage other people to help her with this task, as she did by encouraging a relationship between Sharif and myself. In turn, when regressive behaviors do occur in their children, they may be more troublesome because of a reliance upon interpersonal rather than intrapersonal relationships as an organizer of internal states. Certainly several parents in my study are very disturbed and helpless when regressive behaviors are exhibited by their children and/or when they see regressive behaviors in some of the other Nigerian children in the social network.

I believe Sharif established imaging before separating from his grandmother and that he was into the Rapprochement subphase when "low-keyedness" or imaging gives way to actively remembering mother. In this subphase the absent mother is actively searched for and such activities keep the child oriented toward autonomous interests rather than the more passive way of remembering in the earlier subphase (i.e., remembering as certain contexts arise), which is much more dependent upon the environment. The child's activity is a way to defend against sadness as mother is remembered, and serves to bolster self-esteem as a sense of mastery is gained from such exploration. Sharif's sense of mastery is interrupted when Tijani takes his toys, impinging upon his capacity to feel "big."

Sharif has talked to his grandmother on the phone several times, but this does not appear to be sufficient "libidinal refueling" for consolidation of perceptual experiences. He has to "see" her as well. This need is expressed when separation anxiety is aroused and he says, "I want to see my mother." When Sharif's family visits Nigeria during Christmas vacation, his opportunity to "see" his grandmother helps him unify his perceptual experiences with her so that he can symbolize her. This integration, in turn, makes it possible for him to give up having to see his mother when he is separated from her. In addition, seeing and being seen by his mother relate to maintaining self-control so that once he can successfully image his mother, he gains a degree of control over his hostile aggression. He has experienced an interruption in the visual perceptual mode and this is important for his development of self and object constancy. This would confirm Mahler et al.'s stress on the importance of the primary love object's physical and emotional availability during the entire course of the Separation-Individuation Process. Symbolic representation of a differentiated self and other could not be completed until he "saw" his grandmother.

Impact of multiple mothering in our culture

Multiple primary caregiver experiences need not disrupt establishing an autonomous self, yet certain conditions must be met if self and object constancy are to occur. Still, specific compromise formations may vary with different caregiving environments as Volkan suggests and as we see when Sharif's mother is unable to respond flexibly to her sons' sibling rivalry. If the surrogate mother and mother's experiences are mainly pleasurable and both are emotionally available to meet the child's needs, then relationship experiences with multiple caregivers can consolidate into internally stable other and, concurrently, self representations. The child may use consolidated mental representations to symbolize a "good enough" mother and this enables him to sustain his well-being and sense of self during brief separation experiences even when he is angry with his mother.

The child experiences problems when his surrogate caregiver is abruptly lost for a prolonged period before he consolidates his relationships into this "good enough" representation. It appears imperative that the disruption not occur during the course of establishing imaging. Lack of timely imaging development is an impediment to succeeding phases (Mahler et al. 1975). It would seem that all the perceptual modes in which the child experiences the lost love object must be integrated in order for object constancy to be achieved. Both Habiba and Sharif needed to see their lost object.

If a mother is consistently physically and emotionally available after a disruption occurs, and if the child has an opportunity to form an integration either through reunion with the lost object or through working this problem out with a new object (a secondary love object), then psychic development can proceed. It may, however, proceed with some persistent remnant of early object loss that intensifies conflict resolution at each developmental phase and in adulthood in certain contexts. I see evidence of this in Sharif during our final meetings. Habiba's mother's inconsistent emotional availability adds another dimension to Habiba's developmental experience as self-esteem is easily compromised and requires environmental confirmation. Even if the mother is consistently available, both physically and psychologically, an empathic secondary love object is necessary to mediate the intensity of anger during the Rapprochement subphase. Habiba clearly has difficulty with mood regulation when she doesn't get what she wants. Although her father was often in the room with her, his attention was elsewhere (he could be in a crowded room and keep his attention only on his work). For Habiba to get his attention, she had to "show off" or physically intrude into his focus. His attention was not often spontaneously forthcoming. Sharif's need and wish for a secondary love object is seen in his eagerness to experiment with separations from his mother by using me. His father's special relationship to Tijani, as well as fluctuations in his empathy for Sharif, make it impossible for him to feel sure his father will meet his dependency needs if his mother were away.

Sharif's sister, Aisa, experiences multiple caregivers, yet is progressing in her psychological development at ages 5 and 6 with no more than ordinary conflict one sees in a child this age, and certainly less sibling rivalry than I see in American children. Sharif's mother, who had multiple caregivers, has adjusted well to her new role as full-time mother in a new culture. She does, however, experience difficulties regulating sibling rivalry. She enjoys being in the United States and hopes to return in the future when her children are older. The other adults in my study are so lonely they find little pleasure in their new surroundings and have no desire ever to return. Their loneliness interferes with their parental functioning as more of their attention is directed toward themselves, leaving the child's narcissistic needs less consistently and fully responded to (Campbell 1984). Interestingly, Sharif's mother is the only adult in my sample who had not experienced a major traumatic event involving object loss during childhood.

Introducing another caregiver may provide enrichment, and yet may complicate the child's psychological developmental tasks. My data show the important role non-mother caregivers play in the child's assumption of emotional object and self constancy. Separation from these substitutes mean consequences for the Separation-Individuation Process, especially during the Practicing and Rapprochement subphases. Disrupting the child's relationship to the caregiver can lead to developmental impairments. Possibly the child must work through object constancy with both caregivers before self-cohesion can occur (Campbell 1985). Parents may ameliorate the internal conflict if they do not ignore the importance of their child's loss. Parents often deny the importance of the secondary caregiver because they cannot accept that their child loves someone else, perhaps as much or more than themselves. Parents may realize the severity of their child's loss, but choose not to talk about it as a way to avoid painful memories (perhaps for themselves as well as their child). There may be a lag between an event and the onset of unhealthy behaviors, resulting in parental inability to link behavior to a traumatic experience and thereby preventing empathic response to the child's actions. Instead, they may respond with anger and punishment, which only intensifies the dangerousness of the fear, as we saw with Sharif and his father.

Parental anger with the lost caregiver may interfere with the ability to help the child remember loving feelings for that person. We know Freud was haunted by the disruption of his relationship with his *kinderfrau* or nanny at age 2½, who was fired after discovery of a theft. Freud was not sure if the theft were his nanny's or his own. Later, his adult friendships to Breuer, Fliess, Adler, Jung, and others went from great admiration to intense disappointment (Gay 1988). Sometimes, this involved concerns about who claimed what ideas. Even toward the end of his life, Freud's attitude toward religion contained fascination and a need to discredit and destroy its hold on him. It is difficult for a 2½ year old boy to openly express his wish and need for his nanny for fear of also being sent away for the misdeeds he believed he shared with her. Throughout Freud's life, he retained two significant females: a sexual partner, his wife, and an intellectual confidant—first his sister-in-law and then his daughter. It is as though his sense of continuity came only from a split relationship to females. His difficulty with integrating his relationship to his nanny and mother cast a shadow on his oedipal conflict. This promoted a tendency toward difficulties with integrating good and bad aspects of the object. His disappointments continued to destroy some of his personal and professional relationships.

Anna, Freud's youngest daughter, was also raised in a multiple mothering environment. She had her biological mother, aunt, and *kinderfrau*, Josephine. In contrast to her father, she did not experience separation from her *kinderfrau* until age 6 when Josephine married and left the family. Young-Bruehl (1988, 1989) discusses the impact of this multiple mothering experience upon Anna's personality development and relationships. Although Sigmund Freud suggests experiences with other caregivers can "merge into" the maternal representation (1933) he does not comment upon how multiple mothering can affect a little girl's relationship patterns (Young-Bruehl 1989). Young-Bruehl conjectures that Anna's identification with her *kinderfrau*'s childcare sustained a split. She repeated her childhood good and bad split during her final year of life when she retained a housekeeper who was unable to care for her adequately. Young-Bruehl suggests this housekeeper served as her bad caregiver while a colleague served as the good caregiver. She refused to send her housekeeper to a nursing facility despite her friend's insistence. I suggest that earlier in life she also maintained this split relationship to females. This time, she used Dorothy Burlingham as her good colleague and friend while Melanie Klein became her professional enemy and target for hostility.

I cite these examples because they indicate how multiple mothering caregiving experiences during pre-oedipal development may result in structuralization of compromise formations that produce different configurations of oedipal compromises. When early experiences are similar as a result of culturally sanctioned practices, we can expect differences in nuclear complexes as found cross-culturally by Malinowski, Parsons, and Kosawa, as individuals work out compromise formations to resolve fears of object loss, loss of love, castration, and superego injunctions.

Summary

Habiba and Sharif's transferences, as well as their relationships to other family members, lead me to conclude that abrupt and prolonged separation from a non-mother caregiver can delay or arrest certain aspects of psychological development. This is heightened if the event occurs during the Practicing or Rapprochement subphases when mental representations are forming. A somewhat different configuration of compromise formations may result and influence the outcomes of each succeeding phase of psychic development and future compromises. In turn, this may result in aspects of superego functioning retaining a dependency relationship with environmental sources.

When the child sustains a real loss before attainment of object constancy, this experience makes it difficult for him to trust his mother will not also abandon him. Such a traumatic experience continues to cast its shadow on subsequent developmental phases, resulting in problematic differentiation of internal representations. It renders the child less flexible when dealing with new conflicts and interferes with his capacity to explore and experience aspects of reality necessary for stable internalized self and object structures.

In my study, most of my adult subjects experienced such intense loneliness, they were unable to enjoy or use positive aspects of their new environment for pleasure or to relieve their anxiety as they would in Nigeria. Instead, they isolated themselves by forming a tight-knit social network that served to protect their Nigerian selves and strengthen the boundary between themselves and perceived environmental dangers. They used splitting and projection to maintain the good self and viewed the outside world as their enemy and target for hostility.

Multiple mothering in this Nigerian culture has evolved partly in response to the child's greater opportunity to experience psychological and physical loss of their primary caregiver. The death rate in this culture is so high that most adults in the study had experienced losing a parent and/or sibling before age 5. Infant mortality is high and strains the mother's psychological availability to her other children. Extended families thus become important in preserving the child's sense of well-being.

Working through the fear of object loss is one of the first conflicts a child must successfully complete during psychic development. Therefore, we must ensure that our children have the best opportunity to master this phase of their development. This means we must pay special attention to the entire caregiver environment, not merely mother and child.

References

Ainsworth, Mary D. Salter. 1967. *Infancy in Uganda*. Baltimore: Johns Hopkins Press.

Brenner, Charles. 1982. *The Mind in Conflict*. New York: International Universities Press.

Cambor, Charles. 1969. "Preoedipal Factors in Superego Development." *Psychoanalytic Quarterly* 38: 81-96.

Campbell, JoAnn. 1984. "Cultural Isolation among International Non-Student Wives and Its Effect upon Pre-School Children." Presented at the *83rd Annual Meeting of the American Anthropological Association*, Denver.

__________. 1985. *Parental Adaptations and the Separation-Individuation Process in Children in Some Overseas Nigerian Families*. Unpublished doctoral dissertation, University of Washington, Seattle.

__________. 1989. "Multiple Mothers and Separation-Individuation: Evidence from Some Nigerian Children." Presented at the *88th Annual Meetings of the American Anthropological Association*, Washington, D.C., November 18, 1989.

Chasseguet-Smirgel, Janine. 1985. *The Ego Ideal*. Translated by Paul Barrows. New York: W.W. Norton & Co.

Emde, Robert N., Theodore J. Gaensbauer, and Robert J. Harmon. 1976. *Emotional Expression in Infancy: A Biobehavioral Study*. Psychological Issues, Monograph 37. New York: International Universities Press.

Freud, Sigmund. 1933. *New Introductory Lectures on Psychoanalysis*. Standard Edition, 22. London: Hogarth. 1971.

Furman, Robert. 1978. "Some Developmental Aspects of the Verbalization of Affects." *Psychoanalytic Study of the Child* 33: 187-211.

Gay, Peter. 1988. *Freud: A Life for Our Time*. New York: W.W. Norton & Co.

Hunt, Robert, ed. 1967. *Personalities and Cultures*. Garden City, NY: Natural History Press.

Mahler, Margaret S., Fred Pine, and Anni Berman. 1975. *The Psychological Birth of the Human Infant*. New York: Basic Books.

Malinowski, Bronislaw. 1927. *Sex and Repression in Savage Society*. New York: Meridian Books.

__________. 1928. *The Sexual Life of Savages*. New York: Harcourt, Brace and World.

Okonogi, Keigo. 1978a. "Age of the Moratorium People." *Japan Echo* 5: 17-35.

__________. 1978b. "The Ajase Complex of the Japanese (1), the Depth Psychology of the Moratorium People." *Japan Echo* 5: 88-105.

Parsons, Anne. 1967. "Is the Oedipus Complex Universal? A South Italian 'Nuclear Complex.'" In R. Hunt (ed.), *Personality and Culture*. Garden City, NY: The Natural History Press, pp. 352-399.

Spiro, Melford. 1982. *Oedipus in the Trobriands*. Chicago: University of Chicago Press.

Spitz, René A. 1957. *No and Yes*. New York: International Universities Press.

__________. 1965. *The First Year of Life*. New York: Basic Books.

Stern, Daniel. 1985. *The Interpersonal World of the Infant*. New York: Basic Books.

Volkan, Vamik D. 1979. *Cyprus—War and Adaptation*. Charlottesville: University of Virginia Press.

Winnicott, D. W. 1953. "Transitional Objects and Transitional Phenomena." *International Journal of Psychoanalysis* 34: 89-97.

__________. 1958. *Through Paediatrics to Psycho-analysis*. New York: Basic Books.

__________. 1965. *The Maturational Processes and the Facilitating Environment*. New York: International Universities Press.

__________. 1971. *Therapeutic Consultations in Child Psychiatry*. New York: Basic Books.

Young-Bruehl, Elizabeth. 1988. *Anna Freud: A Biography*. New York: Summit Books.

__________. 1989. "Looking for Anna Freud's Mother." *The Psychoanalytic Study of the Child* 44: 391-408.

Chapter Four

Fields of Shame: Anthropologists Abroad[1]

Benjamin Kilborne

Surprisingly, Freud devoted little attention to shame per se, even though feelings of shame and the defenses against them are among the most powerful emotional constellations. Instead, he focused on what has been translated as *guilt*. Why Freud slighted shame is a matter of debate, but that he did so is today generally accepted, especially as the significance of shame dynamics becomes more and more firmly established (see, for example, Jacobson 1964; Lewis 1971; Wurmser 1981; Nathanson 1987; Morrison 1989; and Lansky 1984). This recent psychoanalytic work provides what I think is a most promising approach to psychoanalytic anthropology which, because it lends itself at once to psychological and sociological analyses, offers an opportunity to approach the interpersonal world of anthropologist and informant both phenomenologically and psychodynamically.

In the following pages, I will try to tell the story of Freud's relative neglect of shame and of its growing importance in contemporary clinical work. In doing so, I shall consider briefly some definitions of shame and the evolution of psychoanalytic thinking about shame from Freud to the

---

[1]A version of this paper appeared in *Ethos*, vol.20, no.2, June 1992. The version that appears here is with the permission of the American Anthropological Association. Chapter revisions owe much to the generous comments of Melvin Lansky and David Spain. For a more detailed discussion of the argument adumbrated here, see my forthcoming book on shame.

present, together with the implications of this for our understanding of what constitutes ethnographic evidence. After a brief clinical vignette, I conclude by delineating some of the dimensions of shame dynamics in the anthropological field situation.

Definitions

Let us begin with a working definition of shame phenomena and dynamics. Shame, the felt discrepancy between the way one fears one will be seen and the way one wants to appear, is often associated with an experience of exposure, of vulnerability, of what we fear others see that we do not want them to. As a result of the experience of uncovering, of failure to live up to an ideal, the individual anticipates rejection. What is hidden are particularly sensitive and easily injured facets of the self, of which one feels ashamed (Nathanson 1987:4). Accordingly, shame evokes feelings of having been ostracized, betrayed, abandoned. Shame calls into question some basic quality of the self (Alexander 1938; Lewis 1971; Wurmser 1981), entailing a sort of embarrassment about existing at all. Helen Block Lewis, in *Shame and Guilt in Neurosis* (1971), calls us "shameniks," departing from assumptions characteristic of Freud and others who suggest that we are primarily guilt-driven and that civilization is built on the guilt generated by the renunciation of instinct.

The word *shame* is derived from the Indo-European root *skam* or *skem*, meaning "to hide." From this same root come our two words *skin* and *hide*. The word shame seems to cover three distinct but related concepts: (1) disgrace itself, the fear of disgrace, and the anxiety that others will see how we have dishonored ourself; (2) the feeling that others are looking on with contempt and scorn at everything we do or don't, that there is no place to hide and that all we can do is disappear; and (3) shame as a preventative attitude (I must hide or disappear in order not to be disgraced). In the second case, one hides out of a fear of exposure; in the third, one hides to prevent or ward off exposure.[2]

---

[2]As distinct from narcissism, which Wurmser sees as a point of view rather than a specific dynamic content, shame is, as he so deftly explains (1981:76):

(continued...)

Shame entails a feeling of failure, weakness or what Balint (1968) called "the basic fault" in the self; guilt entails fear of—and a fantasized retaliation for—a fantasized attack on the other. And one can hide shame in guilt and guilt in shame, as Freud, Piers and Singer (1953), and others have noted. Oversimplifying, shame is an affect associated with the self and disgrace; guilt is an affect associated with transgression. Whereas one is ashamed of one's self (of one's state and being), one feels guilty about what one has done (about one's actions) and how this will be seen by an Other. Seen in terms of a shame-guilt dialectic between, on the one hand, the shame-ridden position of weakness and helplessness and, on the other, the guilt-ridden position of power and destructiveness, our Western emphasis on guilt as a cultural category could arguably be seen to rationalize our colonial past and to be reinforced by our dominant military, political and economic position.

Shame, infants and developmental research

Guilt has, in the psychoanalytic literature, been more directly associated with internal psychic processes, as distinct from social interactions. Yet shame and guilt seem to share a dependency upon an ego-ideal in

---

[2](...continued)

caused by a discrepancy between expectancy and realization; an inner or an outer discrepancy, an inner or an outer conflict. It is the polarity, the tension between how I want to be seen and how I am. In its internalized version shame is thus the outcome of a very specific tension between the superego and the ego function of self-perception. The higher the self-expectation and the greater the demand for perfection, the likelier and the greater the discrepancy, and the harsher the need for self-chastisement by self-ridicule, self-scorn and by symbolic or real disappearance and self-effacement. Insofar as "narcissism" refers to the concept of "self-esteem" and "pathological narcissism" to that of "overvaluation" of oneself or of others (something "immoderate," "limitless," "exaggerated," "absolute"), any great discrepancy between self-expectancy ("ideal-self") and self-perception ("real-self") is by definition a "narcissistic conflict," and it is *so ipso* one that is *felt* as shame ("the complex affect of shame").

terms of which the fantasized effects of one's wishes can be felt to be dangerous to the other person as well as to oneself. To understand that the other person (the object) is also a self, and that this person is capable of experiencing pain (see Nathanson 1987:46) is an experience arrived at, I would argue, through shame interactions. The difference between the two concepts tends to focus on shame as an experienced deficiency of some self state, with guilt as more specific and more specifically attached to actions for which one can be held accountable. Whereas shame entails an experience of basic defect, guilt entails remorse for hostile wishes directed at some other person.[3] Jacobson (1964:144) suggests that shame "refers to visual exposure, guilt predominantly to verbal demands, prohibitions and criticisms."

In recent years, the analytic community has witnessed not only the emergence of Kohut and self psychology, which emphasizes the capacity of the mother to mirror the infant's affective states, but also a renewed interest in mother-infant research. The infant research work of the past ten or fifteen years has stressed how much interaction takes place between mother and infant from birth, challenging the inexplicably resilient notion that the infant is simply a blank slate. Today, most researchers (e.g., Bowlby 1969; Tronick, Als, Adamson, Wise and Brazelton 1978; Lichtenberg 1982; Stern 1985) agree that the infant is, from birth, equipped with considerable powers to engage the attention of adults. Many and various have been the descriptions of phenomena dealing with shame, but not always as such. For example, Nathanson maintains that the description of stranger anxiety in infants provided by Spitz (1965) applies equally well to shame, making shame an emotion that apparently exists (or at least is visible) in infants soon after birth.

When approached by a stranger, the infant of 6 to 8 months will:

> show varying intensities of apprehension or anxiety and reject the stranger. . . . He may lower his eyes "shyly," he may cover them with his hands, lift his dress to cover his face, throw himself prone on his cot and hide his face in the blankets, he may weep or scream [Spitz, quoted in Nathanson 1987:7].

---

[3]Melvin Lansky points out to me that conscious shame is experienced as remorse, but unconscious guilt is often seen as loyalty and self sabotage, and is not *felt* at all. This seems to me an extremely important point.

Although these reactions may be fear and anxiety responses, the averted gaze and the covering of the face are clearly reactions which we associate with shame.

In phase one of the "still face" experiment, filmed by and reported in Tronick et al. (1978), mother and two to three month old infant interact normally, in face-to-face situations. In phase two, the mother is instructed to sit opposite the child, making eye contact but no facial expressions whatsoever. For a short while, the child will try to make faces at the mother. Then, when there is no response, the infant will either burst out in tears of distress, or slump down, averting his eyes from the mother's face. It is hypothesized that, since the infant is too dependent on the mother to entertain the idea that she might abandon or disappoint him, the infant tries to evacuate such feelings, and then feels ashamed of what he needs to hide or get rid of, anticipating rejection should his mother know these feelings. And so shame masks shame, which masks still more shame; one becomes ashamed of being ashamed, and defenses against being found out build one on top of another. The very early expression of anxiety in infants would seem to make them "shameniks," too. No less than adults, infants attempt to get away from what is painful in relationships. So they hide, imagine, deceive and pretend.

Freud and his successors on shame and narcissism

It is useful at this point to summarize the ideas of Freud and his successors concerning narcissism because current debates on shame depend so substantially on these ideas. Whereas shame designates a nest of affects (fear of being seen, humiliation, pain over not being noticed, etc.) and has a dynamic context, narcissism designates a fundamentally metapsychological description of the investment of psychic energy in the psychic economy.[4] For our purposes here, let us define narcissism as

---

[4]Even when "narcissism" designates affective stages (e.g., narcissistic vulnerability), the shade of economic and metapsychological theory continues to dominate the concept. Kohut, for example, seldom uses the concept of "narcissism" without designating investments of psychic energy, even though he maintains that he does not use a conflict or drive model of the affects.

an "overinvestment" in the self, rather than (and in opposition to) the investments made in one's relationships with others.[5] Persons exhibiting narcissistic pathologies are characterized by a relatively greater sensitivity to slights. They are particularly shame-prone because of their embarrassment over feeling so easily wounded and because, also, of their experienced inability either to communicate or successfully to hide or obliterate their pain. Consequently, they often describe feelings of imposture, insubstantiality and smallness. An economic description of such wounding leads to the use of the term "narcissism"; an affective description leads to the use of the term "shame."[6]

The term "narcissism" was first used by Freud in 1910 to refer to the object choice of homosexuals who take themselves as sexual objects, although in his later thinking on the subject Freud drops the distinction between auto-erotism and structural/economic theories of narcissism. But, in 1911, Freud began to conceive of narcissism as a stage in psychological/sexual evolution, between auto-erotism and object love. Then, in 1914, in "On Narcissism," Freud attempts to incorporate narcissism within the framework of his theory of drives (the libido). The individual invests energy in himself by withdrawing investment from the object. Relying on a sort of theory of the conservation of energy, Freud hypothesized that, since energy was limited, it had to come from somewhere. Consequently, narcissistic investment was, for Freud, like borrowing from Peter to pay Paul. In "Mourning and Melancholia" (1915), Freud views narcissism essentially as an identification with the object.[7] In the process of mourning, the bereaved has no choice but to

---

[5]This does not mean that for narcissistic personalities, relationships with others are less important. Rather, because these relationships are so problematic, they are often felt to be excruciatingly painful and thereby important because of the affects associated with them.

[6]One of the confusing features of self psychology is the confounding of these two levels of description. Freud himself has things to say about shame when he speaks of narcissism. Generally speaking, the *affects* of shame only very rarely are rigorously distinguished from the metapsychological *theories* of narcissism.

[7]What Freud appears to be referring to in "Mourning and Melancholia" is (continued...)

change objects. Etymologically, the bereaved has been robbed (bereaved comes from the stem *reafian*, to rob). Jacques Lacan (1949), following Sartre, maintains that the narcissistic or mirror stage of development is a necessary part of ego development, an idea which Kohut and the self psychologists would take up years later.[8]

Primary narcissism[9] is generally seen to be both healthy and inevitable. It designates a process in which the infant or young child invests his libido in himself. *Secondary narcissism*, by contrast, tends to be viewed as pathological, since it tends to entail the withdrawal of the libido from objects in order to reinvest it in the ego or self,[10] thereby constituting a defensive regression.[11] In his paper on narcissism, Freud (1914) holds that in the beginning the infant is his own ego-ideal, the ego-ideal being at first an expression and then a kind of substitute for, and repre-

---

[7](...continued)
projective identification in which the object is experienced to regulate self-esteem.

[8]Compare the mirror transference of Kohut, together with the mirroring self-object (e.g., Kohut, 1971, 1984).

[9]For Melanie Klein (1957) and psychoanalytic writers in her school, the very concept of primary narcissism is misleading as they and those belonging to the Object Relations school in general maintain that object relations are established from the beginning. For these writers, the only narcissism is secondary narcissism, and such narcissism designates flawed object relations expressed in an inability to rely on others (e.g., see Fairbairn 1954 and Guntrip 1968).

[10]For this introductory discussion of narcissism, I have relied upon Laplanche and Pontalis's *The Language of Psycho-analysis* (1973).

[11]Federn comments that Hans Sachs "dealt with that type of narcissism which refers to objects of the external world, and the repression and projection of which lead to the animistic conception of the world as found in primitive man" (Federn 1952:293). This comment of Federn's underscores the extent to which thinking about animism serves as a backdrop to psychoanalytic theories about thinking in general. It also highlights the relations to be developed (see Kilborne n.d.b. and n.d.c.) between magical thinking, ideas about individual development, and ideas about cultural categories.

sentation of, infantile narcissism. For Freud, at least in this text, the awareness of guilt, together with the concomitant moral consciousness, is what brings individuals into the social world, weaning them from their infantile narcissism.[12] But in this text, as in others, the line between shame and guilt seems very thin and, sometimes, what we read today as shame Freud calls "guilt."

Although Freud's very earliest theories of psychodynamics gave a key position to shame, based on his work with patients as reported in *Studies in Hysteria* (Breuer and Freud 1892), and although it is striking that all dreams in *The Interpretation of Dreams* reverse narcissistic injuries and are thus all reversals of shaming situations,[13] Freud seldom if ever mentions shame. This may be because he was having difficulty elaborating his ideas about shame in metapsychological terms or, perhaps, conflicts and rivalry within the ranks may have prompted him to focus more exclusively on the details of oedipal dynamics than he might have done had he been left to his own curiosity and devices. In any case, Freud never discusses shame in his great dream book, despite the prevalence of shaming themes in his own dreams.

Instead, Freud skirts the subject and, ignoring themes of humiliation, vulnerability, shame, and impotence, he develops a conflict theory of affect rooted in unconscious, guilt-inducing desires. His emphasis shifted to unconscious fantasy and transgression, and he gave more importance to oedipal dynamics, paying more and more attention to the oedipal fear of punishment or fear of the superego that he called "guilt." This transition can be seen, for example, in *Three Essays on a Theory of Sexuality* (1905), in which he shifts from speaking about shame and embarrassment as affective responses to being seen, to shame as a

---

[12]In my patient (see below), the negative injunctions (you must be like them) work to maintain the split Susan feels between being Chinese and being American; they also contribute to her fears about not being the person others think she is.

[13]As Melvin Lansky has pointed out to me, not only are all dreams in *The Interpretation of Dreams* based on reversals of situations of shame, but also none are primarily expressions of the wish for sexual consummation.

defense against drives (exhibitionism, voyeurism, etc.).[14]

In his writings, with increasing clarity from 1913 on, Freud tended to link scopophilia, exhibitionism and shame.[15] Morrison (1989) suggests that, in the *Three Essays* (and still more markedly with later writings), Freud's views of shame shift significantly. Up until this work, Morrison notes, Freud views shame as (1) a social affect associated with being discovered or found out by another person, (2) a defense against remembering something painful, and (3) a response to actually having been caught engaging in some sexual activity (e.g., masturbation) in one's early childhood. With the *Three Essays*, Freud's "emphasis regarding shame shifted significantly from affective experience to defense" since, in that paper, Freud viewed "the claims of aesthetic and moral ideals" as defenses against disgust and shame (Morrison 1989:23).

As Wurmser (1981), Morrison (1989), and others note, Freud broadened his definition of shame to include not only embarrassment over sexual drives but also the reaction formation against the desire to look. Phenomenologically, neither self psychologists nor other psychoanalytic writers have availed themselves of the possibilities for founding a theory of shame dynamics on the behaviors of looking and being looked at, even though Freud and others have firmly linked shame to exhibitionism and scopophilia. Significantly, even *The Language of Psychoanalysis* (Laplanche and Pontalis 1973) does not contain a single entry on shame, exhibitionism, voyeurism, scopophilia, or scopophobia.

A master of descriptions of the conflicts of shame, Sartre, in *Being*

---

[14]Following Freud, many other psychanalytic writers have subsumed shame under various metapsychological schema. Nunberg (1955:157), for example, observed that "shame is a reaction formation of the ego to the wish to exhibit"—a remark that makes it difficult if not impossible to attend to the phenomenology of shame. Erikson too focused on shame as it related to his theory of developmental modes, which similarly crimped his ability to explore the phenomenology of shame as an affective state.

[15]Freud and Abraham recognized the narcissistic features of obsessional neuroses, linking looking, scopophilia, and exhibitionism to the anal period. Following along these lines, Erikson (1963) conceptualized shame and doubt as the affective consequences of problems in phases of development (e.g., the anal phase, holding on as opposed to letting go).

and Nothingness (1956), provides one of the finest and most subtle descriptions of the relations between shame and looking. Sartre argues[16] that since we fear being seen by the Other as the person we wish we were not, we know others through our own anxieties, through our own uneasiness. Yet our looking and our shame at being looked at constitute an indispensable part of our sense of orientation in time and space. By his look, the Other, Sartre explains, confers upon us our sense of both time and space. "The Other's look insofar as I apprehend it comes to give my time a new dimension" (1956:243). Shame over looking and being looked at creates conflicts and disturbances which we react to in different ways. These may take the form of dreams, symptoms, acting out, or reaction formations, or may be sublimated in, for example, artistic expression. Shame, however, can also serve defensive functions.

Today, as more and more analysts are treating what they see to be narcissistic or narcissistic-borderline disorders, the dynamics of shame are of growing importance.[17] Moreover, the very popularity of self psychology, which has contributed to a renewed interest in shame dynamics in the United States, can be related to our present American values, cultural contexts and concerns, as are the theories of individual development and ideas about the self. Thus, the very prevalence of an awareness of shame dynamics can be studied anthropologically, in terms of cultural values.

Given the clinical prevalence of narcissistic disorders and the consequent effects of the self psychologists in stressing the intersubjectivity and the interpersonal field, it follows that psychoanalysts are likely to be

---

[16]Sartre's arguments are heavily influenced by Hegel's *The Phenomenology of the Spirit* (1807), required reading for those seriously interested in shame.

[17]Increasingly, the translations of Freud's ideas of the psyche as "mental apparatus" appear to be inadequate and, indeed, misleading in the ways they mechanize the metaphors we use to imagine the thinking processes. There is still no adequate study of the phenomenological assumptions underlying Freud's metapsychology or, more accurately, metapsychologies. In psychoanalytic circles there does appear to be a felt need to emphasize the interpersonal field and to make clear the fact that what one is studying (and what one is using to examine it with) is an interactive, interpersonal relationship.

preoccupied with shame for the foreseeable future, bringing them implicitly closer to the concerns of anthropologists. Thus, the works of Kohut and the self psychologists, by emphasizing narcissism and narcissistic vulnerability, have added a new focus to not only psychoanalytic but also anthropological inquiry.[18]

Shame and the ego-ideal

Any discrepancy between the ideal self and the real self is, ipso facto, a narcissistic conflict, felt as shame. In other words, "the more ambitious and peremptory (narcissistic) the ego ideal is, the more painful is the wound about failing and the more pervasive is the narcissistic anxiety" (Wurmser 1981:76). Or, the more demanding one's ideal of oneself, the more subject to shame one is, and the more vulnerable to narcissistic injury, which leads to heightened shame reactions. Also, the more intense the feelings of shame, the more demanding the ideal of total self-sufficiency, and the more inevitable the failure which, in turn, fuels the shame cycle.

In "On Narcissism," Freud develops a theory of the ideal ego and, at least between the lines, of shame as a feeling of failure and disgrace. In that paper, notes Morrison (1989), Freud developed his notion of ego libido and object libido, primary narcissism and reinvestment of libidinal cathexis in the idealized object. The "ideal-ego" emerges as a result of

---

[18]I wish, here, to emphasize the extent to which psychoanalytic ideas about the self, about social relationships, and about psychological development are necessarily rooted in various specific cultural and historical contexts. We cannot assume, for example, that a shift from Freud's drive-defense model of pre-World War I Vienna to the self psychological model in the United States in the 1980s and 1990s represents an objective "advance" in psychoanalytic theory. The values of nineteenth century Vienna are not those of late twentieth century America. The substantive differences in psychoanalysis in Argentina, France, England, and the United States provide concrete indications that psychoanalytic theory and treatment draw upon cultural values. (On this point, see also the chapters by Ingham, Kirschner, Ramanujam, and Spain in this volume; on the relevance of Kohut's views for anthropology, see the chapter by LeVine in this volume.)

attempts to regain the narcissism associated with the sense of "original perfection." Such a sense of original perfection can, however, be shaken by the buffetings of human events. As Freud notes: "When, as he grows up, [the child] is disturbed by the admonition of others and by the awakening of his own critical judgment, so that he can no longer retain that perfection, he seeks to recover it in the new form of an ego-ideal" (Freud 1914:94). And, continues Freud (1914:95): "It would not surprise us if we were to find a special psychical agency which performs the task of seeing that narcissistic satisfaction from the ego ideal is ensured and which, with this end in view, constantly watches the actual ego and measures it by that ideal."

Generally speaking, those who emphasize shame tend to distinguish theoretically an important role for the ego-ideal and for idealization, which they see as quite distinct from the broader notion of the superego. For example, Hartmann and Loewenstein (1964) subsume shame under the concept of guilt, dismissing differences between the two concepts. Kernberg (1975) essentially follows suit, and the term shame is not even indexed in the standard work on object relations by Greenberg and Mitchell (1983). But Jacobson (1964:154-155) speaks of shame as a manifestation of feelings of inferiority and failure to live up to one's ideals. Conflicts between ego and superego "develop from discordance between wishful self images which embody the narcissistic goals of the ego and a self that appears to be failing, defective, inferior, weak, contemptible in comparison." Such an emphasis on the feeling of failure to live up to the ego-ideal characterizes those writers who have recently focused on shame dynamics.

Pride and shame are silent regulators of our emotions to which far too little attention has been paid. In his splendid book *The Mask of Shame* (1981), Wurmser perceptively wrote a decade ago that an understanding of shame is important in every analytic hour. Every therapeutic session contains expressions of shame, humiliation and embarrassment, together with attempts to hide these feelings—all of which are picked up in countertransference reactions. And attempts to hide become shameful in themselves, since patients often feel that these hiding manoeuvres indicate a split or flaw in the sense of self, a failure to live up to the ego-ideal. "I am ashamed of feeling like an imposter, and I am afraid people will see that is what I really am, that they will find out that I am not the person they think," said a patient of mine. As Wurmser notes:

"Shame is the degradation that has already occurred and the enduring sense of self-contempt and unreality that ensues from such humiliation and mortification" (1981:67). To such expressions of shame may be added reactions to feelings of shame and failure. These may take various forms, for example that of contempt.[19] And contempt is often an attempt to rid oneself of shame, sometimes by denial and projection (I am not ashamed, you are or ought to be).

Shame and self psychology

Although one might expect Kohut to have focused explicitly on shame, he did not. Drawing on the Freudian distinction between primary and secondary narcissism, Kohut's views of shame depend on his presuppositions of a bipolar self which, in turn, define as poles the mother and father. Kohut sees the mother's function as that of providing empathic mirroring for the child's grandiose self (the mirroring selfobject function), and the father's function as coming later in the child's life. The father's role, according to Kohut, is empathically to accept the child's ambitions and ideals (the idealizing selfobject function). If the self gets, as it were, a bad rap with the mother, it can make up for this deficiency to some extent in the relationship with the father.[20] Whereas Chasseguet-Smirgel (1985), for example, stresses the importance of shame as a feeling that one has failed one's ideal of what one needed to be, Kohut sees it to be an overpowering of the ego by primitive exhibitionistic wishes. For Kohut, shame is directly linked to grandiosity and exhibitionism. In *The Restoration of the Self* (1971), Kohut explicitly linked shame to grandiosity denied rather than to a sense of failure to live up to one's ideals, or exposure as unlovable. Essentially, Kohut

[19]Contempt is often regarded as the expression of an overactive superego or ego-ideal, which vengefully turns on others so as to defend against feelings of worthlessness, vulnerability, and humiliation. Lansky suggests (personal communication) that contempt can more usefully be seen as passing shame to the other through projective identification.

[20]Stolorow et al. (1987) have clarified the selfobject by suggesting that it exists in a kind of figure/ground relationship with respect to libidinal objects.

views shame as narcissism in the infant which is not responded to. The absence of the expected response in the mother or parent triggers in the infant a wish to hide his needs, to be ashamed of wanting them gratified. For Kohut, shame is herniated exhibitionism.

Nevertheless, Kohut (1979:241) perceptively discusses those who, in late middle age, realize that they have fallen seriously short of their ideals, describing the

> utter hopelessness for some, of utter lethargy, of that depression without guilt and self-directed aggression, which overtakes those who feel that they have failed and cannot remedy the failure in the time and with the energies still at their disposal. The suicides of this period are not the expression of a punitive superego, but a remedial act—the wish to wipe out the unbearable sense of mortification and the nameless shame imposed by the ultimate recognition of a failure of all-encompassing magnitude.

In thinking about Kohut's emphasis on grandiosity and shame, some (e.g., Morrison 1989) have wondered about the extent to which the parent's failure to respond to the need of the child for an idealized selfobject creates a sense of deficiency in the child, making him shame-prone. Shame can, thus, be a kind of secondary reaction to the failure of parents to respond to the child's mirroring and/or idealization needs.[21] The child becomes ashamed of the inadequacy of his parents as well as of his own needs, leading to depression. Bibring (1963) long ago noted that depression sets in when "the fear of being inferior or defective seems to come true, whenever and in whatever way the person comes to feel that all effort was in vain, that he is definitely doomed to be a 'failure'" (p.25). Complicating the picture still further, I might add that shame can be related to *any* discrepancies felt to symbolize fantasized flaws. Shame can be a reaction both to the failure to attain a fantasized merger with the object and the failure to attain autonomy; or, alternatively, a defense against the wish to merge and to be entirely autonomous. As distinct from narcissism, shame is defined by that experienced

[21]This becomes more intelligible in light of Kohut's ideas about the ideal self as indispensable to the sense of a coherent self, the result of transmuting internalizations.

discrepancy between the way I fear I will be seen and the way I want to appear. Therefore, any feeling of discrepancy between my ideal of myself and the way I really am will be felt as shame.

A clinical illustration: shame dynamics in an analysis

Let me briefly illustrate here the kind of clinical questions and issues raised by shame dynamics[22] both in the transference[23] and counter-transference. For months, during my analysis of "Susan," she avoided looking at me. When I asked her why, she replied that if she did not look at me she "could invent me better." Consider this remark in the light of the following comment by Fenichel who, in 1945, was speaking directly about the relation between looking and shame:

> "I feel ashamed" means "I do not want to be seen." Therefore, persons who feel ashamed of themselves hide themselves or at least avert their faces. However, they also close their eyes and refuse to look. This is a kind of magical gesture, arising from the magical belief that anyone who does not look cannot be looked at [p.139].

Susan was ashamed not only of being in analysis but also of what she perceived as a cause of her difficulties: her inability to express feelings.

---

[22]Although Freud and Abraham recognized the narcissistic features of obsessional neuroses, and both linked these to the anal period, Erikson (1963) departed from their emphasis. He conceptualized shame and doubt as the affective consequences of problems in phases of development (anal development). In my use of shame, I wish explicitly to focus on the interpersonal dimensions of shaming dynamics. This does not, of course, mean that there are not anal meanings present, but I will not be concentrating on them.

[23]Of the various dimensions of transference, I shall here be concentrating primarily—and often exclusively—on those that are relevant to the issues of shame dynamics. In no way do I mean to imply that there are not other issues—e.g, of a drive/defense, conflictual, oedipal nature—with which the analysis has had to contend. Indeed, I believe those can be seen more clearly once the shame dynamics are adequately understood and analyzed.

Along with the dynamics of shame, go scorn and contempt. As Susan put it:

> When people, men or women, need me more than I need them I feel they are pathetic . . . because they need me and their needs make them vulnerable and pathetic. It is what happens whenever people want me and I am not sure I want to get close to them. Sometimes I feel as though I want to go away and hide under a stone.

If Susan showed me her feelings, she believed, I would be as contemptuous of her as she was of "pathetic," needy people who wanted her. So she hid them from me.

One of the signs of analytic progress was Susan's increasingly active interest and participation in Asian-American activities. As her sense of personal identity strengthened, so did her sense of ethnic identity and her ability to tolerate and to express the conflicts experienced in both. For example, when she decided to study Chinese, something she had wanted to do for years, Susan feared that if she did not do well enough with the Chinese language, she would fail in being Chinese, and she did not wish to be reminded of this fear by difficulties in speaking a Chinese language. Susan also began to allude to things "Chinese people" do which I, not being Chinese, would not understand.

Shame dynamics are prominent in Chinese families, particularly between mothers and daughters, as Amy Tan's recent novel *The Joy Luck Club* (1989) shows so well. Once the daughter loses face before the disapproving gaze of her mother, it becomes extremely difficult to recover. As an aunt says to one of the daughters in Tan's novel: "When you lose your face, it is like dropping your necklace down a well. The only way you can get it back is to fall in after it" (p.44).

Susan's fears of not being the person she thought she was or ought to be surfaced in the context of trying out for a play. When she experiences a distance between the person she is and the person she feels she needs to be in order to be acceptable, such discrepancies become in themselves shameful. One day, a director from the theater school came to her Chinese class, requesting people to audition for a play about Chinese people. Susan tried out. At first, she was extremely excited. After being called back twice, however, she obsessed about what would happen if she did not do a good enough job. "I was not acting when I did the reading," she explained. "If I play a part which draws on parts of me you have not seen (and which other people have not seen either), then if I play the part badly, that means that maybe I am not what I think I am."

"As a kid," she said, "the Chinese people treated me as though I was not one of them. But the white people in my Catholic neighborhood also treated me as though I was not one of them. This is like . . . I'm stuck; nobody wants me. I'm caught between worlds, and I don't really want to find out that nobody wants me." Does she know herself as others know her? If she does not, if there is a discrepancy and she thinks much of herself, then the discrepancy means (as she fears) that she is defective, that she is stupid, that others are seeing what she is blind to.

In *The Joy Luck Club*, Amy Tan describes the anxieties of the Chinese mother. "I smile. I use my American face. That's the face Americans think is Chinese, the one they cannot understand. But inside I am becoming ashamed. I am ashamed she [my daughter] is ashamed. Because she is my daughter and I am proud of her, and I am her mother but she is not proud of me" (1989:255). Susan knows that what is presented to her as Chinese is something which, as an American, she does not understand, and she is ashamed of this. Certainly Susan has told me that, as an American, I must continually be reminded by her that I do not understand what I think I do about her being Chinese.

Susan feared that I and that other people would see how not-Chinese or not-American she really was. Shame, reinforced by Chinese values, kept Susan's feelings severely repressed. In other words, Susan's negative self-image was defensively maintained through a dynamic of shame, reinforced by uncertainties about ethnic identity. To Americans, she was ashamed of being Chinese; to Chinese, she was ashamed of being American.

It will be helpful to recall, here, observations about the development of feelings of shame in infancy. Learning to be the person one is constitutes a good part of infancy and early childhood. But, just as one might think that is all there is, each of us is saddled also with the task of learning not to be the person he is not. This is more difficult still and requires better developed object relations and more social supports, experience and knowledge. At this extremely shame-prone stage, individuals such as Susan find themselves snared. As Wurmser notes (1981: 87), "to be torn between two ideal images of oneself, and inevitably to fail one or the other . . . [is] an unending source of shame." Whereas Susan knows she is torn between feeling Chinese and feeling American, it is likely that beneath this ethnic definition of the conflict lurks another conflict between, as Wurmser says, two ideal images of herself, such that she inevitably fails one or the other. The real person gets lost in the shuffle, and Susan is as she fears herself to be: unseen, unrecognized.[24]

Anthropological considerations: fieldwork and shame

In the light of the prevalence of shame in all human interactions, and considering how inevitable shame is on the part of both the anthropologist and those he or she is studying, let us briefly consider these "fields of shame." If one were to arrange ethnographic writings from most to least shame laden, the expressions of shame would be confined almost exclusively to unpublished materials such as diaries considered to be primarily personal. Published ethnographies, even those focusing on intersubjectivity (e.g., Crapanzano 1980) make virtually no mention of shame. And none that I know use shame dynamics as a way of understanding field situations, in a manner analogous to the uses of shame in the psychoanalytic clinical situation.

One of the most important anthropological documents that does express feelings of shame and confusion is Malinowski's deeply personal *A Diary in the Strict Sense of the Term* (Malinowski 1967), published years after his death. Significantly, it gave rise to tirades from anthropologists, such as Clifford Geertz, who were troubled by its revelations.[25] Written in Polish between 1914 and 1918, and never intended

---

[24]What Susan shows others is a "false self." Winnicott's concept is directly pertinent to shame-prone individuals, as they feel what they most essentially are they cannot reveal and what they reveal is not really them.

[25]Malinowski's diaries depict, Geertz writes:

> a sort of mental tableau whose stereotyped figures—his mother, a boyhood friend with whom he has quarrelled, a woman he has loved and wishes to discard, another he is now in love with and wishes to marry—are all thousands of miles away, frozen in timeless attitudes which, in anxious self-contempt, he obsessively contemplates. . . . Not

(continued...)

for publication,[26] it constitutes a document at once moving, poetic and honest, and it offers a view into the heart of an ethnographer in the field. In his diary, Malinowski expresses his confused feelings about fieldwork, his reactions to people, situations and places, his not-always-successful attempts to comprehend the hodgepodge of the day's events, and his ambivalence about being in the field at all.

Describing his arrival in New Guinea on September 9th, 1914 (the day before the diary begins), Malinowski writes: "The land was flat at the foot of the mountains; at the end of the bay, thick green mangrove forests, mountains in fog; sheets of rain kept moving down the slopes into the valley and out to sea. Ashore, it was damp with sultry tropical heat, the town small, uninteresting, its people marked with tropical self-conceit . . . " (1967:6). Throughout the diary, he freely expresses his doubts:

> Went into bush. For a moment I was frightened. Had to compose myself. Had to look into my own heart. "What is my inner life?" No reason to be satisfied with myself. The work I am doing is a kind of opiate rather than a creative expression. I am not trying to link it to deeper

---

[25](...continued)

> universal compassion but an almost Calvinist cleansing power of work brought Malinowski out of his own dark world of oedipal obsessions and practiced self-pity into Trobriand daily life [Geertz 1967, cited in Firth 1989:xxv].

Geertz, it appears, has in Calvinistic fashion assumed Malinowski to be guilty of what to him would be indecent exposure, expressing once again the power of shame. In this case, Geertz's misreading of the diaries seems itself to speak volumes. The very contempt (as shame projected onto another) Geertz displays for the expression of emotions and for Malinowski's "practiced self-pity" would seem to place Geertz's comments squarely within the field of shame.

[26]What Malinowski's intentions really were we will never know. A reliable source has indicated to me that the diaries were prepared for publication by his second wife and then subjected to scrutiny by Audrey Richards and several other persons who persuaded Malinowski's wife to delete a number of passages. Such control over materials omitted constitutes one of the elements of which those assessing anthropological evidence need to be more aware. In this case, it might be that shame dynamics can be related to what is left out.

> sources. To organize it. Reading novels is simply disastrous. Went to bed and thought about other things in an impure way [p.31].

Many readers have been shocked at Malinowski's irascibility. "The old man began to lie about burials. I became enraged and got up and went for a walk" (1967:35). "At moments I was furious with them [the natives], particularly because after I gave them their portions of tobacco they all went away. On the whole my feelings towards the natives are decidedly tending to '*Exterminate the brutes*'" (1967:69). Or again: "As for ethnology: I see the life of the natives as utterly devoid of interest or importance, something as remote from me as the life of a dog." Yet it is precisely this unfamiliarity which attracts Malinowski: "This disgusting trait of mine—that whatever I possess with certainty loses all attraction for me—is one of my basic misfortunes" (1967:204). Yet, struggling all the while, he pursues his understanding of these natives, in the process of expressing his "desire to shake Anglo-Saxon dust from my sandals" (1967:207).

He also talks much about his mother, another subject deleted from published ethnographies. "Main interests in life: Kipling, occasionally strong yearnings for Mother—really, if I could keep in communication with Mother I would not mind anything and my low spirits would have no deep foundation" (1967:41). "I thought of Mother—Mother is the only person I care for really and am truly worried about the future" (1967:52). Or again: "My God, my God, how terrible it is to live in continuous ethical conflict. My failure to think seriously about Mother, Stas, Poland's ordeal—is disgusting" (1967:165).

What fieldwork is and means are questions that only recently have begun to attract the attention they deserve. We need to know far more than we do about experiences in the field, what portions of them are packaged in the form of ethnographies and what portions escape description, remaining secret because of a desire to hide them out of shame. The question of what kind of credence to lend to fieldnotes raises once again the question of anthropological evidence. What counts as "evidence" in anthropology? And how is such "evidence" evaluated and interpreted?

In both anthropological fieldnotes and psychoanalytic process notes, the written materials clearly arouse anxiety and shame, calling attention to their problematic status as "knowledge." This is in part because these ill-defined texts are neither fully comprehensible, complete nor capable of easy interpretation; they are contradictory, messy, often inchoate; they overflow with contradictions and information which does not necessarily have any place at all in one's final ethnography; they contain the experiences of the very person who will be interpreting them; and they leave out a lot of what goes on. If we examine what is left out, I would speculate that a great deal depends on shame dynamics.

Conclusions

Because we know others through shame interactions, shame is the medium, the element, required for the understanding of human interactions and of the doings and undoings of the human soul. How we exist in the element of shame is thus as difficult for us to perceive as it is for fish to know the water they live in or birds the air they breathe.

In my clinical work with patients, I have been able to acquire some understanding of the intersubjective, interpersonal meanings of shame in the analytic situation. In the analysis of one patient described elsewhere (Kilborne n.d.c.), whereas I was frightened of her leaving treatment, she was ashamed because she feared that if she hung around she would discover that I did not want her, that nobody ever has. The first implication for anthropological fieldwork, then, consists in noting how prominent and complex are shame interactions, and how difficult and time-consuming it is to trace their effects on relationships. Because shame is often unconscious, veiled by more conscious layers of shame and guilt, neither informants nor anthropologists may be aware of how much is being dissimulated, withheld, distorted or kept secret. Both as analysts and as anthropologists, we need to be capable of assessing deceit together with its motivations, in order to make basic judgments about what constitutes evidence. As Marc Bloch observed in his *The Historian's Craft* (1954), we need to be aware not only of the existence of deceit but also to understand where it comes from, what motivates each manifestation, however diverse. "It is not enough to establish the fact . . . . It is further necessary to discover its motivation, to [seek] out the imposter behind the imposture" (p.93).

Second, the contrast between shame as a term describing affective states such as feelings of painful exposure, humiliation and failure, on the one hand, and the theoretical construct of narcissism, on the other, represents a split in levels of discourse. This split can be seen as symptomatic of the difficulties encountered in both anthropology and psychoanalysis in describing phenomenologically grounded feeling states. Whether in the anthropology of the emotions, or in the works of writers such as Doi (1973), Epstein (1984), and others, the old Cartesian mind/body problem comes back to haunt us in the form of a disjunction between rationalistic theory and an understanding of the emotions. The search for underlying (linguistic?) structures that are "thought by" individuals only displaces the real difficulties with Cartesianism. One obstacle in the way of reaching beyond our Cartesian limitations may lie in the protective functions the Cartesian framework serves—and in the ways in which our drawing of disciplinary boundaries (of psychology and sociology, for example) contributes to the maintenance of our ethnocentric rationalism, which by definition excludes our individual/subjective feelings and anxieties, precisely what we need to evaluate our ideas. Along these lines, then, there can be no real progress in using shame dynamics as an investigative tool in fieldwork unless or until fieldworkers can find ways of utilizing their own anxieties about shame and looking.

Third, cultural defenses related to looking often serve to protect against feelings of shame. For example, let us consider beliefs in the evil eye, prevalent in cultures around the Mediterranean where, as Peristiany (1966) and others have shown, shame and honor dynamics play one against the other. When one is fortunate, incurs success, power, wealth or esteem, one must not show signs of one's fortune, lest it arouse the jealousy of enemies. Others are assumed to be envious and hostile, especially when they are looking. Sartre's descriptions of looking and the shame of being looked at clearly bear upon these beliefs in the evil eye. Furthermore, when dream interpreters interpret dreams, misfortune and anxiety is often attributed to some family member's evil gaze. These cultural beliefs in the evil eye serve to mask individual uses of shame reactions and defenses, which can easily disappear behind them. For informants believe that they are not fearful of the evil eye because they are ashamed; they are fearful because it is something everyone is frightened of. In sum, the various rituals undertaken to protect against the evil eye can also be seen to afford protection against the assumed hostile and envious gaze of the Other, underscoring the prevalence and depth of shame.

Fourth, questions raised by shame dynamics can help elucidate the entire range of ethnographic sources, by focusing attention on what is left out of accounts of fieldwork, and what kinds of evidence fieldnotes, diaries, letters and ethnographies constitute.

Finally, anthropologists go to the field in order to look at the people they will be writing about in their dissertations or books. This definition of anthropologists as those who look, together with the definition of "their people" as those who are looked at, raises the question: what kinds of shame reactions are produced by the very structure of the field situation? As intruders in societies whose principles (and principals) are to be "uncovered," can anthropologists avoid feeling ashamed? And what is the price to be paid for not realizing (i.e., for denying) that the people they study are looking at them all the time, that theirs is not the only eye? Yet, under the guise of scientific objectivity, many fieldworkers minimize or deny altogether the effects of shame on their work. But how can we grasp the many defenses and meanings of shame which are so essential in all human interactions? Shame reactions (our own, those of our informants, and those with whom we interact in the field), I would argue, can be one of the most important resources we have for understanding others.

References

Alexander, Franz. 1938. "Remarks about the Relation of Inferiority Feelings to Guilt Feelings." *International Journal of Psycho-Analysis* 19:41-49.

Balint, Michael. 1968. *The Basic Fault*. New York: Basic Books.

Bibring, Edward L. 1963. "The Mechanisms of Depression." In Phyllis Greenacre (Ed.), *Affective Disorders: Psychoanalytic Contribution to Their Study* (pp.13-48). New York: International Universities Press.

Bloch, Marc. 1954. *The Historian's Craft*. New York: Alfred A. Knopf.

Bowlby, John. 1969. *Attachment and Loss*. New York: Basic Books.

Breuer, Joseph, and Sigmund Freud. 1895. *Studies on Hysteria*. SE 2. London: Hogarth.

Chasseguet-Smirgel, Janine. 1985. *The Ego Ideal*. New York: W. W. Norton and Co.

Crapanzano, Vincent. 1980. *Tuhami: Portrait of a Moroccan*. Chicago: University of Chicago Press.

Doi, L. Takeo. 1973. *The Anatomy of Dependence*, trans. John Bester. New York: Kodansha International.

Epstein, A.L. 1984. *The Experience of Shame in Melanesia: An Essay in the Anthropology of Affect*. London: Royal Anthropological Institute.

Erikson, Erik. 1963 [1950]. *Childhood and Society*. Second edition, revised and enlarged. New York: W. W. Norton and Co.

Fairbairn, W.R.D. 1954. *An Object Relations Theory of the Personality*. New York: Basic Books.

Federn, Paul. 1952. *Ego Psychology and the Psychoses*. New York: Basic Books.

Fenichel, Otto. 1945. *The Psychoanalytic Theory of Neurosis*. New York: W. W. Norton and Co.

Firth, Raymond. 1989. "Second Introduction 1988." In Bronislaw Malinowski, *A Diary in the Strict Sense of the Term* (pp.xxi-xxxi). Stanford, CA: Stanford University Press [orig. 1967].

Freud, Sigmund.[27] 1900. *The Interpretation of Dreams*. *SE* 4 & 5. 1955.

_____. 1905. "Three Essays on the Theory of Sexuality." *SE* 7. 1960.

_____. 1914. "On Narcissism: An Introduction." *SE* 14. 1957.

_____. 1917. "Mourning and Melancholia." *SE* 14. 1957.

Geertz, Clifford. 1967. "Under the Mosquito Net." *New York Review of Books*, September 14.

---

[27]All references to Freud's works in this book are to the English language *Standard Edition of the Complete Psychological Works of Sigmund Freud*, edited and translated by James Strachey, London: Hogarth Press Hereafter cited as *SE*, with the volume number and year of publication of that volume. First date given is the date of original publication. See Bibliography of this book for complete page references.

Greenberg, Jay and Stephen Mitchell. 1983. *Object Relations in Psychoanalytic Theory*. Cambridge: Harvard University Press.

Guntrip, Harry. 1968. *Schizoid Phenomena, Object Relations and the Self*. New York: International Universites Press.

Hartman, Heinz, and Rudolf Loewenstein. 1964. "Notes on the Superego." *Psychoanalytic Study of the Child* 17:42-81.

Hegel, G.W.F. 1807 [1977]. *Phenomenology of the Spirit*. (A. V. Miller, Trans.). New York: Oxford University Press.

Jacobson, Edith. 1964. *The Self and the Object World*. New York: International Universities Press.

Kernberg, Otto. 1975. *Borderline Conditions and Pathological Narcissism*. New York: Aronson.

Kilborne, Benjamin. n.d.a. "Sartre, Shame and the Epistemology of Looking in Psychoanalytic Theory." (unpublished manuscript).

_________. n.d.b. "Guilt and Shame as Cultural Categories: Historical and Anthropological Perspectives on a False Dichotomy." (unpublished manuscript).

_________. n.d.c. "Peek-a-boo Where Are You? Theories of Child Development and Shame Dynamics in the Analytic Situation." (unpublished manusript).

Klein, Melanie. 1957. *Envy and Gratitude*. London: Tavistock.

Kohut, Heinz. 1971. *The Analysis of the Self*. New York: International Universities Press.

_________. 1979. *The Restoration of the Self*. New York: International Universities Press.

_________. 1984. *How Does Analysis Cure?* (Arnold Goldberg, ed.). Chicago: University of Chicago Press.

Lacan, Jacques. 1977 [1949]. "The Mirror Stage as Formative of the Function of the I." *Écrits: A Selection* (pp.1-7). (Alan Sheridan, trans.). New York: W. W. Norton and Co.

Lansky, Melvin R. 1984. "Violence, Shame and the Family." *International Journal of Family Psychiatry*, 5:21-40.

Laplanche, Jean, & J-B. Pontalis. 1967. *The Language of Psycho-Analysis* (Donald Nicholson-Smith, Trans.). London: Hogarth (1973).

Lewis, Helen B. 1971. *Shame and Guilt in Neurosis*. New York: International Universities Press.

Lichtenberg, J. D. 1982. "Reflections on the First Year of Life." *Psychoanalytic Inquiry* 1:695-729.

Malinowski, Bronislaw. 1989. *A Diary in the Strict Sense of the Term.* Stanford, CA: Stanford University Press [orig. 1967].

Morrison, Andrew P., ed. 1986. *Essential Papers on Narcissism.* New York: New York University Press.

_________, ed. 1989. *Shame: The Underside of Narcissism.* Hillsdale, NJ: Analytic Press.

Nathanson, Donald L. 1987. "A Time Table for Shame." In Donald L. Nathanson, ed., *The Many Faces of Shame* (pp.1-63). New York: Guilford Press.

_________, ed. 1987. *The Many Faces of Shame.* New York: Guilford Press.

Nunberg, Herman. 1955 [orig. 1932]. *Principles of Psychoanalysis.* New York: International Universities Press.

Peristiany, J.G. (Ed.). 1966. *Honour and Shame: The Values of Mediterranean Society.* Chicago: University of Chicago Press.

Piers, Gerhardt, and Milton Singer. 1953. *Shame and Guilt: A Psychoanalytic and a Cultural Study.* Springfield, IL: Chas. C. Thomas.

Sartre, Jean-Paul. 1956. *Being and Nothingness: An Essay on Phenomenological Ontology* (H.E. Barnes, trans.). New York: The Philosophical Library.

Spitz, Rene A. 1965. *The First Year of Life.* New York: International Universities Press.

Stern, Daniel N. *The Interpersonal World of the Infant: A View from Psychoanalysis and Developmental Psychology.* New York: Basic Books.

Stolorow, Robert D., B. Brandchaft, and G. Atwood. 1987. *Psychoanalytic Treatment: An Intersubjective Approach.* Hillsdale, NJ: Analytic Press.

Tan, Amy. 1989. *The Joy Luck Club.* New York: Putnam.

Tronick, E., H. Als, L. Adamson, S. Wise, and T. Berry Brazelton. 1978. "The Infant's Response to Entrapment between Contradictory Messages in Face to Face Interaction." *Journal of Child Psychiatry* 17:1-13.

Wurmser, Leon. 1981. *The Mask of Shame.* Baltimore: Johns Hopkins Press.

Chapter Five

Implications of Some Psychoanalytic Concepts in the Indian Context

B.K. Ramanujam

Introduction

Indian psychiatrists are very ambivalent about accepting psychoanalytic theory and therapy in their classical form. Unfortunately, those who hold strong negative feelings base their opinions on their familiarity with the literature—not on having gone through a personal analysis. Consequently, their opinions are of doubtful validity. In this paper I present theoretical propositions of only those who have psychoanalytic training or background. The evolution of psychoanalytic thinking indicates that the Freudian drive-theory is inadequate to explain human behavior in the Indian context. Indeed, the subtle nuances of object-relations, and their impact on our understanding of the development of the sense of self, end up having a more important place in the theoretical framework. After sketching the development of psychoanalysis in India, a case report is presented to illustrate the profound effect of such issues on personality development.

Historical background

Historically speaking, it is interesting to note that psychoanalysis made its entry into India in the 1920s. A psychiatrist named Girindrasekhar Bose started corresponding with Freud in December 1920

(Sinha 1966:427). From Bose's letters it appears that he kept himself informed of the development of psychoanalytic theories. Since no organized theory of human behavior was available then, Bose experimented with hypnotism, contemplation, introspection, etc. In 1921, after struggling for nearly a decade, he published *The Concept of Repression*, a monograph that earned him the degree of Doctor of Science in Psychology, the first such degree to be bestowed by Calcutta University (Sinha 1966:428). With this recognition and his obtaining the stewardship of the psychology department, Bose introduced psychoanalysis as a regular subject. He also maintained correspondence with Freud until 1937 (Sinha 1966:430). During the course of this correspondence Bose differed from Freud's ideas on the concept of the Oedipus complex. In his response Freud seemed to imply that the theory was still evolving. For instance, in a letter dated March 9, 1929, Freud stated, "But I confess I am by no means more convinced of the validity of my own assumptions. We have not yet seen through this intricate Oedipus matter. We need more observations" (Sinha 1966:434).

Indeed, in connection with this Bose offered his own "theory of the opposite wish." According to this theory, for every expressed wish there is an unconscious opposite wish that can be observed in various life situations. This is different than Freud's concept of ambivalence. Much of the theory of opposite wish was further elaborated in the paper "A New Theory of Mental Life" (Bose 1948). From this brief review it can be seen that Bose was quite productive during those years; he was also responsible, during this period, for training a number of early analysts. It must be admitted, however, that psychoanalysis in its classical form has not found many protagonists in India even to this day. Even in the major urban centers, there are few practitioners.

The works of two British analysts need to be mentioned because they were Bose's contemporaries and their writings are not so well known (Hartnack 1987). Owen Berkeley-Hill's works are still referred to by some authors as significant. Berkeley-Hill was a psychiatrist and the Superintendent of the European Mental Hospital in Ranchi, India. Although he developed novel methods of treatment for British psychiatric patients (since the native Indians were not admitted to that hospital), it is claimed that he also left his mark on psychoanalysis in India because he was responsible for training second generation analysts. One may sense the nature of his influence by reviewing his theoretical papers. His theories were ethnocentric and not based on any deep understanding of the Indian psyche. In order to appreciate his biased views we must remember that he appeared on the scene as a representative of the British government. In spite of the fact that he had married a Hindu woman, there is very little known about their relationship. He was a friend of Ernest Jones and acted as a liaison between the Bengali analysts and the International Psychoanalytic Association. What interests us here is his application of psychoanalytic concepts to understand the Hindu psyche. His autobiography and other papers reflect his deep prejudice against Indians. Three essays are of theoretical significance: "The Anal-erotic Factor in the Religion, Philosophy and Character of the Hindus" (1921), "A Short Study of the Life and Character of Mohammad" (1921), and "Hindu-Muslim Unity" (1925). In the paper on anal eroticism he seems to have been influenced by Jones's work on the same subject. He interpreted the classic Hindu texts and came to the conclusion that Hindus were preoccupied with the "flatus complex." He had a penchant for broad generalizations. For example, to quote Hartnack, "he stated that the Hindu has all the disadvantageous traits of the anal-erotic personality, such as irritability, bad temper, unhappiness, hypochondria, miserliness, meanness, pettiness, slow mindedness, a tendency to bore, a bent for tyrannizing and dictating, and obstinacy" (Hartnack 1987:242). An impressive list indeed. No scholar with any credibility would offer such an hypothesis without adequate proof.

Claude Danger Daly was neither a psychiatrist nor a physician. He was an army officer. His only claim to be an expert on psychoanalytic theories was that he was Freud's patient in 1924, and was treated by Sandor Ferenczi between 1928 and 1929. One of his theoretical papers was titled "Hindu Mythology and Castration Complex" (Daly 1927). Instead of providing any insight into the Hindu way of thinking, the article reflects Daly's own obsessions with castration fears, incest wishes, anal eroticism and menstruation. He was a classic example of a man who held the colonial subjects in abject contempt without making any serious attempt to understand them. His writings do not deserve any serious attention, except as a good example of the worst in ethnocentric, prejudicial (mis)use of Freud's ideas.

Among the scholars familiar with the Indian social system, Morris Carstairs must be recognized. He has the distinction of being not only a psychiatrist who underwent personal analysis but also one who trained in anthropological field methods. He lived in a Rajasthan village and studied upper class Rajputs closely (Carstairs 1957:67-70). He noted that there was a certain emotional distance between fathers and sons. Indeed, any show of affection in public was considered socially unacceptable. Carstairs theorized that this lack of intimacy did not allow manifestation of both positive and negative feelings. This, he felt, rendered the resolution of the oedipal conflict more difficult.

While treating Indian men, I have been repeatedly impressed by the fact that, even as adults, these patients experienced a sense of deprivation regarding the nonavailability of empathic fathers. An illustration is provided by the case of Mr. M who came to me for treatment because of his inability to sit in a closed room with others for any length of time. In fact, the very prospect of a meeting or a conference would precipitate severe anxiety attacks. If forced into such a situation he would leave because he could not control passing wind. During the course of therapy I learned that he was the younger of two sons. His father was an authoritarian individual who enforced a strict code of conduct. The only time the children saw their father was during meal times when conversation was forbidden. The father was perceived as a distant, unempathic, punitive object. This image was so persistent that even as an adult Mr. M constantly felt that his father was watching all his actions despite the fact that the father was dead. Since all authority figures represented the father image he could not tolerate any closeness with them. His symptoms reflected his aversion.

Such situations are not uncommon in Indian families. The paradigm is that it is not the child competing with the father for the mother's attention. The mother is always available. Hence, the intensity of the oedipal struggle in a triadic structure—father, mother, son—is due to the close interaction between the actors. In the Indian extended family there are many male members who can and do, at least partially, satisfy the affectional needs of the child. Gurus and mentors, for example, can take on the same role in the absence of fathers, thus enabling the individual to direct his loves and hates towards different objects, thereby permitting diffusion of the intensity of conflicts.

Sudhir Kakar has been one of the major contributors to the development of psychoanalytic theory in India. In his book, *The Inner World* (Kakar 1978), he has outlined his propositions extensively. Throughout this work he adhered to the drive-theory model. Instead of emphasizing the essential polarity between instinctual demands and restrictions placed by the culture, however, Kakar offers the model of adaptation. He states: "It is now generally accepted that the newborn infant brings with him an innate capacity or readiness to adapt to the culture into which he is received" (Kakar 1978:10). He posits the idea that in the development of the ego there is a contributing cultural component. Although he accepts Freud's model of the ego, he extends its function to include society and institutional aspects of life. Essentially the ego and the id are not always in conflict but are necessary elements in evolution towards an ideal. Finally, he makes a distinction between the psychoanalytic concept of reality and the Hindu vision of reality. According to this position, the psychoanalytic view of reality envisions a scenario in which human experience is perceived as full of conflicts and unfulfilled desires. The Hindu view, on the other hand, does not deny conflicts but offers the hope that it is possible to overcome them and achieve transcendental bliss.

The Hindu society being male oriented, Kakar deals in considerable detail with the development of the male child. The male child, after having been brought up in an indulgent milieu with love and protection during the early years, is suddenly thrust during the oedipal phase into an environment where demands are made upon him of an inflexible nature. There is no transitional phase where he can gradually harness his coping mechanisms to deal with ever new demands. So far he has known only the mother's unsolicited love. The father, being a distant figure, has not prepared him to negotiate adequately in a male world. There is a great need for father's empathic presence to navigate in this unfamiliar milieu. Kakar proposes that instead of the oedipal conflict there is a need for "oedipal alliance." According to him, "oedipal alliance refers to the deeply buried and unfulfilled need of many male patients for the firm support, guidance and emotional availability of the father who was needed by the little boy at the oedipal stage of his life so that the boy could separate and free himself from an overwhelming, omnipresent and especially the sexually threatening preoedipal mother" (Kakar 1980:47).

At the outset I had mentioned that in his early works Kakar had followed the drive psychology model. In subsequent writings, however, he seems to sense the need to emphasize the relationship model in non-western cultures. For example, he states: "Hindu persons, then, in the dominant image of their culture are constituted of relationships: all affects, needs and motives are relational and their distresses are disorders of relationships—not only of relationships with their human but also with their natural and cosmic orders" (Kakar 1985:445).

The term 'cosmic order' is of special relevance. The Hindu psyche is as deeply affected by cosmic events as with more temporal events of this world. The person is not an individual in the western sense of the term but "dividual," as Marriott has termed it, in constant interaction with the environment, forever transforming himself and, in the process, the environment itself (Marriott and Inden 1977). Unfortunately, adherence to such a mystical model has been presented as a pathological process by western analysts. Kakar perceives the danger of the mystically oriented scholars denying the psychoanalytic insights in the same way as analysts belittle the mystics' profound understanding of the human dilemma. This would be counterproductive, Kakar suggests (1982), as both models have elements of truth.

Alan Roland is a psychoanalyst with extensive experience in working with Indian patients both in India and the United States. He has studied and written extensively about identity issues in modern India (e.g., Roland 1988). Roland hypothesizes that the British colonial presence in India left an indelible impression on the Indian sense of identity, especially upon urban educated individuals. In some subtle ways and with some not so subtle methods, the British denigrated the Indians as superstitious, uncultured and barbarian. In order to presume colonial legitimacy, they had to represent themselves as belonging to a superior race whose mission was to help Indians become more mature and cultured. As Nandy (1982) has pointed out, the British sense of superiority was equated with masculinity and maturity. In this equation, political dominance became the prerogative of men and masculinity the preferred symbol (as opposed to women and femininity). This contrasted with the Indian image of bisexuality or androgyny as represented, for example, by Gandhi. Another variant of this denigration was to present Indians as child-like (if one is generous) or childish (if one wants to be derogatory). Obviously, both these attributes precluded the Indians playing any role in politics. The denigration of the Indian self was reinforced by the educational philosophy of Macaulay and proselytizing Christian missionaries. Not surprisingly, some Indians identified with this imposed image.

Roland's clinical experience leads him to suggest that Indians have two layers of identity, a core self incorporating the values of Indian culture and another self influenced by exposure to Western values. Needless to say, accommodating to the two antithetic value systems brings about conflict. Roland describes three mechanisms by which Indians have tried to resolve this conflict. One is through identification with the aggressor—i.e., they became more British than the British themselves, denigrating everything Indian. Others attempted to solve the problem by totally rejecting everything Western and overvaluing Indian spiritual culture. The third group attempted to bring about a synthesis incorporating the best in both cultures. Roland contends that all three mechanisms operate simultaneously with varying degrees of emphasis in individuals.

One of Roland's major contributions is the development of the concepts of the "familial self," "individualized self" and the "spiritual self." The underlying basis for such conceptualization is that the sense of self of people in different cultures varies because of the impact of different social and cultural patterns. He argues that, in order to make sense of such a concept, psychoanalysis and the social sciences should come together in a partnership. The concept of familial-self is based upon the relational model which envisions intense emotional relationships within the family and jati. These relationships are of a symbiotic nature involving mutuality and reciprocity. In such a configuration, in contrast with the sense of self in Western culture, the sense of self is a 'we-self' which is a resultant of strong identification with the values of the family and other groups. In other words, there is not only a private self but also a public self which follows traditionally determined rules of behavior where context is the reference point.

Roland contends that the individualized self is modeled on the American psychological organization in which considerable autonomy is available and varieties of options are available to choose from. Individualism and self-actualization are the cherished ego ideals. Beyond the family, many extrafamilial organizations are available to relate to. In Indian society, an individualized self forms only a small part of a person's psychic organization. This is not to say there is no individuality in Indians, but to emphasize that there is an integration of familial-self and spiritual-self in varying degrees. The spiritual-self is explained as the inner spiritual reality experienced through worship of gods and goddesses and various rituals. Although the spiritual-self may be experienced by only a few individuals, it is deeply embedded in the psychic structure of all Hindus.

Roland describes the evolution of the familial-self along developmental lines. In spite of the fact that a woman may have a subordinate position in an extended household, her status as a mother is highly regarded. There is an intense emotional relationship between the mother and son not only during infancy and childhood but throughout life. It is based on providing instant gratification to prevent frustration, anxiety and unhappiness. Such involvement leads to a great sense of connectedness with others.

This also results in developing great sensitivity to others and enhances the value of non-verbal communication. Dependency needs are reinforced, leaving the child with a sense of well-being. This does not leave much room for individuation. At the same time, individuation in the social sphere is not only expected but encouraged. This is accomplished in two ways: the child is taught to behave properly and to observe the nature of hierarchical relationships and, secondly, the child is conditioned to develop a high degree of sensitivity involving such relationships. Thus the development of the 'we-self' in childhood is maintained through adolescence where the individual remains in the extended family maintaining various degrees of empathic relationships. The adolescent phase is essentially a preparatory stage for learning the skills one needs in order to assume adult responsibilities. In developing this schema, Roland has used his own clinical experience to attempt to integrate many psychoanalytic concepts with those grounded in sociological and anthropological data.

Hindus have been preoccupied with the concept of self since the Vedic period. Although various ideas have been presented at different times, two concepts of self can be identified. Desai and Collins classify them as "atman" and "ahamkara" defined as transcendental self and ego self, respectively (Desai 1986). The atman is the self beyond the confines of temporal limits or personality structure. In this sense it has a positive valence as opposed to ahamkara which evolves out of ignorance. Atman represents the totality of the inner-life principle and proclaims the unity of the body and its psychological faculties. Contrary to the Western, and particularly the psychoanalytic concept of individuality in a stable environment, the Hindu concept of the world and personality structure is more fluid with permeable boundaries.

India as a "field society"

From the above discussion it is obvious that no single model is adequate to understand the Hindu psyche. I have described in more detail elsewhere my concept of Hindu India as a field society (Ramanujam 1986). In such a society, an individual comes into this world with the imprint of past karma. The field agents act as facilitators to help the individual navigate through the life cycle. In such a system the individual sense of self is not personally generated but derives from the collective expectations of others. Throughout the life cycle, transformations take place both in the individual and the field as well. Implicit in this whole discussion is the notion that relationships are very important. These relationships are measured along a family paradigm depending upon the degree of intimacy one can achieve as well as how one's dependency needs are satisfied. Since dependency has a pejorative connotation, it is perhaps better to refer to this phenomenon as interdependency since it is, in fact, mutual and reciprocal. In such a system, emphasis is not on individual selfhood but on the capacity to integrate into the corporate selfhood which offers one a sense of belongingness. A case report of one of my patients will illustrate how encompassing and overwhelming these relationships can be. This report also reflects in a more dramatic form how many contemporary Indians, in spite of believing that they have escaped from the traditional bonds, have not done so.

Mr. B, a thirty-five year old man, was referred to me because of severe depression and suicidal ideation. He was the youngest of three children, one girl and two boys. He came from a very wealthy family in India. His father was a relatively passive member, his mother was the more dominant one in the family. Although this was a nuclear household there was an extensive extended family network. Mr. B was a bright boy and his mother's favorite. She was the one who supervised his education and attended to all his needs, whereas the father remained a remote figure. He did very well in school and, after completing high school, was sent to the United States for advanced studies. He successfully completed graduate studies in business administration. At first he worked for a corporation and, after gaining some experience, established his own consulting firm. His life style was that of a typical corporate executive which included tennis on Sunday mornings, concerts in the evenings and sailing on weekends in good weather. For a number of years he was living with a divorced lady and had separated from her about two years before he came to me for consultation.

Mr. B reported that for the first few years he was in constant touch with his family, including regular phone contacts. As time elapsed, these contacts gradually diminished until they amounted to little more than sending New Year's greetings once a year. He had informed the family that he was not interested in the family business and would not claim his share of the property. He had decided to stay in this country and did not feel any attachment to his country of origin or his people. He felt that he had broken all ties.

Almost fifteen years after he had left the country he did, however, go back for a visit. This visit was to last only a month and he was excited by the prospect because he wanted to get reacquainted with his family members. He found he had to absorb new smells, sounds and sights and noticed he felt strange in his own native land. He made a second visit about two years before my contact with him. This was necessitated by his father's illness. He had planned to stay for a short while but his father's lingering illness forced him to stay for almost a year.

The unfolding scenario would be a story-teller's delight if not for the tragic consequences. The first month he continued to wear western clothes and to eat only non-spicy foods. When it became apparent that his stay would be prolonged, he decided to switch to Indian-style clothing more suitable to the hot climate. He also began to eat Indian foods and visit movie houses. Although a gradual transformation was taking place in his outward appearance and behavior patterns, Mr. B claimed that his identification with the American value system remained strong. There were subtle suggestions that he should think of marriage when the family members realized that his stay would be lengthy. He categorically told them that he was not interested in marriage, especially with an Indian girl. Gradually, however, pressures were mounted in a very subtle way. Some days the topic would never be discussed, and then, after an interval, the issue would come up during meal times. During all this period, negotiations were going on with another wealthy family for a likely alliance. This family had an only daughter of marriageable age. Both families felt that such an alliance would not only bring the two families together but also would further their business interests. Mr. B claimed that, at the time, he was totally unaware of these developments.

One day his mother announced that the family had been invited for tea by some friends. Apprehending no consequences, Mr. B agreed to go. He and the intended bride met socially in the presence of both the families. A few weeks passed when his sister suggested that, as a friendly gesture, he may want to take the lady to a movie. Still not sensing any designs, he agreed and went to a movie with her. A few days later his sister asked if he would consider the lady for a marital partner. This made him very angry and he made it clear in no uncertain terms that he was not ready for marriage and would not even consider the lady. After having met her a few times he had realized that there was nothing in common between them. She was intellectually inferior to him and her interests were limited. Furthermore, he was planning to return to the United States since his father was recovering from his illness. She had no place in his life.

In spite of his strong objections, pressures continued. Finally the ultimate argument was presented: since both of them had been seen in public together, her whole future would be compromised if he failed to marry her. A relentless campaign to arouse his guilt was mounted. Eventually he felt so overwhelmed with guilt and anxiety that he submitted to the family pressure. He reported to me that doing so was the most stupid act on his part but in his state of mind his judgment was poor. Taking advantage of his wavering mind, the family hurried through the wedding. In a confused state, he returned to the United States with his bride.

From the start, conflicts between the two surfaced. Mr. B had his own work hours and social activities. His wife always wanted to know the details of his activities. If he received a phone call she would want to know who the caller was. She would open his mail. Evenings would be spent watching television. Weekends were spent visiting relatives, mostly hers since he hardly associated with the members of his community. All this was distasteful to Mr. B. One weekend, he was persuaded to visit his wife's cousin. Throughout his stay he was constantly subjected to rhetoric by the cousin about the duties and responsibilities of a Hindu husband towards his wife. By the time he returned home, he experienced violent rage. Apprehensive that he might physically hurt her if he stayed with her longer, he sent her back to India. By now, his total life was in disarray: since he had not pursued his business aggressively, he incurred financial loss; he had lost all his friends, he would spend evenings walking the streets, and he would spend sleepless nights experiencing nightmares.

While he was trying to bring some order into his life, his mother arrived with his wife without any warning. She tried to convince him that since the deed was done he should give some more time so that his wife could adapt to his requirements. By now, however, he was so exhausted and defeated that he did not even want to try. He sent both mother and wife back to India. For some time, phone calls from India and in this country kept coming. When he made it clear that he was not willing to make any compromises, the calls ceased. His mental state continued to be disturbed, however, and, at times, he felt that he was going insane. Many times the idea of committing suicide occurred to him. Fearing that he might do something foolish, he asked for help. He was only separated from his wife but not divorced.

The most significant point to be noted in this case report is that the classical drive-theory does not help us to understand the dynamics of Mr. B's struggles. We see conflicts at different levels. These conflicts revolve around culturally determined duties and responsibilities. Mr. B had identified with, as he firmly believed, a value system in which individual autonomy, productivity and success were the ideals. His stay in India had reawakened in him the Hindu virtues of duty to the family and obligations towards his wife, for which he would have to sacrifice his autonomy. Essentially, it was an existential conflict between two opposite ideologies. The basic error in his thinking was that he had abjured all the cultural values. At the same time, however, the need for belongingness was so great that he was willing to go through re-enculturation, but only up to a certain point.

There is a term—"sanskar"—in the Hindu lexicon which is difficult to translate. It poignantly conveys the whole gamut of duties and responsibilities which a Hindu is heir to if he is brought up in a respectable family. There is no greater pejorative expression than someone saying, "The man has no sanskar." It is not only a reflection on him as an individual but also represents failure on the part of the family. Mr. B's transgressions from accepted codes of behavior were many. By breaking all connection with his family he had alienated himself. When he did return and agreed to stay in India for an extended period, the family concluded that all was not lost. It was not only a duty but an obligation to facilitate the return of the prodigal son into the family fold.

Going to a movie or visiting a restaurant may be an ordinary event in the West. In the social class to which Mr. B belonged, however, such a harmless activity signalled an important message. His strong assertions against marriage were seen as a natural response under the circumstances, but it also was assumed that it would be only a matter of time before he would accept the family verdict.

I mentioned the permeability of the Hindu psyche. As time passed and persuasions continued, Mr. B did begin to yield. The final stroke was to arouse his sense of guilt regarding the fate of his bride if he did not accept her. The most unforgivable act was his sending back his wife after having lived with her in a state of matrimony. Such a scenario arouses strong passions among Hindus fed on stories of mythical heroes and heroines. In this case report, one can see how non-verbal patterns of communication play a significant role in inter-personal interactions. Any Hindu child absorbs this fact almost by osmosis. The irony was that Mr. B had forgotten this basic premise. He wrongly considered himself to be invulnerable and impervious to the family and social pressures and, as a consequence, paid a heavy price.

Conclusion

In this paper, in presenting the developments of psychoanalytic theory in India, I emphasized the way it differs from the reductionist approach of Freud's classical drive-theory. Until recently, the classical theory was applied not only to individuals but also to whole cultures. The fallacy of this approach is being increasingly recognized by social scientists of all disciplines. Indian society, which I have described as a field society, has many familial and kinship bonds. These have pervasive influence on individual behavior. They envisage certain ideologies which are imprinted onto the individual psyche from a very early age. A case report is presented to illustrate the profound impact of such a value system.

References

Berkeley-Hill, Owen. 1921a. "The Anal-Erotic Factor in the Religion, Philosophy and Character of the Hindus." *International Journal of Psycho-Analysis* 2:306-338.

_____. 1921b. "A Short Study of the Life and Character of Mohammad." *International Journal of Psycho-Analysis* 2:31-53.

_____. 1925. "Hindu-Muslim Unity." *International Journal of Psycho-Analysis* 6:282-287.

Bose, Girindrasekhar. 1948. "A New Theory of Mental Life." *Samiksa* 2:108-205.

Carstairs, G. Morris. 1957. *The Twice-Born: A Study of a Community of High-Caste Hindus*. Third printing. Bloomington: Indiana University Press, 1975.

Daly, Claude Danger. 1927. "Hindu Mythology and the Castration Complex." *Imago* 13:145-198.

Desai, Prakash, and Alfred Collins. 1986. "Selfhood in Context: Some Indian Solutions." In M. I. White and S. Pollak, eds., *The Cultural Transition* (pp. 261-286). London: Routledge and Kegan Paul.

Hartnack, Christiane. 1987. "British Psychoanalysts in Colonial India (pp. 233-251). In Mitchell G. Ash and William R. Woodward (eds.), *Psychology in Twentieth Century Thought and Society*. New York: Columbia University Press.

Kakar, Sudhir. 1978. *The Inner World: A Psychoanalytic Study of Childhood and Society in India*. Delhi: Oxford University Press.

_____. 1980. "Observations on the 'Oedipal Alliance' in a Patient with Narcissistic Personality Disorder." *Samska* 34: 47-53.

_____. 1982. "Reflections on Psychoanalysis, Indian Culture and Mysticism." *Journal of Indian Philosophy* 10:269-297.

_____. 1985. "Psychoanalysis and Non-Western Cultures." *International Review of Psychoanalysis* 12:441-448.

Marriott, McKim, and Ronald B. Inden. 1977. "Towards an Ethnosociology of South Asian Caste Systems." In Kenneth David (ed.), *The New Wind: Changing Identities in South Asia* (pp. 227-238). Chicago: Mouton.

Nandy, Ashis. 1982. "The Psychology of Colonialism: Sex, Age and Ideology in British India." *Psychiatry* 45: 197-218.

Ramanujam, B. K. 1986. "Social Change and Personal Crisis: A View from an Indian Practice." In Merry I. White and Susan Pollak, eds., *The Cultural Transition* (pp.65-86). London: Routledge and Kegan Paul.

Roland, Alan. 1988. *In Search of Self in India and Japan: Toward a Cross-Cultural Psychology*. Princeton, NJ: Princeton University Press.

Sinha, T. C. 1966. "Development of Psychoanalysis in India." *International Journal of Psycho-Analysis* 47:427-439.

PART TWO

THEORETICAL AND CRITICAL STUDIES

Chapter Six

Freud in a Forest of Symbols: The Religious Background of Psychoanalytic Anthropology[1]

John M. Ingham

The Oedipus complex, the nucleus of classical psychoanalysis, was associated in Freud's thinking with religion. The one seemed to be a Rosetta stone for deciphering the other. Two book-length studies locate the Judaeo-Christian tradition at the center of Freud's concern with oedipality in religion. *Moses and Monotheism* (1939) conjectures a patricidal killing of Moses, followed by collective guilt and a renewed personification of him in a Midianite Moses. *Totem and Taboo* (1913), arguably the inaugural work in psychoanalytic anthropology, considers the phylogenetic origins of the Oedipus complex and, in Freud's own words, "the psychology of religious faith and ties" (Jones 1955:350). As Robert A. Paul (1986:486) has noted, Christianity is the vanishing point of Freud's perspective in *Totem and Taboo*: the lines of interpretation and speculation converge on original sin and the Crucifixion. Psychoanalytic anthropology, in effect, began with an oedipal interpretation of the two principal moments in Christian thought.

Less apparent, but no less interesting for the history of psychoanalytic anthropology, are the ways in which the very discovery of the Oedipus complex may have been grounded in Freud's experience with western culture, including the Judaeo-Christian tradition. Rudnytsky (1987) contends that Sophocles' plays and later literary and philosophical

---

[1]I wish to thank Tom Conley, David Spain, David Lipset, and Sylvia Rosen for reading earlier drafts of this chapter.

reflections on Oedipus were part of the cultural background of oedipal theory. Roith (1987) observes that concern with incest is strong in Jewish sources, and suggests that the traditional Jewish family tends to promote the male Oedipus complex. She also argues that ancient Jewish prejudices about women biased Freud's theorizing about the Oedipus complex and female psychology. In this paper I explore the influence of Roman Catholicism on Freud's thinking. I suspect that Freud's experience with Catholicism sensitized him to oedipal phenomena, but I also think that the peculiar nature of his encounter with Catholicism, in combination with certain features of his personality, tended to limit his theoretical imagination in important respects.

Totem and Taboo was in part a response to Jung's *Wandlungen und Symbole der Libido* (1912; see Jung 1956), a study of the roles of myth and religion in mental life in which Jung equated the libido with all psychic energy and proposed that incestuous imagery serves to symbolize spiritual return and rebirth. Freud had discussed the project with Jung and had read the first part in draft (Jones 1955:351). Viewing it as an attack on cardinal features of psychoanalytic theory, Freud answered on Jung's own ground—that of religion. Whereas Jung discussed Christianity by way of Greek myth and comparative religion, Freud addressed it through interpretations of the beliefs and customs of various primitive peoples. But there may have been deeper, more personal reasons for engaging Jung on the question of Christianity.

Vitz (1988) argues that Freud's relationship with his Catholic nanny during his first three years was a major formative experience in Freud's development. The nanny took Freud to Mass and perhaps to Catholic celebrations, and she may have baptized him. The nanny was suddenly dismissed from the Freud household, perhaps for stealing. The attachment to, and separation from, the nanny, according to Vitz, left Freud with a lifelong fascination with Catholicism.

The evidence for this unlikely thesis is various and impressive. Among other things, Vitz notes that Franz Brentano, a former priest, was Freud's favorite professor; that Freud had an avid interest in Christian churches, art, and sculpture; that he was preoccupied with Pentecost and with visiting Rome during Easter week (presumably the season when his parents dismissed his nanny); that his private correspondence often reads as if he were a Christian; and that on vacations with his family in the mountains, he would urge his daughter Anna to offer flowers to an image of the Virgin in a small chapel before she and the other children went into the forest to search for mushrooms.

According to Vitz, Freud was tempted to convert to Catholicism but was unable to overcome certain emotional inhibitions. In Vitz's reading of Christianity, Adam is an oedipal figure inasmuch as he disobeys God, whereas Christ, who submits to God's will, is anti-oedipal. Citing evidence for Freud's ambivalence about his father and his identification with Oedipus, Vitz contends that Freud could not fully identify with Christ. Indeed, he tries to show that his ambivalence about paternal authority translated in some contexts into identifications with the Devil and the Anti-Christ (1988:160-170).

I would assess the implications of Freud's "Christian unconscious" somewhat differently. Catholicism is, as I will try to show in a moment, subject to a more dialectical reading than the one Vitz gives it. By this alternative reading, there is opposition but also similarity between Eden and Golgotha: unconsciously, the Crucifixion may signify the realization as well as the transcendence of oedipal wishes. Viewed in this way, Catholicism subsumes an understanding that human beings have oedipal impulses and, therefore, corresponding needs for expiation. It also implies that culture and society require sublimation of the reproductive impulse, that is, a redirection of the impulse away from biological reproduction and toward cultural production and reproduction. This in turn suggests that Freud's early experience with Catholicism may have influenced his thinking about the Oedipus complex and sublimation. If Freud sometimes identified with the Devil, it was perhaps because he thought that by opposing religion he could rescue its psychological truth for science. He once said,

> Do you not know that I am the Devil? All my life I have had to play the Devil, in order that others would be able to build the most beautiful cathedral with the materials that I produced [quoted in Bakan 1975:181].

Freud's ambivalence about conversion is inconsequential for our purposes. The important issue here is the way in which Freud's experience with Catholicism may have influenced his psychoanalytic thinking, although we will also see that Freud's experience with his Catholic nanny and his ambivalence about Catholicism may have prevented him from taking psychoanalysis further than he did.

The argument begins with an examination of the reproductive

metaphor in the Judaeo-Christian tradition as a whole and the oedipal connotations of the metaphor in the Christian tradition in particular. Then I note the similarity between the Judaeo-Christian scheme and the classical psychoanalytic thinking about instincts and sublimation. In educing the oedipal nuances in biblical stories and Christian lore and ritual, I am not trying to reduce Christianity to the Oedipus complex, nor am I implying that Christianity has been equally or similarly oedipal in all times and places. Rather, I merely wish to suggest that the nuances may have encouraged Freud's creativity.

The argument does not rest simply on similarity between psychoanalysis and Catholicism. I also show that Freud was influenced in a personal way by Judaeo-Christian themes. We will see that the subjective meaning of work for Freud reiterated an association between the word and spiritual reproduction in the Judaeo-Christian tradition. We will also see that his thinking about incest and primordial moments was laced with references to Eden and Golgotha. Indeed, biblical imagery tended to enter Freud's writing precisely when he was concerned with the Oedipus complex or when the complex was structuring his experience.

Reproduction in the Judaeo-Christian tradition[2]

Reproduction is a key metaphor in Judaism and Catholicism. In Judaism, according to Goldberg (1987), Abraham represents the biological progenitor and spiritual father of the Jews, whereas reproduction and spiritual continuity are associated with the Torah and Moses. The Torah scroll is the word of God transmitted through Moses. Citing customs and usages pertaining to the Torah in various Jewish communities, Goldberg shows that the Torah is identified with male offspring and kings in some contexts and with bridegrooms in others. In marital imagery, the Jewish people are the brides of the Torah. Less often, the Torah is likened to a woman who is married to Jewish men. Goldberg also notes that the transmission of the Torah from one generation to the next has been phrased as oral ingestion in some Jewish traditions.

The Catholic symbolic scheme evinces a similar opposition between

[2]Another version of this section appeared in Ingham (1989).

natural procreation and spiritual regeneration. Adam and Eve personify the former, Jesus and Mary the latter. Jesus is the word "made flesh" (John 1:14).[3] The church is the "bride of Christ." In addition to being wedded to Christ in this sense, Christians partake of His blood and body in Communion. The role and words of Christ, then, resemble Moses and the Torah. Adam and Eve bring sin into the world whereas Christ and Mary offer redemption: Christ through his sacrifice on the cross and Mary through her own Immaculate Conception and the asexual procreation of Jesus. Original sin has nuances of incest and of rebellion against the father. The Crucifixion, which alludes to a spiritual union of Jesus and Mary, both recalls and expiates oedipal guilt.[4]

Let us begin at the beginning. After eating the forbidden fruit, Adam and Eve were ashamed of their nakedness and Eve was punished by an increase in the pain of childbearing. The implication may be that original sin entails sexuality. Augustine attributed the transmission of original sin to sexual intercourse. The rites of blessing the baptismal font on Holy Saturday and baptism also imply that there was something sexual about the Fall. In the traditional rite on Holy Saturday, the font is likened to a womb; the Paschal candle and Holy Spirit, meanwhile, seem to represent the paternal principle. In contrast to sexual intercourse, which reproduces original sin, baptism, which commemorates the death and resurrection of Christ, cleanses original and actual sin and regenerates the person as a spiritual being.

Original sin also involves power. Augustine and other writers concluded that Eve's pride, greed, and lust for power made her vulnerable to the serpent's solicitations (Phillips 1984:59). Eating the fruit was an act of insubordination. When God learned what Adam and Eve had done, he said they had become "like one of us" (Genesis 3:22). The stories of Cain, Noah, and Babel, which illustrate the heritage of original sin, also implicate power in the Fall: a sense of inferiority

---

[3]The Greek *logos* (the word) has seedlike properties. In Stoic philosophy, this seed-word, the *Logos spermatikos*, created the world by fertilizing a moist, feminine matter.

[4]My understanding of Catholicism draws on Watts (1960). It has also benefitted from reading Badcock (1980), Carroll (1986), Dundes (1981), Jones (1959, 1964a, 1964b), Leach (1988), Parsons (1964), Paul (1986), and Russell (1984).

motivated Cain's anger; God sent the flood as punishment for both arrogance and lewdness in the time of Noah; and God was disturbed by the growing power of the people at Babel.[5]

The symbolism of the tree or trees at the center of the garden is part of the enigma of original sin. It would appear that the tree of knowledge and the tree of life are aspects of a single tree. Both trees are in the garden, and both bear forbidden fruit. In an old Christian legend, Seth returns to Paradise for the oil of mercy and sees the tree in two forms: initially without bark or leaves and embraced by a skinless serpent, and then with bark and leaves and with a baby, God's son, wrapped in swaddling clothes in the upper branches (Morris 1871:xiii).

In this legend, an angel gives Seth three seeds from an apple which he was to put under Adam's tongue after Adam died. From the three kernels, three trees would grow—a cedar, a cypress, and a pine. The three would represent the Trinity: the cedar, the Father; the cypress, the Son; and the pine, a fruit-giving tree, the Holy Ghost. In the time of David the three wands grow into one tree (Morris 1871:xiii-xv). The legend seems to link the tree with God.

The tree in the garden, however, also has feminine qualities. Biblical passages identify the Holy Ghost, the Third Person in the Trinity, with wisdom and truth (Acts 6:3; John 14:16-17, 15:26; see Jones 1964a). Wisdom or Sophia is a feminine figuration. Trees in the Bible symbolize Wisdom. Ecclesiasticus 24 identifies Wisdom with a cedar on Lebanon, a cypress on Mount Hermon, a palm in Engedi, the rose bushes of Jericho, a "fine olive" in the plain, and a plane tree (see Watts 1960). It also seems that Wisdom is linked with the tree in the garden. The tree embodies knowledge of good and evil. Similarly, Wisdom is associated with knowledge (Wisdom 8). A passage in Ecclesiasticus (37:17-25) about Wisdom says, "Thoughts are rooted in the heart, and this sends out four branches: good and evil, life and death;" it also notes that understanding produces "fruits." The fruits of understanding recall the fruit of the tree of knowledge, and the four branches growing from the heart resemble the four rivers that originated near the tree in the garden.

During Creation, Wisdom is by God's side, "delighting him day after day, ever at play in his presence" (Proverbs 8:30-31). The Seth legend

[5]On Eve and original sin, see Pagels (1988) and Phillips (1984).

places both the serpent and the infant Son of God in the tree, implying that the tree is mother to them both or that she plays a maternal role in relation to each of them. Wisdom, we may infer, is God's consort, and one of her manifestations is the tree in the garden.

These associations suggest that eating the forbidden fruit is an appropriation of the mother. The serpent who takes fruit from the tree engages in something akin to incest as well as rebellion against the father. Eve serves the serpent's purpose. In Medieval art the serpent is often portrayed as having a snake's body and a woman's head (Phillips 1984:61-62). The name "Eve" in cognate Aramaic and Arabic languages means "snake-woman" (1984:41). Adam takes fruit from Eve, just as Eve takes fruit from the tree or the serpent. Evidently, Eve overlaps both tree and serpent in relation to Adam. Snakes were associated with "wisdom" or magic in the religions of the Near East (1984:41), and the name "Eve" may involve a pun meaning "lady of Life," suggesting a connection with the tree (1984:28). According to Genesis 3:20, Eve is the "mother of all those who live," which implies that she is Adam's mother and that she somehow participates in the feminine principle in the tree.

A gnostic text, "The Reality of the Rulers," states that Eve is Adam's mother. It also says that before the Fall, the spirit of Eve became the tree when "authorities" tried to rape her. Then she, the "female principle" (Eve), came in the form of the serpent, speaking to Adam and carnal Eve (Layton 1987:70, 71). In the gnostic poem, "The Thunder—Perfect Intellect," Eve is simultaneously Wisdom and mother, daughter, and sister to her husband (1987:80). Gnostic texts, to be sure, are not part of orthodox scripture, but they reveal understandings which were possible in early Christianity and which may still occur in the Christian unconscious.

Mary, the Second Eve, is also associated with the tree and Wisdom. In medieval paintings and stained glass depictions the lineage of Jesse grows like a tree from his phallus to link David, Mary, and Jesus. The Lesson at Mass in the feast of the Assumption of the Virgin is Ecclesiasticus 24, the passage that identifies Wisdom with trees. The identification of Joseph as a carpenter fits this connection between Mary and wood (see Watts 1960:160).

Just as Eve is Adam's consort and the "mother of all those who live" (Genesis 3:20), Mary is the "bride" of Christ in her role as representative of the church, the "mother" of God, and the spiritual mother of human beings. *The Song of Songs*, a Hebrew love poem, is, in Catholic liturgy, a dialogue between Christ and his bride the Church; it is also a source of symbols for the Blessed Virgin (Watts 1960:105). Christian legend also traces the cross to the tree of life in Eden.

Mary, then, is connected to two trees—the one in the garden and the tree of the cross—through her association with Wisdom. In an Old English lament, Mary accuses the cross of being an unkind tree, her son's "stepmother." The cross replies that she owes Mary the honor of bearing the fruit that blossomed in her branches. At the end of their conversation, they express their unity as Mary kisses the cross (Morris 1871:131-149; quoted in Jung 1956:270-271).

The figure of Jesus on the cross thus suggests a union of mother and son. And indeed, Augustine wrote:

> Like a bridegroom Christ went forth from his chamber; he went out with a presage of his nuptials into the field of the world. . . . He came to the marriage-bed of the cross, and there, in mounting it, he consummated his marriage. And when he perceived the sighs of the creature, he lovingly gave himself up to the torment in place of his bride, and he joined himself to the woman for ever [quoted in Jung 1956:269].[6]

The woman here is both the church and Mary inasmuch as Mary symbolizes the church.

Christ is Adam's counterpart. He is also the counterpart of the serpent. Following a line in John (3:14)—"and the Son of Man must be lifted up as Moses lifted up the serpent in the desert"—Christ is sometimes portrayed as a serpent encircling the cross (see Watts 1960:79). The serpent in Eden offers Eve the fruit; similarly, Christ is likened to the fruit of the tree and his blood to wine made from the juice pressed from grapes (Morris 1871:138). The serpent convinces Eve to

---

[6]Abrams (1971:37-46) has discussed this and other instances of marital and nuptial metaphors in Christian writing; see also Dundes (1981:70). The oedipal connotations in the Jesus-Mary relationship were evidently less veiled in the early days of Christianity. Gnostic Christians viewed the mother, sister, and consort of Jesus as aspects of a single Mary (see Leach 1988).

take the fruit and thereby provokes the Fall. The fruit of the tree at Calvary is supposed to redeem humanity.[7]

Psychoanalytic theory and Christianity

Freud viewed the libido as object seeking *and* power seeking: besides motivating desire for objects and substitutive objects, it energizes narcissistic concerns with "the preservation, assertion and magnification of the individual" (1933:96). He also recognized destructive impulses, and noted that they readily combine with narcissistic, power-seeking impulses. Satisfaction of the destructive instinct, he wrote, is "accompanied by an extraordinarily high degree of narcissistic enjoyment, owing to its presenting the ego with a fulfillment of the latter's old wishes for omnipotence" (1930:121). Freud (1930:80 n.1) saw the possibility of displacing narcissistic, aggressive, and even erotic libido into professional work and relationships. Similarly, says Freud, the artist wants "honour, power, wealth, fame and the love of women." Although the artist is an introvert, he turns his fantasy into creations that satisfy his repressed desires as well as those of other persons. In doing so, "he earns their gratitude and admiration and he has thus achieved *through* his phantasy what originally he had achieved only in his phantasy—honour, power and the love of women" (1916-1917:375-377). Freud discerned, of course, that these fantasies about power and love often rework the oedipal fantasies of childhood.

These transformations or sublimations of the libido occur under the influence of cultural rules and moral order. The superego, according to Freud, sustains human society and culture (1930). Artists, to elaborate on Freud's example, must transform their own fantasies into creations that fit the tastes and standards of their patrons. Freud's theory of

---

[7]Róheim (1940) theorized that the taking of the fruit from the tree of knowledge was a challenge to the father. Eve is Adam's mother; as Róheim notes, she is called the mother of all living. Since the tree is ambisexual, the fruit stands for the mother's breasts. Reik (1957) suggested that the eating of the fruit represents eating the father. In this way the Eucharist reenacts the primal patricide. Carroll (1986) argues that Mary's virginity may be a defense against oedipal desire and that Christ's exaggerated suffering represents atonement for oedipal inclinations.

instincts and sublimation thus parallels Christian thinking. Both imply that object- and power-seeking libido must be tamed and sublimated, and both associate the libido with oedipal impulses.

Freud's Christian unconscious

Freud may have been thinking about himself when he wrote about the artist. It is well known that he used himself as an example in his writing. Jones (1955:344) suggests that Freud's interest in artists and creative writers was "tinged" with envy. At the same time, writing for Freud shared connotations with Judaeo-Christian logocentricity. Thus Freud's writing evinces an associative linkage between his theory of sublimation and the Judaeo-Christian tradition.

We have seen that Jesus is the Word, that the Torah has attributes of a woman and child, and that both Word and Torah are associated with spiritual reproduction. Words and books are similarly associated with women, children, and reproduction in Freud's thinking. After observing that Breuer, Charcot, and Chrobak had glimpsed the sexual etiology of neuroses, he writes that it is one thing to mention an idea and quite another to develop it. "It is the difference between a casual flirtation and a legal marriage with all its duties and difficulties," and he adds that "To be wedded to an idea" is a familiar expression, at least in French (1914:15). The paper on narcissism "had a difficult birth" (Gay 1988:339). In his essay on Leonardo Da Vinci Freud writes, "There is no doubt that the creative artist feels towards his works like a father" (1910:121). The anonymous essay on Moses is "a love-child" which he only later legitimizes (Jones 1955:367). He notes that writing may become inhibited when infected with too much eroticism: the ink flows out of a tube onto white paper (1926:90), and he states that "*wood, paper* and objects made of them, like *tables* and *books*" are female symbols (1916-17:156).[8] These reproductive connotations of words, books, and writing inform an interweaving of Catholic imagery, oedipal

[8]I am indebted to works by Mahony (1987:4-5, 154-155) and Gay (1988) for calling my attention to reproductive metaphors in Freud's comments on his writing and publications.

theory, and personal experience in *The Interpretation of Dreams* and *Totem and Taboo*. These two texts are especially pertinent here, for the former includes Freud's initial public discussion of the Oedipus complex while in the latter he attempts to theorize about its anthropological implications.

The Interpretation of Dreams

Freud discovered his own Oedipus complex through analyses of his dreams and memories of childhood. The course of the self-analysis is chronicled in letters to Fliess. In a letter dated October 3, 1897, Freud writes that his father "plays no active part in my case" and asserts instead that the "prime originator" was his nanny, who told him everything about God and hell. And then in the same sentence he goes on to describe how his libido was first aroused toward his "*matrem*" during a train ride from Leipzig to Vienna when he saw her in the "*nudam*" (Masson 1985:268). In a letter to Fliess twelve days later he announces his discovery of the Oedipus complex. Again he seems to associate his mother with the nanny. He recalls a time, when crying for his mother, he asked his older half-brother Philipp to open the cupboard or wardrobe, thinking that if the nanny was locked up for thievery, maybe the missing mother was locked up also (Masson 1985:270-273).

Swan (1974) thinks that these letters, the Irma dream of 1895, and Freud's dream life in the summer of 1897 implicate the nanny in Freud's Oedipus complex. Freud interprets one dream about a father's excessively affectionate relation with his daughter as a wishful attempt to settle doubts about the roles of seduction and imagination in recollections of incest. A second dream implies that the nanny both aroused and shamed his sexuality. In a third dream the nanny bathes him in reddish water in which she has just bathed and has him take money from his mother (something the nanny did). The fourth dream about a one-eyed doctor apparently associates ambivalence about paternal figures and injury to the self with the wish to eat something forbidden.

Swan (1974:38-39) thinks that the reddish water dream represents shame and fear of feminine engulfment but also identification with the nanny. Swan in fact finds a persistent tendency on Freud's part to identify with the nanny. Vitz (1988:17-22), following a personal communication from Robert R. Holt, offers an alternative interpretation of the reddish water, although one still consistent with identification with the nanny. The nanny may have privately baptized Freud: the memory of the red water may have been a conflation of menstrual blood and the thought of being "washed in the blood of the Lamb."

In the October 15 letter announcing the discovery of the Oedipus complex, mention of the one-eyed doctor dream follows a discussion of the bath dream and the scene where Philipp opens the cupboard to help Freud find his mother. Swan (1974:45-46) notes that Freud later offered a second explanation for wanting to look into the cupboard. He wanted to be sure that there were no siblings inside (his mother was pregnant at the time). Swan also notes that Freud wanted Philipp, who was his mother's age, to open the cupboard because he suspected Philipp was the father. Krull (1986:124-128) finds various reasons for thinking that Philipp and Freud's mother were sexually involved with each other. The cupboard incident in effect conflates desire for the lost nanny with desire for the mother and associates both desires with the spectacle of a half-brother (the father's son) having an affair with the mother (the brother's stepmother).

Erikson (1954) discerned in the Irma dream a Catholic framework of religious conversion or confirmation: the dreamer merges with Irma, the victim of an improper injection by another doctor. He thus sacrifices his masculinity, but for this he is accepted into a brotherhood, receives grace, and earns the right to oppose the wrongdoer (the Devil). Erikson traced the religious framework to the nanny, but Swan goes beyond Erikson's interpretation to show that Freud associated Irma with the nanny. Thus Freud again identifies with the female object who is penetrated by a male rival. Swan (1974:33) suggests that the split between the sexually arousing, scolding nanny and the pure but naked mother foreshadowed the later split between the "humiliating father" and the "pure mother" in the oedipal situation.

Catholicism and the Oedipus complex also intertwine in *The Interpretation of Dreams*. Schorske (1980), Vitz (1988), and others have commented on Freud's concern with Catholicism in his dreams about Rome, but there are other telling references to Catholicism in the dream book. In a paragraph added to the first chapter in 1909, Freud notes that for several years before publishing the book he dreamed about a simple church tower, and he goes on to say that while continuing his dream studies, his dreams often included various grotesque figures which he associated with a chapel for the Madonna dell' Arena in Padua (1900: 14-15). In a section on moral sense in dreams, Freud observes that wishes in dreams are commonly immoral in character, and throughout the book he shows that dreams express desires for power and sexual gratification, the two motives that figure in original sin. Freud favorably mentions Hildebrandt's idea that "immorality in dreams" can be traced to the "evil impulses" or "temptations" that pass through the mind during waking hours (1900:70), and he quotes the passage in which Hildebrandt repeated Jesus' statement that evil thoughts come from the heart (Matt. 15:19).

Freud traces evil thoughts in dreams to childhood, but first he argues that dreams of being naked derive from the early, shameless period when children are given to exhibitionism.

> When we look back at this unashamed period of childhood it seems to us a Paradise; and Paradise itself is no more than a group phantasy of the childhood of the individual. That is why mankind were naked in Paradise and were without shame in one another's presence; till a moment arrived when shame and anxiety awoke, expulsion followed, and sexual life and the tasks of cultural activity began [1900:245].

Freud then discusses the Oedipus complex as a source of dreams about the deaths of parents and siblings. In other words, he anticipates his more explicit oedipal reading of original sin in *Totem and Taboo*.

In giving oedipal impulses a leading role in the motivation of dreams, Freud places the mother or mother figure at the center of his text (Mahony 1987:110). Pontalis (1974:127) says that to Freud "the dream was a displaced maternal body"; in penetrating the secret of dreams, he "committed incest." Hyman (1966:332-333) argues that the imagery in *The Interpretation of Dreams*—particularly Freud's organizing metaphor of a trek through the woods and a cavernous defile—represents an exploration of the body of the woman or mother. Freud himself provides support for this interpretation, according to Mahony (1987:111), when he observes that female genitalia are often represented as landscapes (i.e., as rocks, woods, and water), and when he discusses the etymological connections among the words "material," "mother," and "wood" (1916-17:156, 159-60; 1900:355, 684).

Other data not mentioned by Mahony strengthen this affinity between dream and woman and link Christian imagery with the symbolic nexus of tree, forest, wood, book, and maternal object. The material includes Freud's pseudonymous recollections of his childhood in his screen memory paper, his presentation and analysis of "The Language of Flowers" dream, and his recurrent dreams about the church tower and the figures which he associated with the Arena chapel.

In "Screen Memories," Freud offers an explanation for vivid memories of childhood that seem devoid of emotional content. He proposes that such memories are retained because they refer to something else that was significant at the time or because they acquire significance retrospectively through associations with later, emotionally charged events. Freud illustrates the hypothesis with an example. Freud's informant—Freud himself—recalls the following scene: the narrator and two cousins, a boy and girl, play in a green, sloping meadow full of yellow flowers. The children pick bunches of the flowers. The two boys fall upon the girl and snatch her flowers. She runs up the hill in tears to two women, a peasant woman and nursemaid at the cottage. The peasant woman gives pieces of bread to the girl and boys.

Freud recollects the occasion that led to the recovery of this and other scenes from his early childhood. When he was seventeen he returned to his birthplace for a vacation, staying with family friends. He explains that his family had left the town when he was about three because of the economic depression in his father's business. Although he says the rest of his childhood was difficult and not worth remembering, he confesses that "I was never free from a longing for the beautiful woods near our home [i.e., his birthplace], in which (as one of my memories from those days tells me) I used to run off from my father, almost before I had learnt to walk" (1899:312-13).

The vacation was evocative also because the young Freud fell in love with the host family's fifteen-year-old daughter. After she left for school, he spent many hours taking solitary walks in the woods fantasizing about her. The yellow dress she was wearing when they first met recalled the yellow flowers in the childhood scene. Freud says that the dress was a less vivid yellow but he remembers that flowers with a light coloring in the lowlands are darker in the Alps. He also suggests that the taking of flowers from the cousin was an allusion to childhood masturbation (1899:319).

A holiday visit with an uncle three years later also revived the meadow scene. During this second vacation Freud became reacquainted with the two cousins. He did not fall in love on this occasion because he was by then "a slave" to his books and "had nothing left over" for his cousin. Yet he was aware that his uncle and father were toying with the thought of his marrying his cousin and giving up his university studies for a practical occupation (1899:314). This relationship, Freud wrote, would have been a "bread-and-butter" relationship. It thus accounted for the almost "hallucinatory" memory of the bread in the childhood scene.

The screen memory paper links an illicit erotic moment—falling on the cousin and taking flowers from her—with woods, a nursemaid, and the father-son relationship; it contrasts romantic love with practical marriage; and it reveals books as substitutes for love objects. The deflowering, as it were, of the cousin in an idyllic natural setting, moreover, recalls Adam taking the fruit from Eve in the garden of Eden. Freud says that taking bread at the top of the hill conflates the fantasy of a prosperous life with the girl in the yellow dress with the thought of being married to the cousin. Replacing flowers with bread, he says, refers to father's scheme of replacing impractical ambitions with a "bread-and-butter" occupation. But there are additional possibilities. The bread, which is juxtaposed with an illicit moment and which soothes the distress of that moment, may be an allusion to Communion. This transition from transgression to a possible reference to Communion is paralleled by another dialectic: the girl in the yellow dress is assimilated to the Edenic figure of the cousin, whereas the latter is linked with bread and legitimate marriage.[9]

These ambiguities regarding flowers recur in the language of flowers dream in *The Interpretation of Dreams*. The dream assumes a key position in the text. It is offered as a prime example of the way in which dreams combine opposites through similarity, and it illustrates the symbolic fulfillment of erotic desire in a convincing manner. Since the dream features flowers and trees and reproduces the Catholic opposition

---

[9]Vitz (1988:134-135) thinks that Freud's screen memory represents the loss of the nanny. As he notes, though, it is not clear that the nursemaid was Resi Wittek, his Catholic nanny. She could have been Wittek's replacement or his cousins' nursemaid. If Wittek was dismissed in January, then she could not have been the nursemaid in the screen memory, but Vitz (1988:12-16) thinks she may not have been dismissed until after the meadow incident.

between innocence and sexuality, its presentation and analysis in the pages immediately preceding the comments on the symbolism of wood suggests that Freud may have been aware of the symbolic associations of trees in Christianity.

The dream was reported by a female patient named Maria. In the main part of her dream, Maria descends from on high over a palisade-like structure, feeling thankful that she does not tear her dress and so remains respectable. She holds in her hand a branch or, rather, a tree covered with red blossoms. As she descends, the blossoms fade. She encounters a manservant who is combing tufts of hair from another tree. Other men had cut branches from other trees, and she asks if it is proper to take one. A young man stands in the garden, and she asks how might the branches of his tree be transplanted into her garden. He embraces her; she asks if that is acceptable and he assures her that it is. He offers to go to her garden to show her how the planting is done but he seems to want something in return, as if he intends to break a law (1900:315, 347-48).

Maria gave her associations to the dream: an angel holding lilies, as in paintings of the Annunciation, and girls in white robes in Corpus Christi processions along streets covered with green branches. Freud surmises that the flowers allude both to innocence and, as they fade, to loss of sexual purity (1900:319). The dream, in other words, incorporates a repetition of Freud's concern with trees and flowers in the screen memory and what appears to be a reference to the opposition between Eve-as-tree (loss of innocence in the garden) and Mary-as-tree (Maria, the Annunciation, the Corpus Christi procession).

Freud's mention of his recurrent dreams in the opening pages of *The Interpretation of Dreams* is a cryptic prelude to the book's submerged Catholicity. The dream that recurred during the writing of the first edition hints that the book may involve a working through of Freud's experience with Catholicism. Freud traced the second recurrent dream—the one that featured grotesque sandstone figures—to the time he had wanted to see Giotto's frescos in the Arena chapel. Unable to find the chapel, he turned back. Years later, on a second attempt, he realized that he must have seen the grotesque figures on the street leading to the chapel. While he had a vague memory of them at the entrance to a beer cellar, it turned out that they were "at the entrance to the garden of a restaurant." In his *Introductory Lectures on Psychoanalysis*, Freud writes that churches and chapels in dreams are female symbols (1916-17:156). This second dream, in other words, refers to the opposition between garden and Mary or church.

Totem and Taboo

In *Totem and Taboo* Freud advances an oedipal theory about the origins of human culture and human society: In the beginning, an aggressive male patriarch monopolizes the females and drives away the sons. The sons then band together, slay and eat the father, and appropriate the mothers. Feeling guilty, they institute exogamy, taboos, and commemorative sacrificial meals. The salient detail is that Freud equates the primal crime with original sin. Christ, Freud writes, "sacrificed his own life and so redeemed the company of brothers from original sin" (1913:153).

Krull (1986) thinks Freud may have modeled the primal crime after relations among Freud, Adler, Stekel, and Jung. In a letter dated December 18, 1912, Jung accuses Freud of acting the part of the "father" and bearded prophet and of treating his students as "slavish sons" or "impudent puppies." Jung also portrays Adler and Stekel and their friends as "an insolent gang." Playing the role of the jealous father, Freud drove the dissidents away, just as his father Jacob banished Philipp (Krull 1986:193).

The woman in this second drama combined Lou Andreas-Salomé and the rest of the psychoanalytic community. In a letter to her, Freud writes:

> I missed you in the lecture yesterday and I am glad to hear that your visit to the camp of masculine protest played no part in your absence. I have adopted the bad habit of always directing my lecture to a definite member of the audience, and yesterday I fixed my gaze as if spellbound at the place which had been kept for you [Pfeiffer 1972:11; quoted in Mahony 1972:58].

The rebellion of Freud's disciples had placed the possession of the psychoanalytic movement in dispute. In a letter to Jung written in 1910, Freud refers to psychoanalysis as his "lady" (McGuire 1974:292). Writing about psychoanalysis evoked thoughts of fermentation, procreation, and women. During the work on *Totem and Taboo* he wrote, "I read and read and it ferments" (Jones 1955:352).[10] And he complained about how slowly the work was going, "With all that I feel as if I had intended only to start a little liaison and then discovered that at my time of life I have to marry a new wife" (Jones 1955:352). The last chapter was a "Princess" who slept behind the "thicket" of the preceding chapters (Jones 1955:354; see Mahony 1987:154-155). The rivalry and romance surrounding the writing of *Totem and Taboo*, moreover, had illicit, perhaps Edenic, connotations. Freud engaged in a "liaison" in working on the book, and a sense of transgression shadowed the writing of its fourth and final section. "It is the most daring enterprise I have ever ventured. . . . God help me!" (Jones 1955:353).

Overview

In summary, Torah scrolls are associated with Moses, and they resemble male offspring, bridegrooms, and women. Thus they represent the reproduction of Jewish culture. For Catholics, Jesus was the Word of God made flesh, Mary is associated with the tree of the cross, and Christ's sacrifice laid the basis for spiritual regeneration. Jesus, Freud noted, plays a role in Christianity analogous to the role of Moses in Judaism (1939:89-90). Freud identified with Moses, which implies that he may also have identified with Jesus (Bakan 1975; Robert 1976). We also know that, for Freud, books were substitutive objects, mother symbols, and children, and that Freud associated love objects and books with woods and trees.

In a letter to Fliess, Freud refers to *The Interpretation of Dreams* as his "dream-child" and says that Fliess is its "godparent." He mentions being in a depressed state and says ". . . it is my cross, I must bear it; and God knows that in adapting to it, my back has become noticeably bent" (Masson 1985:405-406). The depression, apparently, was brought on by the reception given the book, by difficulties in his practice, and by

---

[10]Thass-Thienemann (1968:134-136) suggests that fermentation is variously associated with corruption, digestion, impregnation, and gestation in European languages.

doubts about his ideas (1985:403-404). The identification with the Passion and Crucifixion is clear: Freud returns to the maternal tree and regenerates culture. And, like Christ, he suffers. The conclusion, moreover, is redemptive; Freud says that we need not feel guilty about wishes that are only expressed in dreams. In interpreting dreams and discovering the Oedipus complex, Freud eats the forbidden fruit; in writing he reconstitutes the relation with the mother on the plane of culture.

Discussion

Western culture, it seems, provided a supportive milieu for the discovery of the Oedipus complex and the elaboration of oedipal theory. Freud's reading of Sophocles and his experience with the Judaeo-Christian tradition may have sensitized him to reproductive imagery and oedipal themes. Allusions to Eden and Golgotha, both of which have oedipal nuances, are present in *The Interpretation of Dreams*, Freud's first public discussion of the Oedipus complex, and again in *Totem and Taboo*, an attempt to understand society and culture in terms of the Oedipus complex. The role of the Catholic nanny in Freud's nuclear complex must have imbued Catholic symbolism and imagery with special salience.

Freud's portrayal of the Oedipus complex and Catholicism are not in perfect agreement, however. Freud tends to focus on the father-son relationship, whereas Catholicism foregrounds the mother and her relationship with her son. Freud may have had a dim apprehension of the oedipal connotations of the Jesus-Mary relationship, but he suppresses any recognition of either them or Mary's importance in his writings about Christianity.

The reasons for this bias may lie in Freud's early experience as well as cultural values. Freud theorized that children identify with lost objects, yet Swan (1974) notes that Freud was uneasy about the child's tendency to identify with early maternal objects. Such identifications for Freud implied emasculation and passivity, whereas concern with father-son rivalry and identification with the father were more congruent with patriarchal valuation of masculinity and assertiveness. Freud's failure to more fully consider the pre-oedipal period, according to Swan, was one consequence of Freud's uneasiness. Another may have been the decision to minimize the importance of parental seductiveness, for Freud's early objects were sexual beings. The nanny was "his teacher in sexual matters" (Masson 1985:269) and his mother may have had an affair with her stepson. Freud, the dreams imply, identified with the nanny, yet his phrasing of oedipal theory allowed him to suppress his identification with her (and perhaps his interest in Mary) and to downplay the seductive behavior of maternal figures. At the very outset of psychoanalysis, in other words, theory was facilitated and constrained by an intricate and idiosyncratic blending of culture, experience, and defense, with important consequences for the history of psychoanalytic thought.

References

Abrams, M. H. 1971. *Natural Supernaturalism: Tradition and Revolution in Romantic Literature*. New York: W. W. Norton.

Badcock, Christopher R. 1980. *The Psychoanalysis of Culture*. Oxford: Basil Blackwell.

Bakan, David. 1975. *Sigmund Freud and the Jewish Mystical Tradition*. Boston: Beacon Press.

Carroll, Michael P. 1986. *The Cult of the Virgin Mary: Psychological Origins*. Princeton, NJ: Princeton University Press.

Dundes, Alan. 1981. "The Hero Pattern and the Life of Jesus." *The Psychoanalytic Study of Society* 9:49-83.

Erikson, Erik H. 1954. "The Dream Specimen of Psychoanalysis." *Journal of the American Psychoanalytic Association* 2:5-56.

Freud, Sigmund.[11] 1899. "Screen Memories." *SE* 3, 1962.

---

[11]All references to Freud's works in this book are to the English language *Standard Edition of the Complete Psychological Works of Sigmund Freud,* edited and translated by James Strachey, London: Hogarth Press. Hereafter cited as *SE*, with the volume number and year of publication (continued...)

_____. 1900. *The Interpretation of Dreams*. *SE*, 4 & 5, 1955.
_____. 1910. "Leonardo Da Vinci and a Memory of his Childhood." *SE*, 11, 1957.
_____. 1913. *Totem and Taboo*. *SE*, 13, 1955.
_____. 1914. *The History of the Psychoanalytic Movement*. *SE*, 14, 1957.
_____. 1916-17. *Introductory Lectures on Psychoanalysis*. *SE*, 15 & 16, 1953.
_____. 1926. *Inhibitions, Symptoms and Anxiety*. *SE*, 20, 1959.
_____. 1930. *Civilization and its Discontents*. *SE*, 21, 1961.
_____. 1933. *New Introductory Lectures on Psychoanalysis*. *SE*, 22, 1964.
_____. 1939. *Moses and Monotheism: Three Essays*. *SE*, 23, 1964.
Gay, Peter. 1988. *Freud: A Life for Our Time*. New York and London: W. W. Norton.
Goldberg, Harvey E. 1987. "Torah and Children: Some Symbolic Aspects of the Reproduction of Jews and Judaism." In Harvey E. Goldberg, ed., *Judaism Viewed from Within and from Without*, pp. 107-130. Albany: State University of New York Press.
Hyman, Stanley Edgar. 1966. *The Tangled Bank: Darwin, Marx, Frazer and Freud as Imaginative Writers*. New York: The Universal Library/Grosset and Dunlap.
Ingham, John M. 1989. "Chalma and Tepoztecatl: Further Reflections on Religious Syncretism in Central Mexico." *L'Uomo* 2:61-83.
Jones, Ernest. 1955. *The Life and Work of Sigmund Freud, Vol. 2. The Mature Years, 1901-1919*. New York: Basic Books.
_________. 1959 *On The Nightmare*. New York: Evergreen/Grove Press.
_________. 1964a. "A Psycho-Analytic Study of the Holy Ghost Concept." In *Essays in Applied Psycho-Analysis*, Vol. II (pp. 358-373). New York: International Universities Press.

[11](...continued)
of that volume. First date given is the date of original publication. See Bibliography of this book for complete page references.

_________. 1964b. "The Madonna's Conception Through the Ear." In *Essays in Applied Psycho-Analysis*, Vol. II (pp. 266-357). New York: International Universities Press.

Jung, Carl G. 1956. *Symbols of Transformation: An Analysis of the Prelude to a Case of Schizophrenia*. R. F. C. Hull, trans. Princeton, NJ: Bollingen Library/Princeton University Press.

Krull, Marianne. 1986. *Freud and His Father*. Preface by Helm Stierlin. Arnold J. Pomerans, trans. New York and London: W. W. Norton.

Layton, Bentley, ed. and trans. 1987. *The Gnostic Scriptures*. Garden City, N.Y.: Doubleday.

Leach, Edmund. 1988. "Late Medieval Representations of Saint Mary Magdalene." *Psychoanalytic Review* 75:95-109.

Mahony, Patrick J. 1987. *Freud as a Writer*. Expanded edition. New Haven, CT: Yale University Press.

Masson, Jeffrey M., ed. and trans. 1985. *The Complete Letters of Sigmund Freud to Wihelm Fliess, 1877-1904*. Cambridge, MA: Belknap Press/Harvard University Press.

McGuire, William, ed. 1974. *The Freud/Jung Letters: The Correspondence between Sigmund Freud and C. G. Jung*. Ralph Manheim and R. F. C. Hull, trans. Princeton, NJ: Bollingen Library/Princeton University Press.

Morris, Richard. 1871. *Legends of the Holy Rood: Symbols of the Passion and Cross-Poems*. London: Early English Text Society/Trubner.

Pagels, Elaine H. 1988. *Adam, Eve, and the Serpent*. New York: Random House.

Parsons, Anne. 1969. "Is the Oedipus Complex Universal? The Jones-Malinowski Debate Revisited and a South Italian 'Nuclear Complex.'" In W. Muensterberger and Sidney Axedrad, eds., *The Psychoanalytic Study of Society*, vol. 3, pp. 278-328. New York: International Universities Press.

Paul, Robert A. 1986. "Lina Wertmüller's 'Seven Beauties': An Analysis and Reevaluation." *Journal of Psychoanalytic Anthropology* 9:447-492.

Pfeiffer, Ernst., ed. 1972. *Sigmund Freud and Lou Andreas-Salomé: Letters*. William and Elaine Robson-Scott, trans. London: Hogarth Press.

Phillips, John A. 1984. *Eve: The History of an Idea*. San Francisco: Harper and Row.

Pontalis, J.-B. 1974. "Dream As an Object." *International Review of Psycho-Analysis* 1:125-133.

Reik, Theodor. 1957. *Myth and Guilt: The Crime and Punishment of Mankind*. New York: George Braziller.

Robert, Marthe. 1976. *From Oedipus to Moses: Freud's Jewish Identity*. Ralph Manheim, trans. Garden City, NY: Anchor Press/Doubleday.

Róheim, Géza. 1940. "The Garden of Eden." *The Psychoanalytic Review* 27:1-26, 177-199.

Roith, Estelle. 1987. *The Riddle of Freud: Jewish Influences on His Theory of Female Sexuality*. London and New York: Tavistock Publications.

Rudnytsky, Peter L. 1987. *Freud and Oedipus*. New York: Columbia University Press.

Russell, John C. 1984. "Family Experience and Folk Catholicism in Rural Ireland." *Journal of Psychoanalytic Anthropology* 7:141-170.

Schorske, Carl E. 1980. *Fin de Siècle Vienna: Politics and Culture*. New York: Alfred A. Knopf.

Swan, Jim. 1974. "*Mater* and Nannie: Freud's Two Mothers and the Discovery of the Oedipus Complex." *American Imago* 31:1-64.

Thass-Thienemann, Theodore. 1968. *Symbolic Behavior*. New York: Washington Square Press.

Vitz, Paul C. 1988. *Sigmund Freud's Christian Unconscious*. New York and London: The Guilford Press.

Watts, Alan W. 1960. *Myth and Ritual in Christianity*. New York: Grove Press/Evergreen.

Chapter Seven

Anglo-American Values in Post-Freudian Psychoanalysis[1]

Suzanne R. Kirschner

As psychological anthropologists, our interest in psychoanalysis can lead us in two different directions. On one hand, we utilize psychoanalytic theories and methods in order to study the meanings of, and the motives behind, many different aspects of cultural and social life. Psychoanalytic approaches help us to articulate dimensions of experience and meaning which are not accessible via the use of other interpretive systems.

At the same time, there is another way in which psychoanalytic theories may be of interest to us as students of culture. This second type of interest is exemplified in the question of how psychoanalytic thought *itself* bears the imprint of the culture or cultures in which it has been developed. It is this latter approach to psychoanalysis which I shall take in this essay. More specifically, I will explore the "borrowing" of psychoanalytic theory by the cultures of the United States and Great

---

[1]An earlier version of this paper was published as "The Assenting Echo: Anglo-American Values in Contemporary Psychoanalytic Developmental Psychology," *Social Research* 57(4):821-857 (Winter 1990). This version appears here with the permission of *Social Research*. I would like to thank James Walkup, Robert A. LeVine, Gananath Obeyesekere, Robert A. Paul, and Louis A. Sass for their helpful feedback and/or kind encouragement of this project.

Britain, and its consequent transformation into a system congruent with these host cultures' ideologies, concerns, and values.

As a great many commentators have noted, Freud continually revised and added to his theories so that, taken overall, his writings contain many points of ambiguity and even self-contradiction. Another way of saying this is that Freudian texts are shot through with myriad cultural discourses, both "high" or esoteric and ethnopsychological (see, e.g., Holt 1978, 1984; McGrath 1985; Trosman 1973; Vermorel and Vermorel 1986:15-37). Thus, subsequent psychoanalytic theorists have had a rich collection of discourses from which (tacitly) to select and upon which to expand. This situation has helped to facilitate the mutation and development of "psychoanalysis" into multiple "psychoanalyses," ostensible continuations of Freudianism which actually have diverged radically from one another. As Edith Kurzweil recently noted, "the Freudians primarily are united by their profession rather than by their ideas" (1989: 283).

Psychoanalytic theorists working in the United States and Great Britain have participated in this selective reading and interpretation of earlier psychoanalytic texts. They have emphasized and extended certain aspects of "classical"[2] psychoanalytic theory, and deemphasized or discarded other aspects. Specifically, those versions of psychoanalysis which have been emphasized and elaborated in Anglo-American culture areas, particularly during the past twenty or thirty years (and arguably since the 1930s), have come more and more to focus on the development of the "ego" and/or the "self" and its modes of relating to objects,

[2]I use this term to refer to what is written in Freudian texts, recognizing that "classical psychoanalysis" itself is a problematic and ambiguous term and cannot be used to refer to a unitary body of theory. As I have noted, Freud's psychoanalytic writings taken as a whole are replete with revisions, internal inconsistencies and even contradictions. Hence these writings are constituted by myriad sometimes-conflicting cultural discourses (including Enlightenment rationalism, evolutionary theory, 19th century neurology and psychophysics, German Classicism, and Romanticism, among others). My principal argument is that in the United States and the United Kingdom, some of these discourses and themes—many of which were not as prominent, or scarcely to be found at all, in the Freudian corpus—have been "selected," elaborated and in some cases extended or altered beyond their original meaning.

principally other persons. Increasingly, in these post-Freudian theories, the primary imperative of reality is no longer considered to be instinctual renunciation, but rather separation and individuation. Correspondingly, a person's degree of pathology or maturity has come to be assessed not in terms of his or her present-day relationship to the vicissitudes of the instincts and the Oedipus complex, but rather in terms of how successfully he or she has negotiated the separation-individuation process and its vicissitudes.

In this essay I shall highlight the influence of Anglo-American culture on this "reshaping [of] the psychoanalytic domain" (to borrow Judith Hughes' phrase). I shall explore how the intensified emphasis on and elaboration of "self and object-relations" (so-called "pre-oedipal") issues and motifs evince a commingling of classical psychoanalytic themes with some characteristically Anglo-American concerns and anxieties about the self's autonomy and individuality. Those psychoanalytic theories which have achieved hegemony in America and Britain have done so because they emphasized and expanded elements in psychoanalysis that are congruent with certain unstated but pervasive Anglo-American cultural values and ideals. Simultaneously, these formal theories have served to "canonize" such ethnopsychological discourses on the self and implicit rules of behavioral display, and have accorded to them the status of desirable realities.

First I will discuss the ascendance, in the United States and Great Britain, of those psychoanalytic theories—"later" ego psychology, object relations theory, and self psychology—which highlight the development of the ego and/or the self. Then I will identify three specific attributes of selfhood which Americans (and, with some qualification, the British) deem desirable and important—self-reliance, self-direction and verbal expression—and explore some ways in which these dimensions have become highlighted in psychoanalytic ideas. At the same time I will connect these *contemporary* values to some *older* cultural traditions—nearly all of them what the historian and sociologist of religion Benjamin Nelson (1965) called "Protestant variants of conscience, character and culture." Of particular import are two different types of Protestantism which have had their fullest and most enduring influence on the culture of the United States but which also have influenced intellectual and cultural life in Great Britain: Puritanism and Nonconformism. The persistence of key elements of these spiritual models, and especially of their secular derivatives, has helped to promote the transformation of Anglo-American psychoanalysis into a more explicit and unambiguous discourse on the development of self-reliance and self-direction than can be found in Freudian psychoanalytic texts or in more recent continental versions of psychoanalysis such as that of Lacan.

So as not to collapse the differences between American and English ethnopsychologies,[3] I have considered restricting this analysis to the cultural borrowing of psychoanalysis by the United States only. However, although significant differences between these two cultures exist, and although psychoanalysis never attracted as widespread interest or as great popularity in Great Britain as in the United States, it is nonetheless clear that there are strong similarities in the theoretical directions taken in both American and British theories. In both nations, psychoanalytic theory has come to emphasize "self" and "pre-oedipal" issues, and to posit a developmental trajectory in which the self moves from a sense of undifferentiatedness to one of autonomy and separate-selfhood as well as the capacity for mature relatedness. In both Britain and America, these formulations bear the strong imprint of nonconforming Protestant doctrines and their secular derivatives, as well as of a more general emphasis on self-sufficiency, emotional restraint and verbal fluency which pervades both cultures.

The pre-oedipal turn in Anglo-American psychoanalysis

Numerous commentators (see, e.g., Guntrip 1973; Greenberg and Mitchell 1984; Eagle 1984; Pine 1985; Kohon 1986; Hughes 1989) have observed that most of the elaborations and innovations in psychoanalytic theory which have come to prominence in the United States and Great

---

[3]Seymour Martin Lipset considers the United States, Canada, the United Kingdom, and Australia to be part of the same culture area, although the United States is deemed the most "individualistic" of the four for both religious and historical reasons (1968). The historian David Hackett Fischer (1989) also emphasizes influence of certain aspects of British culture on the different regional cultures of the United States. For more detailed attention to differences between American and British cultural values, see Geoffrey Gorer (1948, 1955).

Britain during the past several decades have accorded central attention and importance to the development of the "self" (viewed at times as a representation within the ego,[4] at others as a separate structure coexisting with the ego,[5] and at still other times as a construct essentially replacing the classical ego[6]). Not only has the development of the self been of special interest, but also the development of the self's modes of relating to "objects," by which usually is meant other persons. Theorists and clinicians have come to focus upon the self and its patterns of relating to objects, as these patterns are expressed in interpersonal interaction as well as intrapsychic fantasy. The three best-known contemporary schools that exemplify these trends are ego psychology (particularly the "later" ego psychology of Edith Jacobson, René Spitz, Margaret Mahler, and Otto Kernberg, whose theories have achieved strong popularity among American clinicians, intellectuals and educated laypersons since the 1960s and 1970s), object relations theory (a central concern in the work of many British analysts, including W.R.D. Fairbairn, D.W. Winnicott, Michael Balint. Joseph Sandler and others) and self psychology (the brainchild of Heinz Kohut).

Although they vary in some of their particulars, virtually all of these theories chronicle a developmental sequence in which the individual's sense of distinctiveness and separate identity develops out of an original subjective state of "undifferentiation." At this earliest stage the infant is inferred to experience himself not only as essentially in union with the rest of the world, but also as omnipotent (even as his actual situation is one of extreme dependence). By the age of three, the individual is

---

[4]This usage of "self" is found in the writings of Heinz Hartmann, the father of ego psychology and originator of the concept of "self" as a representation within the ego. Another analytic theorist who used "self" in this way was Edith Jacobson (1964).

[5]In her memoirs (Stepansky 1988), Margaret Mahler speaks of the development of self and ego as parallel trajectories, one not reducible to the other. Kohut adopts a similar stance in his two major works, *The Analysis of the Self* (1971) and *The Restoration of the Self* (1977).

[6]This path has been taken in the writings of British object relations theorists such as Fairbairn, Winnicott, and Guntrip.

supposed to have arrived at a provisional appreciation and acceptance[7] of his own separateness, and of the limitations of his powers, as well as of the separateness and limitations of other human beings. The attainment of a sense of separateness and individuality, and of the capacity for relationship, is seen to be effected mainly in the context of the development of the infant's relatedness to his mother (the patterns developed by the child in this one central relationship are seen to be extended to the mode of relating to the rest of the world). Emotional and personality disturbances are attributed to arrests, failures, or distortions of this developmental process.

The increasing prominence of these "pre-oedipal" themes and issues in psychoanalytic theory has not gone unnoticed by analysts themselves. The eminent analyst Hans Loewald, in a 1978 address given in Plenary Session at the Annual Meeting of the American Psychoanalytic Association—an address entitled "The Waning of the Oedipus Complex"—noted "the contemporary decline of psychoanalytic interest in the oedipal phase and oedipal conflicts and the predominance of interest and research in pre-oedipal development, in the mother-infant dyad and in issues of separation-individuation and of the self and narcissism" (Loewald 1980:386).[8]

This declining interest in instinctual and oedipal issues, and its replacement by the elaboration of "self" and "object-relational" themes, is not really new to psychodynamic theory: these themes also were

---

[7]Of course, the process of psychological development, including the consolidation of the sense of individual identity and capacity for relationship, is not considered completed by the age of three. Rather, according to these theories, it is the essential groundwork which must be laid by this time.

[8]In a similar vein, John Gedo has written that "the most recent period in the history of psychoanalysis has been characterized by a gradual shift in focus from a view of . . . archaic phenomena ['fixation behaviors, solutions to the psychological vicissitudes of still earlier phases of development'] as part of the background of nuclear oedipal transactions toward more complex conceptualizations that accord these phenomena degrees of pathogenicity in their own right. . . . Almost everyone [no matter what their specific school or orientation within the psychoanalytic 'community'] seems to agree that the research agenda of our time is the exploration of the deepest layers of the unconscious mind" (1984: 6-7).

prominent in the theories of the neo-Freudians. The neo-Freudians were a loosely affiliated group of theorist-clinicians, most of whom had been psychoanalytically trained, who broke away or were expelled from orthodox analytic circles in the United States during the 1930s and 1940s. Included among them were Harry Stack Sullivan, Karen Horney, Erich Fromm, Frieda Fromm-Reichmann, and Clara Thompson. During their lifetimes their theories were extremely popular in the United States, not only utilized by (non-orthodox) analysts but also widely read by intellectuals and the educated lay public (see Horney 1937, 1939; Quinn 1987; Fromm 1941; Hughes 1968, Roazen 1974; Perry 1983). In particular, Sullivan's theories, and his ideas about clinical practice, have been and continue to be extremely (albeit often covertly) influential in American psychoanalysis.

The psychoanalysts with whom I am concerned in this essay—ego psychologists, most adherents of the "British" schools and Kohutians—have taken pains to distinguish themselves from the "revisionists." Most of these theorists have never explicitly broken from the "classical" analytic tradition. Instead, each has tried (albeit at times ambiguously or ambivalently) to present his or her theory as a continuation or elaboration of, or a supplement to, Freud's ideas, rather than as an outright contradiction of them.[9] Probably the most common means of evading the charge of "revisionism" has been to suggest that the issues raised by these theorists are applicable to a different type of patient than those treated by Freud. The idea here is that the neurotic conditions investigated by Freud involve the vicissitudes of the instincts and the oedipal conflict (and thus classical psychoanalytic theory and technique can account for and treat them), but the more serious disorders (narcissistic disturbances, "borderline" conditions and psychoses) derive from disturbances in the sense of identity and the capacity for relationship. While neurotics are seen to have floundered on oedipal issues (which emerge between the ages of three and five), these more severely disturbed patients are seen to have been derailed at an earlier stage of development. It is during this earlier era (before the age of three, in the context

[9]Greenberg and Mitchell (1984), have extensively explored the strategies employed by post-Freudian Anglo-American analysts to preserve this appearance of theoretical continuity with classical analysis.

of the mother-infant relationship) that the seeds are sown for the sense of bounded, cohesive, realistic "self" and "identity," as well as for the ability to form enduring relationships based on the capacity to integrate "good" (gratifying) and "bad" (frustrating and disappointing) images of both the other and the self.[10] In other words, the rationale for this apparent digression from classical theory is that in order to understand and treat these more "basic" emotional and personality disturbances, more detailed attention to the emergence of the sense of "self and objects" is required.

This might be a viable way of shifting focus while still asserting fundamental agreement with Freudian writings, but for the fact that many theorists have not left it at this. In apparent contradiction of the pre-oedipal/oedipal distinction, some of these same theorists also elaborate upon classical theory in a way which at least implicitly challenges the primacy of instinctual and oedipal themes in *all* emotional disturbance, not only in borderline and narcissistic personalities. In late-career writings by Mahler (1975; 1988)—one of the most lucid and influential of the later ego psychologists[11]—there are suggestions that *all* pathology, including "oedipal" pathology, is conditioned by developmental distortions originating during the pre-oedipal period, for example during what she calls the "separation-individuation" phase.[12] In 1975, Mahler wrote:

---

[10]There are differences in the particulars formulated by these various theorists, but this general depiction of the developmental narrative holds for all.

[11]Kohut (1977) argues a similar point.

[12]In two major books, Mahler and her associates (1968, 1975) chronicle an allegedly necessary and universal developmental sequence by which the initially unself-conscious infant comes to achieve a sense of his own separateness and distinctiveness as well as the separateness and limitations of others. Mahler calls the initial states of psychic "undifferentiation" *autism* and *symbiosis*. This is followed by the *separation-individuation* phase, during which the infant is propelled (by virtue of both innate tendencies and environmental exigencies) in the direction of awareness of himself as a separate and rather helpless being whose interests do not always coincide with mother's. This period has three subphases: *differentiation*, *practicing* and *rapprochement*. This last subphase (continued...)

> It seems inherent in the human condition that not even the most normally endowed child, with the most optimally accessible mother, is able to weather the separation-individuation process without crises, come out unscathed by the rapprochement struggle, and enter the oedipal phase without developmental difficulty [p.190].

And one of Mahler's chief research collaborators, Fred Pine, spoke for many psychoanalytically oriented clinicians and thinkers when he asserted that "it is not that oedipal level dynamics and pathology are inconsequential but I doubt that a child gets stuck on issues of that level . . . if things have proceeded in a satisfactory way until that point" (1985:4).

One might protest that it is possible to reconcile these two seemingly contradictory points of view, i.e.: (1) that pre-oedipal pathology is characteristic of more seriously disturbed individuals, and (2) that individuals who exhibit oedipal pathology tend also (upon closer or more theoretically refined scrutiny) to exhibit that of the pre-oedipal type. To effect such a reconciliation one could invoke the commonly voiced assertion that psychoanalysts today encounter many more of these "lower-level" personalities than in past years—that many if not most of the patients nowadays are "borderlines" or narcissistically disordered, as opposed to the higher-level, better individuated neurotics (hysterics and obsessionals) who consulted Freud and about whom he wrote.

Further weight has been lent to this argument in the writings of Kohut and of the social historian and critic Christopher Lasch, both of whom argued that changed social and childrearing conditions have given rise to a different (and perhaps more developmentally primitive) modal abnormal personality structure (Kohut 1977, 1980; Lasch 1979). In other words, pre-oedipal pathology is pandemic in our contemporary historical situation. A greater proportion of personalities exhibit disorders of the self at this point in history than during Freud's era.

---

[12](...continued)
—*rapprochement*—includes a crisis, during which the toddler (aged 18-24 months) must confront and begin to come to terms with his separateness from mother and the limitations of his own and mother's powers. Only as the rapprochement crisis begins to subside (by age three) is the child considered to be on the road to "identity" and "object constancy." (See Campbell, Chapter 3 in this volume.)

Let us pause at this point to review, and attempt to integrate, the rationales that have been offered to explain the shift from an "oedipal" to "pre-oedipal" emphasis in psychoanalytic theory. "Pre-oedipal" and "self" theories have been elaborated to help us understand and treat those patients whose pathology is developmentally and dynamically more "primitive" than that of neurotics. Freud's theory is applicable to neurotics, but not adequate for these more disturbed patients. A potential contradiction of this rationale surfaces in writings which assert that pre-oedipal dynamics and problems are also detectable in most so-called neurotics—that it seems as if virtually all contemporary patients evince not only oedipal but also pre-oedipal pathology. But this might not be a contradiction after all: it could be due to the fact that, as many have suggested, there are more borderlines and narcissistic personalities, and hence patients, these days. It would appear, then, that changed sociocultural conditions have had an impact on childrearing and personality formation such that borderline and narcissistic characters have become the modal abnormal (or, in a more diffuse way, simply the modal) personalities of our time. No wonder, then, that virtually all patients (even those who at first glance appear, for whatever reason, to be simply neurotic) seem to manifest these disturbances if we look long or closely enough. It is precisely this sociohistorical situation, in fact, which has brought to our attention these more "archaic" aspects of human character and its development, fostering the growth of our knowledge in an area which analysts didn't have need or opportunity to study before. But ultimately this is not a contradiction of classical analytic theory, only an elaboration of some aspects of it that had not been well explored.

This would be a plausible argument, provided that one condition were fulfilled: there still would have to be, or at least to have been (even if only in the past), a population of oedipal neurotics somewhere. And this categorical discrimination of "neurotics" versus "borderlines" would still have to be based on the "oedipal" versus "pre-oedipal" criterion. Otherwise the foundations of classical analysis—to which, as I have noted, these analysts are intent upon pledging theoretical allegiance—are very seriously undermined, and these "later" ego psychologists, object relations theorists, and self psychologists, are open to the dreaded charge of revisionism. That is, they may be seen as deviating from Freudian metapsychology in their devaluation of the primacy of instinctual and oedipal vicissitudes in favor of self and relational ones.[13] I repeat: in order for these contemporary models of psychoanalytic explanation to successfully assert their fundamental continuity with classical theory, the classification "oedipal neurotic," and the Freudian account of the etiology of neurosis, would still have to be applicable to a real patient population somewhere—at the very least, to that population from which the theory was derived.

In fact, however, it is not only *today's* analysands who increasingly are being scrutinized in terms of pre-oedipal issues and found wanting. Gertrude and Rubin Blanck assert in their most recent volume that:

> the many reconsiderations in the literature of Freud's five cases raise questions about whether those patients were truly structured. Schreber was clearly psychotic, which Freud knew. It appears that the Wolf Man was certainly understructured, which Freud overlooked because his investigations were not directed toward borderline phenomena. Whether the Rat Man suffered from a true obsessional neurosis is also in doubt. Similar doubts apply to Dora and Little Hans. Today, the three latter cases would probably be regarded as possessing both neurotic and borderline features [1986:122].

And Harold P. Blum hints of Freud's own borderline or narcissistic features when he suggests that "contemporary evaluation" of aspects of Freud's personality "would include consideration(s) . . . of conflicts related to symbiosis and separation-individuation" (1979:157).

Thus the population of true neurotics is shrinking dangerously, not only in today's degenerate world but also within the roster of Freud's own clinical cases. In the face of this problematic logic, it is difficult to escape the conclusion that this shift from oedipal to pre-oedipal, this "waning of the Oedipus complex," does not result only from a difference in those whom we are observing. Rather, it is also linked, at least as strongly, to a change in the lens through which we are looking. If, indeed, these recent developments in psychoanalytic discourse are related more to a change of vision than to a clear-cut diagnostic difference in

---

[13]Greenberg and Mitchell (1983) make just this point in their book. They do not, however, relate the emergence of what they call "relational" psychoanalysis to a broader cultural context.

what is being seen, then the question is raised as to what the source is of this new psychoanalytic way of seeing.

Kohut (1977) used the phrase "experience-near" to emphasize the fact that recent psychoanalytic theoretical concepts have moved closer to phenomenology, utilizing everyday language. Kohut was more explicit and emphatic than other theorists in his predilection for such language and in his insistence on deriving it from patients' self-reports. In a more general sense, *all* of these theories have become increasingly "experience-near," if by this phrase is meant that psychoanalytic terms such as "self," "identity," and "separation-individuation" correspond closely to their usage and connotations in the language of the wider culture.[14]

Of course, everyday language is not "everyday" everywhere. In making increasing use of more "experiential" or "accessible" terms and concepts, psychoanalytic theorists have introduced into their theories (and strengthened already existing psychoanalytic tendencies that are in accord with) intuitively plausible formulations and commonsense connections which are in fact derived from a *cultural* "logic," a set of assumptions and premises deeply embedded in Anglo-American cultural values and by no means universal.

In other words, to note that these theories have come to utilize words and concepts nearer to our "everyday" ones is really to say that they have become more congruent with Anglo-American ethnopsychology. And indeed, in emphasizing and augmenting psychoanalytic discourse about the development of autonomy and individuality, the theories of Mahler, Erikson, Kernberg, Winnicott and others would seem to have absorbed, and to have rendered still more explicit, some characteristically Anglo-American beliefs and values concerning what a person should be like and how he or she should behave. These cultural beliefs and values are manifest both at the level of formal ideology and in (often unstated or implicit) rules of behavioral display and social interaction. Prominent among these desirable characteristics are *self-reliance* (self-sufficiency, self-confidence, and the avoidance of displays of dependency and of

---

[14]Even American theorists who retain more "classical" psychoanalytic terminology, e.g., Edith Jacobson and Otto Kernberg, have moved such concepts into the realm of the phenomenological, thereby providing a point of entry for ethnopsychological beliefs and cultural values. (See Greenberg and Mitchell, 1983: 304-348.)

strong nonverbal displays of emotion), *self-direction* (the capacity to know what is in one's heart and mind and to act in accord with these inner beliefs and feelings), and *verbal expression*.

As a growing number of cross-cultural researchers point out, these assumptions concerning the self, and rules of behavioral display, are hardly ubiquitous; they are not to be found even in Southern European cultures let alone in non-Western ones.[15] Nor is there a simple causal linkage (in either direction) between these values and a high degree of industrialization and its attendant social institutions.[16] It is mainly in Northern European[17] culture areas that these values and norms are dominant. These Northern European cultural values have their sources both in cultural traditions that have existed for many centuries (Macfarlane 1978; Fischer 1989) and in the basic tenets of Protestantism (Troeltsch 1931, 1958; Lukes 1973; Stone 1979; Nelson 1965). As Steven Lukes (1973:94) points out, Protestantism exemplifies "religious individualism" with its doctrines of the priesthood of all believers (highlighting the individual's personal unmediated relationship with God, and the inner life in general) and the respect for individual conscience (emphasizing the individual's right to his own spiritual practice and responsibility for his own spiritual condition).

---

[15]For basic contrasts between the Northern European (Protestant)"referential" self and the Latin-Mediterranean (Catholic) "indexical" self, see Gaines (1982).

[16]For example, in Japan, a highly industrialized society, "dependency" wishes and behaviors (at all stages of life) are sanctioned to a far greater degree than in the United States and Northern Europe. And qualities such as "independent" thought and its expression, which Americans value highly and consider to be important ends of development, are not similarly promoted in Japan. The primacy we accord to verbal expression also is absent in Japanese culture. Many writers point out that in Japanese relationships, verbalization is rarely the means by which one communicates anything considered really important, and that, correspondingly, Japanese tend to possess a more highly developed empathic sensitivity than do, e.g., Americans. See Doi (1973), Lebra (1976), and Roland (1988).

[17]By "Northern European" I refer to all Western European nations north of the Alps, as well as Switzerland and the Anglo-American culture areas (United Kingdom, Scotland, United States, Canada, Australia).

Although these values are embedded in most versions of Protestantism, they are most strongly elaborated in two branches of radical Protestantism which originated during the sixteenth and seventeenth centuries in Germany and England. The first branch included dissenting sects (I shall refer to them all as "nonconformists") such as the Pietists in Germany and the Netherlands, and the Methodists and Quakers in England. These groups emphasized Luther's doctrines of the priesthood of all believers and respect for individual conscience in a manner that was more radical and often more mystical than in Lutheran or Calvinist versions of these principles. The second branch encompassed the Puritans, a radical Calvinist group. Both branches—nonconformists and Puritans—stressed various aspects of autonomy and the inner life. They were among the first settlers of the United States, and their influence on our cultural values and folkways persists to this day, probably more strongly than anywhere else in the world (Fischer 1989; Perry 1944). Hence the United States may be considered the radical Protestant culture *par excellence*. However, these values also are detectable in certain strands within English (whence came the Puritans and other dissenters such as the Quakers and Methodists) and Scottish (Presbyterian, i.e. Calvinist) culture. In the following section I will discuss how secular transformations of these Puritan and nonconforming doctrines persist in contemporary Anglo-American folk psychological and psychoanalytic ideas.

Three Anglo-American values and their expression in contemporary psychoanalytic developmental psychology

For all that has been written about the "Americanization" of psychoanalysis,[18] there has been surprisingly little attention paid to the rela-

---

[18]Scholars who have examined the influence of American society and culture on psychoanalytic theory (usually focusing on the NeoFreudians and/or ego psychologists such as Hartmann and Erikson) have tended to highlight the influence upon psychoanalytic theory and practice of a few central "American" themes and situations. The first of these is American "meliorism" or "optimism" regarding the perfectibility, or at least the malleability, of human beings and the human condition itself. This is contrasted to the rather more pessimistic and (continued...)

tionship between Anglo-American hyperindividualism (and its radical Protestant ancestry) and the ascendance of self and ego issues in psychoanalytic theory. One can only speculate that the cultural derivation of themes such as self-reliance and self-direction has been overlooked because these values are so pervasive and strong that we all tend to take them for granted. They are so much a part of our cultural fabric that even as social scientists we tend not to subject them to analytic or critical scrutiny.[19] During the past several years, however, interest on the part

---

[18](...continued)
sober estimation of man and his fate voiced in Freud's writings (see Ruitenbeek 1966; Hughes 1968:175; Roazen 1990:139-161). Related to this meliorist strain is an "environmentalist" one—a belief in the malleability of human nature and of individuals that far exceeded Freud's own views. Hence American psychoanalysts—beginning perhaps with the NeoFreudians but continuing to the present day—have been shown to place more emphasis than Freud did on the influence, both positive and adverse, of the environment (particularly the human environment, i.e., the quality of parenting) on personality development. Some commentators have given a more pejorative cast to such observations of Americanized analysts' stronger optimism and environmentalism, suggesting that in absorbing these tendencies into their theories, NeoFreudians and ego psychologists also assimilated American shallowness and conformity, and a "drift toward social and political conservatism" (Hughes 1968:195). See also Jacoby (1983). On the related vicissitudes of the medicalization of psychoanalysis in America, see Hale (1978). A few commentators have noted Puritan elements in American culture that have contributed to the strength of its reception here: Nelson (1965) suggested that the "instrumental activism" (emphasis on worldly activity and excellence of performance as evidence of one's salvation) of our Puritan culture promoted Americans' zealous adoption of psychoanalytic therapy as a regime of self-improvement. Rieff made a related point when he wrote that "there was something about Protestantism itself that made it ready, upon decline, for psychoanalysis. . . . For Protestant culture, it was Calvin, with his doctrine of predestination, who first turned all action into symptom. Only the most careful scrutiny of the outer actions could give even a hint of the inner condition, whether that be of grace or damnation." This imperative of self-scrutiny in Puritan thought is seen by Rieff to have made America fertile soil for the introspective orientation of psychoanalysis (Rieff 1990:12-13).

[19]Robert Bellah et al. (1985) is an exception to this generalization. See also T.C. Heller, M. Sosna and D.E. Wellbery (1986) and Lukes (1973).

of cultural anthropologists in the comparative study of ethnopsychologies has brought to greater prominence the culturally distinctive (and probably rather atypical) nature of these and other "individualistic" assumptions inherent in "Western," and specifically Anglo-American, folk psychology (see, e.g., Geertz 1983; Rosaldo 1980; Heelas and Lock 1981; LeVine and White 1986; Lutz 1988). Exposed to models of the person and the life course which are different from our own, we see our own culture and its belief-systems (both ethnopsychologies and formal theories) in a more self-conscious light.

Below I shall consider three attributes of the self which Americans deem desirable and valuable, and offer some examples of how these beliefs and values have entered into or been strengthened in recent psychoanalytic discourse. First, however, I wish to make one prefatory remark regarding this cultural borrowing process which I have been describing. Thus far, this essay has been framed in terms of how psychoanalytic theory has been altered to "fit in" with American values and world view. In fact, however, one cannot consider how our concerns about autonomy have intensified this emphasis within psychoanalysis without acknowledging that in this commingling the American folk psychological ideas also have been modified, at least as they are manifest in the psychoanalytic discourse. Anglo-American psychoanalytic theory has indeed absorbed, and even serves to rationalize, the imperative of autonomous behavior and thought. But at the same time it also brings to our attention, and cautions us about, the stresses and hazards of too-great independence, suggesting that this style of selfhood, too, bespeaks an incomplete development.

To be more specific: the story of development as told by these theorists is not only conceived as a movement out of "symbiosis" (Mahler) or "hallucinatory omnipotence" (Winnicott) or "absolute dependence" (Fairbairn) towards autonomy and self-reliance. These theories also include the postulate that, on some level, all of us always are struggling with the longing for reunion, and that even if one has developed to a higher, more securely individuated level, one still seeks out relationships where this desire for some sort of "oneness" can be integrated with the imperative of separateness. If we are able to negotiate the painful and difficult but necessary process of separation and individuation, to achieve true identity and the capacity for relationship, then we may be "granted" (or rather, we will have "earned") the capacity to engage in limited and partial experiences of reunion with our objects, but without losing the sense of separate and distinctive identity which we have struggled to achieve. Such reunion-in-separateness is of two basic types: (1) "regression in the service of the ego" (present in falling-in-love, artistic and other types of creativity, orgasm and some aspects of the mother-infant relationship) and (2) a more limited and partial type of reunion with the object which is a part of any intimate relationship. For, in any such relationship, if one does not have the capacity to display some dependency, "regression," and permeability of "ego boundaries," then one also is not considered fully healthy and mature.

The inclusion of this dimension alongside of the dominant emphasis on independence and individuation, then, preserves a non-folk psychological element in these psychoanalytic theories, an element in which we see the persistence of a distinctively "psychoanalytic" way of looking at things. For surely one meaning of the term "dynamic" as it pertains to psychoanalysis is the postulate that, "underneath" what is normal, healthy and mature, there always lurk opposing tendencies and longings, and that maturity and sanity actually consist of a delicate balance of tensions, conflicts, and desires. Introduced into a culture which upholds strong conventions and values concerning separate-selfhood and autonomy, the psychodynamic system—which exposes and articulates points of tension and contradiction—has come to fixate on the tension between oneness and separateness, fusion and individuation. These are now viewed as the vital issues for making sense of, and helping to heal, the limitations and dilemmas of human existence.[20]

---

[20]This is not to suggest that this "dynamic" vision stands outside the flux of culture; in it, too, we can detect older cultural discourses, albeit "high" rather than "folk psychological" ones. In Anglo-American post-Freudian theories, this view of development and maturity as a perennial balance between, and integration of, conflicting forces (now conceived less in terms of instinctual tensions than in terms of simultaneous longings for oneness and separateness) closely resembles a generic high Romantic narrative pattern. This Romantic narrative chronicles the development of the Self and/or Mind as it moves out of an initial sense of unselfconscious unity with the world, through a painful but necessary sense of rupture and self-consciousness, and back to a higher unity with the world in which the Self's individuated distinctiveness is preserved. See Abrams, 1971; Kirschner, 1985, 1990, and 1991.

The three values I shall discuss below are (1) self-reliance, (2) self-direction, and (3) verbal expression. I have chosen to highlight them here because they are very central and pervasive, both in American cultural values and in contemporary Anglo-American psychoanalytic theories. Needless to say, this list is by no means exhaustive either as a set of desirable attributes of the American self or as a set of American values which have become highlighted in contemporary psychoanalytic thought.

1) ***Self-reliance***

To be self-reliant is to not depend upon another for care or for the regulation of one's self-esteem. The opposite of self-reliance is overdependence upon others: one is overdependent if one requires or demands the assistance or support of others in order to function or to be comfortable. To help one's child become independent in a variety of ways is probably the single most important goal of the American parent.

Takeo Doi (1963:266-273; 1973), Alan Roland (1988), and others (e.g., Morsbach & Tyler 1986) have pointed out that Americans tend to evince much more extreme discomfort with displays of dependency, or of what we interpret as dependent behaviors, than do those in at least some Asian or Mediterranean cultures.[21] This discomfort is apparent in many aspects of American psychoanalysis. Concerning the therapeutic relationship itself, Takeo Doi (1963) has pointed out "a cultural assumption which many psychotherapists in this country seem to share unwittingly that they can help the patient only insofar as he helps himself." Robert Bellah and his collaborators, in *Habits of the Heart* (an ethnographic study of contemporary American life), quote their prototypical therapist as saying of her profession, "If you've done a really good job, they don't think you've helped them at all, and they think they've done it themselves—and in a sense they have" (1985:70). Not only must all help for the patient ultimately come from within himself, but the more that a patient is able to express a self-reliant attitude (provided it is not defensive) the better is deemed his progress. In Ernst Kris's famous

---

[21]Atwood Gaines (1982:183) has observed that in Mediterranean cultures, complaining (which Anglo-Americans tend to perceive as evidence of moral weakness and psychological immaturity) in some contexts is perceived as communication of the soul's ennoblement, because to complain is to describe the extent to which one has suffered, and suffering is seen as enhancing one's moral dignity.

paper on the "good hour" (1956), the patient's improvement and movement in the direction of termination is gauged in terms of indications that he has begun to perform for himself the functions of the analyst, most notably the interpretive function.

It is testimony to the centrality of the themes of independence and separate-selfhood in American ethnopsychology that American psychoanalysis has come to view all severe psychopathology (and, for some theorists, *all* psychopathology) as related to failed individuation and failed independence. On one hand, the more extremely "dependent" a patient is seen to be, the more severely disturbed he or she is deemed. But on the other hand, it is not only overtly overdependent behaviors which are explained in these terms, but also certain types of more "withdrawn" and "distant" personalities (e.g., "schizoid" and some narcissistic types). In such cases, the outward appearance of self-sufficiency or detachment is considered to belie an inner world of impaired autonomy (Shapiro 1981), and greatly feared wishes for merger with the object (Meissner 1984:206-208).[22]

As has been noted, virtually all Northern European cultures encourage self-sufficiency and discourage displays of dependency and emotion. These conventions are strengthened and rationalized by the generic Protestant emphasis on individual responsibility. One finds these or similar values in Freud's writings, too. The Kantian ideal of rational autonomy[23] is deemed by Freud an index of maturity and civilization, and there are references scattered throughout his theories to infantile "passivity" versus more mature "activity," as well as to the developmental movement towards greater "detachment" from one's parents. "From the first," wrote Benjamin Nelson, "Freud emphasized that the goal of treatment was the achievement of autonomy on the part of the patient, the ability to regulate his own life by norms of his own devising." This,

[22]Another commonsense linkage that psychoanalytic thinkers tend to take for granted is that between extremely dependent behaviors and poor discrimination between self and others. This seemingly intuitive association of "inappropriately" dependent behaviors with an inference of weak "ego boundaries" and lack of "self-cohesion" bears further philosophical and anthropological study.

[23]Kant's principles of moral autonomy and rationality are in large measure transmutations of Protestant doctrines, especially Pietistic inner light mysticism.

as Nelson also noted, is already a "Protestant" element within psychoanalysis,[24] and thus a preexisting source of congruence between Freudian psychoanalysis and Anglo-American cultural values.

However, "self-reliance" has taken on an even stronger and more central importance, as well as additional meaning, in recent American and British psychoanalytic theories. As was noted above, pathological dependence (whether observed or inferred) has become *the* central diagnostic criterion for discriminating between "normal neurotics" (as they often are called) and lower level characters. Following Max Weber (1958), I would suggest that this extreme preoccupation with and valorization of self-reliance (and the intrapsychic sense of "separateness" which is considered its concomitant), and of related qualities such as self-confidence and self-control, is linked to the Puritan strain in Anglo-American culture, with its distinctive version of the Protestant vision of autonomy. Weber and other scholars (Miller 1937; Perry 1944; Lukes 1973) have pointed out that it was in Calvinist doctrines that Protestant ideas about self-reliance and individual responsibility attained their most extreme form, due to the intimate connection in Calvinism between self-reliance and *salvation*. Weber argued that, in response to the doctrine of predestination, there developed in Calvinist culture areas a very strong emphasis on independent achievement in this world. This is because one's worldly activity and success, apparent confidence, and capacity to improve one's life *through one's own initiative* were construed as evidence that one was among the elect, marked for redemption: "God helps those who help themselves." This was perhaps most extremely true of American Puritanism, i.e. the culture of New England where, as Ralph Barton Perry pointed out, Puritanism could develop "unhampered" upon favorable soil.[25]

---

[24] Nelson (in Klausner 1965) p. 75.

[25] Perry (1944: 93-94), following Miller (1937), also points out that "the form of Calvinism which prevailed in New England was the so-called covenant or federal theology." It is this type of Calvinism which most exemplifies and promotes the notion that one's independent efforts and successes—one's material, moral, intellectual and spiritual achievements—all give evidence of the salvation of one's soul.

Perry wrote of the "Puritan temper of personal independence. For though he was willing to admit his dependence on God, he looked to this as a means of emancipation from dependence on man and on nature. Salvation was the only gratuity he was willing to accept" (1944:301). This view of the individual as very much "on his own" became even more marked as Puritanism became divested of its original communitarian and worldly utopian aspirations, which had perhaps mitigated somewhat the "unprecedented inner loneliness," which according to Weber was the lot of the Puritan and "can even today be identified in the national character and institutions of the peoples with a Puritan past" (1958:105).

The contemporary American analyst Robert Holt has suggested that "autonomy is the utopian ideal of ego psychology" (1989:229). Insofar as he asserts that in psychoanalysis there is a "utopian" ideal at all, of course, one might argue that Freud's message has been somewhat misread, "Americanized." But even if we accept Holt's quasi-salvationist viewpoint (perhaps on the grounds that many Anglo-American psychoanalytic theories are indeed more congenial to utopianism), I would propose that the utopia of ego psychology ("later" ego psychology, at least), self psychology, and object relations theory is not simply autonomy but rather "intimacy." By this term I mean the capacity for relationship, in which one may experience sustained connection to another person and, within limits, longed-for "regression" and "oneness," while simultaneously retaining one's essential distinctiveness, integrity and autonomy. Thus, as was discussed above, Anglo-American psychoanalytic theory has become both an explication and rationalization of the folk ideal of self-reliance, and a subtle critique and tempering of this ideal via acknowledgement of the costs and losses inherent in its promotion.

2) ***Self-direction***

Self-direction encompasses two imperatives: (1) that one should know what is in one's heart and mind and (2) that one should make choices and (insofar as is possible) live one's life in accord with these inner beliefs and feelings, rather than in compliance with some external standard or with another person's wishes. The opposite of self-direction, compliance, signifies not merely behavioral conformity to some external authority but also (and this is considered more pernicious and psychologically undesirable) a confusion of the other's desires with one's own in a way that distorts, constricts or suppresses one's true self and its unique personal experience.

In psychoanalytic theories, there are two eras of life in which the theme of self-direction is particularly emphasized. One is the "pre-oedipal" era and the other is adolescence. During infancy and early childhood, parental failure to encourage and promote in the child a sense of his true needs, feelings and preferences is considered to be highly pathogenic. Winnicott (1960) asserts that the child who is forced to respond too early in life to his mother's needs does not have sufficient attention paid to his own. Consequently his "true self"—the seat of his own wishes, and of his unique and spontaneous feelings and gestures—becomes submerged and inaccessible, and cannot develop properly. Kohut (1971, 1977) claims that the narcissistically disturbed self has not received sufficient empathic responsiveness and "mirroring" from his parents, and that this is why such a child cannot develop an adequate self structure. Erikson (1963) posits an early developmental tension between autonomy on one hand, and shame and doubt on the other. He suggests that if the very young child is denied the "gradual and well-guided experience of autonomy and free choice," as embodied in the proper balance between parental limitation and promotion of his free expression, the child will not grow up to know his own mind and feelings.

The particulars of this miscarriage of development thus are conceptualized differently in the various theories. But whether we are looking at Winnicott's overly compliant false self, Kohut's narcissistically disturbed self, Erikson's imbalance of shame and doubt versus autonomy, or still other clinical entities, we find that despite differences in the timing and severity of these pathologies a feature which they share is an inability on the part of the self to develop or discriminate his true feelings and desires, as well as a stunted capacity for free choice, spontaneity and creativity.

The other era when the individual is supposed to learn a great deal about what is in his mind and heart is, of course, adolescence, which the analyst Peter Blos (1967) has called "the second individuation." Erikson, who devoted so much attention to this stage of life, suggests that the task of the adolescent era is the development of a sense of identity. He defines "the sense of ego identity" as "the accrued confidence that the inner sameness and continuity prepared in the past are matched by the sameness and continuity of one's meaning for others" (1963:263). As I understand him, he asserts that the task of the adolescent and young adult is not only the achievement of a greater separation and individuation from primary object ties, but also the expression and integration of the self within the larger society. One must somehow find a way for the inner sense of self to connect to the world in a meaningful, satisfying and socially responsible way. Erikson's apparent optimism about the possibility (indeed, the imperative) of connecting the inner self to the outer social world indicates one important difference between the idea of individuality in the United States and that in many other culture areas, including Japanese, Mediterranean, and even English societies.[26]

This general emphasis on the psychological and moral value of being attuned to one's true beliefs, feelings and preferences appears in large measure to be a secular, modern-day transformation of the "nonconforming" Protestant doctrines that have played such an important role in American cultural life. I have described how certain non-Puritan dissenting Protestant groups that settled in the New World (including the Quakers and the Methodists) emphasized Luther's principles of the priesthood of all believers and respect for individual conscience. These principles were highlighted even more extremely than in Lutheran and Calvinist versions. Nonconformist doctrines tended to be more "emotional," compassionate and optimistic than those of the Puritans, and often

---

[26]Gaines (1982) has contrasted the Northern European Protestant "referential" self to the Latin "indexical" self of French ethnopsychology. He asserts that for the French, as for other Latin cultures, the inner self is considered to be fixed at birth, immutable, and essentially not in commerce with one's outer self, which changes in relation to the interpersonal and "role" situations in which one finds oneself. Lebra (1976:158) suggests that, despite the common description of Japanese culture as characterized by "groupism" and "social orientation," the Japanese "are not indifferent to individuality and autonomy." However, "individuality for the Japanese is at the opposite pole of social involvement. Individuality lies not in society but away from it." In English society, in spite of its strong radical Protestant and Romantic traditions, the imperative of self-expression and self-actualization in one's daily life is likewise not as strong as it is in America.

had strong mystical overtones.[27] For them, intimations of one's salvation arise not (or not only) as a by-product of worldly achievement, but rather in the experience, accessible to all, of contact with God within one's soul. The individual human spirit can be illuminated by the divine spark such that one may apprehend God and one's connection to Him, and thereby have an intuition and foretaste of a more definitive salvation to come. This is the doctrine of the inner light (Tillich 1972; Nelson 1965), which predated Protestantism by many centuries but also became a centerpiece of these post-Reformation doctrines and thereby took on an increasingly "this-worldly" cast. Eventually, the belief that the individual must look inward to discover God's truth within himself became completely secularized, so that it was not God and an intimation of literal salvation one sought by looking within, but rather one's *self*. In the nineteenth century, American philosopher Ralph Waldo Emerson helped to transform the religion of the inner light into a literal worship of the self, with his exhortation that "a man should learn to detect and watch that gleam of light which flashes across his mind from within....Nothing is at last sacred but the integrity of your own mind." Correspondingly, he asserted, "Whoso would be a man, must be a nonconformist...What I must do is all that concerns me, not what the people think" (Emerson 1990). Today, this creed remains one of the foundations of our culture: Robert Bellah describes "finding oneself," and attempting to be faithful to that self in one's "lifestyle," as central aims of contemporary Americans (Bellah et al. 1985).[28]

---

[27]The powerful influence of worldly mystical Protestant strains on American ethnopsychology and Euro-American high culture has rarely been directly assayed. Benjamin Nelson (1975) exhibited characteristic perspicacity when he noted that "Weber was so intent upon the unique predominance in the West of the penetration and remaking of the world to innerworldly asceticism that he failed to give enough weight to another fact. . . . Weber does not . . . sufficiently stress the significance of *innerworldly mysticism.*"

[28]Of course, in spite of our individualistic ideology, and the use of rationales and judgments (of ourselves and others) which invoke the concepts of "self-direction" and "self-expression," at another level of ethnographic analysis one finds that Americans are no more tolerant of truly deviant behaviors than are

(continued...)

In addition to these Protestant sects' direct bequest to American ethnopsychology of the belief that the individual most look inward to discover (God's or his own) truth within himself, there are at least two other secular transformations of Protestant "inner light" mysticism[29] which also have influenced. American high and popular culture. One is Enlightenment (including Kantian) political and moral philosophy: the social and political principles of liberty and freedom of conscience upon which this country was founded owe a great deal to Protestant sectarian thought. Kantian philosophy, with its idea of the autonomous "will of every rational being which makes universal law" (quoted in Lukes 1973: 45), owes more to the doctrine of the inner light (mediated via German Pietism) than often is acknowledged (Nelson 1965, Taylor 1989). Phrasing the spiritual imperative of self-direction in more explicitly political terms, Thomas Jefferson wrote, "Rebellion to tyrants is obedience to God."

The other secular transformation of this aspect of nonconformism can be found, paradoxically, in a critique of Enlightenment rationalism: high Romantic thought. There is an indigenous Romantic strain in American culture which Robert Bellah calls "expressive individualism" (Emerson and Walt Whitman exemplify this tendency). High-cultural English and German Romantic themes and patterns also are prominent in Anglo-American psychoanalytic theories of development. In part, this is due to the straightforward congruence of some of these European motifs with American Romantic themes (for example, that of self-expression).[30] It

---

[28](...continued)
members of any other society. What is so interesting (and cultural) is that we think we are, should be, or could be.

[29]The influence of nonconforming Protestant ideas on a variety of Northern European and American popular and folk cultural discourses has been noted by Nelson (1965). On the connection between Protestant sectarian mysticism and rationalism, see Tillich (1972). On the transmission of Christian mystical themes to the Romantics via their contact with Protestant sectarian doctrines, see Abrams (1973). See also Taylor (1989).

[30]Sass (1988) has explored how Heinz Kohut's theory embodies Romantic and
(continued...)

is also due to the fact that the high Romantic vision, with its depiction of a quasi-mystical striving towards a "higher" reunion of subject and object in which the subject's individuated distinctiveness also is preserved, provided a dynamic, dialectical (and hence psychoanalytic) "understructure" to the American emphasis on separate-selfhood and independence.[31] For these reasons, English and German high Romantic themes and patterns have become elaborated in Anglo-American psychoanalysis to a greater degree than they were in Freud's texts. [32]

The term "nonconforming" originally was applied to these Protestant groups because they dissented and broke away from the Church of England. It is interesting to note that, of the leading British-born object relations theorists, Winnicott was raised as a Methodist and Guntrip a Congregationalist (both "dissenting" denominations), and Fairbairn's primary religious affiliation was with the Scottish Presbyterian Church. Of course, they also were exposed (particularly Winnicott) to a celebration of the "true" self in English Romantic poetry and literature.

3) *Verbal expression*

The importance which Westerners in general attach to verbalization has been noted by many writers (see Tobin, Wu, and Davidson 1989; Roland 1988). In contemporary American culture, verbalization of one's thoughts, feelings and opinions is encouraged as a means of serving the values of self-expression and freedom of choice, both of which have been

---

[30](...continued)
"expressivist" themes. Perhaps these particular Romantic dimensions were expanded in (and to some extent grafted onto) Kohut's and other, similar psychoanalytic theories in conjunction with these theories' taking root in American cultural soil.

[31]Elsewhere (Kirschner 1985, 1990, 1991), I have explored the emphasis on and elaboration of the Romantic spiral narrative pattern in Anglo-American psychoanalysis.

[32]High Romantic themes present in German literature and philosophy are by no means absent from Freudian texts: see Thomas Mann (1931, 1939), Trosman (1973), Holt (1978, 1989), McGrath (1985), Vermorel and Vermorel (1986).

discussed above. The anthropologist Joseph Tobin and his associates have described how, in the contemporary American preschools they studied, the use of language is emphatically encouraged as a means of expressing one's opinions and feelings in a way that it is not in the mainland Chinese or Japanese settings which they also studied. Tobin reports a bit of dialogue from an American school in which the teacher asks, "Do you want juice, Rhonda? Milk? A cracker? What do you want? Don't just keep shaking your head. How am I supposed to know what you want if you don't tell me?" (Tobin et al. 1989:134). Embedded in this utterance are two assumptions: (1) everyone is entitled to freedom of choice and a variety of options; (2) you cannot expect another to intuit or anticipate your preferences; you must state them explicitly.

As a substitute for the acting out of impulses, and as an expression of insight, verbalization has always been deemed of central importance in psychoanalysis. But in the context of American culture, where verbal communication has come to connote an acknowledgement of one's radical separateness, and to serve as a vehicle for one's freedom of choice and self-expression, verbalization in psychoanalysis has acquired additional import: the use of language for communication is now highlighted as an expression of one's awareness that one is separate and different from the other. To communicate verbally is a sign of higher development because it is taken to mean that one is aware that preverbal gesturing or empathic communication (associated with lower-level fantasies of symbiosis and merger with the object) cannot be relied upon to communicate needs and wishes to the other. This emphasis is evident in the developmental theories of ego psychologists Rene Spitz and Margaret Mahler. Spitz (1959), in his genetic field theory of ego formation, asserts that semantic communication is the third (relatively advanced) level of ego development:

> The use of speech for semantic communication involves awareness that object images are separate from self-images, and includes the intention to communicate across ego boundaries. This will remain the principal mode of communication throughout life, with certain exceptions when there is a temporary and reversible merger for pleasure or for artistic creation [Blanck and Blanck 1986:12].

Verbal communication is emphasized in British culture at least as much as in America, but verbalization of feelings is not: Britons are not known for their emotional expressiveness, verbal or otherwise (McGill and Pearce 1982). As for Americans, it may be that the dissemination of psychological and psychodynamic ideas in the United States over the past several decades has helped to promote the idea that such emotional expressiveness is desirable and "healthy." (This would be another example of the characteristically psychoanalytic endeavor to effect a better balance between manifest and repudiated cultural elements, while still fundamentally upholding the status quo.) Certainly there are older Anglo-American sources of expressiveness too, such as the aforementioned Romanticism and expressive individualism. In any case, the emphasis on the *verbal* expression of sentiment preserves and reinforces assumptions about our radical separateness, even as it to some extent challenges or modifies views about the appropriateness of expressive and emotional display.

Conclusion

If my analysis is correct—that the ascendance of "ego" and "self" theories in North American and British psychoanalysis is a testament to our hyperindividualism, which in turn is traceable to our radical Protestant heritage and its secular offshoots—then we would not expect to find that psychoanalytic theory has developed along similar lines (if indeed it has caught on at all) in a non-Protestant nation. The case of psychoanalysis in France would seem to confirm this hypothesis. Marion Olinor (1988:12) points out that "concepts such as separation-individuation, object constancy, or self-object...are foreign to...French" analytic theorists, Lacanian and non-Lacanian alike (see also Turkle 1981). This is not a superficial linguistic difference. In general, the Anglo-American preoccupation with strengthening the ego and/or the self is absent from the French analytic attitude. This is of course most radically true in the case of that most notorious and celebrated of French analysts, Jacques Lacan, for whom the self or subject is an illusion to be dissolved, itself the problem (or rather the symptom). Particularly the notion of self-direction I described above—the idea of a "true" or "real" self which is the repository of one's "authentic" feelings and may even be present in nuclear form at birth—is disdained by many French analysts, even those who are not exclusively Lacanian. In commenting on the initial foreignness and distastefulness of the emphasis in recent Anglo-Saxon psychoanalysis on the "self" (for which there is no precisely equivalent word in French), J.-B. Pontalis wrote: "Thus the French psychoanalyst is, from the start, disconcerted by the notion of *self*....One should therefore talk of a return of the *repressing* rather than that of the repressed: a return masked by nostalgia, a nostalgia for the good old self which would have been lost through too much analysis" (Pontalis 1977:127).[33]

Finally, one might wonder how it could be that a group of analysts, many of whom were neither born nor trained in the United States or England, and many of whom were not even Christian let alone Protestant, could have become the bearers of these quintessentially Anglo-American ideals. In response to this question, I invoke the autobiographical reflections of Margaret Mahler herself: "If I had not come to America," she wrote, "I would have accomplished very little." In Vienna, "I reached an impasse, unable to find a voice to express the developmental and clinical insights toward which I was then groping." In America, however, she found "vital new sources of collegial support." Thus, she asserted:

> It was only in America, and only owing to the tremendous professional encouragement I received in America, that I no longer felt I was laboring under the shadow of titans. If I had not come to America, where I felt free to formulate insights at which I had empathically arrived,

---

[33]While one would hardly want to call Lacanian analysis a French folk psychology, it *is* true that not only is it extremely un-Protestant (in spite of Sherry Turkle's characterization of it as "psychoanalytic protestantism") but also it embodies certain assumptions about the person which are characteristic of the Latin self as described by Gaines (1982). He asserts that "the boundary of the Latin self is not drawn around a single biological unit, but around the 'foyer.' The self consists in part of significant others, primarily family. Thus, the self is partly composed of elements over which the individual has no control....This self stands in stark contrast with the bounded, autonomous and, therefore, self-regulated and self-reflective protestant individual.... The unchanging and unchangeable self which is in part composed of seemingly external social and spiritual elements is the self of Lacan's French version of psychoanalysis" (p. 184).

> I would have accomplished very little. I would never have begun to publish, to teach, to undertake research. Because if one does not find an assenting echo to one's ideas, if one is passed over, as I was in Vienna, then one cannot create. To create, after all, is to believe that what one says will count [1988:120-22].[34]

It was this "assenting echo," I have argued, which made it possible for her to find her "voice" and become professionally productive and influential. As I have attempted to demonstrate, themes of the self and its individuation, of oneness and separateness, are highly salient for Anglo-Americans because of their relation to our ideals of independence and self-direction. American mental health professionals no doubt discerned in Mahler's preexisting interests and interpretive tendencies a resonance with some of their own ingrained ethnopsychological concerns. Thus provided with the necessary support of all kinds, she was induced to further pursue these issues and to elaborate upon her original insights to a far greater extent than she had before. It would appear that in so doing she not only absorbed and underscored the fundamental American concern with self-reliance and separateness, but also drew upon her acquaintance with the high Romantic literary and philosophical discourses about oneness and separateness which were part of the cultural background of any educated Austro-Hungarian (in fact she had studied philosophy).

A similar dialectic of reception and creation may be found to obtain for other celebrated immigrant analysts such as Erikson and Kernberg (and Horney before them). In spite of the initial resistance of Anglo-American psychoanalytic orthodoxy to the paradigm shift embodied in their theories, its ascendance over the past several decades would appear to have been inexorable. I have argued in this essay that this is due to the pressure of selection exerted by Anglo-American ethnopsychological themes.

---

[34]Mahler was not herself referring to the influence of cultural values on the cultivation and reception of her work, which she considered to be universally important and applicable. Rather she emphasized that the "psychoanalytic politics" in Vienna at that time (dominated by Anna Freud and Helene Deutsch) were antipathetic to her and her ideas.

References

Abrams, M.H. 1971. *Natural Supernaturalism: Tradition and Revolution in Romantic Literature*. New York: W.W. Norton.

Bellah, Robert N., Richard Madsen, William M. Sullivan, Ann Swidler, and Steven M. Tipton. 1985. *Habits of the Heart*. Berkeley: University of California Press.

Blanck, Rubin, and Gertrude Blanck. 1986. *Beyond Ego Psychology*. New York: Columbia University Press.

Blos, Peter. 1967. "The Second Individuation Process in Adolescence," in *The Psychoanalytic Study of the Child*, vol. XXII. New York: International Universities Press, pp.162-186.

Blum, Harold P. 1979. "The Prototype of Preoedipal Reconstruction," in Mark Kanzer and Jules Glenn, eds., *Freud and His Self-Analysis*. New York: Jason Aronson.

Doi, L. Takeo. 1963. "Some Thoughts on Helplessness and the Desire to be Loved." *Psychiatry* 26(3):266-272.

_________. 1973. *The Anatomy of Dependence*. (John Bester, Trans.). New York: Kodansha International.

Eagle, Morris N. 1984. *Recent Developments in Psychoanalytic Theory*. Englewood Cliffs, NJ: McGraw-Hill.

Emerson, Ralph Waldo. 1990. "Self-Reliance," in *Selected Essays, Lectures and Poems*. New York: Bantam.

Erikson, Erik. 1963. *Childhood and Society*. New York: W. W. Norton.

Fischer, David Hackett. 1989. *Albion's Seed: British Folkways in America*. New York: Oxford University Press.

Fromm, Erich. 1941. *Escape from Freedom*. New York: Avon Books (1965).

Gaines, Atwood. 1982. "Cultural Definitions, Behavior and the Person in American Psychiatry," in A. J. Marsella and G.M. White, eds., *Cultural Conceptions of Mental Health and Therapy*. Dordrecht, Holland: D. Reidel.

Gedo, John. 1984. *Psychoanalysis and Its Discontents*. New York: The Guilford Press.

Geertz, Clifford. 1983. "From the Native's Point of View: On the Nature of Anthropological Understanding," in *Local Knowledge*. New York: Basic Books.

Gorer, Geoffrey. 1948. *The American People*. New York: Norton.

__________. 1955. *Exploring English Character*. New York: Criterion.

Greenberg, Jay, and Stephen Mitchell. 1984. *Object Relations in Psychoanalytic Theory*. Cambridge, MA: Harvard University Press.

Guntrip, Harry. 1973. *Psychoanalytic Theory, Therapy, and the Self*. New York: Basic Books.

Hale, Nathan G., Jr. 1978. "Berggasse XIX to Central Park West: The Americanization of Psychoanalysis, 1919-1940." *Journal of the History of the Behavioral Sciences* 14:299-315.

Heelas, P, and A. Lock. 1981. *Indigenous Psychologies: The Anthropology of the Self*. Lancaster: Academic Press.

Heller, T.C., M. Sosna, and D.E. Wellberry, eds. 1986. *Reconstructing Individualism: Autonomy, Individuality and Self in Western Thought*. Stanford, CA: Stanford University Press.

Holt, Robert R. 1978. "Ideological and Thematic conflicts in the structure of Freud's Thought," in S. Smith, ed., *The Human Mind Revisited: Essays in Honor of Karl A. Menninger*. New York: International Universities Press, pp.51-98.

__________. 1989. "Ego Autonomy and the Problem of Human Freedom," in *Freud Reappraised: A Fresh Look at Psychoanalytic Theory* (pp. 220-221). New York: The Guilford Press.

Horncy, Karen. 1937 *The Neurotic Personality of Our Time*. New York: W.W. Norton.

__________. 1939. *New Ways in Psychoanalysis*. New York: W. W. Norton.

Hughes, H. Stuart. 1968. *The Sea Change*. New York: Harper and Row.

Hughes, Judith M. 1989. *Reshaping the Psychoanalytic Domain*. Berkeley: University of California Press.

Jacobson, Edith. 1964. *The Self and the Object World*. New York: International Universities Press.

Jacoby, Russell. 1983. *The Repression of Psychoanalysis: Otto Fenichel and the Political Freudians*. New York: Basic Books.

Kirschner, Suzanne R. 1985. "Margaret S. Mahler's Separation-Individuation Theory as a Transmuted Version of an Originally Theological Narrative." Unpublished Qualifying Paper, Harvard University.

_________. 1990. "Sources of Redemption in Psychoanalytic Developmental Psychology," paper presented at the Annual Convention of the American Psychological Association, Boston, MA, August.

_________. 1991. *Judaeo-Christian Mystical Themes in Psychoanalytic Developmental Psychology: From Cosmology to Personality*. Unpublished doctoral dissertation, Harvard University Graduate School of Education.

Kohon, Gregorio. 1986. *The British School of Psychoanalysis*. New Haven: Yale University Press.

Kohut, Heinz. 1971. *The Analysis of the Self: A Systematic Approach to the Psychoanalytic Treatment of Narcisstic Personality Disorders*. New York: International Universities Press.

_________. 1977. *The Restoration of the Self*. New York: International Universities Press.

_________. 1980. "Summarizing Reflections," in Arnold Goldberg, ed., *Advances in Self Psychology*. New York: International Universities Press.

Kris, Ernst. 1956. "On Some Vicissitudes of Insight in Psychoanalysis." *International Journal of Psycho-Analysis*, 37:445-455.

Kurzweil, Edith. 1989. *The Freudians: A Comparative Perspective*. New Haven: Yale University Press.

Lasch, Christopher. 1979. *The Culture of Narcissism: American Life in an Age of Diminishing Expectations*. New York: W.W.Norton.

Lebra, Takie. 1976. *Japanese Patterns of Behavior*. Honolulu: University of Hawaii Press.

LeVine, Robert A., and Merry I. White. 1986. *Human Conditions*. New York: Routledge and Kegan Paul.

Lipset, Seymour Martin. 1968. "Anglo-American Society," in *International Encyclopedia of the Social Sciences*. New York: Macmillan Co./The Free Press, pp.289-301.

Loewald, Hans. 1980. "The Waning of the Oedipus Complex," in *Papers on Psychoanalysis*. New Haven: Yale University Press.

Lukes, Steven. 1973. *Individualism*. Oxford, England: Basil Blackwell.

Lutz, Catherine. 1988. *Unnatural Emotions: Everyday Sentiments in a Micronesian Atoll and Their Challenge to Western Theory*. Chicago: University of Chicago Press.

Macfarlane, A. 1978. *The Origins of English Individualism*. Oxford, England: Basil Blackwell.

Mahler, Margaret S. 1975. "On the Current Status of the Infantile Neurosis," in *The Selected Papers of Margaret S. Mahler* vol 2. New York: Jason Aronson.

_________. 1988. "Epilogue," in Paul Stepansky, ed. *The Memoirs of Margaret S. Mahler*. New York: The Free Press.

Mahler, Margaret S., Fred Pine, and Anni Bergman. 1968. *On Human Symbiosis and the Vicissitudes of Separation-Individuation*. New York: International Universities Press.

_________. 1975. *The Psychological Birth of the Human Infant*. New York: Basic Books.

Mann, Thomas. 1931. "Freud's Position in the History of Modern Thought," in *Past Masters and Other Papers* (pp.167-200). New York: Alfred Knopf.

_________. 1939. "Freud and the Future," in *Freud, Goethe, Wagner* (pp.3-45). New York: Alfred Knopf.

McGill, David and John K. Pearce. 1982. "British-American Families," in Monica McGoldrick, John K. Pearce, and Joseph Giordano, eds., *Ethnicity and Family Therapy*. New York: The Guilford Press, pp.457-479.

McGrath, William J. 1985. *Freud's Discovery of Psychoanalysis*. Ithaca: Cornell University Press.

Meissner, William. 1984. *The Borderline Spectrum: Differential Diagnosis and Developmental Issues*. New York: Jason Aronson.

Miller, Perry. 1937. "The Marrow of Puritan Divinity." *Publications of the Colonial Society of Massachusetts*, XXXII:245-300.

Morsbach, H., and Tyler, W.J. 1986. "A Japanese Emotion: *Amae*," in Rom Harre, ed., *The Social Construction of Emotion*. Oxford, England: Basil Blackwell.

Nelson, Benjamin. 1965. "Self-Images and Systems of Spiritual Direction in the History of European Civilization," in S.Z. Klausner, ed., *The Quest for Self-Control*. New York: Free Press.

_________. 1975. "Max Weber, Ernst Troeltsch, George Jellinek as Comparative Historical Sociologists," *Sociological Analysis* 36(3):229-240.

Olinor, Marion. 1988. *Cultivating Freud's Garden in France*. New York: Jason Aronson.

Perry, Helen Swick. 1983. *Psychiatrist of America*. Cambridge, MA: Harvard University Press.

Perry, Ralph Barton. 1944. *Puritanism and Democracy*. New York: Vanguard Press.

Pine, Fred. 1985. *Developmental Theory and Clinical Process*. New Haven: Yale University Press.

Pontalis, J-B. 1977. *Entre Le Rêve et La Douleur*. Paris: Gallimard.

Quinn, Susan. 1987. *A Mind of Her Own*. New York: Summit.

Rieff, Philip. 1990. "The American Transference from Calvin to Freud," in *The Feeling Intellect* (pp.12-13). Chicago: University of Chicago Press.

Roazen, Paul. 1974. *Freud and His Followers*. New York: New American Library.

_________. 1990. "Ego Psychology." In *Encountering Freud: The Politics and Histories of Psychoanalysis* (pp.139-161). New Brunswick, NJ: Transaction Publishers.

Roland, Alan. 1988. *In Search of Self in India and Japan: Towards a Cross-Cultural Psychology*. Princeton, NJ: Princeton University Press.

Rosaldo, Michael Z. 1980. *Knowledge and Passion: Ilongot Notions of Self and Social Life*. Cambridge, England: Cambridge University Press.

Ruitenbeek, Hendrik. 1966. *Freud and America*. New York: Macmillan.

Sass, Louis A. 1988. "The Self and Its Vicissitudes: An Archaeological Study of the Psychoanalytic Avant-Garde," *Social Research* 55(Winter):551-607.

Shapiro, David. 1981. *Autonomy and Rigid Character*. New York: Basic Books.

Spitz, René. 1959. *A Genetic Field Theory of Ego Formation*. New York: International Universities Press.

Stepansky, Paul, ed. 1988. *The Memoirs of Margaret S. Mahler*. New York: The Free Press.

Stone, Laurence. 1979. *The Family, Sex and Marriage in England 1500-1800*. New York: Harper and Row, 1979.

Taylor, Charles. 1989. *Sources of the Self*. Cambridge, MA: Harvard University Press.

Tillich, Paul. 1972. *A History of Christian Thought from Its Judaic and Hellenistic Origins to Existentialism*. New York: Touchstone.

Tobin, Joseph J., David Y.H. Wu, and Dana H. Davidson. 1989. *Preschool in Three Cultures: Japan, China and the United States*. New Haven: Yale University Press.

Troeltsch, Ernst. 1931. *The Social Teachings of the Christian Churches*, vol. 1. New York: Macmillan.

_________. 1958. *Protestantism and Progress*. Boston: Beacon Press.

Trosman, Harry. 1973. "Freud's Cultural Background," in *The Annual of Psychoanalysis* 1, New York: Quadrangle Press.

Turkle, Sherry. 1981. *Psychoanalytic Politics: Freud's French Revolution*. Cambridge, MA: Harvard University Press.

Vermorel, Madeleine, and Henri Vermorel. 1986. "Was Freud a Romantic?" *International Review of Psycho-Analysis* 13:15-37.

Weber, Max. 1958. *The Protestant Ethic and the Spirit of Capitalism*. New York: Charles Scribners' Sons.

Winnicott, D. W. 1960. "Ego Distortion in Terms of True and False Self." In *The Maturational Process and the Facilitating Environment* (pp.140-152). New York: International Universities Press.

Chapter Eight

Oedipus Rex or Edifice Wrecked? Some Comments on the Universality of Oedipality and on the Cultural Limitations of Freud's Thought[1]

David H. Spain

Just two months after Freud's death on 23 September 1939, *The American Journal of Sociology* published, as one of its regular issues, a major tribute to the founder of psychoanalysis. In it were articles by (among others) Havelock Ellis, A. A. Brill, Gregory Zilboorg, Harold Lasswell, Kenneth Burke, Karen Horney, and A. L. Kroeber. Kroeber's essay (1939) was, of course, his now famous reassessment of *Totem and Taboo*. This choice of subject was fitting on that occasion not only because of the stinging review Kroeber had given this work two decades earlier (Kroeber 1920) but also, and more importantly, because that book of Freud's contained one of the most forceful and dramatic of his many statements about oedipality—arguably the most important and certainly the most disputed of his contributions to knowledge.

Since then, *Totem and Taboo* has been reassessed again and again by various anthropologists (for example, Fox,1967; Lévi-Strauss 1963 [1958]; and Paul 1976) and others (e.g., Wallace 1983) for, like all

---

[1]Many people have read an earlier version of this paper and made comments on it that have resulted in improvements. For their suggestions and encouragement, I would like to thank John Ingham, Lorna Rhodes, and various members of the Seattle Psychoanalytic Society, and the Anthropology and Analysis Study Group. Although I doubt, somehow, that the changes I have made will prove satisfactory to him, kindly offered comments by Marvin Harris did force me to rewrite footnote 9 entirely. I am *very* grateful to him for those comments.

oedipal theory. Instead of yet another review of *Totem and Taboo* or his other books grounded in the oedipal leitmotif, however, I comment on two of the most common anthropological objections to Freud's views-and, in contrast to the usual pro-psychoanalytic review, I will *accept* them. I do so not because of any aim, on this occasion, to (re)bury Freud by piling up still more criticism; neither do I wish to resurrect him by showing that his thought was flawless. Rather, I want to see if it is possible today, after all the scholarship in the half century since Freud's death and in the three-quarters of a century since the publication of *Totem and Taboo*, to shed some new light on some old issues central to both psychoanalysis and psychoanalytic anthropology.

Thus, I will suggest that many anthropologists (and others) *can* be understood to have uttered an important truth when they assert that the Oedipus complex is not a universal. I will also argue, along with his more vehement critics, that some of Freud's most basic assumptions about oedipality were in error because, in part, he was blinded by his culture and personality to other, perhaps better, viewpoints. I do not, however, take what some of Freud's critics apparently believe is the next logical step for anyone who would accept such critiques—namely, the jettisoning of either psychoanalysis or psychoanalytic anthropology. I do not because accepting such criticisms, when they are valid, must eventually reinvigorate these fields. Only if advocates of psychoanalysis continue to dismiss criticisms out of hand will the decline of these fields be assured.

Listed below are eight statements that I believe are reasonable, both individually and when considered as a set, even though they may seem crassly anti-psychoanalytic and/or ludicrously contradictory. The first six bear directly on the question of the universality of oedipality; the last two pertain broadly to the question of whether psychoanalytic theory, both in general and regarding Freud's oedipal theory specifically, is limited by Freud's culture and/or his personality.

1. Leslie White was right: one cannot explain cultural variety with a constant.
2. *The* Oedipus complex is not a universal.
3. No two Oedipus complexes are alike.
4. Oedipality is found in people in all cultures but it is not true that to be human is to be oedipal.

5. There are many humans—indeed, millions of them—who do not have and have never had an oedipal experience or an Oedipus complex.
6. Harris, in an insightful anti-psychoanalytic essay, is correct when he suggests that anthropologists should try to discover the causes of variability in Oedipus complexes.
7. Some of the sternest critics of psychoanalysis are right when they claim that some of Freud's most basic ideas about oedipality (and other psychoanalytic issues) are either plainly wrong or seriously misleading because they were rooted in and, in this sense, culture-bound derivatives of, both his personality and culture.
8. There is, I believe, at least one other psychological complex that is as universal and important for human development as the Oedipus complex.

In the remainder of this paper, I suggest why these statements seem reasonable to me.

Universals and constants (Statements 1-3)

The first three statements may be considered together as they are aspects of the same broader point—namely, that much needless debate has been engendered by what, to me, is a puzzling habit of anthropological discourse: two very distinct words, *universal* and *constant*, are used as though they are equivalent. Consider this example from Harris's *Cultural Materialism: The Struggle for a Science of Culture* (1979:264-265) [please, dear reader, read this quote; it is, I regret, long and tedious but it also happens to be absolutely central to the point I am trying to make, so bear with me and read it word for word to the end]:

> The central weakness of the Freudian notions of psychodynamic *universals* is precisely the same as the weakness lying at the heart of sociobiology and structuralism. In each case, *universal* components of human nature are said to account for a remarkably variable set of institutions. And in each case *uniformity* has to be translated into diversity by intervening variables. . . . In cultural materialistic perspective, the problem of the intervening variables looms larger than that of the alleged *universals*.

> In order to explain why the *constant* yields such variable results, the causes of variation necessarily become the focus of research. And once these causes have been grounded in the infrastructure, the heuristic value of the *constant* becomes increasingly dubious. Finally, the *constant* loses all strategic value as more and more puzzles involving both similarities and differences find their solution in the similarities and differences of the etic and behavioral infrastructure [emphasis added].

Now where, I ask you, has it been shown or claimed that universal oedipal experiences are uniform? On what grounds can one shift, as Harris does, without comment and therefore seemingly without effect, from "universal" to "uniform" and "constant"?

This is not an isolated instance. Harris expressed essentially the same view more than a decade earlier in *The Rise of Anthropological Theory* (Harris 1968:457) and it is the central thread of his concluding argument in chapter 6 of *Cannibals and Kings* (Harris 1977:66). Neither is his view ignorable simply because it seems to be merely one more polemical pronouncement in support of cultural materialism since it also can be found in the theoretically contrasting work of Lévi-Strauss (1969 [1949]:8).[2] Although not found all that often in print in words so direct as Harris's, I have *heard* many people—students as well as some of the most distinguished anthropologists in America—launch into their criticisms, of psychoanalysis in general and oedipality in particular, from this muddled starting point. Indeed, fallacious as it is, this sort of argument may well be one of the most time-honored in all of anthropology. Be that as it may, it is fatally flawed because oedipality is not a constant but a variable or, more precisely, a set of them.

The origin of this facet of our largely oral tradition is unclear, at least to me. If not introduced to anthropology by Leslie White, it certainly appears to have been made famous by him through his incessant reminders that one cannot explain cultural variation in terms of biopsych-

---

[2]"Likewise," says Lévi-Strauss in the opening chapter of *The Elementary Structures of Kinship* (1969:8), "it is easy to recognize *universality* as the criterion of nature, for what is *constant* in man falls necessarily beyond the scope of customs . . ." [emphasis added].

ological constants (see, for example, chapters 6-12 of *The Science of Culture*, White 1949). Although indisputable, it is unreasonable to move from this to the quite different but seemingly similar claim that one cannot explain myriad cultural differences in terms of human oedipality. It fails as an argument because no two Oedipus complexes are alike.[3]

Consider, for example, the impact of the "White argument" on Harris's theory about the worldwide importance for human affairs of various demo-econo-techno-environmental factors. Since all human groups have populations, exchange systems, tools and environments, these are universals. Given this and the time-honored line of thought being critiqued here, one would be forced to conclude that Harris should cease studying these "constants" because information about them will not yield answers to what he thinks is the most important question in the science of anthropology—namely, what causes cultural variation.[4]

---

[3]White, of course, is also attempting to show that anthropological researchers must grant certain variables strategic priority—a viewpoint that survives not only in the work of cultural materialists like Harris but also in the work of other cultural anthropologists who believe that adequate explanations of human actions can be achieved without a theory of the person (cf., Paul 1984).

[4]It must be acknowledged, of course, that variables like *population* differ from *oedipality* in several important ways. For one, population, by definition, is not the property of an individual. Similarly, a considerable amount of definitional dexterity would be required if one wished to say that an individual had a technology, an economy, or an environment. These variables are far more easily and typically understood to be properties of groups. For oedipality, however, the reverse is usually the case: typically it is thought of as being the property of individuals, although group values for a variable like oedipality obviously could be developed.

Second, it is *relatively* easy to develop valid and reliable measures of variables like *population* or even *population density*. Such features certainly have been measured many times for hundreds of years by (and for) groups all over the world. This is not to say there is no debate about particular measurement "how-to's" in demography, nor is this groundwork for the somewhat tempting but needless retort that "any fool can count people but it takes a psychoanalyst to measure oedipality." Rather, it simply acknowledges that we may expect more debate regarding how one is to measure oedipality than some other kinds of

(continued...)

By the same token, psychoanalysts could hardly have found Freud's ideas about oedipality useful if he had identified an important constant in human affairs. What made the idea important was that, with it, one could make sense of the diverse symptoms of equally diverse patients. True, Freud did think (perhaps erroneously at times) that oedipality was highly relevant in the lives of all his patients, but that does not transform the variable into a constant. For neurotics (and others), oedipality may be a "constant problem" but a constant problem does not a constant make.[5]

In short, although one cannot explain variation in terms of a constant and although oedipal experiences as well as oedipal derivatives are

---

[4](...continued)
variables, such as population density.

Even so, it would be a mistake to see these comments as a basis for concluding either that oedipality is not a useful variable for those wanting to differentiate human groups or that it neither can nor has been measured reliably and with some precision. Even anthropologists hostile to psychoanalysis have obtained data useful for making such distinctions, and they have been doing so for many years. One of Malinowski's greatest achievements, for example, was his account of the way Trobriand Islanders, as a group, were distinctive oedipally—a view only reinforced, by the way, by Spiro's ringing critique of the more polemical of Malinowski's objectives in that research (see, for example, Spiro 1982:162ff). And even Harris seems to have understood that some of his data support the suggestion that groups may be differentiated in oedipal terms (see Harris 1977:66—a point to be discussed again below).

Nevertheless, and for reasons not entirely clear to me (but see Spiro, 1982:174ff for some hints as to why this may be so), the definite article in the phrase "the Oedipus complex" seems to have an impact on people that is far more powerful—and misleading—than when it is used in phrases like "the population density," "the class structure," or "the IQ." It may, therefore, be wise, for a time at least, to utilize the less familiar but reasonably euphonious "oedipality" in places where one might usually expect to say "the Oedipus complex." It is this, in part, that prompts the inclusion of statement number 2 in the list above. That is, insofar as the word "the" in "the Oedipus complex" implies that oedipality is a constant, then the phrase is misleading and should be avoided.

[5]In a sense, oedipality and other such variables are "constant variables" (i.e., variables that are constantly important).

constantly in evidence in the human situation, it does not follow that oedipality is a constant that can be of no interest to those who, like Harris, wish to identify the causes of cultural variety.

Millions discovered with no oedipal complexes (Statements 4-5)

Over the years, Freud's premise about the universality of oedipality has been challenged on numerous grounds. Of these, none is more common than the claim that its status as a *scientific* principle may be doubted because, as a universal, there would be no individuals lacking an Oedipus complex and, therefore, that conclusions based on oedipal theory could not be falsified since the theory precludes the finding of counter cases. Although the grounds for such an argument have already been largely demolished by what has been said regarding oedipality as a variable, anthropologists and others remain fascinated by the possibility that individuals might be found who have no Oedipus complex. What motivates such a search is itself an interesting matter. Perhaps it is because so much human angst seems linked to oedipal experiences and strivings. Thus, the search for people who lack oedipal experiences may really amount to an attempt to see if it might be possible to identify the social conditions that would prevent oedipal conflict and unhappiness.

To put it another way, the universality of oedipality might still be questioned by those who, although they understand the variable nature of this factor in current human affairs, believe that any amount of oedipal conflict and striving is such a source of angst and unhappiness that, in the best of all possible worlds, it ought to be eliminated. From this perspective, oedipality is like crime or poverty—i.e., it may be a variable that so far has been found everywhere, but it still would be worthwhile trying to find instances when the value on this variable is zero. Anthropologists and others holding such a view may think of themselves as optimists who never stop hoping that somewhere people will be found who have managed to achieve this admittedly rare condition and so they continue to search.[6]

---

[6]Such searches have long been central to the anthropological endeavor. For (continued...)

For this and other reasons, most people I know express some surprise on being told that there are in fact millions—indeed millions and millions—of human beings who have had no oedipal experiences and/or who neither have nor have had an Oedipus complex. For many, the surprise is coupled with considerable puzzlement when it is added that thousands of such individuals have been studied intensely by psychologists and anthropologists (among others) and that, as a result of this research, a great deal is known about such people. And the mystery deepens still further when it is noted that by far the vast majority of these individuals were found to be quite normal—i.e., these Oedipusless individuals are neither psychopaths nor sociopaths.

If not abnormals, who are they? Why have they remained so obscure? Should not anthropologists be spreading the word about them in order to enhance the efforts of those trying to reduce social and psychic conflict and other unwanted products of oedipality? Perhaps. You be the judge. The millions of intensely-studied non-oedipal normal humans I have in mind are small children—*people* who are under 3 or so years of age.

For some years now, I have presented thoughts along these lines to colleagues and students. As can be imagined, I have encountered a wide variety of reactions to the denouement. Some smile and say something like "Oh sure; I forgot. Of course." Others, being well aware of the anthropological tradition of trotting out an obscure culture to refute any and all generalizations about human beings, say they thought I must have been thinking about some unknown tribe somewhere. Some, however, are clearly quite disappointed, often, it seems, because they have been holding fast to the hope that such people would show us all how to avoid oedipal conflict.[7]

---

[6](...continued)
psychological anthropologists, if not for the whole field, the precedent was established most forcefully, I would argue, by Margaret Mead's attempt to prove that there were adolescents who did not exhibit the "storm and stress" thought to be typical for persons at this "stage" of development.

[7]I have also been accused of playing a (mere) verbal trick. If this seems to be so, then I can respond only by saying that this certainly was not unintended. My (continued...)

But, given Freud's ontogenetic, developmental theory, one cannot completely avoid oedipality and remain healthy. Oedipus is about growth, about human maturation. Oedipality is no more avoidable or necessarily an abnormality (cf. Kohut 1984:27) than theories about human dentition can be about avoidable milktooth loss. In normal growth, oedipal experiences and, if you will, *an* Oedipus complex—i.e., one that is uniquely configured for each of us—is, from Freud's developmental perspective, inevitable.[8]

The oedipal period is that time-span during which an individual moves, psychologically, beyond the intra-psychically dyadic mother-child relationship. It is the period when the foundation is laid for life after having fully confronted, intra-psychically, the discovery that "real life" involves not only dyads (the mother-child dyad being primordial and prototypic) but triads (me, parent-of-same-gender and parent-of-opposite-gender being the prototype). As well, oedipality is about seeking and accepting emancipation, of achieving a sense of agency and responsibility and, perhaps most importantly, about developing a responsive and therefore responsible superego (Loewald 1979:758-61).

---

[7](...continued)
aim was to show, *experientially*, that the claims I am making are not about the views of some indefinite, perhaps less well-informed, "Others," but rather are about those very readers who feel "tricked." The "trick" will not work if one does not, to some extent, hold the views being critiqued. With the *experience* of being "tricked," therefore, the common "it may be true for them but it isn't true for me" escape is closed off. This too, of course, may contribute to the annoyance some people feel with the denouement.

[8]It used to puzzle me when I encountered people who thought Mead proved, with her research in Samoa, that adolescence was not a universal. It also used to amaze me that it took Mead, via her sojourn in the South Pacific, to show American psychologists that not all adolescents are troubled. Knowing now that people often confuse constant and universal and that many others are engaged in an almost wistful search for a culture without oedipality, these reactions to Mead's work are easier to understand. Given, however, Mead's knack for asking the right questions (and for "finding" the right data to answer them in the way she believed to be correct), one can only marvel that she never found a place where people passed through the Oedipal years without a trace of *angst*.

Oedipality is also about the continuing effort to be male or female. The formation and fleshing out of a gender identity is a lengthy process. In humans, the maturational course centrally involves becoming a male or female by repeated attempts to *be* male or female because "becoming" is in fact a succession of moments of "being." Accordingly, one of the potentially more painful aspects of the oedipal years is discovering that some of the most important of all the facets of *being* male or female are not only beyond one's reach and grasp but also are in fact actively denied us, especially by our parents. It is here, in the face of this frustration and disappointment, that we find children creating fantasies about seduction, murder, babies, castration and marriage.

It is incorrect to say, however, that to be human is to be oedipal because, quite simply, there are many humans who are not oedipal. Similarly, it is incorrect to suggest, as Harris (1977) does, that oedipality is found everywhere today because social conditions everywhere are now, and have been for some time, so stressful and at least potentially if not actually so warlike as to require the rearing of what Harris mistakenly calls "oedipal"—i.e., brutal—males. Harris errs, as do many others, in assuming that oedipality *per se* is a matter of where you are in the world when in fact it is primarily a matter of where you are in the human developmental process.

By much the same token, when Spiro says: "If there were a human society in which mothers did not have male consorts—so that the son had no adult rival for the love of the mother—in such a society the Oedipus complex (by definition) would not exist" (1982:162), it would be incorrect to conclude that oedipality is a universal because there are no consortless mothers. On the contrary, oedipality is a universal *and also* there are, in fact, millions upon millions of consortless mothers. There is, let me stress, no paradox here. That it appears paradoxical to so many is merely further evidence, though none is needed, of the adverse effects of the common but entirely unwarranted assumption that Freud claimed oedipality was a feature of all humans. However common, it is unwarranted because such a belief is fundamentally at odds with his *developmental* viewpoint.

If, however, you now find yourself asking who these consortless mothers are and why they have not been studied and widely publicized, I would at first respond only indirectly and suggest that both the question and the answer ought to sound familiar. If that did not work, I would then note that the consortless people I have in mind are mothers of children who are under about 3 years of age. And I would hasten to add that these mothers are not found only among the Nayar or certain Caribbean and American so-called matrifocal groups (cf. Spiro 1982: 162) nor are the many unwed American teenagers the mothers I have in mind. Rather, I mean to include *all* mothers—but (and this caveat is of central importance) from the viewpoint of their pre-oedipal children. And, although the point should be obvious, I might add for the sake of completeness that whether those mothers are male or female (Chodorow 1978) or have one spouse or ten or none is, for the point being made here, almost completely irrelevant because, from the pre-oedipal child's viewpoint, there are no parent-generation rivals (*yet*).

In short, we find oedipality when intrapsychic unconscious dyadicality gives way to intrapsychic unconscious triangularity. It is *not* true, therefore, that to be human is to be oedipal. Oedipality is a developmental emergent for all (normal) humans and, *therefore*, is not found in all people.

The origin of oedipality (Statement 6)

Harris asserts, in words of the sort that throughout his distinguished career have deservedly brought him both acclaim and opprobrium, that while Freud was "definitely on to something" in his attempt to link sex roles and aggression, "unfortunately his causal arrows were running backwards" (Harris 1977:65). "What is poppycock," he adds (ibid.), "is the idea that the oedipal situation is caused by human nature rather than by human cultures." In the midst of his essentially anti-psychoanalytic essay, however, Harris does voice at least one opinion that should not be dismissed as the idle musing of an anti-Freudian, cultural-materialist Johnny-one-note. The "Oedipus situation," he states, although "widespread if not universal," does have "*variable features*" (Harris 1977:66, emphasis added).

Unfortunately, instead of considering what the causes of the variablity in the oedipal situation might be—a question that fits squarely within his quasi-paradigmatic desire to account for the "origin, maintenance, and change of the global inventory of sociocultural differences and similarities" (Harris 1979:27), Harris merely asserts that the "Oedipus situation" is not part of human nature but, instead, is found everywhere because "all of the conditions for creating castration fears and penis envy are present in the [equally widespread] male supremacy complex" (1979:27)—a complex complex that he sees as "derivative of the attempt [made by all known human groups] to control ecological and reproductive pressures" (Harris 1977:65-66). Given this, Harris seems to be forced to conclude that "The Oedipus complex was not the cause of war; war was the cause of the Oedipus complex" (1977:65).

Although some may feel the urge simply to ignore such "poppycock," we would do well, I think, to acknowledge that Harris can be read as having raised an issue that psychoanalytic anthropologists are well prepared to probe with insight—namely, how cultural and oedipal variability are related. Thus, while Harris may perhaps be ignored insofar as he intends to explain the origin of oedipality *per se*, he is "on to something" insofar as he is asking for research about the origins of *variability* in the "oedipal situation."[9] To pursue the latter question, we will need to know a great deal more than we do now about the nature

---

[9]Given Harris's assessment of the work of Kardiner and the Whitings (see, for example, Harris 1968:422-463), some cultural materialists may see in my comments the basis for claiming victory in a long-standing debate. That is, some may read me as having granted not only that oedipality varies more-or-less directly with TEDE (techno-econo-demo-environmental) variables of the sort emphasized in cultural materialism, but also that the TEDE variables are the more powerful independent variables and that oedipality is merely a weak, dependent variable.

For those who read me this way, I need to note two things. First, in the absence of studies showing, in some detail, how TEDE variables account for variations in oedipality, claims about what causes changes in what would seem to be premature. It is for this reason, in part, that I refer, simply, to the need to find out how cultural and oedipal variability are *related*. Careful empirical inquiries into the questions raised by this debate would, of course, be most useful. I look forward to the day when cultural materialists and psychoanalytic anthropologists have embarked upon the necessary research.

Second, even if it can be shown that variations in oedipality are directly caused by variations in TEDE variables, the statements about oedipality of the sort made by Harris and cited in this paper (e.g., "The Oedipus complex was not the cause of war; war was the cause of the Oedipus complex") would still be misleading for reasons that have, I think, been spelled out fairly clearly in the body of this essay.

and amount of oedipal variability there is. In an insightful discussion, the import of which tends to be overshadowed by other parts of his widely discussed reassessment of Malinowski's data from the Trobriands, Spiro (1982:163-174) notes that oedipality varies in structure, intensity and outcome. This is a useful beginning, but it is only that. Much more theoretical and empirical work needs to be done.[10]

Freud's thought is culture-bound (Statement 7)

Anthropologists and others who are sensitive to the power of culture often express one version or another of what I propose to call the "psychoanalysis as culture-bound syndrome" critique—i.e., the claim that the value of psychoanalysis is, at best, limited because it is both a product and expression of Freud's particular, time- and place-bound, culture. Thus, Freud has been described as having produced a theoretical edifice that is both expressive of and consistent with what at the time was typical male misogyny, of having had a "failure of nerve" regarding the sexually abusive behavior of adults generally and, perhaps, of his father in particular, of having over-emphasized "sex" in part because he lived in a sexually repressive "Victorian" society, of having misunderstood the "myth" that names and (mis)informs his central organizing concept, of having generalized to all of humanity from a culture-bound myth that just happened to fit well the psyches of certain paternalistic Eastern Europeans, of having come up with a theory that gained acceptance only because it was consistent with bourgeois, capitalist familism, and so on through a seemingly endless catalogue of errors, distortions and their ostensible cultural and/or personal origins.

---

[10]After this paper was written, Gananath Obeyesekere's *The Work of Culture* (1990) was published. Although the book is about far more than oedipality, Obeyesekere does masterfully lay out in great detail many of the most basic variants of oedipality using some ethnographic material on family life in South Asia and a great deal of very rich material on the oedipal themes presented in the great myths, dramas, and rituals of South Asia. Another publication relevant to this point that appeared after this paper was written is Stanley Kurtz's fascinating and largely convincing reassessment of the Trobiand oedipal scene (Kurtz 1990). See also his forthcoming book *All the Mothers Are One: Hindu India and the Cultural Reshaping of Psychoanalysis*.

Clearly, these studies cannot be accepted or rejected as a class; their merits must be assessed individually. Some people however, do tend to reject such studies as a type on the grounds that the impact of culture on the theoretical shape of an *empirical science* can at most be trivial. Although such an argument might have had some credibility prior to the early 1960s and the work of scholars as different as Kuhn and Foucault, it simply is no longer sustainable. *All* scientific viewpoints, in both their details and general character, are expressive in numerous non-trivial ways of both the cultural context in which they emerge and of the psychological characteristics of those who develop and adopt them.[11]

Critics bent on discrediting an entire science have sometimes been unsparing in their exploitation of this fact. Some Marxists, for example, have attempted to discredit Darwinism by this means (a literature reviewed, all too favorably at times, in Sahlins 1977). Such efforts, however, tend to be fairly easy to recognize for what they are: extreme and, usually, desperate attempts to pillory a science by holding it up to a standard which no theory, including that of the authors of such critiques, could ever meet.

Nevertheless, this general line of attack, even in its most extreme forms, continues to appeal to the opponents of psychoanalysis—so much so, in fact, that more than a few of my students and colleagues have been taken aback not only by my willingness to accept some of these critiques but also by my insistence that psychoanalysis can only benefit from them. These days, however, with the work of (among others) Rieff (1959), Gallop (1982), Mitchell (1975), Sagan (1988), Foucault (1973, 1977, and 1979), Lerman (1986), Ellenberger (1970), Masson (1984), Balmary (1979), Vitz (1988), Rudnytsky (1987), Roazen (1971), Sulloway (1979), Lerman (1986), Krull (1986), Anzieu (1986), Gay (1978, 1986, 1987, and 1988), Deleuze and Guattari (1977) and Bakan (1958), the only reasonable view is not whether but what kind of influence Freud's personality and culture had upon the development of psychoanalysis. Perhaps more telling than the work of all these scholars, however, is the

---

[11]There are, now, many studies that document this both ethnographically and historically. Latour and Woolgar (1979), Traweek (1988), and Haraway (1989) are among those who have made this point recently and quite powerfully. Also on this point, see Spain (n.d.b.).

effect of Freud's theory itself on this argument. If one accepts Freud's theory, then one could not possibly deny that Freud's theoretical ideas were, at least in part, derivatives of his personality especially but also his culture.[12]

Two things tend to be lost sight of by those who worry that the entire theory could be destroyed by accepting such a conclusion. First, Freud's ideas were not merely unchecked personal and/or idiosyncratic fantasies but were and still are rather routinely subjected to various often successful empirical checks by literally hundreds of other psychoanalytic researchers (for reviews of this literature see Fisher and Greenberg 1985; and Kline 1981). It may be presumed, therefore, that the ideas that survive these efforts reflect far more than fin-de-siècle Vienna or Freud the man. Second, Freud is not the whole of psychoanalysis. Despite the fact that it often takes on organizational qualities not unlike some religions, modern psychoanalysis is no more a Freudian cult than modern biology is a Darwinian one. The reasons are the same in both cases: there is more to each field than the legacy of the explicator of its now dominant paradigm.

This is not to say that the authors cited above have correctly identified the personal and cultural sources of Freud's insights. This would be impossible since the results of their efforts are mutually contradictory, and explicitly so. Debates as to the relative merits of these studies will surely rage for years. In the meantime, however, one trend needs to be noted: too many of these works express or entail the belief that the entire edifice will be wrecked if some cracks can be found in the Freudian foundation. Since Freud is not the whole of psychoanalysis, such attempts to discredit the psychoanalytic paradigm are no more likely to succeed than would an effort to show that modern American anthropology is fatally flawed because Boas's viewpoint has roots in, say, a sword phobia.

---

[12]For those for whom textual grounds for this claim might be of use, one could consider Brenner (1982) who contends (see pp. 213-253) that all cultural products, and this surely would include scientific theories, are compromise formations and hence are expressions of a personal nature about "nature."

Sigismundu Freud-san (Statement 8)

What if Freud had been Japanese and not Viennese? Would psychoanalysis be essentially the same as the discipline created in late nineteenth century Vienna or would it be different? Although such questions are usually dismissed as sophomoric invitations to idle speculation, certain historical materials make it possible not only to explore this possibility more realistically but also to illustrate more concretely the general issues raised above regarding statement number 7.

To begin, we must first pause to note the obvious: Freud was often unable to accept certain psychoanalytic ideas when he was first exposed to them. In many cases, of course, his reaction was grounded in his often far greater experience or for other similar "good" reasons. At other times, however, his resistance appears to have been directly related to the way in which his personality blinded him to the utility of the new idea. His stormy relationships with Adler, Jung, and Rank (among others) are well known in this regard. When these early followers were seen as having rejected one or another central psychoanalytic premise, Freud responded by rejecting them and their revisionist ideas. These events, which were so important for the history of psychoanalysis, are now routinely interpreted as being at least partly the outcome of aspects of Freud's character (e.g., his perhaps excessive narcissism). Although cultural issues are invoked sometimes, they seldom are depicted as the key factors.[13]

By the early 1930s, however, Freud's fame was worldwide and, accordingly, he was attracting eager listeners from quite different cultures. Little is known at present of the ideas offered by these early and truly "foreign" supporters of psychoanalysis. The experience of one

---

[13]One wonders, of course, why this should be so. I suspect this is due in part to the tendency of historians and other scholars to assume that Jung, Rank, Fliess, and others in the inner-circle, by virtue of being so close to Freud, shared his culture. Culture, in other words, does not become an important explanatory factor until the differences are much greater than those characterizing Freud's associates. That this is inadequate from an anthropological viewpoint is, I trust, self-evident. At other times, however, culture *is* considered but it goes by other names (e.g., as "history" or "religion").

such visitor, however, graphically illustrates how cultural differences could have but apparently did not enrich Freud's theoretical viewpoint.

In 1932, the Japanese psychoanalyst Heisaku Kosawa presented a paper to Freud, in German, entitled "Two kinds of guilt feelings: The Ajase complex [of the Japanese]" (see Kosawa 1931). In it, Kosawa described what he believed was a distinctive Japanese form of guilt that was at the heart of a psychological complex "peculiar to the Japanese" (Okonogi 1978:93). I know of no record telling us specifically about Freud's response to Kosawa's paper. At this point, all that can be said with confidence is that there was no reference to this idea or to Kosawa or to the Ajase complex in the psychoanalytic literature until a very few years ago. I believe this may well reflect what should be a sobering fact: that, for reasons of cultural background, Freud and Kosawa simply did not understand each other.

From the recent account provided by Kosawa's student (Okonogi 1978 and 1979), it would appear that Kosawa saw the Ajase complex as an *alternative* to the Oedipus complex—i.e., that it was the Ajase complex and not the Oedipus complex that was central to the psychic life of the Japanese. Given Freud's behavior in previous basically similar circumstances (one thinks, for example, of his response to Rank's doubts about the centrality of the Oedipus complex), one can easily imagine how Freud would have reacted to such a proposal. I can be less speculative, however, by describing *my* encounter with Kosawa's theoretical suggestions.

I first came to know about Kosawa's work in 1979, when Shusuke Yagi, then an anthropology graduate student, suggested I should read the papers by Okonogi. He made the suggestion after a course in which I had lectured about the universality of oedipality. He thought (and hoped) that Okonogi's papers would convince me that such universality claims rested on thin ice (at best). I read the papers with interest and distinctly remember thinking that they did not really challenge psychoanalytic theory. Note the shift I had made: from having been presented with Okonogi's papers as a challenge to claims about the universality of oedipality to seeing the papers as a failed attempt to challenge psychoanalysis as a whole. This was the first of my several misunderstandings of Kosawa's work.

My student soon pointed out my mistake and so I began to reexamine the essays and, recalling the title of Kosawa's paper, to focus on his discussion of the two forms of guilt. For reasons having to do with assumptions I then had regarding the pre-oedipal roots of shame, I saw Kosawa's comments about the centrality of non-oedipal guilt as "really" about the centrality of shame in Japan—a claim that, of course, was anything but novel to an anthropologist. This was my second misunderstanding, but at the time I did not appreciate this because I was so interested in the possibility that I had in my hands not only a Japanese but also a psychoanalytic source that seemed to support Benedict's still controversial view that Japan was a shame culture.

Several years went by. I then happened to read a psychoanalytic paper describing the difference between structural and object relations conflict (Dorpat 1976). Although the full impact was not immediate, I did sense that the theoretical distinction Dorpat was making resonated with the Okonogi papers. Eventually, I managed to understand that the supposedly unique Japanese form of guilt that Kosawa had discussed with Freud in 1932 was the same as the ostensibly new form of guilt Dorpat had identified forty years later. This guilt, which Dorpat saw as the product of "object relations conflict," was all but equated by him with "separation guilt" which was first described, in 1965, by Modell (Modell 1965; cited by Dorpat).

At this point, I felt I finally had understood Kosawa and Okonogi and, moreover, that I also could more readily understand why Freud had been unable to appreciate fully the significance of the theoretical ideas Kosawa had presented (if in fact that is what happened; the lack of a concrete record on this point forces me to rely on what is clearly only an inference, however plausible it may be). Freud's cultural background, I believe, led him to privilege Oedipus and structural conflict over Ajase and object relations conflict. Using the terminology of Okonogi's account of the difference between the Ajase and Oedipus complexes, I suspect Freud would have had difficulty fully appreciating Kosawa because he was, by virtue of the accident of his birth, deeply—one might well say "all too"—familiar with the "paternal principle latent in the depths of the Western mind" (Okonogi 1978:96) and far less familiar with "the [Japanese] maternal principle of forgiving and being forgiven, which is diametrically opposed to the Western paternal principle of punishing sin and making the sinner atone" (Okonogi:94-95).[14]

The Ajase complex, with its emphasis on dyadic mother-child ties and murderous rage directed at the mother by the child when his/her idealized image of her is lost (as it inevitably must be), gets its name from a Japanized Indian-Buddhist story about a young prince named Ajase. This story, which appears to have played much the same role for Kosawa that the Oedipus dramas did for Freud, depicts a complex that stands in relation to the so-called pre-oedipal years as the Oedipus complex does to the oedipal years. Because the pre-oedipal years impinge so significantly on the later oedipal ones, it can now be appreciated that the distinctive particulars of one's Ajase complex will necessarily and significantly shape the course of one's development in the oedipal period.[15]

---

[14]Separation guilt and object relations conflict clearly are concepts Freud could have understood. Indeed, Modell's comparison of his formulations to Freud's suggestion in *Civilization and Its Discontents* that guilt could be present before structuralization of the superego (Modell 1965:327) makes this a very reasonable claim. Even so, it remains a fact that psychoanalysis in the 1930s was *far* from having a coherent and well-articulated version of what we now know as object relations theory. Indeed, there are many who would argue that this worthy goal still eludes us (see Hamilton 1988, however, for a useful general discussion). That this was the case is, I am suggesting, at least in part a consequence of the character of European culture at the time Freud was developing his version of psychoanalysis.

[15]In other contexts (e.g., in reaction to Spain n.d.a.), some have sensed that the Kosawa-Okonogi formulation of the Ajase Complex, like Freud's regarding Oedipus, was biased along gender lines. I am not completely certain just what prompts this reaction because the issue at the heart of the complex is equally relevant for both boys and girls. Although one of the most dramatic and, therefore, clearest aspects of the Ajase complex does involve a wish by *Prince* (not Princess) Ajase to kill his mother or at least to be rid (i.e., independent) of her once he discovers that he is not her only love or purpose in life, the key feature of the complex is the separation guilt felt by Ajase because he violated an internalized norm or expectations about seeking independence. Clearly, both girls and boys will face this conflict as they mature. Chodorow's observations (1978) about the impact of having females for mothers do, however, provide

(continued...)

I am speaking here of a *universal* complex and, in this, am perhaps going beyond what Okonogi might say since he seems to perceive Kosawa's view as entailing the claim that the Ajase complex is "peculiar to the Japanese" (1978:93). In contrast to this, I am suggesting that this is *not* a uniquely Japanese complex even though it may well be the one that, for many Japanese, is the greater source of stress and unconscious guilt.[16]

---

[15](...continued)
excellent grounds for both expecting and explaining differences in the intensity and outcome of the Ajase complexes of boys and girls.

[16]This particular claim needs to be explored empirically far more than it has been to date. The research of others, however, seems to me to provide good grounds for expecting it to be supported. One study by Lebra (1983) contains references to (an undefined) "Japanese version of guilt" (p.207) that, from the context, appears to emerge "from the awareness that one might possibly betray the social group one belongs to" (Doi 1971:49, as cited by Lebra). Similar comments about special forms of guilt can be found in DeVos's work. His projective test data, for example, prompt him to suggest that guilt in Japan is often due "to the realization of having injured a love object toward whom one feels some degree of unconscious hostility" (DeVos 1973 [1960]:148)—an event very nearly the same as the one that led to Ajase's guilt.

Issues regarding the universality claim are broached by Dale (1986), who criticizes the Kosawa-Okonogi formulation for being part of a wider effort to keep alive the "myth of Japanese uniqueness." For this and other reasons, therefore, it is of more than passing interest that there are additional grounds for support of this claim in the work of others from nonwestern cultures besides Japan. Of special interest in this regard is Bouhdiba's *Sexuality in Islam* (Bouhdiba 1985). In a stunning concluding chapter, entitled "In the kingdom of the mothers," he proposes a psychological complex "specific to Arabo-Muslim culture" (1985:228)—a syndrome he refers to as the Judar complex after a tale, also with roots in India, involving the struggle of a boy for independence from his mother. Research efforts by Kakar (e.g., 1978) also point to the great salience of the Ajase years among South Asians (although he does not use the term or cite the Kosawa-Okonogi literature). Roland (1988) also compares Japan and India in ways that echo the points being made here; he refers to Kosawa's theory but makes rather different use of it than I do.

(continued...)

This discussion of the Ajase complex has been introduced to make two points. In addition to lending cross-cultural concreteness to the claim that Freud's thought was limited by his culture and personality, it has value also because it resonates with the observations of numerous analysts who have suggested, directly and indirectly, that Freud's conception of oedipality is far from being free of the limitations of his personal qualities and cultural milieu—e.g., Loewald (1979), Schafer (1960 and 1974), Sagan (1988) and many others from within psychoanalysis (not to mention scores from outside it). Freud's conception of superego, for reasons that now seem oddly self-evident and even unexceptional but which in fact were elusive and are still being debated, entails an over-brutalized conception of human nature. Harris's contention that war causes oedipality is only one of the more prominent anthropological ramifications of Freud's error. Similarly, Freud's claims about the centrality of oedipality in human affairs is also, for complex but now somewhat more evident reasons, an error. It is now clear, therefore and in a way that it neither was nor could have been to Freud, that we must understand *both* Ajase and Oedipus if we are ever to fathom the human experience (again, see Loewald 1979, for a powerful expression of a similar point).

---

[16](...continued)

These and related issues are discussed in greater detail in Spain n.d.a. In that paper, I suggested (among other things) that it would be useful to cease referring to the period prior to the oedipal years as the *pre*oedipal period. That this marked term is in such widespread use and was an outgrowth of the impact of Freud's culture on this theoretical viewpoint is no justification for continuing to use it when there is a perfectly good unmarked term for this developmental period—namely, the Ajase period. It is not a period notable merely because it precedes oedipality (although this is what is implied by its current name); it is significant in its own right (cf. Loewald 1979).

Finally, given the problems that derive from using the definite article in phrases like "the Oedipus complex" (see footnote 4, above), it would seem only logical that "the" should also be avoided when one is about to say something like "the Ajase complex." The problem is finding the appropriate word. Although not yet common, the word oedipality is at least moderately euphonious, but ajasity. . . ? I am indebted to Bob Bergman for pointing out this problem and for suggesting ajasity (with no enthusiasm whatsoever).

In sum, Freud, like so many others, found it difficult to appreciate fully the value of theoretical ideas and critiques that were deeply rooted in and expressive of dominant psychological themes characteristic of other, contrasting individuals and cultural traditions. His personal and cultural scotoma were, *as ours are*, virtually inevitable. They are surmountable, of course, but first they must be brought into consciousness. That it took nearly 40 years longer for western than non-western Freudians to provide a well-developed formulation of Ajase guilt shows how significant such blind spots can be.

Conclusion: Oedipus or edifice?

In *Psychoanalyzing Psychoanalysis*, Balmary suggests that the faults of psychoanalysis as a whole can be identified by discovering the "faults of the [founding] father." "Psychoanalysis," she opines, "is an edifice in which questions are posed at every floor. But the architect is dead. We have no alternative but to examine the foundations and to try to understand" (Balmary 1982:5). Were psychoanalysis an edifice, this might be so, but her choice of metaphor, while common enough regarding the sciences, is infelicitous in this instance. Her contention entails the assumption that Freud *is* psychoanalysis. Psychoanalysis, in my opinion, is and must be far more than Freudian thought; by the same token, it also must be more widely acknowledged that it is far more than a theory about oedipal conflict. Freud thought of himself as a revolutionary and, in this context, compared himself to Darwin. This apt observation should perhaps be taken more seriously by psychoanalysts and psychoanalytic anthropologists. Darwin's place in biology is assured but Darwin is not biology. Indeed, he is not even evolution. The same must be said of Freud—and Oedipus—in relation to psychoanalysis.

In short, Freud is not a dead architect. He did not lay the foundation for what has turned out to be an intellectual Leaning Tower of Pisa. Psychoanalysis is not an edifice wrecked. If we need metaphors, then perhaps we ought to reconsider his own. Freud was an archaeologist. He was, as Rudnytsky (1987) so forcefully demonstrates, an Oedipus digging hard for self-knowledge.[17] That we can now see that he failed to excavate the site fully does not mean we must abandon the effort altogether. Indeed, as Balmary herself shows, it is only by the methods Freud developed for such excavations that we can appreciate how incompletely he probed . . . and how much more there is to discover.

References

Anzieu, Didier. 1986. *Freud's Self-Analysis* (Peter Graham, trans.). Madison, CN: International Universities Press [orig. 1975].

Bakan, David. 1958. *Sigmund Freud and the Jewish Mystical Tradition.* Boston: Beacon Press.

Balmary, Marie. 1979. *Psychoanalyzing Psychoanalysis: Freud and the Hidden Fault of the Father*. (Ned Lukacher, trans.). Baltimore: Johns Hopkins University Press (1982).

Bouhdiba, Abdelwahab. 1985. *Sexuality in Islam* (Alan Sheridan, trans.) London: Routledge & Kegan Paul.

Brenner, Charles. 1982. *The Mind in Conflict*. New York: International Universities Press.

Chodorow, Nancy. 1978. *The Reproduction of Mothering: Psychoanalysis and the Sociology of Gender*. Berkeley: University of California Press.

Dale, Peter N. 1986. *The Myth of Japanese Uniqueness*. New York: St. Martin's Press.

Deleuze, Gilles, and Felix Guattari. 1977. *Anti-Oedipus: Capitalism and Schizophrenia*. (Robert Hurley, Mark See, and Helen R. Lane, trans.). New York: Viking Press [orig. 1972].

DeVos, George. 1973. "Some Observations of Guilt in Relation to Achievement and Arranged Marriage." In George A. DeVos, ed.,

[17]And in this context, it may be hypothesized that Kosawa may well have been an Ajase, fighting hard to balance his urge to merge with his desire for guiltless separation.

Socialization for Achievement: Essays on the Cultural Psychology of the Japanese. Berkeley: University of California Press.

Doi, L. Takeo. 1971. *Amae No Kozo* [The Structure of Amae]. Tokyo: Kobundo.

Dorpat, Theodore L. 1976. "Structural Conflict and Object Relations Conflict." *Journal of the American Psychoanalytic Association* 24:855-874.

Ellenberger, Henri F. 1970. *The Discovery of the Unconscious: The History and Evolution of Dynamic Psychiatry*. New York: Basic Books.

Fisher, Seymour, & Greenberg, Roger, P. 1985. *The Scientific Credibility of Freud's Theories and Therapy*. New York: Columbia University Press.

Foucault, Michel. 1973. *The Order of Things: An Archaeology of the Human Sciences*. New York: Vintage Books.

_________. 1977. *Madness and Civilization: A History of Insanity in the Age of Reason*. London: Tavistock.

_________. 1979. *The History of Sexuality, Vol. I: An Introduction*. London: Allen Lane.

Fox, Robin. 1967. "*Totem and Taboo* Reconsidered." In E. Leach, ed., *The Structural Study of Myth and Totemism* (pp. 161-178). London: Tavistock.

Gallop, Jane. 1982. *The Daughter's Seduction: Feminism and Psychoanalysis*. Ithaca: Cornell University Press.

Gay, Peter. 1978. *Freud, Jews and Other Germans: Masters and Victims in Modernist Culture*. New York: Oxford University Press.

_________. 1984 and 1986. *The Bourgeois Experience: Victoria to Freud*. (two vols.). New York: Oxford University Press.

_________. 1987. *A Godless Jew: Freud, Atheism, and the Making of Psychoanalysis*. New Haven, CT: Yale University Press.

Hamilton, N. Gregory. 1988. *Self and Others: Object Relations Theory in Practice*. Northvale, NJ: Jason Aronson, Inc.

Haraway, Donna J. 1989. *Primate Visions: Gender, Race and Nature in the World of Modern Science*. London: Routledge, Chapman and Hall, Inc.

Harris, Marvin. 1968. *The Rise of Anthropological Theory*. New York: Thomas Y. Crowell Company.

_________. 1977. *Cannibals and Kings: The Origins of Cultures*. New York: Random House.

_________. 1979. *Cultural Materialism: The Struggle for a Science of Culture*. New York: Random House.

Kakar, Sudhir. 1978. *The Inner World: A Psychoanalytic Study of Childhood and Society in India*. London: Oxford University Press.

Kline, Paul. 1972. *Fact and Fantasy in Freudian Theory*. London: Methuen.

Kohut, Heinz. 1984. *How Does Analysis Cure?* Arnold Goldberg, ed. Chicago: University of Chicago Press.

Kosawa, Heisaku. 1931. "Zaiaku—Ishiki No Nishu—Ajase Conprekkusu. [Two Kinds of Guiilt Feelings—Ajase Complex]. *Koryo* (The Magazine of the Department of Medicine, Tohoku Imperial University). Reprinted in *Gendai No Esupuri*, 148:166-173.

Kroeber, A. L. 1920. "Totem and Taboo: An Ethnologic Psychoanalysis." *American Anthropologist* 22:48-55.

_________. 1939. "Totem and Taboo in Retrospect." *The American Journal of Sociology* 45(3):446-451.

Krull, Marianne. 1979. *Freud and His Father*. (Arnold J. Pomerans, trans.). New York: Norton.

Kuhn, Thomas. 1962. *The Structure of Scientific Revolutions*. Chicago: University of Chicago Press.

Kurtz, Stanley N. 1990. "Polysexualization: A New Approach to Oedipus in the Trobriands." *Ethos* 19:68-101.

_________. (in press). *All the Mothers Are One: Hindu India and the Cultural Reshaping of Psychoanalysis*. New York: Columbia University Press.

Latour, Bruno, and Steve Woolgar. 1979. *Laboratory Life: The Social Construction of Scientific Facts*. Beverley Hills, CA: Sage Publishing Co.

Lebra, Takie Sugiyama. 1983. "Shame and Guilt: A Psychocultural View of the Japanese Self." *Ethos* 11:192-209.

Loewald, Hans W. 1979. "The Waning of the Oedipus Complex." *Journal of the American Psychoanalytic Association* 27:751-775.

Lerman, Hannah. 1986. *A Mote in Freud's Eye: From Psychoanalysis to the Psychology of Women*. New York: Springer.

Lévi-Strauss, Claude. 1963. "The Structural Study of Myth." In *Structural Anthropology* (pp. 206-231). (C. Jacobson and B.G. Schoepf, trans.). New York: Basic Books [orig., 1958].

_________. 1969. *The Elementary Structures of Kinship*. (J.H. Bell, J.R. von Sturmer, trans.). R. Needham, ed. Boston: Beacon Press [orig., 1949].

Masson, Jeffrey Moussaieff. 1984. *The Assault on Truth: Freud's Suppression of the Seduction Theory*. New York: Farrar, Straus, and Giroux.

Mitchell, Juliet. 1975. *Psychoanalysis and Feminism: Freud, Reich, Laing, and Women*. New York: Vintage.

Modell, Arnold H. 1965. "On Having the Right to a Life: An Aspect of the Superego's Development." *International Journal of Psycho-Analysis* 46:323-331.

Obeyesekere, Gananath. 1990. *The Work of Culture: Symbolic Transformation in Psychoanalysis and Anthropology*. Chicago: The University of Chicago Press.

Okonogi, Keigo. 1978. "The Ajase Complex of the Japanese (1)." *Japan Echo* V(4):88-105.

_________. 1979. "The Ajase Complex of the Japanese (2)." *Japan Echo* VI(1):104-118.

Paul, Robert A. 1976. "Did the Primal Crime Take Place?" *Ethos* 4:311-352.

_________. 1984. "Editorial." *Ethos* 12:99-104.

Rieff, Philip. 1959. *Freud: The Mind of the Moralist*. Chicago: University of Chicago Press.

Roazen, Paul. 1971. *Freud and His Followers*. New York: New American Library.

Roland, Alan. 1988. *In Search of Self in India and Japan: Toward a Cross-Cultural Psychology*. Princeton, NJ: Princeton University Press.

Rudnytsky, Peter L. 1987. *Freud and Oedipus*. New York: Columbia University Press.

Sagan, Eli. 1988. *Freud, Women, and Morality: The Psychology of Good and Evil*. New York: Basic Books.

Sahlins, Marshall. 1977. *The Use and Abuse of Biology: An Anthropological Critique of Sociobiology*. Chicago: University of Chicago Press.

Schafer, Roy. 1960. "The Loving and Beloved Superego in Freud's Structural Theory." *Psychoanalytic Study of the Child* 15:163-188.

_________. 1974. "Problems in Freud's Psychology of Women." *Journal of the American Psychoanalytic Association* 22:459-485.

Spain, David H. n.d. a. "White Knight vs. Trojan Horse or, On the Dispensibility of the Term "Pre-Oedipal." Manuscript.

_________. n.d.b. "Anxieties about Hypotheses and Hypotheses about Anxiety: Steps to a Psychocultural Reading of Method in the Human Sciences." Paper presented at the 1988 Annual Meeting of the American Anthropological Association, Phoenix, AZ.

Spiro, Melford E. 1982. *Oedipus in the Trobriands*. Chicago: The University of Chicago Press.

Sulloway, Frank J. 1979. *Freud: Biologist of the Mind*. New York: Basic Books.

Traweek, Sharon. 1988. *Beamtimes and Lifetimes: The World of High Energy Physics*. Cambridge: Harvard University Press.

Vitz, Paul C. 1988. *Sigmund Freud's Christian Unconscious*. New York: The Guilford Press.

Wallace, Edwin R., IV. 1983. *Freud and Anthropology: A History and Reappraisal*. New York: International Universities Press.

White, Leslie. 1949. *The Science of Culture: A Study of Man and Civilization*. New York: Grove Press.

Chapter Nine

Psychoanalysis and Materialism: Do They Mix?[1]

Allen Johnson

Anthropologists have historically been cautious about embracing materialism and, as we shall see, this has certainly been true in the anthropological response to Freud. For my own part, I have never felt that psychoanalysis excluded or was incompatible with the materialist approaches of anthropologists, including cultural evolutionism, evolutionary biology, ecological anthropology, and Marxism. Indeed, I came to psychoanalysis from cultural ecology, and one of the appeals to me of psychoanalysis from the beginning of my clinical training (at the Southern California Psychoanalytic Institute) was its firm grounding in human biology and its concern with the problem of adaptation.

I had clear evidence early on, however, that others do view psychoanalysis and materialism as an unlikely partnership. Nearly every one of my anthropological colleagues who knew of my work in cultural ecology expressed outspoken surprise on learning I had undertaken psychoanalytic training: the most common question was, "Why did you do that?" But the implicit question was, Why have you gone off in an entirely different direction? The bioecological bases of Freud's thought are, perhaps, not apparent to those who have not studied him closely, or else people may have thought that modern psychoanalysis has cast off such nineteenth

---

[1]The title of this paper was suggested by David Spain and the subtitle emerged from our discussion about how to signal our sense that the recent trend away from materialist approaches in anthropology has affected psychoanalytic anthropology as well.

century baggage. Of course, much of the surprise behind the question might simply have reflected a widespread opinion of psychoanalysis, as though the real question were: "Why did a sensible fellow like you do something crazy like that?"

Of more relevance is the strong theoretical move in anthropology over the past ten or fifteen years away from positivism toward relativism, reflexivity, and ultimately, "postmodern deconstructionism" (Shweder 1991:109). These trends have led away from efforts to locate the causes of cultural phenomena in biology, ecology, or even in interactions between the self and the environment. Causality itself has come to be viewed as an outmoded concept, and culture is seen as essentially independent of biology, like some sort of alien lens placed between the individual and his nature such that he never perceives his own biological make-up except through this distorting lens. The lens itself comes from somewhere else, say History or Creativity, and, being free from biology, distorts it in essentially random ways.

In this paper I examine the importance of biologically based materialism in Freud's thought, and argue that it is essential to his contribution. I have no wish to question the value of or turn the clock back on the hermeneutic advances of recent years in anthropology. But I hold that psychoanalytic anthropology (and psychoanalysis itself) should not lose touch with the materialist vision either.

The problem

Freud's tendency to find explanations for human practices in biological sources has always met with disagreement, both in psychoanalysis and in anthropology. It is this tendency to be a biological determinist (but not necessarily a biological reductionist), that I will call "materialism" in this paper. By materialism I mean a theoretical orientation in the social sciences which seeks to explain patterns of human thought and behavior by reference to fundamental biological needs relentlessly clamoring for fulfillment. The upwelling biological impulses to satisfy needs for food, shelter, defense, and sexual reproduction are referred to by materialists as primary causes of a huge array of human phenomena, from systems of technology to social and political organization and even value systems and religious beliefs.

This materialism is not identical to materialism in the physical sciences (Barzun 1958; Bohm 1957), although both are related in being largely deterministic world views that leave little room for human choice or creativity in shaping the world. The use of the term in anthropology does not stress so much the original materialist idea that all nature is composed of sheer matter, without vital force, spirit, or purpose but rather stresses the role of biological evolution, adaptation, and need fulfillment in explaining cultural phenomena. This anthropological materialism takes many forms, from explicitly biogenetic explanations, as in sociobiology or evolutionary biology (Williams 1981), to the also very biological "human ecology" (Moran 1979), to the less deterministic "cultural ecology," which may be very eclectic (Johnson 1982). Marx, of course, described himself as a materialist and some Marxists in anthropology follow him in this regard; many Marxists in anthropology, however, are now "structural Marxists" who disavow the primacy of biological/ecological causality and thus are not materialists (Friedman 1974).

Freud the materialist. Freud was a materialist in my sense of a theorist who refers to biological processes to explain patterns of human thought and behavior. To avoid misunderstanding, it might be better to say that he used materialist reasoning, just as he used structuralist (de George and de George 1972:xvi-xvii) and dialectical (Murphy 1971:128) reasoning, yet he was never merely a materialist, structuralist, or dialectician.

Freud's materialism had two facets. One was his stress upon the fundamental importance of instinctual life, and especially upon sexual pleasure as a motivation for behavior. Freud was more prepared than many later writers, within psychoanalysis as well as anthropology, to view human behavior as biologically determined. In *Civilization and its Discontents* (Freud 1930), as elsewhere, he locates the source of human suffering and neurosis in the intrinsic, unavoidable clash between biology (id impulses) and culture (superego controls). The biological part is given: we cannot eliminate the needs that clamor within us. We can try to control or deflect them, but (on the famous archaeological analogy; Freud 1930:69) they never disappear; they remain in the foundations of our character and will out, one way or another.

The second aspect of his materialism is found in his explanation of why superego controls are just as inevitable as id impulses. For Freud, human biology is to a considerable degree antagonistic to the maintenance of social life and cultural community. Powerful, biologically rooted passions like lust, greed, and violent self-assertion would destroy the sociocultural order. Yet, that order is necessary if humans are to survive. Thus, Freud takes for granted the materialist tenet that culture is part of humankind's adaptive tool-kit: with culture, we become "Prosthetic Gods" (Freud 1930:92), capable of considerable mastery over nature.

Thus, Freud was a late nineteenth century version of both an evolutionary biologist (there is a human nature that has resulted from biological evolution) and a cultural materialist (culture is adaptive and human survival depends on it). Although what he added with his concepts of repression, the unconscious, and the mechanisms of defence may have alienated him forever from both evolutionary biologists and cultural materialists, that does not change the fact of his underlying materialism.

Freud's materialism, holding both id impulses and superego controls to be necessary and inevitable, accounts for his fundamentally tragic view of the human condition. All animals must suffer pain and frustration, but at least they live in harmony with their own natures. Humans cannot live except in society, which cannot survive except in opposition to human nature. Thus humans have the tragic fate that they must live at odds with themselves. The Oedipus complex is the prototype of this inevitable clash of incompatible necessities.

Rejection of materialism. Both within psychoanalysis and among generally sympathetic anthropologists there has been a persistent erosion of Freud's biological determinism. Although Malinowski (1927) accepted the idea of "nuclear complexes" arising from family life, he rejected the idea that in all cases the complex had to be oedipal. This challenged the idea of a pan-human, inherited Oedipus complex, replacing it with culturally flexible, locally adapted nuclear complexes of unknown number and variety. We will return to this idea in the section below called "Ecological/Functionalist Approaches."

Psychoanalytic revisionists took a similar stance: the Oedipus complex was not a human universal but a culturally (historically) specific response to hierarchical, competitive society: the Greek Oedipus himself was caught in the transition from egalitarian matriarchal society to stratified patriarchal society (Fromm 1948) or suffered from a homosexually abusive father (Devereux 1953); oedipal strife today, as well as sibling rivalry, simply reflect the hierarchical competitiveness of modern capitalist society, not human nature (Horney 1937); indeed, some societies, such as the Marquesas, do not have an Oedipus complex (Kardiner 1939:246).

These and other critiques of Freud's oedipal determinism are often quite explicit about shifting the blame for oedipal conflict from the innocent child to the parents or society at large. Hence, in addition to the conditions of patriarchy and capitalism, our attention is drawn to the Laius Complex (Devereux 1953) and to Jocasta's complicity (Bross 1988). The underlying feeling seems to be that if the Oedipus complex is universal and rooted in human biology, then each of us has very little freedom to avoid the complex and the blame that comes with harboring homicidal and incestuous impulses toward family members. On the other hand, if oedipal feelings are only brought about by the child's experience in certain types of society, then: first, I may not have oedipal feelings at all, since my family may have been the sort that does not cause oedipal feelings; second, if I do have oedipal feelings, they are not my fault but the result of my bad treatment at the hands of parents and society; and, third, to whatever degree I do have oedipal feelings, they are not biologically determined and may indeed be changed through new interpersonal experiences and reconstituted personal meanings.

It should be apparent that one constant element in these revisions of Freud has been the Nature vs. Nurture controversy. Freud took, or has been treated as if he took, the Nature pole, while the revisionists have taken the Nurture pole. In anthropology, Nurture is largely Culture, and the anthropological response to Freud has had the effect, even in the case of friendly revisions, of weakening the role that biology is seen to have in human behavior while strengthening the role ascribed to culture and to personal choice. Thus, among some psychoanalysts and psychoanalytic anthropologists, the response to Freud has been an enthusiastic acceptance of much of his thought along with a persistent watering down of its materialist content.

Materialism in psychoanalytic anthropology

Insofar as this move signifies the sloughing off of outmoded aspects of nineteenth century materialism, and a growth toward richer conceptions of what it is to be human, it is an improvement. For example, Freud seems at times to reduce general qualities such as the desire for affection to the narrower biological impulse of sexual drive, as he was criticized for doing from the earliest days of the psychoanalytic movement (Roazen 1974:253-4). Still, we must ask what we may be losing in not pursuing paths of research indicated by Freud's materialism, which was as central to his genius as any of his other philosophical commitments.

I will organize my comments around three very different kinds of materialism, two of which we have already introduced and the third of which we have hinted at: first, most controversially, is the possibility that features of our behavior, including not only impulses and desires but also aspects of symbolic and fantasy life, are biostructurally based, hard-wired in the human genome; next is the ecological-functionalist idea that adaptation to particular environments at specific technological levels sets the basic conditions under which child development takes place and character structure is formed; and last is the Marxian dialectical materialist idea that class relations in the political economy are embedded in and require such character attributes as competitiveness, dominance, and loyalty to help maintain unequal access to the means of production, reproduction and exchange.

Biostructuralism. This first type of materialism may be the most difficult to defend. On the one hand, readers may question whether biostructuralism is a form of materialism, and on the other hand whether it has any role to play in a psychoanalytic anthropology. To deal with the first problem very briefly, biological structures, to the extent that we can demonstrate that they exist and influence cultural behavior, presumably came into existence according to the principles of evolutionary biology. That is, they reflect the natural selection of gene frequencies via selective reproductive success, and hence were adaptive during human prehistory if not necessarily today. Such evolutionary processes conform to my earlier definition of materialism.

The second difficulty merits more detailed discussion. Freud assumed that the Oedipus complex was an intrinsic human trait passed across all the generations since the primal crime occurred (Freud 1913:158). He located it in what he called the "collective mind." This idea, that so complex and specific a structure as the Oedipus complex is human nature, very likely "hard-wired" (to use a modern phrase), is a case of what I am calling a biostructural argument. An argument like this requires that we accept two debatable propositions: first, that such a structure somehow exists in every human mind and, second, that it is biological, not cultural, in origin.

We have already seen that many critics, both in psychoanalysis and anthropology, have questioned the universality of the Oedipus complex, and we will return to these criticisms in the next two sections. But what are the implications for psychoanalytic anthropology if it *is* universal?

I must admit, the evidence for the universality of the Oedipus complex is not very strong. Spiro (1982) has made a very strong argument, but his evidence is mainly found in his detailed re-analysis of Malinowksi's Trobriand data. Stephens (1962) has surveyed a large cross-cultural literature and found support for the widespread occurrence of the Oedipus complex, but his argument ultimately supports the idea of cultural variation in the complex and hence falls in the category of "ecological-functionalist" approaches to be discussed next.

The most compelling evidence on this issue comes from the worldwide occurrence of oedipal-type folktales. Edmunds and Dundes (1983) have asserted that the oedipal tale is universal, and have compiled an impressive collection of such tales from many world regions. Most of the tales in their collection, however, come from eastern Europe and are clearly related to one another historically. The possibility that most such tales are historically related, diffused throughout Europe, the Mediterranean, Asia, and even the Pacific, must be considered (Lessa 1956). Pollock (1988) has also asserted the universality of the tale, but offers little concrete evidence.

For my own part, I had been quite skeptical about the universality of the Oedipus complex until forced to consider the possibility by my work with colleagues at UCLA on the worldwide occurrence of oedipal-type tales. These tales, which involve incest or culturally inappropriate closeness between mother and son along with father-son aggression, and which usually depict physical violence, mutilation, or homicide, do indeed occur in every world region and at every level of societal complexity. Our collection of such folktales now exceeds one hundred, and contrary to the frequently argued idea that the Oedipus complex arises with complex society and male-dominated class structure, we find them to be very common in nonstratified societies, including very small-scale foragers and tropical forest villagers.

Owing to lack of space and the incompleteness of our analyses of our collection of folktales, I cannot deal here with the many objections that can be made to such a "finding." We are currently grappling with the problem of how to define what an "oedipal-type tale" is and how to decide if any given tale is an instance or not. We also recognize that the presence of an oedipal tale does not automatically prove the existence of an Oedipus complex.

Still, I am increasingly led to conclude that there is a universal human fascination with a tale which is both complex and specific and cannot have arisen over and over again around the world simply by chance. The common conjunction in the same tale of inappropriate mother-son intimacy, generally of an explicitly sexual nature, along with physical violence between father and son, is not the sort of thing the proverbial infinite number of monkeys at an infinite number of typewriters would crank out over and over again.

Indeed, I can think of only three explanations that would account for the extraordinarily widespread, if not universal, occurrence of oedipal-type tales. One, that such tales were told early in human culture history and have spread around the world with the expanding human migration, seems plausible to me but begs the question of why this tale and perhaps a handful of others that are equally widespread should be so stable and enduring. After all, over a period of tens of thousands of years languages have so diverged as to be impossible to recognize as relatives, yet the same basic tale is still being told.

Another explanation, perhaps the most acceptable to anthropologists, would find the origins of the Oedipus complex, and oedipal tales, in the common human experience of growing up in a family with a mother, and usually a father; I will argue that this is a version of ecological-functionalist logic and I will return to it momentarily.

That leaves me with the controversial but interesting possibility that oedipal tales are the external reflection of some innate property of the human mind. The only anthropologist I am aware of who has seriously discussed this possibility is Robert A. Paul (1976, 1982). His development of the idea of a universal Oedipus complex based on a "precultural atom" of competition between males of different generations for access to females is an excellent starting point for thinking about how such a structure might have had evolutionary significance in human prehistory. Yet, although a biostructural basis for the Oedipus complex is clearly implied by his argument, Paul (1982:12) carefully avoids committing himself on this point:

> What the ontological status of this structure may be it is not my purpose to propose: whether it is in the genes, or in a Lamarckian remembrance of things past, or in a realm of archetypes, or Platonic ideas.

In both of our nearest primate relatives, the chimpanzees and the gorillas, competition between males for fertile females is a basic structuring principle of social organization. Although incest is rather rare, and mother-son incest appears rarest of all in both primates, a main cause of this is that adolescent males are either prevented from mating with the females of the group by dominant, "alpha" males, or are allowed to mate only after the alpha male has exercised what de Waal (1982:167) calls his *droit du seigneur*, or right to first mating. In sociobiological terms, males are competing for the opportunity to have the females produce their own offspring rather than those of another male. The competition is such that de Waal was moved to comment that the group of chimpanzees he observed seemed just like Freud's "primal horde."

It is interesting, however, that chimpanzee mothers actually reject their sons when they try to mount them during estrus (de Waal 1982, Goodall 1971). The mothers appear to have an aversion to mating with their sons, although the sons show no such reluctance to attempt to copulate with their mothers. Spain (1987) has dealt very convincingly with the important problem posed by this, namely finding a way to reconcile Freud's and Westermarck's views on the existence of incest desires among humans.

For our purposes, a crucial aspect of chimpanzee sexual behavior has to do with its complexity and what that says about chimpanzee mental structure. Let us look at just three aspects. First, chimpanzees do recognize one another (each has a distinctive face), and mothers and their offspring know each other even after the offspring mature. The same is true for brothers and sisters, but not for fathers and children, since paternity is obscured by a female's multiple matings during estrus.

Second, even though alpha males do compete with less dominant males and try to exclude them from mating, females nonetheless welcome matings with other males if they can be arranged. Especially striking is the degree to which females will conspire with nondominant males to deceive the alpha male, by mating in hiding or when the alpha male is otherwise occupied. If they did not deceive him, he would charge into them and disrupt their mating, hopefully (from his standpoint) before ejaculation.

And, third, males form coalitions with one another that result in some sharing of access to females. Males will use a coalition to depose an alpha male and replace him (although, after some time, one partner to the coalition will emerge as dominant over the other). A male who is friendly to an alpha male can actually soothe him, through frequent grooming and gestures of dependence, into allowing him to mate openly with a female without the alpha male's interference.

Such complex and specific behavior has led psychologists (Tooby and Cosmides 1989; Cosmides and Tooby 1989) to conclude that chimpanzees have mental structures, which they label as "algorithms," of matching complexity and specificity. The bargaining implied in conspiring to deceive an alpha male, and in coalition formation between males, requires a number of cognitive capabilities, including face recognition, memory of transactions over time, and some ability to recognize and interpret the "values" of one's partner.

To this emphasis on cognitive capabilities we must add emotional content. Both the mating and the competition between males are clearly heavily emotionally charged for chimpanzees. These are matters of great importance and powerful feelings are aroused that lead to outbursts of calling, posturing and fighting, as well as compensating efforts to soothe and restore friendly feeling (Goodall 1971).

What I am suggesting is that we need a language and research strategies for studying the biostructural aspects of human family and community relations. Terms like Jung's "collective unconscious," "archetype," and "imago," Freud's "collective mind," and Campbell's (1959) "engram," or "inherited image," seem unacceptable today, but they attempt to describe something that still needs describing.

For example, psychoanalysts find it helpful to refer to "good enough mothering" (Winnicott 1965), or an "average expectable environment" (Hartmann 1958:23). These refer to a newborn infant's "expectations" of finding appropriately empathic and responsive parenting. Winnicott (1965:43) refers to this as "the inherited potential." Such potential is flexible enough to permit adaptation to culturally variable parenting behaviors ("...the inherited potential of an infant cannot become an infant unless linked to maternal care"), and yet also sets limits on what can be tolerated by an infant before serious health consequences become likely. Such expectations are very complex and imply definite biological structure.

I consider it likely that the seemingly universal oedipal-type tale is evidence of a biostructural human substrate that includes the kind of "complex and specific" structure labelled by Cosmides' and Tooby's algorithms. These are not determinant in the reductionistic sense that there is a gene (or a portion of a chromosome) devoted to the Oedipus complex: obviously, humans have great tolerance for variety in their environments, can accommodate to many kinds of interpersonal field, and show remarkable individual differences. But they are something quite different from a *tabula rasa* or even some such highly general and elemental traits as a capacity for "Trust" or a need for "Mirroring." They are substantial, definite structured potentials which must be activated or completed by interpersonal experiences of the growing child. Like a glove for a hand, the cultural setting into which the individual is born need not be a perfect match, but must have an appropriate size and shape or the individual will not be able to fit.

Ecological functionalism. We have already seen how Freud, especially in *Civilization and its Discontents*, saw culture as providing a degree of mastery over nature and hence as essential for human survival. The price paid for this powerful adaptive advantage was impulse control. By means of symbols, impulses could be controlled and redirected, a great achievement but one that placed the individual forever in the midst of a conflict between Nature and Culture. This approach seeks to explain cultural phenomena in two ways: first, culture is a set of rules and beliefs for controlling impulsiveness, and second, culture is a set of defensive products, or "projective systems" (Whiting and Whiting 1975:1). For example, rules against incest and aggression in the family reflect the first process (actual incest could destroy the family by violence); the oedipal theme in folktales and other art forms reflects the second (it is not we the audience who possess incestuous and violent impulses, says the play, but the tragic figure Oedipus, who is appropriately punished for his crimes).

This basic model came to characterize, with relatively minor variations, virtually the whole field of culture and personality studies in anthropology. Specific versions of the model can be found in Kardiner (1939, 1945), Malinowski (1927), Mead (1954), Erikson (1963), Fromm and Maccoby (1970), and Edgerton (1971). The similar goal in each such study was, in effect, to examine how children are brought up to be the kind of people they have to be to behave reasonably appropriately in their society (Harrington and Whiting 1972). These authors vary in the degree to which they examine repression and subsequent production of cultural materials through defense mechanisms such as projection, but they participate in a similar ecological functionalist framework.

For example, in Erikson's (1963:111-186) famous comparison of the Sioux and the Yurok, we are presented with a contrast in personality styles that can be related to differences in underlying economy and patterns of child rearing. The Sioux, traditionally mobile hunters under constant threat of war, build strong, expressive characters with early "indulgent" child care, but follow this with frustrations that intensify anger, which can then be channeled toward enemies. Their "centrifugal" social character is seen not only in the necessary adaptive strategies of meat sharing and fighting courage, but also in the religious expressions of the vision quest and self mortification.

The Yurok, by contrast, being sedentary salmon fishers along the north California coast, are taught early restraint, leading to an emphasis on orderliness and careful management of resources. Their "centripetal" social character is seen in food storage and stinginess, as well as in a cultural preoccupation with acquisition and display of wealth symbols.

While many would agree that such analyses played a major role in American anthropology well past the end of World War II, many would also hold that such an approach is outmoded today. Advances in cultural theory, both in the increased formalism in psychological anthropology and in the many layered richness of interpretative anthropology, show more evidence of vitality today than the tradition of culture and personality studies. In his comprehensive criticism of Malinowski, for example,

Sahlins (1976) seems to have not merely buried ecological functionalism but to have jumped up and down so vigorously on the grave as to ensure that even its ghost may never see the light of day again. Shweder (1991:269-312) has now attempted to bury the "culture and personality" version of the larger paradigm with the same enthusiasm.

It would be an error to dismiss such a productive approach, however, on the grounds that it is no longer new. Work from this general research tradition continues to make valuable contributions to anthropology (e.g., Barry 1976; LeVine 1973; Johnson and Johnson 1988; Murphy and Murphy 1985). The general idea that distinct patterns of human adaptation, which always implicate family structure, will influence the formation of adult character, including the typical conflicts shared by members of a community, is valid and will continue to generate new research.

Historical materialism. Marx's materialism had in common with the ecological functionalists the idea that human behavior (and thought; Mao Tse-Tung 1961) is largely determined by the need to sustain life with food, shelter, and other necessities. Marx's materialism was made more interesting than that of many of his contemporaries by his addition of the dialectic, especially as seen in his concept of Class Struggle. If for Freud the contradiction between id impulses and superego controls underlay human suffering, for Marx it was the contradiction between a large, wealth generating working class and a small, parasitic ruling class that underlay human suffering. The greed and aggression of a small group of men caused class inequality, and the need to develop a political system that would control such exploiters justified Marx's revolutionary political program.

In psychoanalysis, Marx's thought is clearly descernible quite early in the American psychoanalytic movement, in the work of Erich Fromm (1946) and Karen Horney (1937). We have seen how both denied that the Oedipus complex was a human universal, believing instead that it was limited to patriarchal societies, and particularly industrial capitalism. With an actually distant and harsh father who controlled the family wealth and the lives of his wife and children, it was no wonder that young boys grew up fearful and angry at their fathers and frustrated by a feeling they could not grow to full manhood while under his control. Furthermore, in a highly competitive society built on the celebration of greed and self-aggrandizing displays of wealth, it was understandable if siblings were also competitive with one another, as fathers were with their sons.

Thus, Fromm (1948:445-46) wrote:

> We arrive at the result that the complex centered around the boy's incestuous strivings toward his mother and his resulting hostility against the father is wrongly called an Oedipus complex. There is a complex, however, which fully deserves to be called an Oedipus complex, the rebellion of the son against the pressure of the father's authority—an authority rooted in the patriarchal, authoritarian structure of society.

This general approach, emphasizing the role of political economy in the formation of individual character and intrapsychic and interpersonal conflict, has had a significant impact in anthropology. It may be found in Devereux's (1953, 1963) analyses of Sophocles' *Oedipus Rex* in relation to the emerging patriarchal political structure in Classical Greece, and in Kardiner's (1939) account of *The Individual and His Society*. Fromm and Maccoby (1970) apply the approach in *Social Character in a Mexican Village*, arguing that three different character types found in the village (Passive, Hoarding, and Exploitative) reflect adaptations to three different political-economic positions (tenant farmer, smallholder, and modern capitalist, respectively).

Michael Maccoby (1976) transfered the method to his research on American business managers, as reported in *The Gamesman*. As in other psychoanalytic social studies that have a Marxian cast to them, this one sees management styles as adapted, or at least fitted, to different states of the political economy. For example, the "Company Man" is oriented largely toward finding a secure position within a company that has stability and longevity. His company loyalty and desire for approval from superiors are well-suited to a former stage in industrial capitalism. By contrast, the "Gamesman" finds his greatest pleasure in the competition to be first in an ever changing economy, where innovation and an ability to shift quickly into new product lines are rewarded. The Gamesman has few loyalties, whether to friends or company, is quick to jump to a new company if his personal interests dictate, and lacks a commitment to a set of guiding or transcendent values. The Gamesman is well-suited to the intensely competitive, innovative, fast-moving market-place that is increasingly dominated by international firms.

Of psychoanalytic interest is Maccoby's description of the intrapsychic differences between such distinct types of managers. The Company Man was primarily motivated by the search for security. He was fearful of failure because it could cost him his chance at job permanence, and thus he sought to please his superiors above all else. The Gamesman is primarily motivated by the desire to control what he explicitly views as a game, in order to win that game. He feels little real connection to other people, although he may be very popular in the public arena, and he feels most alive when actually playing the game to win. He hates the thought of being a "loser," which turns out to be primarily a fear of humiliation: others will see him as a loser and no longer respect him. He does not seek to work within a team to please his superiors, but rather to control that team in order to make it win.

What makes this a materialist analysis is, of course, the implication that some phenomenological level of a sociocultural system, in this case individual character, is explainable with reference to the economic base of society. It is not necessary to argue that the Gamesman's personality is created somehow by the economy. It is sufficient to argue that the labor market for managers is selective and, as the economy changes, the criteria for selecting managers undergo changes as well. There are still places in management for the Company Man, and even for other types identified by Maccoby, such as the Craftsman, but certain areas of the economy, like electronics, increasingly call for managers of the Gamesman type. It may be that some Gamesmen are "amoral, manipulative confidence men, lonely hustlers who drift apart after the game is over" (p. 109), but others do try to be fair and, "given our socioeconomic system with its stimulation of greed, its orientation to control and predictability, its valuation of power and prestige above justice and creative human development, these fair minded gamesmen may be as good as we can expect from corporate leaders" (p. 120).

The intrapsychic and interpersonal dynamics of class relations are deserving of further attention by psychoanalytic anthropologists. I have recently had an opportunity to find this out for myself during a re-visit to a Brazilian plantation some twenty years after my original field study in 1966-67 (Johnson 1971). At that time I had documented a class relationship between the landlord and his tenant farmers that they themselves cast in terms of a parent-child relationship: the tenants feel the landlord should be a "father" (*pai*) to them, and the landlord feels that in some ways they are like his "children" (*filhos*).

On the other hand, on both sides of this class divide is a strong recognition that their economic relationship is in the nature of a contract with obligations on both sides. The landlord expects hardworking, sober, productive tenants. Tenants expect a reliable, generous, and protective landlord. The tenants do not expect *noblesse oblige* gifts from the landlord, but a fair exchange: "The landlord gives us a house and land, but we give him the strength of our arms. Without our arms he could do nothing" (Johnson 1971:131).

Thus the tenant recognizes his poverty and dependence upon a wealthy and powerful elite, and at the same time expects to pay his way and be treated with respect. Indeed, he strongly desires complete independence from the plantation. Men continually remove their families from the plantation in order to try to live independently: bright and strong young men migrate to a big city like Sao Paulo to seek higher wages in the industrial sector; craftsmen move into rural towns and attempt to ply their trades as self-employed skilled labor; and men who may inherit or manage to purchase a small plot of land will try to live on it by raising subsistence crops supplemented by wage labor or crafts production. Some of them succeed, but most do not and must return to the more protective dead-end of the plantation. Thus, I wrote in 1971:140, "This conflict between two contradictory goals [security vs. independence] gives the workers' total behavior an ambivalent aspect, which they themselves feel perhaps more keenly than anyone."

In restudies of the same plantation, still owned by the same landlord, in 1988 and 1989, with more psychoanalytic experience under my belt, I had an opportunity to enrich my understanding of this class relationship. I was struck by the underlying hostility that each side held toward the other, in spite of a generally peaceful and respectful relationship on the surface. I am sure this was there twenty years ago, when indeed I noted the tenants' displeasure with the landlord for his failure to be amply protective and generous (1971:123-128). But I took it more at face value then, assuming the landlord had indeed failed them, and did not fully appreciate the extent to which both tenant and landlord have their separate and very distinct class ideologies.

These ideologies are rooted in family feelings and amount to a splitting up of the world into two partial, distorted viewpoints. The landlord, for example, recently said in one moment that he loves his tenants and sees them as part of his big family, and in the very next said, "these tenants, they do nothing [at that moment several were constructing an irrigation canal a few meters away, in the tropical noonday sun, where they worked for him every day from 7 am to 2:30 pm without a lunch break]. They don't want to work, they want everything to be given to them free. In the United States you don't have such things, do you? There, everybody works." For their day of labor he gives them the equivalent of $U.S. 0.35 and no food.

His anger was not directed so much at the men who were working for him at that very moment, but at the slowly growing possibility that under Brazil's agrarian reform law, some tenants may agitate to occupy and take possession of part of his plantation. But, it goes deeper than that, and back to a past where agrarian reform was inconceivable. The landlord knows very well that his tenants find him stingy and weak. They are not shy about asking for things from people they perceive as being wealthy; the North American visitor discovers this soon enough, as well as how persistent they can be. In their view, the landlord is so wealthy and powerful that there is no reason for his not helping them except his stinginess. The landlord reacts to this as though his plantation were a nest full of baby birds all with their beaks open crying "more, more." He believes that he could never be protective or generous enough to please them, and this is why he says they are lazy and want something for nothing.

The tenants do not only view the landlord as stingy. They view the elite class in general as capable of eliminating their poverty yet unwilling to do so. They tend to split the elites into two idealizations: the noble rich who help the poor, and the stingy rich who do not. I have felt both of these idealizations directed at me. Not seeing myself as rich, but rather as an impoverished graduate student in 1966, I was astonished to have the tenants call me a rich man. I had to come to terms with the fact that, for all my limited means, I had all the trappings of wealth: untorn and unmended clothes, shoes and dark glasses, wristwatch and pocket-knife and a seemingly unlimited supply of pens and notebooks.

I learned of their idealization of me a bit when I was there the first time: I would overhear snippets of conversation in which I was seen as expert and wise. But it was later when I realized the full extent of the unrealism of which these very sensible, intelligent, and productive farmers are capable. When my student and colleague Carlos Soares visited the planation fifteen years after my original study, two dramatic changes had taken place: local health clinics had been established that provided free medical care, and the government had instituted a social security program that paid significant and desperately needed income to the elderly, even to nonliterate tenant farmers who could only sign their registration forms with an "X." This was stunning enough, but the truly unexpected part was that the tenants told Carlos that it was I who had arranged these benefits for them! They had perhaps read my sympathies right, but had invested me with a political power that was of course completely unrealistic.

As regards negative idealization, during my last two visits, I noticed that these short research periods, of two to four weeks in length, followed a similar emotional rhythm. After an initial high of friendliness during the first evening and subsequent day, work settled down to a cordial routine in which our research team was courteously received and graciously assisted. We found ways to recompense with money or gifts all such assistance, at rates three to five times above the local going wage. But, as the research neared its final three or four days, people began confronting us with their needs in increasing frequency, asking what we were going to do for them, or what we would leave them when we went away. Strangers would crowd our house in the evening asking for help, and friends would come into our rooms and finger our clothes and other belongings. Some participants in our project, who were not much experienced at anthropological fieldwork but who had felt great warmth for and from the people, expressed the feeling they were being invaded and made exquisitely uncomfortable.

The negative idealization became apparent at the very end, when we performed our final gift giving, only to be responded to in many cases with disappointment. "Is that all?" sums up the reaction of many people who, by local standards, we abundantly rewarded. As I see it, the tenants apply different standards to those whom they see as rich and powerful: they tend to view them as infinitely rich and powerful. Hence, any gift seems ordinary because it does not really put much of a dent in their persistent poverty and hopelessness. The giver is like a parent who is idealized to the point where any discomfort or frustration is viewed as the parent's stinginess rather than as a realistic limitation on what a parent can do for a child.

Thus, we came to have some understanding of the way the landlord comes to feel over time: it is as if we started to say to ourselves, "you can give these people *everything* and they still are not satisfied!" This, however, is just as distorted as the tenants' view that elite people are infinitely rich and powerful. For some reason, it appears that both the landlord and the tenants have split their images of the other into positive and negative idealizations. Any real tenant disappoints a landlord by resenting his low wages and wanting more help. Any real landlord disappoints his tenants by refusing some requests for help and running his plantation as a profit-making business. I believe there are at least two sources of this splitting.

One is rooted in the reality of the class relationship. In this (north-eastern) section of Brazil, class differences are sharp and rigid. The wealthy elite is a small percentage of the population, probably around 5%, and it is extremely difficult for a lower class individual to rise into it. The poor constitute the large majority of the population, probably over 70%, and live in extreme poverty, such that they may have only one Sunday best set of clothes plus a few well-mended hand-me-downs, no shoes, and a very restricted and often inadequate diet. They see the great wealth of their landed elite, driving powerful new cars and trucks that cost perhaps one hundred times a poor family's annual income, and they recognize that they could have a much better life with but a small part of that elite family's wealth. But, recognizing also that they cannot have any part of that wealth, they are left with envy and rage. Their envy is expressed in their idealization of the rich into infinitely-rich, and their rage in their disappointment even when they are given to.

The landlord knows all of this on some level. His absurd position that the workers are lazy can only be explained as a defensive effort to justify his greater wealth (the poor are characterologically, probably genetically, unworthy) and to deflect their envy from its target. He is really not a bad man and does try to help out, but he is afraid of opening what he fears will be the floodgates of their neediness, until he will be drained completely and they still will not be satisfied. So he complains about their lazy, greedy irresponsibility and imagines a United States in which everyone works hard and supports himself in comfort (he is a knowledgeable man but was plainly startled when I revealed to him that there are thieves and homeless people on the streets of Los Angeles where I live; it did not jibe with his splitting of nations into a bad Brazil and a good United States).

It is possible that patterns of upbringing in the peasant household stimulate envy, and thus splitting, in the sense suggested by Foster (1972). If so, it does not appear likely to happen during the first year of a child's life, when he is treated with great warmth, nurturance, and love by older family members. Since women tend to have many pregnancies, however, weaning is likely to be during the second year and to be abrupt, with sibling caretakers assuming parental roles. From here on, a child will experience the chronic scarcity of food and maternal attention in the household. Such deprivation is likely to stimulate envy and splitting.

We have also noted a moderate amount of sadistic teasing of toddlers by their sibling caretakers. For example, sibling caretakers may pretend to walk away from the toddler, causing it to cry; or they may frustrate the toddler almost to the point of tears before hugging and soothing him, then begin frustrating him all over again.

Thus, envy with splitting into positive and negative idealizations may indeed be stimulated in children through deprivation, and that may account in part for their being key aspects of class ideology in northeastern Brazil. It is not enough, however, to regard the elements of class ideology as simple projections of attitudes wholly created in the nuclear family. These must also be seen as arising out of the class relationship itself. Envy, splitting, and idealization are present in the peasant household (indeed, I would speculate they may be human universals but that could bring us back to biostructuralism!), but they are intensified and reach their fullest development in the class relationship itself.

Discussion

Materialism is intrinsic to Freud's thought. It energizes his theory of intrapsychic conflict and is one of the roots of his pessimism. Indeed, one of the reasons for the rejection of materialism by some psychoanalysts and psychoanalytic anthropologists may have been a felt need to retain optimism that the individual can take a stand against both biological urges and social conditions in order to live a creative and reasonably satisfying life.

Nonetheless, few psychoanalytic theorists today conceive of human beings without some essential strivings that explain broad aspects of their behavior. If it is not the sexual and aggressive urges central to Freud's conceptions, it is something else, such as a seemingly intrinsic and powerful will to grow and become, or a need to be understood, "mirrored," and sustained by others. Although a need for "empathic" mothering, for example, may be phrased in such a way that it hardly sounds biological, if we examine it closely we will see that it implies a very complex and relatively precise set of expectations on the part of the growing child. To be held, soothed, and delighted in when little, to be allowed opportunities for independent action and risk taking when a little older, to be expected to be able to take responsibility and acquire skills when still older: these are hardly vague and indeterminant expectations, even though there is a huge variety of different, culturally appropriate possibilities for meeting them satisfactorily.

Beyond this, it would push relativism and reflexivity to an absurd extreme to suggest that the child's growing environment (and, too, the adult's continually unfolding world) do not set conditions that the self must adapt to. Such adaptation requires not just strategies or scripts, but outlooks, attitudes, and motivations. Adaptation is not a game of mastery played by a free and private self, but a challenge that requires the self to take on certain fundamental shapes, including the characteristic values and shared meanings of a community. As Freud saw, this challenge always involves the individual in a powerful conflict between selfish strivings and social standards.

Finally, the psychoanalytic tradition in anthropology has encouraged an examination of the development of the self in the political economy. As society becomes more complex, the family becomes less and less autonomous and self-sufficient. As in our Brazilian example, the emotional content of the class relationship is not a mere projection of preexisting family attitudes. But neither is the family of either the poor tenant farmer or the wealthy landlord just a creation of social class. The idealization, splitting, and projection that shape class attitudes are both created in the family (at least in part by processes common to human families everywhere) and intensified and given unique shape through the family members' interactions in the political economy.

In all these cases the materialism of Freud is most valuable when placed in a context of competing orientations. Biological structures may profoundly influence us, but culture gives us many alternatives and ensures that virtually no human act can be seen as purely biological in origin. Ecological realities make certain social and economic arrangements highly likely, but individuals in any society find ways to avoid expectations, pursue personal goals, adopt one political stance as opposed to another, in short to deviate in manifold ways. And, if class relations reflect the underlying relations of production in society, class ideology and class consciousness can become vehicles for transforming those relations and fundamentally shaping the whole of society. This willingness to accept that seemingly contrary processes may coexist is what makes Freud's thought continually dynamic and provocative, and can help ensure that psychoanalytic anthropology retains its dynamism and ability to provoke.

References

Barry, J. W. 1976. *Human Ecology and Cognitive Style*. New York: Sage.

Barzun, Jacques. 1958. *Darwin, Marx, Wagner: Critique of a Heritage*. Garden City, NY: Doubleday. Second Edition.

Bohm, D. 1957. *Causality and Chance in Modern Physics*. New York: Harper.

Bross, M. 1988. "Oedipus and Jocasta: A Re-examination of Freud's Drama of Destiny." In G. H. Pollock and J. M. Ross, eds., *The Oedipus Papers*. Madison, WI: International Universities Press.

Campbell, Joseph. 1959. *The Masks of God: Primitive Mythology*. New York: Viking Press.

Cosmides, Leda, and John Tooby. 1989. "Evolutionary Psychology and the Generation of Culture, Part II: Case Study: A Computational Theory of Social Exchange. *Ethology and Sociobiology* 10:51-97.

de George, R. T., & F.M. de George. 1972. *The Structuralists: From Marx to Lévi-Strauss*. Garden City, NY: Doubleday.

Devereux, George. 1953. "Why Oedipus Killed Laius: A Note on the Complementary Oedipus Complex in Greek Drama." *International Journal of Psychoanalysis* 34:132-141.

_____. 1963. "Sociopolitical Functions of the Oedipus Myth in Early Greece." *Psychoanalytic Quarterly* 32:205-214.

de Waal, F. 1982. *Chimpanzee Politics: Power and Sex Among Apes.* New York: Harper and Row.

Edgerton, R. B. 1971. *The Individual in Cultural Adaptation.* Berkeley: University of California Press.

Edmunds, L., & Dundes, A., eds. 1983. *Oedipus: A Folklore Casebook.* New York: Garland.

Erikson, Erik. 1963. *Childhood and Society.* New York: W. W. Norton.

Foster, George M. 1972. "The Anatomy of Envy: A Study in Symbolic Behavior." *Current Anthropology* 13:135-202.

Freud, S. 1913. *Totem and Taboo.* In James Strachey, (Ed. and Trans.), *The Standard Edition of the Complete Psychological Works of Sigmund Freud* 13:1-161. London: Hogarth.

_____. 1930. *Civilization and Its Discontents. Standard Edition* _21:57-145. London: Hogarth.

Friedman, J. 1974. "Marxism, Structuralism, and Vulgar Materialism." *Man* 9:444-69.

Fromm, Erich. 1948. "The Oedipus Complex and the Oedipus Myth." In Ruth N. Anshen, ed., *The Family: Its Function and Destiny.* New York: Harper and Brothers.

Fromm, Erich, & Maccoby, M. 1970. *Social Character in a Mexican Village.* Englewood Cliffs, NJ: Prentice-Hall.

Goodall, Jane. 1971. *In the Shadow of Man.* Boston: Houghton Mifflin.

Harrington, C. and J. W. M. Whiting. 1972. "Socialization Process and Personality." In F. L. K. Hsu, ed., *Psychological Anthropology.* Cambridge, MA: Schenkman.

Hartmann, Heinz. 1958. *Ego Psychology and the Problem of Adaptation.* New York: International Universities Press.

Horney, Karen. 1937. *The Neurotic Personality of our Time.* New York: W. W. Norton.

Johnson, Allen. 1971. *Sharecroppers of the Sertao.* Stanford, CA: Stanford University Press.

_________. 1982. "Nonreductionist Cultural Ecology." In J. G. Kennedy & R. B. Edgerton, eds., *Culture and Ecology: Eclectic Perspectives.* Washington, D.C.: American Anthropological Association.

Johnson, Allen, and Orna Johnson. 1988. "Oedipus in the Political Economy: Theme and Variations in Amazonia." In R. R. Randolph,

D. Schneider, and M. N. Diaz, eds. *Dialectics and Gender: Anthropological Approaches*. Boulder, CO: Westview.

Kardiner, Abram. 1939. *The Individual and His Society*. New York: Columbia University Press.

_________. 1945. *The Psychological Frontiers of Society*. New York: Columbia University Press.

Lessa, William A. 1956. "Oedipus-Type Tales in Oceania." *Journal of American Folklore* 69:63-73.

LeVine, Robert A. 1973. *Culture, Behavior, and Personality*. Chicago: Aldine.

Maccoby, M. 1976. *The Gamesman*. New York: Simon and Schuster.

Malinowski, Bronislaw. 1927. *Sex and Repression in Savage Society*. [Reprinted by World Publishing Co., NY 1955]

Mao Tse-Tung. 1961. "On Practice." In, A. P. Mendel, ed., *Essential Works of Marxism*. New York: Bantam Books.

Mead, Margaret. 1954. "Theoretical Setting." In Margaret Mead & Martha Wolfenstein (eds.), *Childhood in Contemporary Cultures*. Chicago: University of Chicago Press.

Moran, E. 1979. *Human Adaptability*. Belmont, CA: Wadsworth.

Murphy, R. 1971. *The Dialectics of Social Life*. New York: Basic Books.

Murphy, Y. and R. Murphy. 1985. *Women of the Forest*. New York: Columbia University Press. Second Edition.

Paul, Robert A. 1976. "Did the Primal Crime Take Place?" *Ethos* 4:311-352.

_________. 1982. *The Tibetan Symbolic World*. Chicago: University of Chicago Press.

Pollock, G. H. 1988. "Oedipus: The Myth, the Developmental Stage, the Universal Theme, the Conflict and Complex." In G. H. Pollock & J. M. Ross, eds., *The Oedipus Papers*. Madison, WI: International Universities Press.

Roazen, Paul. 1974. *Freud and His Followers*. New York: New American Library.

Sahlins, Marshall. 1976. *Culture and Practical Reason*. Chicago: University Chicago Press.

Shweder, Richard A. 1991. *Thinking Through Cultures*. Cambridge, MA: Harvard University Press.

Spain, David H. 1989. "The Westermarck-Freud Incest-theory Debate: An Evaluation and Reformulation." *Current Anthropology* 28:623-635; 641-645.

Spiro, Melford. 1982. "Is the Oedipus Complex Universal?" In *Oedipus in the Trobriands* (pp. 144-181). Chicago: University of Chicago Press.

Stephens, W.N. 1962. *The Oedipus Complex: Cross-Cultural Evidence.* New York: Free Press.

Tooby, John, and Leda Cosmides. 1989. "Evolutionary Psychology and the Generation of Culture, Part I: Theoretical Considerations." *Ethology and Sociobiology* 10:29-49.

Whiting, B.B., and J.W.M. Whiting. 1975. *Children of Six Cultures: A Psycho-Cultural Analysis.* Cambridge, MA: Harvard University Press.

Williams, B. 1981. "A Critical Review of Models in Sociobiology." *Annual Review of Anthropology* 10:163-92.

Winnicott, Donald W. 1965. "The Theory of the Parent-Infant Relationship." In *The Maturational Processes and the Facilitating Environment* (pp. 37-55). NY: International Universities Press.

Chapter Ten

Freud's Findings in the Context of Recent Evolutionary Theory

Christopher R. Badcock

Freud and Darwin. The fifty years since Freud's death in 1939 have been long enough to allow for some far-reaching reformulations in our understanding of his work, but none is likely to be more significant or more fundamental than that now occurring in what is perhaps one of the most surprising contexts: that of overlap between Freud's findings and modern evolutionary theory.

In a way that may suggest an ultimate precedent for Freud, only recently, thanks to major advances in genetics and to modern field studies of animal behavior, have we really begun to understand what Darwin really said, as opposed to what it was imagined he said. Furthermore, these new insights into authentic Darwinian ideas are highly pertinent to Freud and will probably do much to bring about a very different attitude to the founder of psychoanalysis in the twenty-first century as compared to that current in the twentieth.

The most important aspect of our modern insight into evolution is that natural selection is essentially a question of *differential reproductive success.* What this means, fundamentally, is that what Darwin proposed—and all that Darwin proposed—is that organisms which have heritable traits resulting in their leaving a larger number of descendants than others will become increasingly represented in future generations, thereby subtly changing the genetic makeup of a species, or, in other words, directing its evolution. This means that reproductive success—the total number of descendants which an organism has—is the ultimate arbiter and driving force of evolution. As we shall see later, this has deep and immediate implications for Freud's insistence on the importance of what he called the *libido*. Evolution, we now know, is less a question of "the survival of the fittest" than it is one of the reproductive success of the reproductively most successful, and this puts the libido theory center stage where human beings are concerned, both in evolution and in psychology.

A second way in which Darwin was misunderstood—or rather, misrepresented, which might be a more accurate word—was in relation to the *unit* of selection. Darwin took a largely individualistic view of the workings of natural selection and saw it in terms of the struggle of individual organisms to survive and ultimately to reproduce. Yet, for the best part of this century, a quite different view gained widespread implicit acceptance. This was so-called *group selection*, the belief that natural selection could operate on entire families, groups or even species without taking account of individual differences. The problem with this idea is that it made cooperation in general, and self-sacrifice or *altruism* in particular, far too easy to explain and evaded Darwin's deepest insight into the evolution of behavior. This was the realization that if natural selection acted on individuals it would appear to reward self-interest, rather than the interests of the group, family or species (Badcock 1991).

Finally, Darwin was frequently misrepresented as being a believer in evolutionary progress: the idea that evolution by natural selection implied some inherent *improvement, perfecting* or *advancement* of species or individuals. In large part, this was probably because such ideas appealed to Victorian social prejudices which saw Western, industrialized nations as "more highly evolved" than others and because such non-Darwinian concepts of evolutionary progress had been popularized by writers such as Jean Baptiste Lamarck (1744-1829) and Herbert Spencer (1820-1903). According to these, essentially non-Darwinian, views of evolution as a process of gradual advancement of organic creation towards some higher end, human beings in general, and the human consciousness in particular, were ultimate achievements of evolution, pinnacles of *progress, development* and *adaptation* understood as a perfecting process.

But here again, recent and authentic Darwinian insights have gone far towards correcting such errors and, in doing so where human consciousness is concerned, have converged critically on fundamental Freudian insights into the unconscious. Far from being seen as the pinnacle of psychological perfection in a simple, obvious sense of its ability to perceive truth and to reason honestly and correctly, recent ideas originating in modern evolutionary thought have instead pointed out a very different adaptive background for the evolution of human consciousness.

The leading evolutionary theorist Robert Trivers (b.1942) has pointed out that it is a mistake to imagine that animal communication, once it exists, will inevitably evolve to convey true information for the benefit of others, the group or the species. On the contrary, the example of camouflage should remind us that very often misinformation can pay an individual, and the more complex and critical the communication, the greater the scope for using it to disseminate both information and misinformation. In the case of human beings, laboratory experiments have shown that conscious misrepresentation of the truth creates stresses and discrepancies in individual behavior that other individuals can often detect. For example, false smiles tend to be exaggerated because the muscles surrounding the eyes which contract in genuine smiles cannot be voluntarily contracted in insincere ones, and people who know that they are telling lies often give the fact away by subtle changes in the pitch or intonation of their speech, are more likely to gesture below the body center-line, and so on. Given the enormous value of verbal communication to human beings, Trivers concluded that the most effective misinformers are likely to be *those who do not know that they are lying*, or, in other words, *those who have become unconscious of their true motives by means of self-deception.*

Such self-interested suppression of some thoughts in favor of others is the essence of the true, Freudian concept of *repression.* Like Freudian repression, this is a dynamic process: one in which one does not become unconscious of certain things merely because one does not remember them, but because one has actively excluded them from consciousness (Badcock 1988).

However, the truth has to be registered somewhere since to ignore it altogether would hardly serve the self-interest of the exploiters of others' belief in their self-deceiving fictions. The consequence is a view of consciousness that is not merely dynamic, but also *topographical* in the Freudian sense. In the words of Robert Trivers, "The mind must be structured in a very complex fashion, repeatedly split into public and private portions, with complicated interactions between the subsections" (1981:35).

It is not difficult to see that the outcome is essentially what Freud discovered: a consciousness which is both topographical in the sense that it has many different levels or regions, and also dynamic in the sense that what is not conscious has been made unconscious by an active force of repression. But this is by no means the only instance in which recent advances in the evolutionary understanding of behavior have re-opened findings originally made by Freud (Badcock 1986:37-47).

The libido and the selfish gene. As is well known, Freud's so-called "libido theory" pictured the child developing through three stages of infantile sexuality: the oral, anal and phallic/oedipal. What Freud did not know, but what we know today, is that *oral behavior* understood as *compulsive sucking independent of need for food* probably evolved because human mothers, like most mammals, do not ovulate (and therefore do not conceive) if their nipples are persistently stimulated by sucking, at least for about two years after giving birth. The birth of another offspring within the first few years of the life of an existing one is the major single threat to the life of an existing child in third world and hunter-gatherer conditions. The latter case is especially significant because it is as hunter-gatherers that human beings have spent at least 99 percent of their total existence on earth, and so it seems likely that human infants have evolved oral behavior principally to safe-guard themselves against the very real threat to their survival posed by the appearance of siblings within the first few years of their lives (Badcock 1990:72-77).

Paradoxically then, a form of behavior for which Freud appeared to have good grounds to describe as *sexual* because it seemed independent of nutritive need, turns out, on closer inspection, probably to have evolved to promote the survival of a child. In other words, far from being involved with infantile libido as such, oral behavior now seems to have more to do with a child's survival during childhood.

Yet, from another point of view, Freud's insistence on calling such things as oral behavior sexual seems justified in a more fundamental way, at least if we interpret the word sexual here in the wider sense indicated by the term libido. Indeed, it indicates that Freud's view of such behavior was in fact much closer to the modern, evolutionary view than others which, for example, interpreted oral behavior in terms of mere *attachment*.

What I have in mind here is the surprisingly recent realization that natural selection actually selects, not so much for the survival of the organism in itself, as for the survival of the genes for which the organism is little more than temporary, bio-degradable packaging. This insight explains a wealth of findings about animal and human behavior, including some which seem to contradict it (such as the evolution of sterile castes of workers in insect societies), and, as we shall see later, also probably provides the true biological foundation for Freud's speculations about a *death instinct*.

But the point at issue here is that, once one realizes that evolution by natural selection is ultimately a matter of differential reproductive success, with some genes leaving more copies of themselves in future generations than others, then Freud's insistence on the central role of the libido in human psychology becomes wholly understandable and exactly what one might have predicted. In other words, if organisms are nothing more than the temporary packaging of their genes, the ultimate aim of the organism must normally be reproduction which, in a sexually reproducing species, inevitably makes sex and reproduction central to the organism's behavior.

As Freud himself put it in a strikingly modern sounding passage at the beginning of one of his *Introductory Lectures on Psychoanalysis* devoted to "The Libido Theory and Narcissism": "The individual organism, which regards itself as the main thing and its sexuality as a means, like any other, for its own satisfaction, is from the point of view of biology only an episode in a succession of generations, a short-lived appendage to a germ-plasm endowed with immortality—like the temporary holder of an entail which will outlast him" (1916:413-414).

Making due allowances for obsolete terminology like "germ-plasm," one could not wish for a better or more accurate statement of what has since become known as the *selfish gene* view of evolution: the realization that, from the ultimate point of view of natural selection, organisms are nothing more than the temporary carriers of the genetic information which they contain.

Looked at from this point of view, oral behavior might indeed be called sexual in the sense that it—like all other behaviors—must have evolved in the first place because infants who manifested it enjoyed greater ultimate reproductive success than those who did not. Oral behavior in infancy, in other words, evolved because of its implications for the reproductive success of the adults such "oral" infants grew into and this, essentially, is how Freud conceived it. Today we may be able to fill in details to the picture of which he was quite unaware, but, fundamentally, the libido theory seems vindicated. Reproductive success evidently rules, both in evolution, and in human psychology.

Evolution of the primal scene. If these suggestions about the evolutionary background of oral behavior are to be relied upon, it is worth considering the possibility, unknown to Freud but apparent from this line of research, that what he saw as sexual feelings directed towards the parents might in fact have more to do with the child's survival in primal conditions than anything else. This is because, as I pointed out earlier, modern findings show that the birth of a sibling within four or five years is the single greatest threat to the survival of an existing child in primitive conditions such as would certainly have typified our ancestors for the vast majority of the time our genus, *Homo,* has existed on earth. But since mothers' sensitivity to nipple-stimulation as a means of inhibiting the female sexual cycle declines after about two years, it is perhaps not surprising that Freud discovered that oral behavior began to abate after that time and that oedipal tendencies soon succeeded it.

If the parents' sexual activities pose such a potential threat to the existence of an existing child of three or four years of age, it is perhaps not surprising that such children should both attempt to monopolize their parents' interest and to sabotage any attempts they may make to conceive a sibling. The term *primal scene* is used in psychoanalysis to describe the frequently reported real or imagined scenes of parental intercourse which seem to play a central role in the Oedipus complex of both sexes and in which the child appears to be motivated to interfere.

Freud may have taken primal scene material more or less at face value and interpreted it as evidence of infantile sexual interest in the parent of the opposite sex and rivalry with that of the same sex. In fact, such a concern to monitor and perhaps intervene in parental sexual activities may reflect an evolved tactic in parent-offspring conflict over the conception of siblings. It may simply be that, in primal conditions where, presumably as among hunter-gatherers of recent times, parents and children bedded down together around camp fires at night, children who could no longer interrupt their mother's reproductive careers by sucking at their nipples attempted to do so by intervening in their attempts at sexual intercourse. In modern, Western cultural conditions where parents and children often sleep in different rooms, such an intense interest in the parents' sexual lives might seem unambiguous evidence of infantile sexuality but may in reality have evolved—as oral behavior almost certainly did—to safeguard the existing child's survival, rather than to serve its own, immediate sexual interest (Badcock 1990:78-94).

To put the matter succinctly, we might say that, taking the more realistic view which sees child-development from the point of view of the child as well as from the conventional view of the parent, children can be expected to feel with regard to their parents in general but with regard to the same-sex parent in particular a notable, if unconscious, *ambivalence.* By this I mean that we can expect to find *powerful feelings of love and hate directed at the same object.*

Conflict, cooperation and oedipal ambivalence. Ambivalence is important because some have argued that the findings of modern evolutionary biology have disproved Freud's belief that oedipal conflict could occur, for example between sons and fathers. Statistics relating to homicide prove conclusively that relatives preferentially avoid killing one another. This is an important point in itself because others have claimed Freud as a member of the recent school of thought which sees the family as the quintessential home and origin of conflict and violence of all kinds.

However, such a view is easily disposed of if the figures for violent crime are examined with the distinction between relatives by blood, as opposed to marriage, in mind. For example, in 1972, 75 percent of all murders of relatives in Detroit were by non-blood related persons, and whereas 30 percent of collaborative murderers in Miami were found to be blood-relatives, only 2 percent of murder victims were blood-relatives of their murderers. Nor are such figures in any way exceptional, because the degree of relatedness between collaborative killers is far higher than that between victim and murderer in all societies for which data are available. Furthermore, they are thrown into tragic relief by the finding that, where parental murder of children is concerned, an adopted child living in modern Western societies such as the USA, Canada or Great

Britain is one hundred times more likely to be killed by a step or substitute parent than by a natural one (Daly and Wilson, 1988:87-88).

The biological, evolutionary rationale for these findings is interesting in itself, and worth a brief digression because it is probably critical to a correct understanding of Freud's findings regarding the Oedipus complex. Basically, the idea is this: Performing acts that benefit others—or forgoing acts that injure them—amounts to an expression of *altruism.* In modern behavioral science *altruism* is defined as *an act which is likely to promote the reproductive success of the recipient at a cost to the reproductive success of the actor.* Clearly, forgoing injuring someone as the figures above suggest relatives do is likely to be a notable contribution to the reproductive success of those so benefited. Yet, how could such forbearance evolve if, as I pointed out earlier, natural selection selects acts which enhance, rather than reduce, the reproductive success of the actor?

The answer to this question is that a gene for forbearing doing violence to relatives could evolve if the cost to it in the actor was less than the benefit to identical copies of that gene in the relatives concerned. For example, suppose that I had a gene which made me forego food if my children were starving and that I thereby benefited them. I would only have to save the lives of three of my children in this way for that gene to have been selected because each of my offspring receives one half of my total complement of genes. If I perish because of my act of altruism, 100 percent of my genes for altruism have been wiped out (that is, those in my own body), but if at least three of my children survive because of it, 150 percent of my genes will have been preserved (that is, three times the 50 percent present in each child), and this is a net gain for the genes in question. In short, natural selection at the level of the gene will have selected my act of altruism because the reproductive success of the genes in question will have been enhanced by my sacrifice. (Specifically, a gene for altruism can evolve by natural selection if, all other things being equal, $Br > C$, where B is the benefit to the reproductive success of the gene for altruism in the recipient of the act, C is the cost to the copy of the same gene in the altruist, and r is the degree of genetic relatedness between them [Badcock 1991:61-87].)

Applying reasoning like this, and facts relating to family violence like those set out above, critics have pronounced Freudian findings regarding oedipal conflict as biologically unacceptable. Of course, if

Freud really had believed that sons routinely murdered their fathers, or daughters their mothers, such criticisms would be to the point and correct. However, what Freud really found is not that children do in fact regularly murder their parents (and no one doubts that they very exceptionally do), but that children normally harbor *ambivalent* feelings about their parents, especially about the parent of the same sex.

These critics overlook that the other side of such feelings as envy, hate, and resentment is love, compassion, and esteem and that ambivalence means that *both* kinds of feelings are present in children with regard to their parents, and not least in regard to the parent of the same sex. Furthermore, as Robert Trivers has pointed out, "close association permits more altruism but also throws individuals into closer competition, thus engendering more opportunities for selfishness. A classic example is sibling conflict for parental investment" (Trivers 1985:119).

Insofar as oedipal behavior may be related to soliciting preferential parental investment at the expense of siblings, it would be an illustration of Trivers's general principle. Indeed, the finding that oedipal behavior is usually more pronounced and persistent in males may be a consequence of the fact that sons may have more to gain by it. This is because it is generally true of most sexually reproducing species, human beings not excepted, that males can have vastly greater reproductive success than females. In other words, a man with twenty wives is likely to have many more children than a woman with twenty husbands. An important principle of evolutionary biology holds that parents who had some way of reliably knowing what the ultimate reproductive success of their offspring was likely to be would find their own reproductive success enhanced by making the "right" decisions about the allocation of their investment in those offspring.

Here parental investment is defined as *anything contributed by a parent which benefits the reproductive success of its offspring at a cost to the remaining reproductive success of the parent.* It is an abstract concept which covers everything from the sex cell from which the offspring grows to parental behavior such as guarding, instructing, transporting and, of course, feeding the young. According to another fundamental principle of evolutionary biology, the female is defined as the sex with the larger sex cell and this almost always results in females devoting much more effort to parental investment as such, which perhaps explains why mothers appear to be the archetypical figures of oedipal attachment in both sexes and certainly are such in early childhood, as I mentioned earlier (Badcock 1991:123-181).

However, it also means that mothers have more to gain by strategic choices relating to the allocation of their parental investment and never stand in exactly the same relation to their male offspring as do their husbands. This is because a father almost always has the option—at least in principle—of adding directly to his reproductive success which, as we have just seen, can theoretically be enormous if only he can find enough females to impregnate. A mother, however, never has that option because the best she can do is to have one pregnancy at a time.

But if a woman has sons who show unmistakable signs of exceptional potential where their personal reproductive success is concerned, perhaps by way of exhibiting precocious sexuality in childhood directed towards her and the other females of the family, she may find that her own ultimate reproductive success would be rewarded by preferential investment in them. Once started, such a cycle might become self-sustaining, with precociously sexual, *oedipal* sons attracting preferential parental investment from their mothers and perhaps thereby securing greater reproductive success in adult life than they might otherwise have enjoyed. In this way, mothers whose personal reproductive potential might be limited by being female would find their male offspring could add grandchildren to the benefit of their own reproductive success at a rate impossible if they had invested preferentially in their daughters.

If this line of reasoning is correct, it might explain, not merely why males in particular exhibit precocious "infantile" sexuality preferentially directed towards their mothers and sisters, but also why they might direct aggression towards their fathers and brothers. This is because an inevitable aspect of male reproductive success is conflict with other males.

Data on murder from 35 societies throughout the world show that on average, out of every one hundred murders of a person of one sex by a person of the same sex, ninety-five will be murders of males by other males. In the case of the Yanomamö Indians of South America, approximately 30 percent of deaths among adult males was attributable to violence and almost half of all men aged 25 or more had participated in a killing, while 70 percent of all adults over forty years of age had lost a close relative because of violence.

Furthermore, such violence was directly related to male reproductive success: killers had on average two and half times as many wives and three times as many children as non-killers. That such findings are not limited to so-called "primitive" societies is suggested by the fact that today violence is the chief cause of death among African-Americans under age forty. A recent study of the available data concluded that "There is no known human society in which the level of lethal violence among women even begins to approach that among men" and added that *"Intrasexual competition is far more violent among men than among women in every human society for which information exists"* (Daly and Wilson 1988:161).

With aggression against other males such an important fact in recent societies, it is likely to have been just as significant a factor, if not even more significant, in the primal hunter-gatherer societies in which our ancestors evolved the behavioral responses which they have bequeathed to us. Set against such an evolutionary background as this, Freud's finding of aggressive rivalry directed at the father by the son may not be quite so biologically impossible as some have supposed.

On the contrary, if it succeeded in suggesting future prowess in competition with other males for females in the same way in which precocious sexuality may have suggested future reproductive success, then such oedipal behavior may have been rewarded by preferential parental investment, perhaps especially on the part of mothers. Far from actually wanting to murder their fathers, then, oedipal sons may in reality be sending signals which, like comparable signals to do with sexual precocity, are aimed essentially at securing preferential parental investment, perhaps principally on the part of the mother.

Penis-envy. An approach to the problem of the Oedipus complex in terms of parental investment might explain another strange finding of Freudian psychology, the phenomenon of *penis-envy*. This term describes a latent envy of the male's possession of the penis on the part of the female.

Because secondary sexual characteristics only develop at puberty, a little girl could not use them to ascertain the sex of her siblings as an adult might evaluate the sex of another adult. Only the primary sex differences exist in childhood, and here the presence of the penis—so much more obvious by comparison with the female genital—would be a wholly reliable indicator and indeed one which could not be concealed in cultures where, almost certainly, total nudity was the rule, especially for young children. If her own and her siblings' sex were critical to what kind of parental investment was forthcoming, natural selection might favor the evolution of a reliable and independent means of determining it. Along with this would go a counter-strategy to preferential parental investment in males: one which might motivate a little girl to resent the preference her brothers might be shown and to compete accordingly.

Very significantly for the interpretation of his finding which I am putting forward here, Freud remarks that, along with "the reproach that her mother did not give her a proper penis"—that is, did not make her male—a woman's free associations often include the feeling "that her mother did not give her enough milk, did not suckle her long enough ... did not feed her sufficiently" (Freud 1931:234). In most cultures such a reproach would have be the sober truth: boys are indeed breast-fed longer than girls and no one needs to be told that in later childhood sons normally enjoy all kinds of privileges not extended to their sisters.

If common human envy evolved simply because those who felt envious of others were usually more likely to do better than those who were more accepting of others' advantages in the struggle for survival and reproductive success, it is not far-fetched to suggest that penis-envy may have evolved by a similar means. The difference would be that this was a specialized kind of envy, one specifically adapted to sibling rivalry related to preferential parental investment in males and one which motivated females both to form reliable judgments about their own and other siblings's sex, and to compete accordingly (Badcock 1990:94-103).

Resolution and identification. In Freud's view the Oedipus complex in both sexes was dissolved when the child was forced to resolve its infantile ambivalence by means of identification with the parents and their values. *Identification* is a psychological process by means of which one associates oneself with someone or something on the basis of a subjective feeling of similarity with him, her, or it. Freud saw the typical pattern whereby sons identified with their fathers and daughters with their mothers essentially as an if-you-can't-beat-them-join-them tactic by means of which the negative, hating side of the oedipal ambivalence was suppressed by the positive, loving side. This resulted in a son giving up feeling resentful of his father by subjectively seeing himself *as* his father and a daughter doing a similar thing with regard to her mother. Where oedipal conflicts did not work out this way, other possibilities existed. For example, a son might *not* identify with his father, but with his mother, and a similar, so-called *negative* resolution of the Oedipus complex could occur in a girl who identified with her father.

Freud was not alone in finding that parents in general, and fathers in particular, were critical individuals where the psychological development of their children was concerned. Non-analytic psychologists too have found that there is much evidence suggesting a link between the father and the son's masculinity. Fifteen separate studies have shown that boys raised without fathers are less masculine and six others that many fatherless boys alternatively exhibit compensatory hyper-masculinity and aggressiveness. "When the age of father-child separation is considered, studies show that father absence has the greatest effect on the masculinity of boys separated from their fathers in early childhood ... An inadequate father-child relationship often appears to be a major factor in the development of homosexuality in males ... homosexuals who take a passive, feminine role in sexual affairs have a particularly weak identification with their fathers and a strong one with their mothers" just as Freud would have predicted (Lamb 1981:335-336).

What is less clear is why this should be so. One possible explanation, wholly consistent with modern evolutionary biology, might be that identification with the father by the son is the psychological equivalent of what is known in animal behavior as *phenotypic matching*. This simply means assessment of genetic similarity by means of physical and behavioral resemblance on the grounds that two organisms which look and act alike probably share similar genes. If the genes concerned code for cooperative behaviors such as avoiding injuring kin, it follows that sensing a resemblance with oneself might be critical in determining how cooperative one might be with someone who may indeed be a relative.

This is all the more crucial where fathers are concerned, as opposed to mothers, since mammals typically know who their mothers are in a way they never do their fathers, simply because they directly issue from their mother's body and normally have plenty of opportunity to taste and smell her. Comparison of taste and smell is usually a prime means of detecting genetic relationships in animals, mammals no less, and experiments show that human babies can discriminate their own mothers after a few days of breast-feeding.

However, fathers are different, and here matching by identification may be critical—after all, it could always have been the mailman! If we make the reasonable assumption that genetic factors play a major role in determining a man's ultimate reproductive success and that the success of his father is usually a reliable guide to his own, then the findings quoted above would immediately make sense. They would suggest that sons who could find an adequate father with whom to identify could unconsciously conclude that there were good grounds for feeling confident in their own reproductive success in life but that the contrary would be the case for sons lacking such a father.

The finding that lack of a father in early childhood is associated with infrequent orgasms in married women and that "inappropriate or inadequate fathering seems to be a major factor in the development of homosexuality in females as well as males" (Lamb 1981:28) might at first seem paradoxical here, but further reflection shows that it may be part of the same overall pattern. It may be that girls in primal, hunter-gatherer societies evolved to judge their own chances of securing an adequate mate by the success of their own mothers.

If this were so, and if the situation with regard to father-absence in the development of men were as I have suggested, then in both sexes what may seem to be an archetypical case of home-environmental determinism turns out in reality to be critically linked to genetic factors. Indeed, if the interpretation of Freud's findings regarding the Oedipus complex suggested here are anything to go by, it seems that they are far more profoundly rooted in biology and evolution than many of Freud's critics may have suspected (Badcock 1990:110-119).

Evolution beyond the pleasure principle. In his book of 1920, *Beyond the Pleasure Principle*, Freud's concern was to deal with findings that left little doubt that, although the pleasure principle might reign in the unconscious, its writ did not run everywhere there. Three findings in particular made Freud doubt that everything which went on in the unconscious did so under the rule of the pleasure principle.

First was *masochism*, the finding that pain inflicted on the self could be pleasurable. Admittedly, this could be reconciled with the pleasure principle if the latter were made elastic enough to stretch to pleasure which resulted from pain, but the problem still remained of why things which were pleasurable to some because they caused pain were normally not in the least pleasurable to others for that same reason.

A second finding casting doubt on the completeness of the pleasure principle was the so-called *negative therapeutic reaction*. This was the finding that some patients could not be made to want to recover in psychoanalysis, but seemed to insist unconsciously on remaining ill, or even on deteriorating further. A real element of self-destruction seemed to motivate these cases which was puzzling if, as otherwise seemed to be the case, a desire for health and recovery could normally be counted on as one valuable factor contributed by the pleasure principle to the process of the analytic cure.

Finally, the so-called *traumatic neuroses* seemed to contradict the pleasure principle because their chief symptom was often recurrent dreams or distressing memories of the shocking event which had precipitated the illness in the first place. A large number of such cases (sometimes called *war neuroses*) came to the attention of psychotherapists like Freud in the aftermath of the World War I and seemed to involve a compulsive repetition of the horrifying event without the slightest possibility of its yielding any kind of pleasure.

Freud's answer began with the last consideration. He concluded that there must be something more fundamental than the pleasure principle in the unconscious, and called it *the compulsion to repeat.* He suggested that the compulsion to repeat in these cases originated in the fact that the mind had not been prepared for the shock it had experienced. In re-living the trauma, the unconscious was, so to speak, trying to *reset to zero* in the sense of attempting to get back to the event, but this time to master it. The fact that such attempts always failed was a result of the fact that, in reality, such a reset-to-zero was not possible, even though it might be repeatedly attempted in fantasy—during dreams for example. Such traumatic dreams might be cases where the pleasure principle attempted such a reset, but always failed. Yet its failure would not prove that the pleasure principle did not exist, merely that there was something more fundamental going on: a compulsion to repeat, irrespective of pleasure or unpleasure.

As an extension of this line of argument Freud then went on to argue that instincts as such are always specific instances of the more general compulsion to repeat and that *they aim to restore an earlier state of things,* the ultimate restoration being that state which preceded life:

namely, death. According to his final instinct theory set out in this book and retained for the remainder of this life, there are ultimately two sources of instinct: Eros, which strives to unite and whose chief expression is the libido, and Death, which strives to destroy and whose most obvious manifestation is aggression.

Such a metaphysical formulation did not allow for much in the way of factual confirmation, and it is hardly surprising that, of all Freud's ideas, that relating to the death instinct has been the least widely accepted. Indeed, even Freud himself admitted to being "not convinced myself" and expressed the expectation that "the deficiencies in our description would probably vanish if we were already in a position to replace the psychological terms by physiological or chemical ones." He adds that "Biology is truly a land of unlimited possibilities. We may expect it to give us the most surprising information and we cannot guess what answers it will return in a few dozen years to the questions which we have put to it. They may be of a kind which will blow away the whole of our artificial structure of hypotheses" (Freud 1920:59-60).

It might be worth pointing out in conclusion that, whatever the merits of his own formulation regarding the death instinct, it seems that his prediction regarding biology has indeed been fulfilled in approximately the time-span he foresaw. This is because, as I pointed out earlier, modern biology has come to see the organism as little more than the biodegradable packaging for its genes and is able to explain self-sacrifice on the part of individuals in terms of the ultimate benefit that such altruism might have for identical copies of the genes which code for it in near kin. In my earlier discussion I put the matter in terms of avoiding doing harm to kin at a cost to oneself, but the fundamental principle will work equally well if it is instead a question of doing harm to oneself in the interests of kin.

Here, the supreme example would be workers and soldiers in insect societies who sacrifice their own personal reproductive success or even survival for the benefit of near relatives who do reproduce (the queens and drones). Such extreme cooperation evolves basically for the same reason that complex multi-cellular organisms like human beings find that their individual cells normally also cooperate with one another. Ultimately, this is because all such cells are genetically identical. Brain or liver cells can leave reproduction to the sex cells because the genes being reproduced by those cells are identical to those present in non-reproducing cells. Such non-reproductive cells, like sterile worker bees or ants, may not have any personal reproductive success of their own, but the genes which they share with those that do carry out the reproductive function are sufficiently alike for the reproductive success of the genes in question to be favored, rather than harmed, by such a reproductive division of labor.

Indeed, it becomes readily apparent that, once such a division of labor where reproduction is concerned evolves at either the level of the cell in a multicellular organism or at that of the individual in a social species, the mortality of certain individuals is an inevitable corollary of the reproductive success of others. Only in unicellular, asexual species where the entire organism reproduces by dividing in its entirety is this fundamental link between death and sex avoided.

Looked at from this point of view, the destruction of the individual, which Freud would have seen as the workings of the death instinct, makes perfect sense in terms of evolution. Talk of *Eros* and *Death instinct* may now sound hopelessly out of date, but the fundamental insight that there is a biological imperative underlying at least some instances of self-destruction is one wholly validated by modern biological research. Indeed, perhaps the very findings which led Freud to postulate an instinct of death—masochism, negative therapeutic reaction, extreme guilt—may in reality be behaviors which have evolved in human beings by a similar effect to those which promote self-sacrifice and self-destruction for the benefit of near kin in other organisms. Perhaps those who unconsciously assess their own reproductive prospects as poor for any reason will implicitly take the view that evolution does of their existence and see themselves as existing to reproduce, rather than reproducing to exist.

But since the very fact of one's existence would imply costs as well as benefits for other near relatives in the primal conditions in which human beings first evolved (for example, in consuming food which others could eat), individuals who unconsciously despaired of their reproductive prospects might also feel their existence to be no longer justified and act accordingly. What would look like a death instinct in these circumstances would actually be an expression of the fundamental truth that natural selection is driven by the survival, not of individuals as such, but of the genes which they contain and which they may share with near relatives better placed than they to carry on the fight for reproductive success.

Incest-avoidance. Similar considerations may explain another of Freud's findings which has been regarded as biological heresy. This is his insistence that human beings are ambivalent about incest. Here, it seems, biology has proved Freud wrong, since it is hard to see how natural selection could reward inbreeding and the deleterious effects it usually brings. Again, we now know that incest-avoidance is not a purely cultural factor as Freud seems to have supposed, but is widespread and common in animal behavior.

But however that may be, the considerations immediately above relating to the genetics of altruism illustrate that, however undesirable inbreeding may be genetically, close relatedness does bring great benefits where cooperation is concerned. In-breeding—or incest, to give it its other name—can pay if the result is to make individuals so closely related to one another that the likelihood of their sharing common genes for social cooperation reaches very high levels. (In other words, it raises the discount parameter, r, to very high levels in the inequality which governs the evolution of altruistic traits: $Br > C$.)

Indeed, one might predict that the greater the degree of parental investment, especially provided by the father, the more critical it might be that he is even more closely related to his offspring than normal. Since human beings have attained unprecedented levels of parental investment, not least by fathers, this might create an evolutionary tendency for human beings to favor marriage to near kin, thus explaining one side of the ambivalence Freud discovered.

The other side of the ambivalence about incest, of course, would be easily explained by the conventional observation that inbreeding, whatever its benefits for social cooperation—and many highly cooperative organisms do seem to be inbred—nevertheless carries heavy costs in terms of the effects on the offspring.

However, the social benefits may compensate to some extent and set up a complex interaction between two contradictory evolutionary imperatives: one which says, "avoid incest in the interests of genetic diversity in your offspring," and another which says, "marry near kin whose cooperation in raising your offspring you can rely upon." Perhaps both programs run simultaneously in the human unconscious and perhaps the result of their conflicting interaction is the ambivalence which Freud observed.

If this were so, it would parallel closely what I argued earlier when I presented Freud's findings regarding the Oedipus complex in the new setting of modern parental investment theory. There too, Freud's belief that oedipal behavior was based on incest and parricide has been a cause of scandal to biologists. But again, if oedipal behavior is actually all about soliciting parental investment, rather than parricide and incest, a major difficulty is removed and Freud's findings—as opposed to his theories about them—instead appear as something very modern: an insight into parent-offspring conflict over the allocation of investment. Again, it does not seem to me to require anything specifically 'cultural' to explain incest-taboos in childhood. After all, if oedipal behavior is all about soliciting parental investment, it is obvious that parents can resist in part by erecting taboos—that is, arbitrarily contrived rules—against it, and this they evidently do, at least in some cultures, such as our own.

Inheritance and transference. "In my opinion there is an almost complete conformity . . . between the individual and the group: in the group too an impression of the past is retained in unconscious memory-traces. . . . My position, no doubt is made more difficult by the present attitude of biological science, which refuses to hear of the inheritance of acquired characters by succeeding generations. I must, however, in all modesty confess that nevertheless I cannot do without this factor in biological evolution" (1939:94). In these words, written at the very end of his life, Freud expressed what has been taken as his most notorious offence against biology: his apparently unshakable belief in the inheritance of acquired characteristics. Had this been merely a private opinion, peripheral to the central concerns of psychoanalysis, we might be justified in ignoring it, but unfortunately Freud goes on to add that "If it is not so, we shall not advance a step further along the path we entered on, either in analysis or in group psychology" (1939:100).

The problem with this view of Freud's is that we now have an extensive knowledge of the processes and substances involved in heredity. Today we know that inheritance is brought about by the transmission of information coded in DNA (deoxyribonucleic acid) and nothing else. Admittedly, we also now know that parents can mark their DNA in various ways, but these bio-chemical markers are reset by each generation and do not seem to influence the basic units of inheritance, the genes. Because the genetic information present in a woman's egg cells is copied before her birth, no experiences which she has could possibly alter it. Again, even though men's sex cells—sperm—are continuously produced in vast profusion and there is some evidence (at least in rats) that factors like high alcohol consumption can affect the viability of sperm as such, there is absolutely no evidence that anything that happens to a man can be recorded, as it were, in his DNA. On the contrary, our whole modern understanding of evolution and genetics rejects such a possibility because, as we have already seen, modern biology sees the individual organism as little more the biodegradable packaging of its genes, with the organism existing ultimately for the benefit of the DNA it contains, rather than the DNA being modified directly by the organism for the organism's own purposes.

Freudian psychoanalysis, both of the individual and of entire groups and cultures, therefore appears to founder on an issue where the judgment of modern science has decisively found against Freud: acquired characteristics cannot be inherited. It seems that only by dint of a belief in a completely outdated and discredited genetic mechanism can Freud succeed in explaining anything. By his own admission psychoanalytic explanation remains permanently stalled where he left it in the 1930s and, some would say, everything that has happened to it since has only underlined the point.

However that may be, recent research has shown that he got the idea, not from the works of Lamarck as has been commonly supposed up until now, but from Darwin himself, who also believed it. Indeed, it was not until the 1920s and 30s—when Freud was in his mid-sixties, seventies, and eighties—that biologists in general rejected it. "Freud learned his views of the inheritance of acquired characteristics from . . . the study of Darwinian biology in the era before it became controversial. Nor, having abandoned the study of zoology before this controversy arose, was he aware until the last year of his life that inheritance through use and disuse had been called into question and found wanting" (Ritvo 1990:148).

Significantly, Freud's longest and most detailed discussion of what he termed the *archaic heritage* is found in the last of his books of applied psychoanalysis, *Moses and Monotheism.* Here he refers to "the instincts of animals" as an example of such a heritage, evidently following "Darwin's definition of 'instinct as acquired learning'" (Freud 1939:100; Ritvo 1990:117). Today no one would reject Darwin's concept of an evolutionary basis for animal behavior merely because the discoverer of natural selection had been unclear about the actual mechanism of inheritance involved (believing, for example "that a woman's children by a second marriage could resemble her first husband!" [Ritvo 1990:69]). Similarly, it seems to me that we should interpret Freud's insistence on the importance of what he termed "the archaic heritage" as an implicit recognition of the ultimate significance of evolutionary factors in shaping human behavior, rather than, as has been the case up until now, seeing it merely as a complete impossibility.

Summarizing his work, Lucille Ritvo expresses the view that Freud

> did not relinquish completely what he regarded as his "great discovery" of the importance of the experiential—the trauma of childhood seductions—but displaced it from ... the childhood experience of the individual to the childhood experience of the race. The discoverer of the Oedipus complex followed Darwin in assuming that an innate or inherited characteristic had behind it the developmental or experiential history of the species [Ritvo 1990:41].

In other words, what Freud called "memory-traces in the archaic heritage" can be regarded today as evolved, unconscious foundations of behavior. The fact that he saw these as bridging the gulf between individual and group psychology suggests an altogether modern view of the interrelation between individual and social behavior of the kind sketched out earlier in this section and in my previous discussion of the possible evolutionary foundations of oedipal behavior.

Indeed, it may well be that what must have appeared even to Freud to be the most obvious case of environmental circumstance shaping behavior, what we have termed *transference,* may turn out in reality to reflect, not so much the impact of personal experience, as the primacy of the genetic determinants of behavior. Transference is based on the unconscious re-modelling of existing situations and relationships on earlier ones, usually experienced in childhood. This makes such early experiences look decisive, and doubtless they are. But the fact that human beings seem compulsively to expect repetitions of early experiences in circumstances where they are reminded of them may suggest a different idea.

This is that, in the primal, small-scale societies in which human beings originally evolved, anyone who reminded one of someone else, or of some previous experience with others, would in all probability be a relative or descendant of the original protagonist. If behavior is largely under genetic control as modern evolutionary research strongly suggests, it may simply be that a compulsive expectation that similar individuals or relationships will produce similar experiences to those one had in the past is fully justified by the probability that, in primal conditions, those with whom one is interacting in the present would in fact have inherited the genetic predispositions to their behavior from those with whom one had interacted in similar circumstances in the past.

In other words, transference would be a subjective psychological equivalent of objective, genetic patterns of inheritance: a tendency to expect similar genes or similar situations to produce similar behavior and comparable outcomes. Since such outcomes could not always be counted on to be pleasurable, the pleasure principle here might give way to what Freud called the *compulsion to repeat* and express an altogether fundamental maxim: that if behavior is shaped by evolution, *the individual's present will always be overshadowed by the past.* This, essentially, seems to have been Freud's most fundamental insight, and it is one whose ultimate validity only the future can decide (Badcock 1992).

References

Badcock, Christopher R. 1986. *The Problem of Altruism*. Oxford and Cambridge, MA: Basil Blackwell.

__________. 1988. *Essential Freud*. Oxford and Cambridge, MA: Basil Blackwell.

__________. 1990. *Oedipus in Evolution*. Oxford and Cambridge, MA: Basil Blackwell.

_________. 1991. *Evolution and Individual Behavior*. Oxford and Cambridge, MA: Basil Blackwell.

_________. 1992. *Essential Freud, second edition*. Oxford and Cambridge, MA: Basil Blackwell.

Daly, Martin D., and Margo Wilson. 1988. *Homicide*. New York: A. de Gruyter.

Freud, Sigmund.[1] 1916. *Introductory Lectures on Psychoanalysis, SE* 16.

_________. 1920. *Beyond the Pleasure Principle, SE* 18.

_________. 1931. "Female Sexuality," *SE* 21.

_________. 1939. *Moses and Monotheism, SE* 23.

Lamb, M., ed. 1981. *The Role of the Father in Child Development*, second edition. New York: John Wiley & Sons.

Ritvo, Lucille. 1990. *Darwin's Influence on Freud: A Tale of Two Sciences*. New Haven, CT: Yale University Press.

Trivers, Robert. 1981. "Sociobiology and Politics." In E. White, ed., *Sociobiology and Human Politcs* (pp.1-43). Lexington and Toronto: D.C. Heath & Co.

_________. 1985. *Social Evolution*. Menlo Park, CA: Benjamin/Cummings.

[1]All references to Freud's works in this book are to the English language *Standard Edition of the Complete Psychological Worls of Sigmund Freud*, edited and translated by James Strachey, London: Hogarth Press. Hereafter cited as *SE*, with the volume number and year of publication of that volume. First date given is the date of original publication. See Bibliography of this book for complete page references.

Chapter Eleven

The "Primary Process" Revisited[1]

Melford E. Spiro

I shall begin by admitting to a parapraxis. When David Spain invited me to participate in this symposium, I read his proposed title not as *Psychoanalytic Anthropology*, but as *Psychoanalysis* "Fifty Years after Freud's Death." Consequently, this paper addresses a technical issue in psychoanalytic theory, as such, and although it has important anthropological implications, most especially for the understanding of cultural symbols and their meanings, I do not address them here.[2]

Human mentation, according to Freud, is characterized by two types of functioning, which he called the "primary" and "secondary" processes.[3] These types differ along two related dimensions. One dimension consists of the mode in which desires are satisfied; the other consists of the mode in which thoughts are represented in the mind. Because of time

---

[1]A version of this paper also appears in *The Psychoanalytic Study of Society*, vol. 17, L. Bryce Boyer and Ruth Boyer, eds.. Hillsdale, NJ: Analytic Press, 1992, pp.171-180, by mutual agreement of both publishers.

[2]Since these implications may not be entirely obvious, I intend to address them explicitly in a separate publication. In the meantime, I apologize for the misunderstanding.

[3]Although Freud stressed the distinction between these "processes" in virtually all of his major theoretical works, from his first (Freud 1895) to his last psychological publication (Freud 1940), nevertheless the locus classicus is his "Formulations on the Two Principles of Mental Functioning" (Freud 1911).

constraints, I shall address the second dimension exclusively, and henceforth the terms "secondary process" and "primary process" will refer to that dimension only.

The differences between these two types of mental representation, as viewed both by Freud and by standard psychoanalytic theory, can be briefly summarized as follows. In the secondary process mode, the representational medium usually, but not always, consists of words: they are combined by normal rules of syntax, and the thoughts they represent are related to each other by normal canons of (Aristotelian) logic. In normal adults, this mode of mental representation characterizes the representation of conscious thoughts.

In the primary process mode, the representational medium usually, but not always, consists of images: they are combined by a syntax of their own; and the thoughts they represent are related to each other in ways that are often nonlogical if not illogical. Thus, for example, the primary process is characterized by the absence of negation and of time, by the identity of opposites, by the reversal of normal causation, and by other seemingly bizarre features. If in normal adults, the secondary process mode characterizes the representation of conscious thoughts, then the primary process mode characterizes the representation of unconscious thoughts.

Although I believe that Freud was brilliantly correct regarding the different *functions* that he attributed to the primary and secondary processes, of which more below, I also believe, however, that his delineation of the *formal* differences between these two types of mental functioning is critically flawed. More specifically, I argue here that some of the critically important features that, according to Freud, uniquely characterize the representation of unconscious thoughts characterize the representation of conscious thoughts as well.[4]

Since, however, thoughts—whether conscious or unconscious—are represented by signs, before examining that thesis it is first necessary to briefly discuss some characteristics of signs and their meanings. If the discussion seems elementary, which it is, that is because I shall address only those characteristics of signs that are relevant for demonstrating the

---

[4]Because of space limitations, this argument is a summary of a much longer manuscript (Spiro, mimeo) that not only develops each of its points in greater detail, but also discusses others that we have not been able to discuss here.

formal similarities between conscious and unconscious mental representation.

Although the signs by which thoughts are represented in the mind are (what might be called) *internal* signs, nevertheless I propose to classify them in accordance with Charles Peirce's typology of external signs which, as we shall see below, is especially useful for a semiotic understanding of unconscious mental representation.

If a sign is viewed as any object or event that denotes some other object or event, or some class of objects or events—the latter to be designated as its *denotatum*—then, following Peirce (1932), we may distinguish three types of signs: indices, icons, and symbols.

An index is an object or event that functions as a sign in virtue of a relationship of *factual contiguity* between that object or event and its denotatum. A cloud, for example, is a sign (an index) for rain.

An icon is an object or event that functions as a sign in virtue of a relationship of *factual similarity* between that object or event and its denotatum. A painting of a cloud, for example, is a sign (an icon) for a cloud.

A symbol is an object or event that functions as a sign although it has no obvious relationship, either of contiguity or similarity, to its denotatum. For many, perhaps most, symbols—those designated as "cultural"—the relationship between symbol and denotatum is established by convention. Hence, anthropologists usually characterize cultural symbols as "arbitrary." In any event, if a painting of a cloud is an icon for a cloud, then by the criterion just enunciated, the English lexeme "cloud" is a cultural symbol for a cloud. Contrary, however, to received anthropological opinion, I shall argue below that cultural symbols, whether verbal or any other, comprise only one class of symbols, which may be distinguished from another class that I shall call "private." Meanwhile, I shall employ the term "symbol" to designate cultural symbols exclusively.

Any object or event can function as an external sign, I have said, so long as it denotes some other object or event, or a class of objects or events. Let us now observe, however, that the word "denotes" is doubly ambiguous. In the case of indices, denotes means "to signal the occurrence" of some object or event, while in the case of icons and symbols it means "to represent the concept" of an object or event, or else of a class of objects and events. Thus, when it is said that a cloud (of a particular type) denotes rain, "denotes" signifies that the occurrence of the cloud signals the occurrence of rain. When, however, it is said that the word "cloud" or that a painting of a cloud denotes clouds, "denotes" signifies that they represent the concept of a cloud or of the class of clouds.

In what follows, this discussion of signs will be confined to icons and symbols exclusively because we are concerned here not with external, but with internal signs, and although internal signs can be classified as icons or symbols, they cannot be classified as indices, at any rate not very easily. Before turning, however, to internal signs, we must briefly deal with the "meaning" of signs, more particularly that of verbal symbols, because they constitute the type of signs that (by definition) are employed for the representation of thoughts in the secondary process mode.

The meaning of verbal symbols, or words, like that of any other kind of sign, consists of their denotata. Insofar as most words are cultural symbols, their meaning is established by social convention. But words may have not one, but three, kinds of conventional meanings: denotative, connotative, and figurative. If, for example, the denotative and connotative meanings of the English word "father" consist of genitor and pater, respectively, and if jointly they comprise the *literal* meanings of that cultural symbol, then the other cultural meanings of "father"—God, Catholic priests, George Washington, etc.—comprise its *figurative* meanings. Notice now that all of these figurative meanings of "father" are also *cultural* because they are no less conventional than the two literal meanings of that symbol.

When cultural symbols represent or convey figurative meanings, they are called *tropes*. If, however, the figurative meanings of such a symbol, as in the case of the aforementioned figurative meanings of "father," are cultural, then in such a case that symbol is employed as a *cultural trope* (as I shall call it), as opposed to (what might be called) a *private trope*, of which more below.

As sign users, we not only respond to external signs, but we also produce signs, both external and internal—external signs to communicate our thoughts to others, internal signs to represent our thoughts to ourselves (in our minds). The latter type, with which we are concerned here, consist both of words and images. If they consist of words (cultural symbols), the thoughts that they represent usually correspond to the conventional meanings, either literal or figurative, of the words. Thus, if a thought regarding either a father or a priest is represented in the mind, both may be represented (if the actor is an English speaker) by the word "father."

Often, however, our thoughts do not correspond to the conventional, or cultural, meanings of the words by which we represent them in our minds. Suppose, for example, that I wish to be with father, but suppose that, conceiving of him as brave, I represent that wish by the thought "I want to be with the lion." Since the (consciously) intended denotatum of "lion" is not an African carnivorous feline, but father, in such a case the meaning of this cultural symbol is figurative. Unlike, however, a previous example, in which the figurative meanings that attributed to the word "father" are *cultural*, in this example the figurative meaning of the word "lion" is *personal*. In short, in this case, the cultural symbol is here employed not as a cultural, but as a private trope.

As all of the above techniques of mental representation are employed by normal adults for the representation of *conscious* thoughts in waking life, they are all (by definition) characteristics of the secondary process mode of mental representation. We may now compare them with the techniques which, according to Freud, make up the primary process mode, the mode that is allegedly employed for the representation of *unconscious* thoughts. Because the dream, or so Freud maintained, is the royal road to the unconscious, for the purpose of this comparison I propose to examine the representational techniques employed in dreams. It must be emphasized, however, that the techniques employed to represent unconscious thoughts in dreams are also employed to represent unconscious thoughts in waking life, even though the representational medium is different.

Because the representational medium employed in dreams consists of images (visual signs), if the conscious meaning of a dream image is literal—if, for example, an image of a lion is consciously intended by the dreamer to represent a lion—then such an image (to employ Peirce's typology of signs) is an icon. Often, however, dream images are not icons because frequently their meanings, for at least two reasons, are figurative.

First, if the thoughts represented in a dream are conscious, then the meanings of the dream images may be figurative because, as Freud explicitly recognized, the representational constraints inherent in a visual medium may preclude the literal representation of certain thoughts, more particularly abstract thoughts. Thus, how else, if not figuratively, might such thoughts as "father is dependable," or "father is wise," be represented in a dream? Indeed, if the representational medium consists of images, then how else, if not figuratively, might such thoughts be represented in waking life?

Second, if the thoughts represented in a dream are unconscious, then the meanings of the dream images may be figurative because the thoughts are represented by means of the three representational techniques that Freud designated as "displacement," "condensation," and "symbolization." For the sake of brevity, but also because condensation and symbolization (for reasons too complex to explain in brief compass) are merely special cases of displacement,[5] I shall confine the discussion of this second reason to displacement alone.

Displacement in dreams is a representational technique by which an image that *iconically* denotes one object or event is employed instead to represent another object or event, one that iconically is denoted by a different image. Thus, if a dreamer has an unconscious thought regarding his father, then if he employs displacement, he may represent his father, for example, by an image of a lion. Since the (unconsciously) intended denotatum of the image is father, not lion, its meaning is not literal, but figurative. In the event, the image of the lion is employed not as an icon, but as a symbol—not, to be sure, a cultural symbol, but a private one.

It will now perhaps have been recognized that, viewed *formally*, displacement in dreams is identical with private tropes in waking life. A private trope— whether a metaphor, a metonymy, a synecdoche, or any other—is a representational technique by which an object or a thought is represented not by a conventionally appropriate word, but by one that *conventionally* denotes some other object or thought. Similarly, displacement (as it is found in dreams) is a representational technique by which

[5]On this point, as well as others, I am indebted to the pioneering discussions of the primary process by Gill (1965) and Holt (1965).

an object or a thought is represented not by an iconically appropriate image, but by one that *iconically* denotes some other object or thought.

In sum, just as in waking life a private trope represents an object or a thought by substituting a conventionally inappropriate word for a conventionally appropriate one, so also in dreams displacement represents an object or a thought by substituting an iconically inappropriate image for an iconically appropriate one.

That is not the only formal similarity between private tropes and displacement. In both techniques the substitution of one sign for another is governed by the same logical principles. In the case of tropes, as students of rhetoric have long recognized, the substitution of one *verbal symbol* for another is governed by the principles of "similarity" and "contiguity," and these same principles, it can easily be demonstrated, govern the substitution of one *image* for another in the case of displacement. In other words, in both techniques one sign is substituted for another just in case the denotata of both signs are either similar in one or more attributes, or else are spatially or temporally contiguous.

Although tropes are employed for the representation of conscious thoughts, whereas displacement, according to Freud, is employed for the representation of unconscious thoughts, seeing as displacement and tropes are formally identical, it would appear that there are no *formal* differences, *pace* Freud, between the representation of conscious thoughts (in regard at least to their figurative representation) and that of unconscious thoughts. If that is so, then since (by definition) displacement is a technique of the primary process mode of mental representation, and tropes are techniques of the secondary process mode, it would also appear, *pace* Freud, that there are no *semiotic* differences (so far, at least, as these techniques are concerned) between the primary and secondary processes.

Having said that, it must also be said that there is one critical difference between tropes and displacement, hence between the representation of conscious and unconscious thoughts. If sign-substitution is employed to represent a conscious thought—that is, if sign-substitution is employed as a trope—then the *figurative* meaning of the substitute sign is conscious. If, however, this technique is employed to represent an unconscious thought—that is, if sign-substitution is employed as displacement—then the *literal* meaning of the substitute sign is conscious.

To understand the import of this difference, we must turn from the formal characteristics of sign-substitution to its motivation. Whether the representational medium consists of images or words, and whether the thoughts to be represented occur in waking life or in dreams, the motivation for employing this technique of mental representation is radically different, depending on whether the thoughts are conscious or unconscious.

If sign-substitution is employed to represent a conscious thought, then the motive is to *reveal* or express the thought more effectively, whereas if this same technique is employed to represent an unconscious thought, the motive is to *conceal* the thought by representing it in symbolic disguise. Since everyone is aware of the expressive power of tropes, whatever I might say on this subject would be redundant. Hence, let us proceed directly to explicate the motive for sign substitution for the representation of unconscious thoughts.

Unconscious thoughts are thoughts that at one time were conscious, but which, because they arouse anxiety, are repressed, that is, removed from conscious awareness. Suppose, now, that an actor has the thought "I wish that father was dead," and suppose, because such a thought arouses moral anxiety, that it is repressed by the actor. Suppose, too, that while he is asleep this unconscious thought attempts to reenter consciousness in a dream, but is blocked from doing so by (what Freud called) the "dream censor."

If, however, "father" is replaced, for example, by "lion"—so that the thought is represented as "I wish that the *lion* was dead"—then in that disguised form the thought can reenter consciousness without arousing anxiety, and since, as a consequence, the father is represented in the dream by an image of a lion, the thought can be expressed (and fulfilled) in the dream without being blocked by the dream censor. Because in that case sign-substitution is motivated by the actor's wish to protect himself from the painful affect of moral anxiety, this technique is employed as a *psychological defense* .

Using this example as paradigmatic, we may now return to my thesis that the meaning of a substitute sign differs according to whether sign-substitution is employed for the representation of conscious or of unconscious thoughts because the motivation for employing this representational technique is different.

If sign-substitution is employed to represent a conscious thought—in which case the motive is to more effectively express a thought—then the figurative meaning of the substitute sign is the consciously intended, and the only, meaning of the sign. Thus, if I conceive of my father as someone on whom I can always depend, and if, as a consequence, I represent him in waking life as "a tower of strength," or if in a dream I represent him by an image of a tower, then the conscious and only meaning of both signs, the verbal and the visual, is *figurative*.

If, however, sign-substitution is employed to represent an unconscious thought—in which case the motive is defensive, i.e., to conceal the thought—then the substitute sign has not one, but two, intended meanings, one conscious, the other unconscious. Moreover, unlike the representation of a conscious thought, in this case the conscious meaning is not figurative, but *literal*, and it is its *unconscious* meaning that is figurative. Thus, in the lion dream, the image of the lion consciously represents a lion, while unconsciously it represents the father. That is why, of course, the substitution of lion for father can perform its defensive function, for since consciously the image represents a lion, it is the lion, not the father, whose death the dreamer consciously desires.

On the basis of the foregoing analysis, and employing Peirce's typology of signs, it is instructive to compare the semiotics of the lion dream with that of the tower dream. Since both the image of the tower and that of the lion are intended to represent father, both images are employed as a *metaphor* for father—not, however, a cultural metaphor, but a private one. Since, however, the image of the tower is consciously intended to represent the father, the tower is a *conscious metaphor* for father. On the other hand, since the image of the lion is consciously intended to represent a lion, the lion is both an *icon* for a lion, and an *unconscious metaphor* for father.

To round out this analysis, it should be added that unconscious thoughts are present not only in dreams, when the representational medium consists of images, but also in waking life, when the medium consists of words. Consequently, if the unconscious wish for the father's death threatens to reenter consciousness in waking life, seeing as this wish is consciously represented as a wish for the death of a lion, the substitution of "lion" for "father" is defensively motivated. Hence, although the conscious meaning of "lion" is literal, it also has a figurative meaning—father—which, however, is unconscious. In that case, while consciously the verbal symbol "lion" is employed as a cultural metaphpor, unconsciously it is employed as a private one.

We may now summarize the conclusions of this analysis, which I shall formulate in five propositions. In addition, I shall propose a terminological change. First the conclusions.

1. If displacement, a characteristic that Freud viewed as the distinctive feature of the primary process mode of mental representation, and tropes, a characteristic of the secondary process, are representational techniques by which thoughts are represented by means of sign substitution, then there are no differences, *pace* Freud, between the primary and secondary processes of mental representation, at least insofar as this technique is concerned.

2. If unconscious thoughts, according to Freud, are represented by means of displacement, i.e., sign substitution, and if conscious thoughts, insofar as they are represented by tropes, are also represented in that fashion, then there are no formal differences, *pace* Freud, between the mental representation of conscious thoughts (in regard at least to their figurative representation) and that of unconscious thoughts.

3. Although sign-substitution is *formally* the same, whether employed to represent conscious or unconscious thoughts (in both cases it is governed by the principles of similarity and contiguity), *motivationally* this technique is radically different depending on whether the thoughts are the one or the other. Thus, if it is employed to represent a conscious thought, then the motive is to more effectively *reveal* the thought, i.e., to express it with greater cognitive, affective, or dramatic force. If, however, it is employed to represent an unconscious thought, then the motive is to *conceal* the thought by representing it in symbolic disguise.

4. As a consequence of this motivational difference, there is also a *functional* difference between the representation of conscious and unconscious thoughts by means of sign-substitution. Thus, if this technique of mental representation is employed to represent a conscious thought, its function is *communicative*. If, however, it is employed to represent an unconscious thought, then its function is *defensive*; that is, it permits the thought to reenter consciousness without, however, arousing painful affects, such as anxiety or guilt.

5. From the perspective of Peirce's typology of signs, we may say that the defensive function of sign substitution is made possible by the fact that if this representational technique is employed for the representation of unconscious thoughts, then whether the representational medium consists of words or images, the substitute sign has a dual semiotic status. Consciously, the word and image are employed as a *cultural symbol* and an *icon*, respectively, but unconsciously both are employed as a *private symbol* .

Following from these five propositions, I now wish to propose some terminological changes for the designation of the key concepts of this paper. If both "displacement" and "trope" designate the same technique of mental representation (sign substitution), and if the same principles (similarity and contiguity) govern this technique whether the representational medium consists of words or images, whether employed in waking life or in dreams, whether employed to represent conscious or unconscious thoughts, and whether, therefore, its function is communicative or defensive, then to avoid conceptual and terminological confusion, I would propose the following terminological changes.

I propose that *displacement* be employed as a generic term for any and all of these instances of sign substitution. I further propose, however, that we distinguish two types of displacement, depending on whether this technique is employed for the representation of conscious or unconscious thoughts. If displacement, i.e., sign substitution, is employed to represent conscious thoughts, I propose that it be designated as a *trope*, but if it is employed to represent unconscious thoughts, then I propose that it be designated as a *defense*.

References

Freud, Sigmund. 1895. *Project for a Scientific Psychology. Standard Edition*, 1:283-398. London: Hogarth Press, 1961.

_____. 1940. *An Outline of Psychoanalysis. Standard Edition*, 23:141-208. London, Hogarth Press, 1964.

Gill, Merton M. 1967. "The Primary Process." In Robert R. Holt (ed.), *Motives and Thought: Psychoanalytic Essays in Honor of David Rapaport. Psychological Issues*, Monograph 18/19:260-298.

Holt, Robert R. 1967. "The Development of the Primary Process: A Structural View." In Robert R. Holt (ed.), *Motives and Thought: Psychoanalytic Essays in Honor of David Rapaport. Psychological Issues*, Monograph 18/19:344-384.

Peirce, Charles S. 1932. "The Icon, Index and Symbol." *Collected Papers*, Volume 2. Cambridge, MA: Harvard University Press.

Spiro, Melford E. n.d. "Tropes, Defenses, and Unconscious Symbols: Some Critical Reflections on the Primary Process" (mimeo).

Notes on the Contributors

Christopher R. Badcock (Ph.D., sociology, 1973), is Associate Professor of Sociology at the University of London. He is the author of numerous books including *Evolution and Individual Behavior: An Introduction to Human Sociobiology* (1991), *Oedipus in Evolution* (1990), and *Essential Freud: An Introduction to Classical Psychoanalysis* (1988; revised second edition 1992). Dr. Badcock, who at one time was in didactic analysis with Anna Freud, is seeking to complete the synthesis of Freudian findings and modern evolutionary theory and to develop it as a new paradigm for human behavioral science.

JoAnn F. Campbell (Ph.D., anthropology, 1985), is a Research Consultant residing in Seattle, Washington. She recently was involved in a research project focusing on the development and implementation of a curriculum for grades 2-5 in selected Seattle public schools designed to aid children in the management of social-emotional experiences (the "PATHS Project," Dr. Carol A. Kusche, Principal Investigator) and is currently working on a project devoted to the study of the appeal cycle in an Asian-American population, a project of the San Francisco Psychoanalytic Institute.

John M. Ingham (Ph.D., anthropology, 1968), is Professor of Anthropology at the University of Minnesota and is the author of *Mary, Michael, and Lucifer: Folk Catholicism in Central Mexico* (1986) and "Chalma and Tepoztecatl: Further Reflections on Religious Syncretism in Central Mexico," (*L'Uomo* 1989), among numerous other papers.

Allen Johnson (Ph.D., anthropology, 1968), is Professor and Chair, Department of Anthropology, University of California, Los Angeles. He is the author, with Timothy Earle, of *The Evolution of Human Societies* and, among other papers, of "Oedipus in the Political Economy" (with

Orna R. Johnson, 1988). He is senior co-author of *Oedipus Ubiquitous: The Family Romance in World Folk Literature*, which is in press. In October 1991, he was graduated from the Southern California Psychoanalytic Institute.

Benjamin Kilborne (Ph.D., anthropology, 1973), is in private practice of psychoanalysis in the Los Angeles area. He has published numerous papers, especially on dreams (e.g., "Dream Interpretation and Culturally Constituted Defense Mechanisms" and "Pattern, Structure, and Style in Anthropological Studies of Dreams," both in *Ethos* 1981). He was graduated from the Southern California Psychoanalytic Institute in 1990 and is now a member of their faculty. He also is a Visiting Lecturer, Deptartment of Psychiatry at The University of California at Los Angeles and a member of the faculty in Clinical Studies at the California Institute of the Arts.

Suzanne R. Kirschner (Ph.D., anthropology, 1991), is Lecturer on Social Studies at Harvard University. She has published "'Then What Have I to do with Thee?' On Identity, Fieldwork, and Ethnographic Knowledge" (*Cultural Anthropology* 1987) and is writing a book on religious and romantic sources of the post-Freudian psychoanalytic narrative of development.

Robert A. LeVine (Ph.D., anthropology, 1958), is Roy E. Larsen Professor of Education and Human Development, and Professor of Anthropology at Harvard University. He is a 1971 graduate of the Chicago Institute for Psychoanalysis. He is the author of numerous books including *Culture, Behavior and Personality* (1982, 2nd edition) and the author of many articles including "Infant Environments in Psychoanalysis: A Cross-cultural View" (in Stigler et al., eds., 1990) and "Psychoanalytic Theory and the Comparative Study of Human Development" (in Munroe et al., eds. 1981).

B.K. Ramanujam (Diploma in Psychological Medicine, Royal College, London, 1965), is Chief, Mental Hygiene Clinic, West Side VA Medical Center in Chicago and Assistant Professor of Psychiatry, University of Illinois School of Medicine. In 1963, he was graduated from the Menninger School of Psychiatry. He has published several papers, including "Problems of Identity seen in the Clinic Setting" (in S. Kakar, ed., 1979) and "Social Change and Personal Crisis: A View from an Indian Practice" (in White and Pollak, eds. 1986).

David H. Spain (Ph.D., anthropology, 1969) is Associate Professor of Anthropology and Adjunct Associate Professor, Department of Psychiatry at the University of Washington. He graduated from the Seattle Institute of Psychoanalysis in 1986 and is now a member of the faculty. In addition to having published a reader in cultural anthropology, he has co-authored two books, one on Africa and one on research design in anthropology. He also has published numerous papers, among them several recent and controversial essays on incest theory, including "The Westermarck-Freud Incest-theory Debate: An Evaluation and Reformulation" (*Current Anthropology* 1987) and "Taboo or Not Taboo: Is That the Question?" (*Ethos* 1988).

Melford E. Spiro (Ph.D., anthropology, 1950) is Emeritus Professor of Anthropology at the University of California, San Diego. He has published many books and articles including *Oedipus in the Trobriands* (1982) and, most recently, *Anthropological Other or Burmese Brother? Studies in Cultural Analysis* (1991). Some of his papers have been published in a collection entitled *Culture and Human Nature: Theoretical Papers* (1987, Kilborne and Langness, eds.). He is a past President of the Society for Psychological Anthropology and of the American Ethnological Society. He was a candidate at the San Diego Psychoanalytic Institute from 1973-1978 and practiced psychoanalysis from 1977-1981.

Margaret Trawick (Ph.D., anthropology, 1978) is Professor and Chair of the Department of Social Anthropology, Massey University, New Zealand. The author of numerous papers on ethnopoetics, spirit possession, and science and culture in India, she is currently at work on a book on Indian feminism. The issues raised in her paper for this volume are discussed in a broader context in her recent book, *Notes on Love in a Tamil Family* (1990).

Bibliography

Abrams, M.H. 1971. *Natural Supernaturalism: Tradition and Revolution in Romantic Literature*. New York: W.W. Norton.

Ainsworth, Mary D. Salter. 1967. *Infancy in Uganda*. Baltimore: Johns Hopkins Press.

Alexander, Franz. 1938. "Remarks about the Relation of Inferiority Feelings to Guilt Feeling." *International Journal of Psycho-Analysis* 19:41-49.

Amsterdam, B., and M. Levitt. 1980. "Consciousness of Self and Painful Self-Consciousness." *Psychoanalytic Study of the Child*, 35:67-84.

Anzieu, Didier. 1975. *Freud's Self-Analysis*. Peter Graham, Trans. Madison, CT: International Universities Press, 1986.

Badcock, Christopher R. 1980. *The Psychoanalysis of Culture*. Oxford: Basil Blackwell.

_________. 1986. *The Problem of Altruism*. Oxford and Cambridge, MA: Basil Blackwell.

_________. 1988. *Essential Freud*. Oxford and Cambridge, MA: Basil Blackwell.

_________. 1990. *Oedipus in Evolution*. Oxford and Cambridge, MA: Basil Blackwell.

_________. 1991. *Evolution and Individual Behavior*. Oxford and Cambridge, MA: Basil Blackwell.

_________. 1992. *Essential Freud: An Introduction of Classical Psychoanalysis*. Second edition. Oxford and Cambridge, MA: Basil Blackwell.

Bakan, David. 1958 *Sigmund Freud and the Jewish Mystical Tradition*. Boston: Beacon Press.

_________. 1975. *Sigmund Freud and the Jewish Mystical Tradition*. Boston: Beacon Press.

Balint, Michael. 1968. *The Basic Fault*. New York: Basic Books.

Balmary, Marie. 1979. *Psychoanalyzing Psychoanalysis: Freud and the Hidden Fault of the Father* (Ned Lukacher, Trans.). Baltimore, MD: Johns Hopkins University Press, 1982.

Barry, J. W. 1976. *Human Ecology and Cognitive Style*. New York: Sage.

Barzun, Jacques. 1958. *Darwin, Marx, Wagner: Critique of a Heritage* (2nd ed.). Garden City, N.Y.: Doubleday. Second Edition.

Bellah, Robert N., Richard Madsen, William M. Sullivan, Ann Swidler, and Steven M. Tipton. 1985. *Habits of the Heart: Individualism and Commitment in American Life* . Berkeley: University of California Press.

Benedict, Ruth. 1946. *The Chrysanthamum and the Sword*. Boston: Houghton Mifflin Co.

Berkeley-Hill, Owen. 1921a. "The Anal Erotic Factor in the Religion, Philosphy and Character of the Hindus." *International Journal of Psycho-Analysis* 2:306-338.

_________. 1921b. "A Short Study of the Life and Character of Mohammad." *International Journal of Psycho-Analysis* 2:31-53.

_________. 1925. "Hindu-Muslim Unity." *International Journal of Psycho-Analysis* 6:282-287.

Bibring, Edward L. 1963. "The Mechanims of Depression." In Phyllis Greenacre, ed., *Affective Disorders: Psychoanalytic Contribution to Their Study* (pp.13-48). New York: International Universities Press.

Bion, Wilfred R. 1963. *Elements of Psychoanalysis*. London: Hogarth.

Blanck, Rubin, and Gertrude Blanck. 1986. *Beyond Ego Psychology*. New York: Columbia University Press.

Bloch, Marc. 1954. *The Historian's Craft*. NY: Alfred Knopf.

Blos, Peter. 1967. "The Second Individuation Process in Adolescence," in *The Psychoanalytic Study of the Child*, vol. XXII (pp. 162-186). New York: International Universities Press.

Blum, Harold P. 1979. "The Prototype of Preoedipal Reconstruction." In Mark Kanzer & Jules Glenn, eds., *Freud and His Self-Analysis*. New York: Jason Aronson.

Boesky, Dale. 1989. "The Questions and Curiosity of the Psychoanalyst." *Journal of the American Psychoanalytic Association*, 37:579-603.

Bohm, D. 1957. *Causality and Chance in Modern Physics*. New York: Harper.

Bose, Girindrasekhar. 1948. "A New Theory of Mental Life." *Samiksa* 2:108-205.

Bouhdiba, Abdelwahab. 1985. *Sexuality in Islam* (Alan Sheridan, Trans.). London: Routledge & Kegan Paul.

Bowlby, John. 1969. *Attachment and Loss*. New York: Basic Books.

Brenner, Charles. 1982. *The Mind in Conflict*. New York: International Universities Press.

Breuer, Joseph, and Sigmund Freud. 1893-1895. *Studies on Hysteria*. In James Strachey, ed. and trans., *Standard Edition of the Complete Psychological Works of Sigmund Freud*, vol. 2. London: Hogarth Press.

Briggs, Jean L. 1970. *Never in Anger: Portrait of an Eskimo Family*. Cambridge, MA: Harvard University Press.

Bross, M. 1988. "Oedipus and Jocasta: A Re-examination of Freud's Drama of Destiny." In G.H. Pollock and J.M. Ross (eds.), *The Oedipus Papers*. Madison, WI: International Universities Press.

Broucek, F. 1982. "Shame and Its Relationship to Early Narcissistic Development." *International Journal of Psychoanalysis*, 63:369-378.

Cambor, Charles. 1989. "Preoedipal Factors in Superego Development." *Psychoanalytic Quarterly* 38:81-96.

Campbell, JoAnn F. 1984. "Cultural Isolation among International Non-Student Wives and Its Effect upon Pre-School Children." Presented at the *83rd Annual Meeting of the American Anthropological Association*, Denver.

_________. 1985. *Parental Adaptations and the Separation-Individuation Process in Children in Some Overseas Nigerian Families*. Unpublished doctoral dissertation, University of Washington, Seattle.

_________. 1989. "Multiple Mothering and Separation-Individuation: Evidence from Some Nigerian Children." Presented at the *88th Annual Meetings of the American Anthropological Association*, Washington, D.C., November 18, 1989.

Campbell, Joseph. 1959. *The Masks of God: Primitive Mythology*. New York: Viking Press.

Carroll, Michael P. 1986. *The Cult of the Virgin Mary: Psychological Origins*. Princeton, NJ: Princeton University Press.

Carstairs, G. Morris. 1957. *The Twice-Born: A Study of a Community of High-Caste Hindus*. Bloomington: Indiana University Press, 1975.

Chasseguet-Smirgel, Janine. 1985. *The Ego Ideal* (Paul Barrows, Trans.). New York: W.W. Norton & Co.

Chodorow, Nancy. 1978. *The Reproduction of Mothering: Psychoanalysis and the Sociology of Gender*. Berkeley: University of California Press.

_________. 1989. *Feminism and Psychoanalytic Theory*. New Haven, CT: Yale University Press.

Cosmides, Leda, and John Tooby. 1989. "Evolutionary Psychology and the Generation of Culture, Part II: Case Study: A Computational Theory of Social Exchange." *Ethology and Sociobiology* 10:51-97.

Crapanzano, Vincent. 1978. "Lacan's Écrits." *Canto* 2:183-191.

_________. 1980. *Tuhami: Portrait of a Moroccan*. Chicago: University of Chicago Press.

Dale, Peter N. 1986. *The Myth of Japanese Uniqueness*. New York: St. Martin's Press.

Daly, Claude Danger. 1927. "Hindu Mythology and the Castration Complex." *Imago* 13:145-198.

Daly, Martin D., and Margo Wilson. 1988. *Homicide*. New York: A. de Gruyter.

de George, R. T., and F. M. de George. 1972. *The Structuralists: From Marx to Lévi-Strauss*. Garden City, N.Y.: Doubleday.

de Waal, F. 1982. *Chimpanzee Politics: Power and Sex Among Apes*. New York: Harper and Row.

DeGroot, J.J.M. 1910. *The Religion of the Chinese*. New York: Macmilan.

Deleuze, Gilles, and Felix Guattari. 1972. *Anti-Oedipus: Capitalism and Schizophrenia* (Robert Hurley, Mark Seem, and Helen R. Lane, trans.). New York: Viking Press, 1977.

Desai, Prakash, and Alfred Collins. 1986. "Selfhood in Context: Some Indian Solutions." In M. I. White and S. Pollak, eds., *The Cultural Transition* (pp. 261-286). London: Routledge and Kegan Paul.

Devereux, George. 1937. "Institutionalized Homosexuality of the Mohave Indians." *Human Biology* 9:498-527.

_________. 1939. "Mohave Culture and Personality." *Character and Personality* 8:91-109.

_________. 1951. *Reality and Dream: The Psychotherapy of a Plains Indian*. New York: International Universities Press.

_________. 1953. "Why Oedipus Killed Laius: A Note on the Complementary Oedipus Complex in Greek Drama." *International Journal of Psychoanalysis*, *34*:132-141.

_________. 1956. "Normal and Abnormal: The Key Problem of Psychiatric Anthropology." In J. Casagrande and T. Gladwin, eds., *Some Uses of Anthropology: Theoretical and Applied* (pp.23-48, plus references). Washington, D.C.: Anthropological Society of Washington. (Also in much expanded version in French in Devereux 1970, pp.1-83; and retranslated into English in Devereux 1980, pp.3-72.)

_________. 1961. *Mohave Ethnopsychiatry: The Psychic Disturbances of an Indian Tribe*. Washington, D.C.: Smithsonian Institution Press.

_________. 1963. "Sociopolitical Functions of the Oedipus Myth in Early Greece." *Psychoanalytic Quarterly* 32:205-214.

_________. 1967. *From Anxiety to Method in the Behavioral Sciences*. The Hague and Paris: Mouton.

_________. 1970. *Essais d'Ethnopsychiatrie Générale*. Paris: Gallimard.

_________. 1976. *Dreams in Greek Tragedy*. Oxford: Basil Blackwell.

_________. 1978a. *Ethnopsychoanalysis: Psychoanalysis and Anthropology as Complementary Frames of Reference*. Berkeley: University of California Press.

_________. 1978b. "The Works of George Devereux." In George D. Spindler, ed., *The Making of Psychological Anthropology* (pp.364-406). Berkeley: University of California Press.

_________. 1980. *Basic Problems of Ethnopsychiatry*. (Basia Miller Gulati and George Devereux, trans.). Chicago: Univeristy of Chicago Press.

DeVos, George A. 1973. "Some Observations of Guilt in Relation to Achievement and Arranged Marriage." In George A. DeVos (ed.), *Socialization for Achievement: Essays on the Cultural Psychology of the Japanese*. Berkeley: University of California Press. [orig. 1960].

DeVos, George, and Bryce L. Boyer. 1989. *Symbolic Analysis Cross-Culturally: The Rorschach Test*. Berkeley: University of California Press.

Doi, L. Takeo. 1963. "Some Thoughts on Helplessness and the Desire to be Loved." *Psychiatry* 26(3):266-272.

_________. 1971. Amae No Kozo [The Structure of Amae]. Tokyo: Kobundo.

__________. 1973. *The Anatomy of Dependence* (John Bester, Trans.). New York: Kodansha International.

__________. 1986. *The Anatomy of the Self: The Individual Versus Society*. Tokyo: Kodansha International.

Dorpat, Theodore L. 1976. "Structural Conflict and Object Relations Conflict." *Journal of the American Psychoanalytic Association* 24:855-874.

Dundes, Alan. 1975. *Analytic Essays in Folklore*. The Hague: Mouton.

__________. 1981. "The Hero Pattern and the Life of Jesus." *The Psychoanalytic Study of Society* 9:49-83.

__________. 1985. *Life is Like a Chicken Coop Ladder: A Portrait of German Culture through Folklore*. New York: Columbia University Press.

__________. 1990. *Parsing through Customs: Essays in Psychoanalytic Folklore Study*. Madison: University of Wisconsin Press.

Eagle, Morris N. 1984. *Recent Developments in Psychoanalytic Theory*. New York: McGraw-Hill.

Edgerton, R. B. 1971. *The Individual in Cultural Adaptation*. Berkeley: University of California Press.

Edmunds, L., and A. Dundes, eds. 1983. *Oedipus: A Folklore Casebook*. New York: Garland.

Ekman, Paul, and W.V. Friesen. 1975. *Unmasking the Face*. Englewood Cliffs, NJ: Prentice-Hall.

Ellenberger, Henri F. 1970. *The Discovery of the Unconscious: The History and Evolution of Dynamic Psychiatry*. New York: Basic Books.

Emde, Robert N., Theodore J. Gaensbauer, and Robert J. Harmon. 1976. "Emotional Expression in Infancy: A Biobehavioral Study." *Psychological Issues, Monograph 37*. New York: International Universities Press.

Emerson, Ralph Waldo. 1990. "Self-Reliance," in *Selected Essays, Lectures and Poems*. New York: Bantam.

Endleman, Robert. 1966. "Reflections on the Human Revolution." *Psychoanalytic Review* 53:169-188.

__________. 1967. *Personality and Social Life*. New York: Random House.

__________. 1981. *Psyche and Society: Explorations in Psychoanalytic Sociology*. New York: Columbia University Press.

________. 1986. "Homosexuality in Tribal Societies." (Overview Essay). *Transcultural Psychiatric Research Review* 23:187-218.

________. 1989. *Love and Sex in Twelve Cultures*. New York: Psyche Press.

________. 1990. *Deviance and Psychopathology: The Sociology and Psychology of Outsiders*. Malabar, FL: Krieger Publishers.

________. 1991. *Eros and Evolution: Prospects for PASO (PsychoAnalytic SOcial Science*. New York: Psyche Press.

________. (Forthcoming). "Review of T. & R. Lidz: *Oedipus in the Stone Age*." *Psychoanalytic Review*.

Epstein, A.L. 1984. *The Experience of Shame in Melanesia: An Essay in the Anthropology of Affect*. London: Royal Anthropological Institute.

Erdheim, Mario. 1982. *Die gesellschaftliche Produktion von Unbewusstheit: Eine Einführung in den ethnopsychoanalytischen Prozess* (The Societal Production of the Unconscious: An Introduction to Ethnopsychiatric Process). Frankfurt am Main: Suhrkamp.

Erikson, Erik H. 1950. *Childhood and Society*. New York: W. W. Norton.

________. 1958. *Young Man Luther: A Study in Psychoanalysis and History*. New York: W. W. Norton.

________. 1954. "The Dream Specimen of Psychoanalysis." *Journal of the American Psychoanalytic Association* 2:5-56.

________. 1959. "Identity and the Life Cycle." *Psychological Issues* 1. New York: International Universities Press.

________. 1963. *Childhood and Society*. 2nd edition, revised and enlarged. New York: W. W. Norton.

________. 1969. *Gandhi's Truth*. New York: W. W. Norton.

Ewing, Katherine P. 1990. "The Illusion of Wholeness: Culture, Self, and the Experience of Inconsistency." *Ethos* 18:251-278.

Faber, M. D. 1980. *Culture and Consciousness: The Social Meaning of Altered Awareness*. New York: Library of Art and Social Science.

________. 1989. *The Withdrawal of Human Projection: A Study of Culture and Internalized Objects*. New York: Library of Art and Social Science.

Fairbairn, W.R.D. 1954. *An Object Relations Theory of the Personality*. New York: Basic Books.

Federn, Paul. 1952. *Ego Psychology and the Psychoses*. New York: Basic Books.

Fenichel, Otto. 1945. *The Psychoanalytic Theory of Neurosis*. New York: W.W. Norton and Co.

Ferenczi, Sandor. 1951. *Sex in Psychoanalysis*. New York: Basic Books.

Feuer, Lewis. 1969. *The Conflict of Generations*. New York: Basic Books.

Fine, Reuben. 1975a. *Psychoanalytic Psychology*. New York: Jason Aronson.

________. 1975b. "The Idea of a Psychoanalytic University." *History of Childhood (Journal of Psychohistory)* 3:103-115.

________. 1977. "Psychoanalysis as a Philosophical System: The Basis for Integrating the Social Sciences." *Journal of Psychohistory* 5:1-66.

Firth, Raymond. 1989. "Second Introduction 1988." In Bronislaw Malinowski, *A Diary in the Strict Sense of the Term* (pp.xxi-xxxi). Stanford, CA: Stanford University Press.

Fischer, David Hackett. 1989. *Albion's Seed: British Folkways in America*. New York: Oxford University Press.

Fisher, Seymour, & Greenberg, Roger P. 1985. *The Scientific Credibility of Freud's Theories and Therapy*. New York: Columbia University Press.

Fortes, Meyer. 1987. *Religion, Morality and the Person; Essays on Tallensi Religion*. Jack Goody, ed. Cambridge: Cambridge University Press.

Foster, George M. 1972. "The Anatomy of Envy: A Study in Symbolic Behavior." *Current Anthropology* 13:135-202.

Foucault, Michel. 1973. *The Order of Things: An Archaeology of the Human Sciences*. New York: Vintage Books.

________. 1977. *Madness and Civilization: A History of Insanity in the Age of Reason*. London: Tavistock.

________. 1979. *The History of Sexuality, Vol. I: An Introduction*. London: Allen Lane.

Fox, Robin. 1967. "Totem and Taboo Reconsidered." In E. Leach (ed.), *The Structural Study of Myth and Totemism* (pp. 161-178). London: Tavistock.

Freeman, Derek. 1967. "Totem and Taboo: A Reappraisal." In W. Muensterberger and S. Axelrad, eds., *The Psychoanalytic Study of Society*, vol.4 (pp.9 33). New York: International Universities Press.

Freud, Anna. 1937. *The Ego and the Mechanisms of Defense*. London: Hogarth Press.

________. 1961ff. *The Writings of Anna Freud*. Vols. 1-6. New York: International Universities Press.

Freud, Sigmund.[1] 1895. *Project for a Scientific Psychology*. *SE* 1, 1961:283-398.

_____. 1899. "Screen Memories." *SE* 3, 1962:301-322.

_____. 1900-1901. *The Interpretation of Dreams*. *SE* 4-5, 1953.

_____. 1901. *The Psychopathology of Everyday Life*. *SE* 6. 1960.

_____. 1905a. "Three Essays on the Theory of Sexuality." *SE* 7. 1960:125-248.

_____. 1905b. *Jokes and Their Relation to the Unconscious*. *SE* 8. 1960.

_____. 1910. "Leonardo Da Vinci and a Memory of his Childhood." *SE* 11, 1957:59-137.

_____. 1913. *Totem and Taboo*. *SE* 13. 1955:1-164.

_____. 1914a. *The History of the Psycho-Analytic Movement*. *SE* 14, 1957:1-66.

_____. 1914b. *On Narcissism; An Introduction*. *SE* 14. 1957:67-140.

_____. 1915-16. *Introductory Lectures on Psychoanalysis (Parts I and II)*. *SE* 15. 1961.

_____. 1916-1917. *Introductory Lectures on Psychoanalysis (Part III)*. *SE* 16. 1961.

_____. 1917. "Mourning and Melancholia." *SE* 14. 1957:237-258.

_____. 1921. *Group Psychology and the Analysis of the Ego*. *SE* 18. 1955:67-145.

_____. 1920-1922. *Beyond the Pleasure Principle*. *SE* 18. 1955:1-64.

_____. 1923. *The Ego and the ID*. *SE* 19. 1961:1-66.

_____. 1924. "The Dissolution of the Oedipus Complex." *SE* 19. 1961: 173-182.

_____. 1925a. *An Autobiographical Study*. *SE* 20. 1959:7-76.

_____. 1925b. "On Negation." *SE* 19. 1961:235-242.

[1]All references to Freud's works are to the English language *Standard Edition of the Complete Psychological Works of Sigmund Freud*, edited and translated by James Strachey, London: Hogarth Press. Hereafter cited as *SE*, with the volume number and year of publication of that volume. First date given is the date of original publication.

_____. 1926. *Inhibitions, Symptoms and Anxiety*. *SE* 20. 1959:77-175.
_____. 1927. *The Future of an Illusion*. *SE* 21. 1961:3-58.
_____. 1930. *Civilization and Its Discontents*. *SE* 21. 1961:59-148.
_____. 1931. "Female Sexuality." *SE* 21. 1961:223-243.
_____. 1933. *New Introductory Lectures on Psychoanalysis*. *SE* 22. 1964: 7-184.
_____. 1937. *Analysis Terminable and Interminable*. *SE* 23. 1964:209-254.
_____. 1939. *Moses and Monotheism: Three Essays*. *SE* 23. 1964:3-140.
_____. 1940. *An Outline of Psychoanalysis*. *SE* 23. 1964:141-208.
Friedman, J. 1974. Marxism, Structuralism, and Vulgar Materialism. *Man* 9:444-469.
Fromm, Erich. 1941. *Escape from Freedom*. New York: Farrar and Rinehart.
__________. 1947. *Man for Himself*. New York: Rinehart.
__________. 1948. "The Oedipus Complex and the Oedipus Myth." In Ruth N. Anshen, ed., *The Family: Its Function and Destiny*. New York: Harper and Brothers.
__________. 1955. *The Sane Society*. New York: Holt, Rinehart and Winston.
Fromm, Erich, and M. Maccoby. 1970. *Social Character in a Mexican Village*. Englewood Cliffs, NJ: Prentice-Hall.
Furman, Robert. 1978. "Some Developmental Aspects of the Verbalization of Affects." *Psychoanalytic Study of the Child*, 33: 187-211.
Gaines, Atwood. 1982. "Cultural Definitions, Behavior and the Person in American Psychiatry." In A. J. Marsella and G.M. White (eds.), *Cultural Conceptions of Mental Health and Therapy*. Dordrecht, Holland: D. Reidel.
Gallop, Jane. 1982. *The Daughter's Seduction: Feminism and Psychoanalysis*. Ithaca, NY: Cornell University Press.
__________. 1985. *Reading Lacan*. Ithaca, NY: Cornell University Press.
Gardner, Allen, and Beatrice Gardner. 1969. "Teaching Sign Language to a Chimpanzee." *Science* 165:664-672.
Gay, Peter. 1978. *Freud, Jews and Other Germans: Masters and Victims in Modernist Culture*. New York: Oxford University Press.
_________. 1984 and 1986. *The Bourgeois Experience: Victoria to Freud*. (two vols.) New York: Oxford University Press.

_________. 1987. *A Godless Jew: Freud, Atheism, and the Making of Psychoanalysis*. New Haven, CT: Yale University Press.
_________. 1988. *Freud: A Life for Our Time*. New York and London: W. W. Norton.
Gedo, John. 1984. *Psychoanalysis and Its Discontents*. New York: The Guilford Press.
Geertz, Clifford. 1967. "Under the Mosquito Net." *New York Review of Books*, September 14.
_________. 1983. "Fron the Native's Point of View: On the Nature of Anthropological Understanding," in *Local Knowledge*. New York: Basic Books.
Gill, Merton M. 1967. "The Primary Process." In Robert R. Holt, ed., *Motives and Thought: Psychoanalytic Essays in Honor of David Rapaport*. *Psychological Issues*, Monograph 18/19:260-298.
_________. 1982. *Analysis of Transference*. New York: International Universities Press.
Goldberg, Harvey E. 1987. "Torah and Children: Some Symbolic Aspects of the Reproduction of Jews and Judaism." In Harvey E. Goldberg, ed., *Judaism Viewed from Within and from Without* (pp. 107-130). Albany: State University of New York Press.
Goodall, Jane. 1971. *In the Shadow of Man*. Boston: Houghton Mifflin.
Gorer, Geoffrey. 1948. *The American People*. New York: Norton.
_________. 1955. *Exploring English Character*. New York: Criterion.
Greenberg, Jay, & Mitchell, Stephen. 1984. *Object Relations in Psycho-an- alytic Theory*. Cambridge, MA: Harvard University Press.
Guntrip, Harry. 1968. *Schizoid Phenomena, Object Relations and the Self*. New York: International Universites Press.
_________. 1973. *Psychoanalytic Theory, Therapy, and the Self*. New York: Basic Books.
Hale, Nathan G., Jr. 1978. "Berggasse XIX to Central Park West: The Americanization of Psychoanalysis, 1919-1940." *Journal of the History of the Behavioral Sciences* 14:299-315.
Hallowell, A. Irving. 1955. *Culture and Experience*. Philadelphia: University of Pennsylvania Press.
Hamilton, N. Gregory. 1988. *Self and Others: Object Relations Theory in Practice*. Northvale, NJ: Jason Aronson Inc.

Haraway, Donna J. 1989. *Primate Visions: Gender, Race and Nature in the World of Modern Science*. London: Routledge, Chapman and Hall, Inc.

Harrington, C., and Whiting, J. W. M. 1972. "Socialization Process and Personality." In F. L. K. Hsu, ed., *Psychological Anthropology*. Cambridge, MA: Schenkman.

Harris, Marvin. 1968. *The Rise of Anthropological Theory*. New York: Thomas Y. Crowell Company.

________. 1977. *Cannibals and Kings: The Origins of Cultures*. New York: Random House.

________. 1979. *Cultural Materialism: The Struggle for a Science of Culture*. New York: Random House.

Hartman Heinz. 1958. *Ego Psychology and the Problem of Adaptation*. New York: International Universities Press.

Hartman, Heinz, and Rudolf Loewenstein. 1964. "Notes on the Superego." *Psychoanalytic Study of the Child* 17:42-81.

Hartnack, Christiane. 1987. "British Psychoanalysts in Colonial India." In Mitchell G. Ash and William R. Woodward, eds., *Psychology in Twentieth Century Thought and Society* (pp.233-251). New York: Cambridge University Press.

Hartshorne, H., and M. May. 1928. *Studies in the Nature of Character: Studies in Deceit, i*. New York: Macmillan.

Heelas, P., and A. Lock, eds. 1981. *Indigenous Psychologies: The Anthropology of the Self*. Lancaster, PA: Academic Press.

Hegel, G.W.F. 1807 [1977]. *Phenomenology of the Spirit*. (A.V. Miller, trans.) New York: Oxford University Press

Heller, T.C., M. Sosna, and D.E. Wellberg, eds. 1986. *Reconstructing Individualism: Autonomy, Individuality and Self in Western Thought*. Stanford, CA: Stanford University Press.

Holt, Robert R. 1967. "The Development of the Primary Process: A Structural View." In Robert R. Holt, ed., *Motives and Thought: Psycho-analytic Essays in Honor of David Rapaport. Psychological Issues*, Monograph 18/19:344-384.

________. 1978. "Ideological and Thematic conflicts in the structure of Freud's Thought," in S. Smith, ed., *The Human Mind Revisited: Essays in Honor of Karl A. Menninger* (pp.51-98). New York: International Universities Press.

_________. 1989. "Ego Autonomy and the Problem of Human Freedom," in *Freud Reappraised: A Fresh Look at Psychoanalytic Theory* (pp.218-252). New York: The Guilford Press.

Horney, Karen. 1937 *The Neurotic Personality of Our Time*. New York: W.W. Norton.

_________. 1939. *New Ways in Psychoanalysis*. New York: W. W. Norton.

Hsu, Francis L.K. 1979. "The Cultural Problem of the Cultural Anthropologist." *American Anthropologist* 81:517-532.

Hughes, H. Stuart. 1968. *The Sea Change*. New York: Harper and Row.

Hughes, Judith M. 1989. *Reshaping the Psychoanalytic Domain*. Berkeley: University of California Press.

Hunt, Jennifer. 1989. *Psychoanalytic Aspects of Fieldwork*. Newbury Park, CA: Sage Publications, Paper #18.

Hunt, Robert, ed. 1967. *Personalities and Cultures*. Garden City, NY: Natural History Press.

Hyman, Stanley Edgar. 1966. *The Tangled Bank: Darwin, Marx, Frazer and Freud as Creative Writers*. New York: The Universal Library/Grosset and Dunlap.

Ingham, John M. 1986. *Mary, Michael, and Lucifer: Folk Catholicism in Central Mexico*. Austin: University of Texas Press.

_________. 1989. "Chalma and Tepoztecatl: Further Reflections on Religious Syncretism in Central Mexico." *L'Uomo* 2:61-82.

Jacobson, Edith. 1964. *The Self and the Object World*. New York: International Universities Press.

Jacoby, Russell. 1983. *The Repression of Psychoanalysis: Otto Fenichel and the Political Freudians*. New York: Basic Books.

Johnson, A. 1971. *Sharecroppers of the Sertao*. Stanford: Stanford Univ. Press.

_________. 1982. "Nonreductionist Cultural Ecology." In J. G. Kennedy and R. B. Edgerton, eds., *Culture and Ecology: Eclectic Perspectives*. Washington, D.C.: American Anthropological Association.

Johnson, A., and O. Johnson. 1988. "Oedipus in the Political Economy: Theme and Variations in Amazonia." In R. R. Randolph, D. Schneider, and M.N. Diaz, eds., *Dialectics and Gender: Anthropological Approaches*. Boulder, CO: Westview.

Johnson, Allen, and Timothy K. Earle. 1987. *The Evolution of Human Societies: From Foraging Group to Agrarian State*. Stanford, CA: Stanford University Press.

Jones, Ernest. 1955. *The Life and Work of Sigmund Freud, Vol. 2. The Mature Years, 1901-1919*. New York: Basic Books.

_________. 1959. *On The Nightmare*. New York: Evergreen/Grove Press.

_________. 1964a. "A Psycho-Analytic Study of the Holy Ghost Concept." In *Essays in Applied Psycho-Analysis*, Vol. II. pp. 358-373. New York: International Universities Press.

_________. 1964b. "The Madonna's Conception Through the Ear." In *Essays in Applied Psycho-Analysis*, Vol. II. Pp. 266-357. New York: International Universities Press.

Jung, Carl G. 1956. *Symbols of Transformation: An Analysis of the Prelude to a Case of Schizophrenia*. R. F. C. Hull, transla. Princeton, NJ: Bollingen Library/Princeton University Press.

Kakar, Sudhir. 1979. *The Inner World: A Psychoanalytic Study of Childhood and Society in India*. Delhi and London: Oxford University Press.

_________. 1980. "Observations on the 'Oedipal Alliance' in a Patient with a Narcissistic Personality Disorder." *Samksa* 34:47-53.

_________. 1982. "Reflections on Psychoanalysis, Indian Culture and Mysticism." *Journal of Indian Philosophy* 10:269-297.

_________. 1985. "Psychoanalysis and Non-Western Cultures." *International Review of Psychoanalysis* 12:441-448.

_________. 1990. "Stories from Indian Psychoanalysis: Context and Text." In James W. Stigler, Richard A. Shweder, and Gilbert Herdt, eds., *Cultural Psychology: Essays on Comparative Human Development* (pp.427-445). New York: Cambridge University Press.

Kanzer, Mark. 1980. "Visual Communication in the Psychoanalytic Situation." *International Journal of Psychoanalysis*, 61:249-258.

Kardiner, Abram. 1939. *The Individual and His Society*. New York: Columbia University Press.

_________. 1945. *The Psychological Frontiers of Society*. New York: Columbia University Press.

Kaufman, Gershen. 1985. *Shame: The Power of Caring*. Cambridge, MA: Schenkman Publishing Co.

Kernberg, O.F. 1975. *Borderline Conditions and Pathological Narcissism*. New York: Aronson.

Kilborne, Benjamin. 1978. *Interpretations du Rêve au Maroc*. Claix: La Pensée Sauvage.

_________. 1981. "Dream Interpretation and Culturally Constituted Defense Mechanisms." *Ethos* 9(4): 294-312

_________. 1981a. "Pattern, Structure, and Style in Anthropological Studies of Dreams." *Ethos* 9:165-185.

_________. 1981b. "Moroccan Dream Interpretation and Culturally Constituted Defense Mechanisms." *Ethos* 9:294-312.

_________. 1987. "In Memoriam: George Devereux." *The Psychoanalytic Study of Society* 11:1-14.

_________. n.d.a. "Sartre, Shame and the Epistemology of Looking in Psychoanalytic Theory." (unpublished manuscript).

_________. n.d.b. "Guilt and Shame as Cultural Catagories: Historical and Anthropological Perspectives on a False Dichotomy." (unpublished manuscript).

_________. n.d.c. "Peek-a-boo Where Are You? Theories of Child Development and Shame Dynamics in the Analytic Situation." (unpublished manuscript).

Kilborne, Benjamin, and L.L. Langness, eds. 1987. *Culture and Human Nature: Theoretical Papers of Melford Spiro*. Chicago: University of Chicago Press.

Kirschner, Suzanne R. 1985. "Margaret S. Mahler's Separation-Individuation Theory as a Transmuted Version of an Originally Theological Narrative." Unpublished Qualifying Paper, Harvard University.

_________. 1987. "'Then what have I to do with Thee?' On Identity, Fieldwork, and Ethnographic Knowledge." *Cultural Anthropology* 2:211-234.

_________. 1990. "Sources of Redemption in Psychoanalytic Developmental Psychology," paper presented at the Annual Convention of the American Psychological Association. Boston, MA.

_________. 1991. *Judaeo-Christian Mystical Themes in Psychoanalytic Developmental Psychology: From Cosmology to Personality*. Unpublished doctoral dissertation, Harvard University Graduate School of Education.

Kleeman, James. 1967. "The Peek-a-boo Game; Part 1: Its Origins, Meanings and Related Phenomena in the First Year." *Psychoanalytic Study of the Child*, 22:239-273.

Klein, George S. 1976. *Psychoanalytic Theory: An Exploration of Essentials*. New York: International Universities Press.

Klein, Melanie. 1948. *Contributions to Psycho-Analysis, 1921-1945*. London: Hogarth Press.

_________. 1957. *Envy and Gratitude*. London: Tavistock.

Kline, Paul. 1972. *Fact and Fantasy in Freudian Theory*. London: Methuen.

Kohon, Gregorio. 1986. *The British School of Psychoanalysis*. New Haven: Yale University Press.

Kohut, Heinz. 1959. "Introspection, Empathy and Psychoanalysis." *Journal of the American Psychoanalytic Association* 7:459-483.

_________. 1971. *The Analysis of the Self*. New York: International Universities Press.

_________.1977. *The Restoration of the Self*. New York: International Universities Press.

_________. 1984. *How Does Analysis Cure?* Arnold Goldberg, ed., Chicago: University of Chicago Press.

_________. 1985. *Self Psychology and the Humanities: Reflections on a New Psychoanalytic Approach*. Edited with an introduction by Charles B. Strozier. New York: W.W. Norton.

Kosawa, Heisaku. 1931. "Zaiaku-Ishiki No Nishu—Ajase Conprekkusu. [Two Kinds of Guiilt Feelings—Ajase Complex]." *Koryo* (The Magazine of the Department of Medicine, Tohoku Imperial University). Reprinted in *Gendai No Esupuri* 148:166-173; 1979.

Kris, Ernst. 1956. "On Some Vicissitudes of Insight in Psychoanalysis." *International Journal of Psycho-Analysis*, 37:445-455.

Kristeva, Julia. 1980. *Desire in Language: A Semiotic Approach to Literature and Art*. New York: Columbia University Press.

_________. 1982. *Powers of Horror: An Essay on Abduction*. New York: Columbia University Press.

_________. 1984. *Revolution in Poetic Language*. New York: Columbia University Press.

Kroeber, A. L. 1920. "Totem and Taboo: An Ethnologic Psychoanalysis." *American Anthropologist* 22:48-55.

_________. 1939. "Totem and Taboo in Retrospect." *The American Journal of Sociology* 45(3):446-451.

Krull, Marianne. 1979. *Freud and His Father*. Arnold J. Pomerans, tr. New York: Norton, 1986.

Kuhn, Thomas. 1962. *The Structure of Scientific Revolutions*. Chicago: University of Chicago Press.

Kurtz, Stanley N. 1990. "Polysexualization: A New Approach to Oedipus in the Trobriands." *Ethos* 19:68-101.

_________. (in press). *All the Mothers Are One: Hindu India and the Cultural Reshaping of Psychoanalysis*. New York: Columbia University Press.

Kurzweil, Edith. 1989. *The Freudians: A Comparative Perspective*. New Haven: Yale University Press.

La Barre, Weston. 1938a. "Native American Beers." *American Anthropologist* 40:224-234.

_________. 1938b. *The Peyote Cult*. New Haven, CT: Yale University Publications in Anthropology, #19.

_________. 1939. "The Psychopathology of Drinking Songs." *Psychiatry* 2:203-212.

_________. 1948. *The Aymara Indians of the Lake Titicaca Plateau, Bolivia*. Menasha, WI: Memoirs of the American Anthropological Association, #68.

_________. 1954. *The Human Animal*. Chicago: University of Chicago Press.

_________. 1968. "Personality from a Psychoanalytic Viewpoint." In E. Norbeck, D. Price-Williams, and W. McCord, eds., *The Study of Personality: An Interdisciplinary Appraisal*. New York: Holt, Rinehart and Winston.

_________. 1969. *They Shall Take Up Serpents*. New York: Schocken.

_________. 1970. *The Ghost Dance: Origins of Religion*. Garden City, NY: Doubleday. Reprinted 1990: Prospect Heights, IL: Waveland Press.

_________. 1978a. "Freudian Biology, Magic and Religion." *Journal of the American Psychoanalytic Association* 26:813-830.

_________. 1978b. "Psychoanalysis and the Biology of Religion." *Journal of Psychological Anthropology* 1:57-64.

_________. 1978c. "The Personal Approach in Culture and Personality Research." In George D. Spindler, ed., *The Making of Psychological Anthropology* (pp.259-299). Berkeley: University of California Press.

_________. 1980a. "The Influence of Freud on Anthropology." In *Culture in Context: Selected Writings of Weston La Barre* (pp.163-200). Durham, NC: Duke University Press (originally published in *The American Imago* 15:275-328, 1958).

_________. 1980b. *Culture in Context: Selected Writings of Weston La Barre*. Durham, NC: Duke University Press.

_________. 1984. *Muelos: A Stone-Age Superstition about Sexuality*. New York: Columbia University Press.

_________. 1985. "George Devereux (1908-1985)." *The Journal of Psychoanalytic Anthropology* 8:209-213.

_________. 1991. *Shadow of Childhood: Neoteny and the Biology of Religion*. Norman: University of Oklahoma Press.

Lacan, Jacques. 1968. *Speech and Language in Psychoanalysis*. Anthony Wilden, trans., comm. and ed. Baltimore: Johns Hopkins University Press.

_________. 1949 [1977]. "The Mirror Image as Formative of the Function of the I." *Écrits: A Selection* (pp.1-7). (Alan Sheridan, Trans. New York: W. W. Norton.

_________. 1977. *Écrits: A Selection*. (Alan Sheridan, Trans.) New York: W. W. Norton.

Lamb, Marshall, ed. 1981. *The Role of the Father in Child Development*, second edition. New York: John Wiley & Sons.

Langs, Robert. 1976. *The Bipersonal Field*. New York: J. Aronson

Lansky, Melvin R. 1984. "Violence, Shame and the Family." *International Journal of Family Psychiatry* 5:21-40.

Laplanche, Jean, and J.B. Pontalis. 1967. *The Language of Psycho-Analysis*. (Donald Nicholson-Smith, trans.) London: Hogarth, 1973.

Lasch, Christopher. 1979. *The Culture of Narcissism: American Life in an Age of Diminishing Expectations*. New York: W.W.Norton.

Latour, Bruno, & Steve Woolgar. 1979. *Laboratory Life: The Social Construction of Scientific Facts*. Beverley Hills: Sage Publishing Co.

Layton, Bentley, ed. 1987. *The Gnostic Scriptures*. Translations, annotations, and introductions by Bentley Layton. Garden City, NY: Doubleday.

Leach, Edmund. 1988. "Late Medieval Representations of Saint Mary Magdalene." *Psychoanalytic Review* 75:95-109.

Lebra, Takie S. 1971. "The Social Mechanism of Guilt and Shame. The Japanese Case." *Anthropological Quarterly* 44:241-255.

_________. 1976. *Japanese Patterns of Behavior*. Honolulu: University of Hawaii Press.

_________. 1983. "Shame and Guilt: A Psychocultural View of the Japanese Self." *Ethos* 11:192-209.

_________. 1984. *Japanese Women: Constraint and Fulfillment*. Honolulu; University Press of Hawaii.

Lemaire, Anika. 1977. *Jacques Lacan*. (D. Macey, trans.). London: Routledge and Kegal Paul [orig. 1970].

Lerman, Hannah. 1986. *A Mote in Freud's Eye: From Psychoanalysis to the Psychology of Women*. New York: Springer.

Lévi-Strauss, Claude. 1949. *The Elementary Structures of Kinship*. Tr. J.H. Bell & J.R. von Sturmer; R. Needham, ed. Boston: Beacon Press (1969).

_________. 1958. "The Structural Study of Myth." In Lévi-Strauss, Claude, *Structural Anthropology* (pp.206-231). (C. Jacobson and B.G. Schoepf, trans.). New York: Basic Books (1963).

LeVine, Robert A. 1973. *Culture, Behavior, and Personality.* Chicago: Aldine.

_________. 1981. "Psychoanalytic Theory and the Comparative Study of Human Development." In Robert L. Munroe and Ruth H. Munroe, eds., *Handbook of Cross-cultural Human Development* (pp.63-72). New York: Garland Publishers.

_________. 1982. *Culture, Behavior and Personality*, 2nd ed. New York: Aldine.

_________. (in press). "Infant Environments in Psychoanalysis: A Cross-cultural View." In G. Herdt, ed., *Cultural Psychology*. New York: Cambridge University Press.

LeVine, Robert, S. Dixon, Sarah LeVine, A. Richman, P.H. Leiderman, and T.B. Brazelton. (in press). *Omwana: Infants and Parents in a Kenya Community*. New York: Cambridge University Press.

LeVine, Robert A., and Merry I. White. 1986. *Human Conditions*. New York: Routledge and Kegan Paul.

LeVine, Sarah. 1979. *Mothers and Wives: Gusii Women of East Africa*. Chicago: University of Chicago Press.

Levy, Robert. 1973. *Tahitians: Mind and Experience in the Society Islands*. Chicago: University of Chicago Press.

Lewis, Helen B. 1971. *Shame and Guilt in Neurosis*. New York: International Universities Press.

Lichtenberg, J.D. 1982. "Reflections on the First Year of Life." *Psychoanalytic Inquiry* 1:695-729.

Lipset, Seymour Martin. 1968. "Anglo-American Society," in *International Encyclopedia of the Social Sciences*. New York: Macmillan Co./The Free Press, pp.289-301.

Loewald, Hans W. 1979. "The Waning of the Oedipus Complex." *Journal of the American Psychoanalytic Association* 27:751-775.

Lukes, Steven. 1973. *Individualism*. Oxford, England: Basil Blackwell.

Lutz, Catherine. 1988. *Unnatural Emotions: Everyday Sentiments in a Micronesian Atoll and Their Challenge to Western Theory*. Chicago: University of Chicago Press.

Lynd, Helen. 1958. *On Shame and the Search for Identity*. New York: Harcourt, Brace.

Maccoby, Michael. 1976. *The Gamesman*. New York: Simon and Schuster.

Mahler, Margaret. 1942. "Pseudoimbecility: a magic cap of invisibility." In *Infantile Psychoses and Early Contributions: The Selected Papers of Margaret S. Mahler*. (1979) New York: Jason Aronson.

_________. 1975. "On the Current Status of the Infantile Neurosis," in *The Selected Papers of Margaret S. Mahler* vol 2. New York: Jason Aronson.

_________. 1988. "Epilogue." In Paul Stepansky, ed., *The Memoirs of Margaret S. Mahler*. New York: The Free Press.

Mahler, Margaret S., Fred Pine and Anni Bergman. 1968. *On Human Symbiosis and the Vicissitudes of Separation-Individuation*. New York: International Universities Press.

_________. 1975. *The Psychological Birth of the Human Infant*. New York: Basic Books.

Mahony, Patrick J. 1987. *Freud as a Writer*. Expanded edition. New Haven, CT: Yale University Press.

Malinowski, Bronislaw. 1927. *Sex and Repression in Savage Society*. New York: Meridian Books.

_________. 1928. *The Sexual Life of Savages*. New York: Harcourt, Brace and World.

_________. 1989. *A Diary in the Strict Sense of the Term*. Stanford, CA: Stanford University Press [orig. 1967].

Mann, Thomas. 1931. "Freud's Position in the History of Modern Thought." In *Past Masters and Other Papers* (pp.167-200). New York: Alfred Knopf.

________. 1939. "Freud and the Future," in *Freud, Goethe, Wagner*. New York: Alfred Knopf.

Manson, William C. 1988. *The Psychodynamics of Culture: Abram Kardiner and Neo-Freudian Anthropology*. New York: Greenwood press.

Mao Tse-Tung. 1961. "On Practice." In A. P. Mendel, ed., *Essential Works of Marxism*. New York: Bantam Books.

Marriott, McKim, & Ronald B. Inden. 1977. "Towards an Ethnosociology of South Asian Caste Systms." In Kennet David, ed. *The New Wind: Changing Identities in South Asia* (pp.227-238). Chicago: Mouton.

Marsella, A.J., G. DeVos, G. and F.L.K. Hsu. 1985. *Culture and Self: Asian and Western Perspectives*. London: Tavistock Publishers.

Masson, Jeffrey Moussaieff. 1984. *The Assault on Truth: Freud's Suppression of the Seduction Theory*. New York: Farrar, Straus, and Giroux.

________, ed. 1985. *The Complete Letters of Sigmund Freud to Wihelm Fliess, 1887-1904*. (Jeffrey M. Masson, trans.). Cambridge, MA: Harvard University Press.

Mcfarlane, A. 1978. *The Origins of English Individualism*. Oxford, England: Basil Blackwell.

McGill, David and Pearce, John K. 1982. "British-American Families," in Monica McGoldrick, John K. Pearce, and Joseph Giordano, eds., *Ethnicity and Family Therapy*. New York: The Guilford Press, pp.457-479.

McGrath, William J. 1985. *Freud's Discovery of Psychoanalysis*. Ithaca: Cornell University Press.

McGuire, William, ed. 1974. *The Freud/Jung Letters: The Correspondence between Sigmund Freud and C. G. Jung*. Ralph Manheim and R. F. C. Hull, trans. Princeton, NJ: Bollingen Library/Princeton University Press.

Mead, George H. 1934. *Mind, Self and Society*. Chicago: University of Chicago Press.

Mead, Margaret. 1928. *Coming of Age in Samoa*. New York: Morrow.

________. 1930. *Growing Up in New Guinea*. New York: Morrow.

_________. 1935. *Sex and Temperament in Three Primitive Societies*. New York: Morrow.

_________. 1949. *Male and Female*. New York: Morrow.

_________. 1954. "Theoretical Setting." In Margaret Mead and Martha Wolfenstein, eds., *Childhood in Contemporary Cultures*. Chicago: University of Chicago Press.

_________. 1963. "Totem and Taboo Reconsidered with Respect." *Bulletin of the Menninger Clinic* 27:185-199.

Meissner, William. 1984. *The Borderline Spectrum: Differential Diagnosis and Developmental Issues*. New York: Jason Aronson.

Meltzer, Françoise. 1987. "Editor's Introduction: Partitive Plays, Pipe Dreams." In *The Trial(s) of Psychoanalysis* (pp.215-221). *Critical Inquiry* 13(2):215-407.

Metge, Joan. 1985. *In and Out of Touch: Whakamaa in Cross-cultural Contact*. Wellington: University of Victoria Press.

Miller, Perry. 1937. "The Marrow of Puritan Divinity." *Publications of the Colonial Society of Massachusetts*, XXXII:245-300.

Miller, Susan. 1985. *The Shame Experience*. Hillsdale, NJ: The Analytic Press.

Mitchell, Juliet. 1975. *Psychoanalysis and Feminism: Freud, Reich, Laing, and Women*. New York: Vintage.

Mitchell, Juliet, and Jacqueline Rose. 1982. *Feminine Sexuality: Jacques Lacan and the École Freudienne*. New York: W. W. Norton.

Modell, Arnold H. 1965. "On Having the Right to a Life: An Aspect of the Superego's Development." *International Journal of Psycho-Analysis*, 46:323-331.

Moran, E. 1979. *Human Adaptability*. Belmont, CA: Wadsworth.

Morris, Richard. 1871. *Legends of the Holy Rood: Symbols of the Passion and Cross—Poems*. London: Early English Text Society/Trubner.

Morrison, Andrew P., ed. 1986. *Essential Papers on Narcissism*. New York: New York University Press.

_________, ed. 1989 *Shame: The Underside of Narcissism*. Hillsdale, NJ: Analytic Press.

Morsbach, H., and W.J. Tyler. 1986. "A Japanese Emotion: *Amae*." In Rom Harre, ed., *The Social Construction of Emotion*. Oxford, England: Basil Blackwell.

Murphy, R. 1971. *The Dialectics of Social Life*. New York: Basic Books.

Murphy, Y. and R. Murphy. 1985. *Women of the Forest*. New York: Columbia Univ. Press. Second Edition.

Muslin, Hyman L. 1985. "Heinz Kohut: Beyond the Pleasure Principle, Contributions to Psychoanalysis." In *Beyond Freud: A Study of Modern Psychoanalytic Theorists* (pp.203-229). Hillsdale, NJ: The Analytic Press.

Nandy, Ashis. 1982. "The Psychology of Colonialism: Sex, Age and Ideology in British India." *Psychiatry* 45:197-218.

Nathanson, Donald L. 1987. "A Time Table for Shame." In Donald L. Nathanson, ed., *The Many Faces of Shame* (pp.1-63). New York: The Guilford Press.

Nelson, Benjamin. 1965. "Self-Images and Systems of Spiritual Direction in the History of European Civilization." In S.Z. Klausner, ed., *The Quest for Self-Control*. New York: Free Press.

_________. 1975. "Max Weber, Ernst Troeltsch, Georg Jellinek as Comparative Historical Sociologists," *Sociological Analysis* 36(3):229-240.

Nunberg, Herman. 1955 [orig. 1932]. *Principles of Psychoanalysis*. New York: International Universities Press.

Obeyesekere, Gananath. 1981. *Medusa's Hair: An Essay on Personal Symbols and Religious Experience*. Chicago: University of Chicago Press.

_________. 1990. *The Work of Culture: Symbolic Transformation in Psychoanalysis and Anthropology*. Chicago: The University of Chicago Press.

Okonogi, Keigo. 1978a. "Age of the Moratorium People." *Japan Echo* V: 17-35.

_________. 1978b. "The Ajase Complex of the Japanese (1), the Depth Psychology of the Moratorium People." *Japan Echo* V: 88-105.

_________. 1979. The Ajase Complex of the Japanese (2). *Japan Echo* VI(1):104-118.

Olinor, Marion. 1988. *Cultivating Freud's Garden in France*. New York: Jason Aronson.

Ortigues, M.-C. and Ortigues, R. (1966) *Oedipe Africaine*. Paris: Plon.

Pagels, Elaine. 1988. *Adam, Eve, and the Serpent*. New York: Random House.

Parsons, Anne. 1964. "Is the Oedipus Complex Universal? The Jones-Malinowski Debate Revisited and a South Italian 'Nuclear Complex.'" In W. Muensterberger and Sidney Axedrad, eds., *The Psychoanalytic Study of Society*, 3: 278-328. New York: International Universities Press. (Also reprinted in Anne Parsons. 1969. *Belief, Magic and Anomie: Essays in Psychosocial Anthropology*. New York: Free Press.)

Parsons, Talcott. 1952. "The Superego and the Theory of Social Systems." *Psychiatry* 15:15-24.

Paul, Robert A. 1976. "Did the Primal Crime Take Place?" *Ethos* 4:311-352.

_________. 1982. *The Tibetan Symbolic World*. Chicago: University of Chicago Press.

_________. 1984. "Editorial." *Ethos* 12:99-104.

_________. 1986. "Lina Wertmüller's 'Seven Beauties': An Analysis and Reevaluation." *Journal of Psychoanalytic Anthropology* 9:447-492.

_________. 1987. "The Question of Applied Psychoanalysis and the Interpretation of Cultural Symbolism." *Ethos* 15:82-103.

_________. 1989. "Psychoanalytic Anthropology." *Annual Review of Anthropology* 18:177-202.

Peirce, Charles S. 1932. "The Icon, Index and Symbol." *Collected Papers*, Volume 2. Cambridge, MA: Harvard University Press.

Peristiany, J.G. 1966. *Honour and Shame: The Values of Mediterranean Society*. Chicago: University of Chicago Press.

Perry, Helen Swick. 1983. *Psychiatrist of America*. Cambridge, MA: Harvard University Press.

Perry, Ralph Barton. 1944. *Puritanism and Democracy*. New York: Vanguard Press.

Peterfreund, Emanuel. 1983. *The Process of Psychoanalytic Therapy*. Hillsdale, NJ: The Analytic Press.

Peterson, Indira. 1986. "The Tie That Binds: Brothers and Sisters in North and South India." Paper presented at the Conference on Religion in South India, Hyannis, MA.

Peto, A. 1969. "Terrifying Eyes: a Visual Superego Forerunner. *Psychoanalytic Study of the Child* 24:197-212.

_________. 1970. "To Cast Away: A Vestibular Forerunner of the Superego: Its Role in Normalcy." *Psychoanalytic Study of the Child* 25: 401-416.

Pfeiffer, Ernst, ed. 1972. *Sigmund Freud and Lou Andreas-Salomé: Letters*. W. and E. Robson-Scott, transla. London: Hogarth Press.

Phillips, John A. 1984. *Eve: The History of an Idea*. San Francisco: Harper and Row.

Piers, Gerhardt, and Milton Singer. 1953. *Shame and Guilt*. Springfield: Chas. C. Thomas.

Pine, Fred. 1985. *Developmental Theory and Clinical Process*. New Haven: Yale University Press.

_________. 1990. *Drive, Ego, Object and Self: A Synthesis for Clinical Work*. New York: Basic Books.

Plottel, Jeanine Parisier. 1985. "Jacques Lacan: Psychoanalyst, Surrealist, and Mystic." In *Beyond Freud: A Study of Modern Psychoanalytic Theorists* (pp.333-351). Hillsdale, NJ: The Analytic Press.

Pollock, G. H. 1988. "Oedipus: The Myth, the Developmental Stage, the Universal Theme, the Conflict and Complex." In G. H. Pollock & J. M. Ross, eds., *The Oedipus Papers*. Madison, WI: International Universities Press.

Pontalis, Jean-Baptiste. 1974. "Dream as an Object." *International Review of Psychoanalysis* 1:125-133.

_________. 1977. *Entre Le Rêve and La Douleur*. Paris: Gallinard.

Quinn, Susan. 1987. *A Mind of Her Own*. New York: Summit.

Rabow, Jerome, Gerald Platt, and Marion Goldman, eds. 1987. *Advances in Psychoanalytic Sociology*. Malabar, FL: Krieger Publishing.

Ragland-Sullivan, Ellie. 1987. *Jacques Lacan and the Philosophy of Psychoanalysis*. Chicago: University of Illinois Press.

Ramanujam, B.K. 1979. "Toward Maturity: Problems of Identity Seen in the Indian Cultural Setting." In Sudhir Kakar, ed., *Identity and Adulthood* (pp.37-55). Delhi: Oxford University Press.

_________. 1986. "Social Change and Personal Crisis: A View From and Indian Practice." In Merry I. White and Susan Pollak, eds., *The Cultural Transition* (pp.65-86). London: Routledge and Kegan Paul.

Rancour-Laferriere, Daniel. 1985. *Signs of the Flesh: An Essay on the Evolution of Hominid Sexuality*. New York: Mouton.

Reik, Theodor. 1957. *Myth and Guilt: The Crime and Punishment of Mankind.* New York: George Braziller.

Reppen, Joseph. 1985. *Beyond Freud: A Study of Modern Psychoanalytic Theorists.* Hillsdale, NJ: The Analytic Press.

Rieff, Philip. 1959. *Freud: The Mind of the Moralist.* Chicago: University of Chicago Press.

__________. 1990. "The American Transference from Calvin to Freud." In Philip Rieff, ed., *The Feeling Intellect.* Chicago: University of Chicago Press.

Ritvo, Lucille. 1990. *Darwin's Influence on Freud: A Tale of Two Sciences.* New Haven, CT: Yale University Press.

Rizzuto, Ana-Maria. 1979. *The Birth of the Living God: A Psychoanalytic Study.* Chicago: The University of Chicago Press.

Roazen, Paul. 1971. *Freud and His Followers.* New York: New American Library.

__________. 1990. "Ego Psychology," in *Encountering Freud: The Politics and Histories of Psychoanalysis* (pp.139-161). New Brunswick, NJ: Transaction Publisher.

Robert, Marthe. 1976. *From Oedipus to Moses: Freud's Jewish Identity.* Ralph Mannheim, transla. Garden City, NY: Anchor Press/Doubleday.

Róheim, Géza. 1925. *Austrailiam Totemism: A Psychoanalytic Study in Anthropology.* London: Allen and Unwin.

__________. 1930. *Animism, Magic and the Divine King.* New York: International Universities Press.

__________. 1932. "Psychoanalysis of Primitive Cultural Types." *International Journal of Psycho-Analysis* 13:150-174.

__________. 1934. *The Riddle of the Sphinx.* London: Hogarth.

__________. 1940. "The Garden of Eden." *The Psychoanalytic Review* 27:1-26, 77-199.

__________. 1941. "Play Analysis with Normanby Island Children." *American Journal of Orthopsychiatry* 1:524-530.

__________. 1943. *The Origin and Function of Culture.* New York: Nervous and Mental Disease Monographs. [Anchor Books Edition, 1971].

__________. 1945. *The Eternal Ones of the Dream: A Psychoanalytic Interpretation of Australian Myth and Ritual.* New York: International Universities Press.

_________. 1947. "Dream Analysis and Field Work in Anthropology." In Géza Róheim, ed., *Psychoanalysis and the Social Sciences*, vol. 1 (pp.87-130). New York: International Universities Press.

_________. 1950. *Psychoanalysis and Anthropology*. New York: International Universities Press.

_________. 1951. "Hungarian Shamanism." In Géza Róheim, ed., *Psychoanalysis and the Social Sciences*, vol. 3 (pp.131-169). New York: International Universities Press.

_________. 1952. "Culture Hero and Trickster in North American Mythology." In Sol Tax, ed., *Indian Tribes of Aboriginal America*, vol.3 (pp.190-194). Chicago: University of Chicago Press.

_________. 1953. *The Gates of the Dream*. New York: International Universities Press.

_________. 1954. *Magic and Schizophrenia*. New York: International Universities Press.

_________. 1972. *The Panic of the Gods*. (Warner Muensterberger, ed.) New York: Harper Torchbooks.

_________. 1974. *Children of the Desert: The Western Tribes of Central Australia*. (Warner Muensterberger, ed.) New York: Basic Books.

Roith, Estelle. 1987. *The Riddle of Freud: Jewish Influences on His Theory of Female Sexuality*. London and New York: Tavistock Publications.

Roland, Alan. 1988. *In Search of Self in India and Japan: Towards a Cross-Cultural Psychology*. Princeton, NJ: Princeton University Press.

Rosaldo, Michaell Z. 1980. *Knowledge and Passion: Ilongot Notions of Self and Social Life*. Cambridge, England: Cambridge University Press.

Rudnytsky, Peter L. 1987. *Freud and Oedipus*. New York: Columbia University Press.

Ruitenbeek, Hendrik. 1966. *Freud and America*. New York: Macmillan.

Russell, John C. 1984. "Family Experience and Folk Catholicism in Rural Ireland." *Journal of Psychoanalytic Anthropology* 7:141-170.

Sagan, Eli. 1988. *Freud, Women, and Morality: The Psychology of Good and Evil*. New York: Basic Books.

Sahlins, Marshall. 1976. *Culture and Practical Reason*. Chicago: University of Chicago Press.

_________. 1977. *The Use and Abuse of Biology: An Anthropological Critique of Sociobiology*. Chicago: University of Chicago Press.

Salzman, L. 1968. *The Obsessive Personality*. New York: Science House.

Sandler, Joseph. 1960. "On the Concept of the Superego." *Psychoanalytic Study of the Child*, 15:139-158.

_________. 1963. "The Ego Ideal and the Ideal Self." *Psychoanalytic Study of the Child*, 18:139-158.

_________. 1987. *From Safety to Superego: Selected Papers of Joseph Sandler*. New Yoprk: Guilford Press.

Sartre, Jean-Paul. 1956. *Being and Nothingness: An Essay on Phenomenological Ontology*. (H.E. Barnes trans.) New York: The Philosophical Library.

Sass, Louis A. 1988. "The Self and Its Vicissitudes: An Archaeological Study of the Psychoanalytic Avant-Garde," *Social Research* 55 (Winter):551-607.

Schafer, Roy. 1960. "The Loving and Beloved Superego in Freud's Structural Theory." *Psychoanalytic Study of the Child* 15:163-188.

_________. 1968. *Aspects of Internalization*. New York: International Universities Press.

_________. 1974. "Problems in Freud's Psychology of Women." *Journal of the American Psychoanalytic Association* 22:459-485.

_________. 1983. *The Analytic Attitude*. New York: Basic Books.

Schiefflin, E. 1983. "Anger and Shame in the Tropical Forest." *Ethos*, 11:1181-1191.

Schneider, Carl. 1977. *Shame, Exposure and Privacy*. Boston: Beacon Press.

Schorske, Carl E. 1980. *Fin de Siècle Vienna: Politics and Culture*. New York: Alfred A. Knopf.

Shapiro, David. 1981. *Autonomy and Rigid Character*. New York: Basic Books.

Shweder, Richard A. 1991. *Thinking Through Cultures*. Cambridge: Harvard University Press.

Schweder, Richard A., and Robert LeVine, eds. *Culture Theory: Essays on Mind, Self and Emotion*. Cambridge: Cambridge University Press.

Sinha, T. C. 1966. "Development of Psychoanalysis in India." *International Journal of Psycho-Analysis* 47:427-439.

Spain, David H. 1987. "The Westermarck-Freud Incest-Theory Debate: An Evaluation and Reformulation." *Current Anthropology* 28(5):623-634; 641-645.

_________. 1988. "Taboo or Not Taboo: Is that the Question?" *Ethos* 16:285-301.

_________. 1989. "The Westermarck-Freud Incest-theory Debate: An Evaluation and Reformulation." *Current Anthropology* 28:623-635; 641-645.

_________. n.d.a. "White Knight vs. Trojan Horse or, On the Dispensibility of the Term 'Pre-Oedipal.'" Manuscript.

_________. n.d.b. "Anxieties about Hypotheses and Hypotheses about Anxiety: Steps to a Psychocultural Reading of Method in the Human Sciences." Paper presented at the 1988 Annual Meeting of the American Anthropological Association, Phoenix.

Spindler, George D., ed. 1978. *The Making of Psychological Anthropology*. Berkeley: University of California Press.

Spiro, Melford. 1982. *Oedipus in the Trobriands*. Chicago: The University of Chicago Press.

_________. 1992. *Anthropological Other or Burmese Brother? Studies in Cultural Analogies*. New Brunswick, NJ: Transaction Publishers.

_________. n.d. "Tropes, Defenses, and Unconscious Symbols: Some Critical Reflections on the Primary Process" (mimeo).

Spitz, René. 1957. *No and Yes*. New York: International Universities Press.

_________. 1959. *A Genetic Field Theory of Ego Formation*. New York: International Universities Press.

_________. 1965. *The First Year of Life*. New York: Basic Books.

Stein, Howard F. 1974. "Envy and the Evil Eye among Slovak-Americans: An Essay in the Psychological Ontogeny of Belief and Ritual." *Ethos* 2:15-46.

_________. 1978a. "Aging and Death among Slovak-Americans." *Journal of Psychological Anthropology* 1:297-320.

_________. 19787b. "Judaism and the Group-Fantasy of Martyrdom." *The Journal of Psychohistory* 6:151-210.

_________. 1979. "The White Ethnic Movement. Panism and the Restoration of Early Symbiosis: The Psychohistory of a Group Fantasy." *Psychohistory* 6:319-360.

_________. 1985. *Psychoanthropology of American Culture*. New York: Psychohistory Press.

_________. 1990a. *American Medicine as Culture*. San Diego, CA: Westview Press.

_________. 1990b. "Psychoanalytic Perspectives. Chapter 4." In T.M. Johnson and C.F. Sargent, eds., *Medical Anthropology: Contemporary Theory and Method* (pp.73-92, plus references). New York: Praeger.

_________. 1990c. "Adapting to Doom: The Group Psychology of an Organization Threatened with Cultural Extinction." *Political Psychology* 11:113-145.

_________. 1990d. "The Internal and Group Milieux of Ethnicity: Identifying Generic Group Psychodynamic Issues." *Canadian Review of Studies in Nationalism* 27:1-2; 107-130.

Stein, Howard F., and Maurice Apprey. 1987. *From Metaphor to Meaning: Papers in Psychoanalytic Anthropology*. Charlottesville: University of Virginia Press.

_________. 1990. *Clinical Stories and Their Translation*. Vol.3, Series in Ethnicity, Medicine and Psychoanalysis. Charlottesville: University of Virginia Press.

Stepansky, Paul, ed. 1988. *The Memoirs of Margaret S. Mahler*. New York: The Free Press.

Stephens, W. N. 1962. *The Oedipus Complex: Cross-Cultural Evidence*. New York: Free Press.

Stern, Daniel. 1985. *The Interpersonal World of the Infant*. New York: Basic Books.

Stolorow, Robert D., B. Brandchaft, and G. Atwood. 1987. *Psychoanalytic Treatment: An Intersubjective Approach*. Hillsdale, NJ: Analytic Press.

Stone, Laurence. 1979. *The Family, Sex and Marriage in England 1500-1800*. New York: Harper and Row, 1979.

Strathern, Andrew. 1977. "Why is Shame on the Skin?" In John Blacking, ed., *The Anthropology of the Body*. London: Academic Press.

Sulloway, Frank J. 1979. *Freud: Biologist of the Mind*. New York: Basic Books.

Swan, Jim. 1974. "*Mater* and Nannie: Freud's Two Mothers and the Discovery of the Oedipus Complex." *American Imago* 31:1-64.

Tan, Amy. 1989. *The Joy Luck Club*. New York: Putnam.

Taylor, Charles. 1989. *Sources of the Self*. Cambridge, MA: Harvard University Press.

Thass-Thienemann, Theodore. 1968. *Symbolic Behavior*. New York: Washington Square Press.

Tobin, Joseph J., David Y.H. Wu, and Dana H. Davidson. 1989. *Preschool in Three Cultures: Japan, China and the United States*. New Haven: Yale University Press.

Tomkins, S. 1963. *Affect, Imagery, Consciousness*. New York: Springer.

Tooby, John, and Leda Cosmides. 1989. "Evolutionary Psychology and the Generation of Cultures, Part I: Theoretical Considerations." *Ethology and Sociobiology* 10:29-49.

Traweek, Sharon. 1988. *Beamtimes and Lifetimes: The World of High Energy Physics*. Cambridge: Harvard University Press.

Trawick, Margaret. 1990. *Notes on Love in a Tamil Family*. Berkeley: University of California Press.

Trilling, Lionel. 1950. *Freud and the Future*. Boston: Beacon Press.

Trivers, Robert. 1981. "Sociobiology and Politics." In E. White, ed., *Sociobiology and Human Politcs*. Lexington and Toronto: D.C. Heath & Co.

_________. 1985. *Social Evolution*. Menlo Park, CA: Benjamin/ Cummings.

Troeltsch, Ernst. 1931. *The Social Teachings of the Christian Churches*, vol.1. New York: Macmillan.

_________. 1958. *Protestantism and Progress*. Boston: Beacon Press.

Tronick, E., H. Als, L. Adamson, S. Wise, and T. Berry Brazelton. 1978. "The Infant's Response to Entrapment between Contradictory Messages in Face to Face Interaction." *Journal of Child Psychiatry* 17:1-13.

Trosman, Harry. 1973. "Freud's Cultural Background," in *The Annual of Psychoanalysis* 1, New York: Quadrangle Press.

Turiel, E. 1967. "An Historical Analysis of the Freudian Concept of the Superego." *Psychoanalytic Review* 54:118-140.

Turkle, Sherry. 1981. *Psychoanalytic Politics: Freud's French Revolution*. Cambridge, MA: Harvard University Press.

Vermorel, Madeleine, and Henri Vermorel. 1986. "Was Freud a Romantic?" *International Review of Psycho-Analysis* 13:15-37.

Vitz, Paul C. 1988. *Sigmund Freud's Christian Unconscious*. New York and London: The Guilford Press.

Volkan, Vamik D. 1979. *Cyprus-War and Adaptation*. Charlottesville: University of Virginia Press.

Wallace, Edwin R., IV. 1983. *Freud and Anthropology: A History and Reappraisal*. New York: International Universities Press.

Wallerstein, Robert S. 1988. "One Psychoanalysis or Many?" *International Journal of Psycho-Analysis* 69:5-21.

Watts, Alan W. 1960. *Myth and Ritual in Christianity*. New York: Grove Press/Evergreen.

Weber, Max. 1958. *The Protestant Ethic and the Spirit of Capitalism*. New York: Charles Scribners' Sons.

White, Leslie. 1949. *The Science of Culture: A Study of Man and Civilization*. New York: Grove Press.

Whiting, Beatrice B., and John W.M. Whiting. 1975. *Children of Six Cultures: A Psycho-Cultural Analysis*. Cambridge, MA: Harvard University Press.

Williams, B. 1981. "A Critical Review of Models in Sociobiology." *Annual Review of Anthropology* 10:163-92.

Winnicott, Donald W. 1953. "Transitional Objects and Transitional Phenomena." *International Journal of Psychoanalysis* 34: 89-97.

_________. 1958. *Collected Papers: Through Paediatrics to Psychoanal- ysis*. New York: Basic Books.

_________. 1960. "Ego Distortion in Terms of True and False Self," in *The Maturational Process and the Facilitating Environment*. New York: International Universities Press, pp.140-152.

_________. 1965. "The Theory of the Parent-Infant Relationship." In *The Maturational Process and the Facilitating Environment* (pp.37-55). NY: International Universities Press.

_________. 1971a. *Therapeutic Consultations in Child Psychiatry*. New York: Basic Books.

_________. 1971b. *Playing and Reality*. New York: Basic Books.

Wurmser, Leon. 1981. *The Mask of Shame*. Baltimore: Johns Hopkins Press.

_________. 1987. "Shame: The Veiled Companion of Narcissism." In Donald A. Nathanson, ed., *The Many Faces of Shame*. New York: The Guilford Press.

Young-Bruehl, Elizabeth. 1988. *Anna Freud: A Biography*. New York: Summit Books.

__________. 1989. "Looking for Anna Freud's Mother." *The Psychoanalytic Study of the Child* 44: 391-408.

Name Index

Subject Index